A Search for Unity in Diversity

A Search for Unity in Diversity

The "Permanent Hegelian Deposit" in the Philosophy of John Dewey

James A. Good

LEXINGTON BOOKS

A division of
ROWMAN & LITTLEFIELD PUBLISHERS, INC.
Lanham • Boulder • New York • Toronto • Oxford

LEXINGTON BOOKS

A division of Rowman & Littlefield Publishers, Inc.
A wholly owned subsidiary of The Rowman & Littlefield Publishing Group, Inc.
4501 Forbes Boulevard, Suite 200
Lanham, MD 20706

PO Box 317
Oxford
OX2 9RU, UK

British Library Cataloguing in Publication Information Available

Library of Congress Cataloging-in-Publication Data

Good, James A. (James Allan)
A search for unity in diversity : the "permanent Hegelian deposit" in the philosophy of John Dewey / James A. Good.
p. cm.
Includes bibliographical references and index.
ISBN 0-7391-1061-6 (cloth : alk. paper) — ISBN 0-7391-1360-7 (pbk. : alk. paper)
1. Dewey, John, 1859-1952. 2. Hegel, Georg Wilhelm Friedrich, 1770-1831—Influence. I. Title.
B945.D44G56 2005
191—dc22 2005026706

Printed in the United States of America

The paper used in this publication meets the minimum requirements of American National Standard for Information Sciences—Permanence of Paper for Printed Library Materials, ANSI/NISO Z39.48–1992.

To Linda, who puts air under my wings

Thanks are due to the following for permission to quote from copyrighted materials: from the letters of John Dewey by permission of the Center for Dewey Studies, Southern Illinois University Carbondale; from manuscript material by John Dewey and Herbert Schneider by permission of the Special Collections Research Center, Morris Library, Southern Illinois University Carbondale; from manuscript material by John Dewey by permission of Houghton Library, Harvard University; from the *Collected Papers of Charles S. Peirce* by permission of the Harvard Department of Philosophy; from manuscript material by James Rowland Angell and Thomas Davidson by permission of Yale University Library; from manuscript material by John Dewey by permission of The Johns Hopkins University; from manuscript material by William Torrey Harris and Thomas Davidson by permission of the Missouri Historical Society; from manuscript material by John Dewey by permission of the University of Vermont; from my article "The Value of Thomas Davidson" by permission of the *Transactions of the Charles S. Peirce Society*; from manuscript material by John Dewey by permission of the Bentley Historical Library, University of Michigan.

Contents

Abbreviations

JSP: Harris, William Torrey, ed. *The Journal of Speculative Philosophy, 1867-1893.* 22 vols. Reprint. Edited by James A. Good. Bristol, England: Thoemmes Press, 2002.

EW: Dewey, John. *The Early Works, 1882-1898.* 5 vols. Edited by Jo Ann Boydston. Carbondale: University of Southern Illinois Press, 1967-1972.

MW: Dewey, John. *The Middle Works, 1899-1924.* 15 vols. Edited by Jo Ann Boydston. Carbondale: University of Southern Illinois Press, 1976-1983.

LW: Dewey, John. *The Later Works, 1925-1953.* 17 vols. Edited by Jo Ann Boydston. Carbondale: University of Southern Illinois Press, 1981-1999.

Preface

While I cannot pinpoint precisely when or why I was originally inspired to write on Dewey's debt to Hegel, it is not as difficult to recall the influences that inspired the way I approached the issues I engage in the following pages. My undergraduate philosophy mentor, Don Wester, schooled me in the history of western philosophy, convinced me of the importance of intellectual history, and introduced me to Dewey during my senior year. Although I am not sure that he would agree with my characterization, I later reminisced that Wester had given me the Rortian cure to the modern philosophical malady before I had contracted it.[1] This meant that I became wary of philosophers who claimed their words mirrored reality, allegedly perennial philosophical problems, and the various dualisms that seemed always to provide the unsteady foundations of those problems. I have no doubt that Wester predisposed me somewhat toward Dewey, and I remember being intrigued from the start by Dewey's connection to Hegel. How could such a resolutely empirical and purportedly anti-metaphysical philosopher have come from the ranks of Hegelian idealists? But when I left Oklahoma Baptist University for the philosophy graduate program at Baylor University, I vaguely described my primary philosophical interests as theories of interpretation and the history of German philosophy.

At Baylor, William Cooper's course in American philosophy attracted my attention more precisely to Dewey for philosophical reasons. I was principally impressed by Dewey's ability to resist the pull of philosophical vortices, in which many philosophers seemed ensnared, by placing dualisms such as mind and body within the context of more inclusive explanatory frameworks. I continue to believe Dewey was remarkably adept at persuasively depicting apparently opposing terms as functions or stages within an ongoing process. Also at Baylor, I was delighted to discover another recent convert to the Deweyan approach to both philosophical and more practical problems in Stuart Rosenbaum. In his laissez-faire manner, Rosenbaum guided my deeper mining of the vast and labyrinthine passages within the Deweyan corpus. Although other philosophers might have questioned my interest in studying Dewey's life and historical context as well his as writings, Rosenbaum accepted it with equanimity. In addition to reading all of Dewey's essays in *The Philosophy of John Dewey,* I read Morton White's *The Origin of Dewey's Instrumentalism,* Neil Coughlan's *The*

Young John Dewey, and George Dykhuizen's *The Life and Mind of John Dewey.*[2] Upon completion of those studies, I felt well prepared to venture into Dewey's most important tomes on my own, which I began to do with great zeal. And Rosenbaum was always ready and willing to discuss Dewey at a moment's notice. I distinctly recall daydreaming while administering a final exam in one of my introductory logic courses about how I might be able to combine my interests in Dewey and German philosophy by writing a doctoral dissertation on his controversial "Hegelian deposit." As an existential crisis led me to question my career plans, Robert Baird, chair of the Baylor Philosophy Department, graciously indulged my desire to take courses in American literature and history. In an American intellectual history course, Gary Hull reinforced my love of intellectual history and unwittingly helped me decide to switch from philosophy to history.

With the gentle prodding of my newfound life partner, I completed my philosophy M.A. at Baylor, and began to pursue an M.A. in American history at the University of Houston, under the direction of Gerald Goodwin. My thesis, which expanded on a paper I had written at Baylor, argued against Bruce Kuklick's effort in *Churchmen and Philosophers* to demonstrate that Dewey was significantly indebted to the New England Theology that emanated from Jonathan Edwards and provided some of the underpinning of the Social Gospel.[3] By then I could draw upon new Dewey biographies by Robert Westbrook and Steven Rockefeller.[4] Although many of the arguments I made in that thesis seem rather simplistic to me now, I am still persuaded that my conclusion was fundamentally correct. Any similarities between Dewey's thought and late-nineteenth-century New England Theology were due more to their common intellectual milieu than to any direct lineage. After a few years of adjunct teaching in philosophy and history, I was given the opportunity to begin doctoral studies in the Rice University History Department under the direction of Thomas Haskell.

In my first conversation with Haskell, I inquired into his primary research interest and without hesitation he earnestly replied with one word: "causation." As he explained that he was fascinated by the ways in which humans have attributed causation and thereby ascribed moral responsibility, I knew instantly that I had found a similarly abstract spirit within the confines of a history department. Haskell's abstract inclination is guided by analytical skills that are legendary among both graduate students and established scholars. But it is his ability to articulate thoughtful interpretative visions of aspects of American intellectual history that has most influenced scholars. Haskell helped me understand the importance of the professionalization of the academy during the late nineteenth century and the pressures that process brought to bear on American intellectuals. Although many historians have documented ways that late-nineteenth-century scientific advances had a profound impact on philosophers, Haskell persuaded me that issues arising from the increasing social and economic interdependence of the time also perplexed many intellectuals.[5] I believe the lessons I learned from Haskell shed light on Dewey's attraction to Hegel's organicism during the early years of his philosophical development and led me to reflect more deeply about each philosopher's conception of his chosen vocation. Despite some initial misgivings about my unusually philosophical dissertation proposal, Haskell agreed to direct my research. The Rice History Department also afforded me the unusual opportunity to work with two historians who have focused, to a large degree, on the history of German philosophy, Richard Wolin and John Zammito. Both taught me more about German intellectual history than I can easily summarize, and both saw merit in my still embryonic dissertation proposal. At Rice I also had the opportunity to read Hegel with three scholars, all of whom helped me see his thought from different angles. I read Hegel's early writings with Zammito, the *Phenomenology of Spirit* with Steven Crowell, and the "Lesser Logic" and *The Philosophy of Right* with Tristram Engelhardt. In the course of those studies, I learned about recent Hegel scholarship that made him seem surprisingly Deweyan to me.

As I sharpened my vision of this project, I was also motivated by three frustrations with previous work on Dewey's debt to Hegel that I address throughout the text. First, many studies of Dewey's philosophical development employ terms such as "idealism," "the absolute," and "Hegelianism" in remarkably ambiguous ways given the complex history of their usage. Second, at least some authors who have addressed this topic seem rather biased against Hegel. And finally, much of the extant scholarship seems to ignore recent readings of Hegel. But even works that paved the way for the present book, such as Thomas Alexander's *John Dewey's Theory of Art, Experience, and Nature,* left me with questions.[6] Although I was persuaded by Alexander's carefully crafted argument that critics who pointed to Hegelian elements in Dewey's aesthetics misunderstood his thought in crucial ways, as I finished reading the book, I still wanted to know how Dewey's aesthetics compared to Hegel's. More recently, John Shook's thoroughly researched *Dewey's Empirical Theory of Knowledge and Reality* substantially clarified Dewey's relationship to the British neo-Hegelians and argued that Dewey never made a clean break from idealism.[7] While I agreed with Shook's overall argument, I wanted to complement his work by focusing on Dewey's American context. Thus I resolved that in order to make significant progress on this question, both philosophers and historians must better define crucial terms, pay closer attention to what Hegel actually wrote as well as recent Hegel scholarship, examine the nineteenth-century American reception of Hegel, and make direct comparisons between the writings and ideas of Hegel and Dewey. With that approach, I believe I have found a much more significant Hegelian deposit in Dewey's mature thought than has been previously identified.

Notes

1. Richard Rorty, *Philosophy and the Mirror of Nature* (Princeton: Princeton University Press, 1979).

2. John J. McDermott, ed., *The Philosophy of John Dewey* (Chicago: University of Chicago Press, 1981); Morton White, *The Origin of Dewey's Instrumentalism* (New York: Columbia University Press, 1943); Neil Coughlan, *Young John Dewey: An Essay in American Intellectual History* (Chicago: University of Chicago Press, 1973); and George Dykhuizen, *The Life and Mind of John Dewey* (Carbondale: Southern Illinois University Press, 1973).

3. Bruce Kuklick, *Churchmen and Philosophers: From Jonathan Edwards to John Dewey* (New Haven: Yale University Press, 1985).

4. Robert B. Westbrook, *John Dewey and American Democracy* (Ithaca: Cornell University Press, 1991); and Steven C. Rockefeller, *John Dewey: Religious Faith and Democratic Humanism* (New York: Columbia University Press, 1991).

5. See Thomas Haskell, *The Emergence of Professional Social Science: The American Social Science Association and the Nineteenth-Century Crisis of Authority* (Baltimore: Johns Hopkins University Press, 2000).

6. Thomas Alexander, *John Dewey's Theory of Art, Experience, and Nature: The Horizons of Feeling* (Albany: State University of New York Press, 1987).

7. John Shook, *Dewey's Empirical Theory of Knowledge and Reality* (Nashville: Vanderbilt University Press, 2000).

Acknowledgments

As one who firmly agrees with Hegel's and Dewey's emphasis on the social nature of the learning process, I recognize that this book would not have been possible without the support and assistance of many people. In addition to essential emotional and financial support, my wife, Linda Good, has proofread chapters, made innumerable photocopies, and even assisted me on runs to the library. All the while, she was nobly engaged in providing critical legal services to impoverished clients in her position as a Managing Attorney of a local legal aid office. Her energy and constant encouragement have been a vast source of inspiration to me. Our children, Ben, Virginia, and Amanda, have taught me more about what is most important in history, philosophy, and everyday life than they will ever know.

The Rice History Department provided me with generous financial support throughout my doctoral studies, including a Sarofim/NEH Fellowship during the 2000-2001 academic year. Peter Caldwell has graciously maintained my status as a visiting scholar at Rice, which provides me continued access to the facilities and capable staff of Fondren Library. At Rice I was also blessed to work with talented graduate students who read more drafts of chapters than I can count and offered constructive criticism of my work. My special thanks go to Tanya Dunlap, Scott Marler, Susan Hanssen, Shane Story, and Kate Kirkland. Although many faculty members contributed to my intellectual and professional development, both Thomas Haskell and John Zammito have provided far more than intellectual influence; they have remained supportive friends who assist and encourage me in a myriad of ways.

In the early stages of this project, I received vital encouragement from Larry Hickman, Robert Westbrook, and John McDermott. The staff at the Center for Dewey Studies at Southern Illinois University in Carbondale, Illinois; Karen Drickamer, Curator of Special Collections at the Southern Illinois University Morris Library; Emily Troxell, librarian at the Missouri Historical Society; and Jeffrey D. Marshall, University Archivist and Curator of Manuscripts in The Special Collections Department of the Bailey/Howe Library, University of Vermont, all provided friendly and essential assistance in my research.

I had the opportunity to offer a series of sessions on "The Lost *Bildung* Tradition in American Philosophy" at the Summer Institute in American Philosophy, held at the University of Vermont in 2001. At the invitation of Christof Mauch, I presented an early version of chapter six at the German Historical Institute's Young Scholars Forum in Washington D.C. in 2002. And the following year, Daniel Tröhler invited me to present a paper I titled "The Hegelian Roots of Dewey's Pragmatism" at the Institut für historische Bildungsforschung Pestalozzianum, Universität Zürich, Switzerland. I received valuable feedback on this project in all three of those venues.

When I completed the manuscript, Hickman, Westbrook, and Wilfred McClay read the final product and provided much needed advice and assistance in getting it published. Many others kindly read and commented on significant parts or all of the manuscript: Tom Burke, Donald Koch, John Stuhr, James Garrison, John Shook, and Philip Jackson. Although I have not taken all of the advice I have received from these people, their comments, criticisms, and suggestions saved me from many errors and helped me reflect more deeply about the arguments I make in the book.

Finally, I have benefited from frequent, wide-ranging conversations over hot chocolate about science, history, philosophy, writing, academic careers, and life in general with my good friend John D. Rogers. I cannot count the times I was baffled about how to write a particular passage or formulate an argument until I discussed the problem with John. Even more importantly than that, his friendship and support sustained my spirit on numerous occasions.

The resulting book is a product of all of these influences, as well as smaller ones too subtle and numerous to list. Despite all of the encouragement, assistance, and sustenance I have received from these sources, I take full responsibility for any and all errors that may remain in the book.

Introduction

The extent to which scholars disagree in their assessments of John Dewey's philosophy is truly remarkable. Recently, James Hoopes argued that an implicit commitment to metaphysical nominalism, the view that only particulars are real, undermined Dewey's emphasis on the social nature of individuals because he could not account for the reality of community, a general notion. Dewey's nominalism, Hoopes claimed, provided a deficient basis for American liberal thought because it inevitably leads to atomistic individualism and undermines community. By way of contrast, Larry Hickman maintains that Dewey formulated a "novel solution" to the "traditional problem of 'universals'" that rejected both nominalism and realism, allowing him to construct a viable theory of values that prevents their stifling reification. And rather than an implicit atomistic individualism, David Fott argues that Dewey so emphasized the social nature of the self that "there is no, or hardly any, psychological room within which [individuals] may withdraw from society" and gain a vantage point for critical evaluation.[1]

At first blush, these author's disagreements about basic points of Dewey's thought do not bode well for a resolution of the issues. They may reveal a focal point around which debate might profitably center, however. The core issue is Dewey's historicization of the self. Is the self, according to Dewey, so inextricably situated within the flux of history that it cannot rise above its context and critique its own society? This book recontextualizes the debate over Dewey's conception of the self's relationship to its social and historical context by examining the crucial transition in his thought during the 1890s with a view toward understanding what Dewey called the "permanent [Hegelian] deposit" in his mature philosophy.[2] A clearer understanding of the influence of Hegel upon Dewey will demonstrate that, despite his historicism, Dewey succeeded in articulating a philosophy that provides for individuality and cultural criticism.[3]

These clashing opinions recapitulate a long-standing controversy about the degree to which Dewey himself successfully maintained critical distance from his culture. The suspicion that he was unsuccessful is somewhat ironic in view of the facts that he was investigated twice by the F.B.I., and at one time or another, condemned by people on all sides of the political and cultural spectrum.[4]

Intellectuals as diverse as Bertrand Russell, Reinhold Niebuhr, Lewis Mumford, and Randolph Bourne claimed that Dewey's thought represented the dark side of American culture, betraying a spirit of compromise and acquiescence to corporate capitalism. Similar assessments of Dewey have recently resurfaced in John Patrick Diggins's *The Promise of Pragmatism* and Brian Lloyd's *Left Out.* Though Diggins's and Lloyd's accounts differ from one another, and from those that precede them, their conclusions are familiar: Dewey was blinded to the critique of ends by an unyielding commitment to bureaucratic efficiency.[5]

Broadly speaking, these criticisms are rooted in three concerns. First, many have objected that Dewey was naïvely sanguine about the prospects of humans sacrificing self-interest for the sake of the public good.[6] But Dewey's most optimistic writings were what Lewis Feuer calls "lay sermons," in which he sought to exhort readers to a democratic way of life, and many scholars seem to overlook the ways that he carefully qualified his optimism.[7] Dewey never categorically asserted that the social sciences would eventually solve all social problems; rather, he held that a specific type of empirical method, if used intelligently, could ameliorate, but never eliminate, social conflicts. For Dewey, it is those conflicts that compel personal and communal growth and development. The second concern is whether Dewey's instrumentalism can critically assess both means and ends, and thus avoid a destructive moral relativism. Critics depict Dewey's instrumentalism as an uncritical reflection of the bureaucratic mentality that accompanied the rise of corporate capitalism, and construe his philosophy of education as a bourgeois attempt at social control that would mold lower-class Americans into pliant factory workers for the good of the whole.[8] The third claim, closely related to the second, is that Dewey abandoned the classical theory of truth as correspondence of our beliefs to actual states of affairs in the world, in favor of the view that truth is made in accordance with processes whereby we adapt to, rather than change, the environment.[9] Dewey frequently replied to the latter two allegations by emphasizing his critique of philosophical dualisms and arguing that his notion of experience was fundamentally distinct from the traditional Western view that reified the subject/object dichotomy. He maintained that the charge of relativism stemmed from an uncritical acceptance of the dualisms of subjective and objective reasoning, relative and absolute truth, and the individual and society, and that the problem of how thought corresponds to actual states of affairs was an insoluble conundrum generated by Cartesian mind/body dualism. If, as Dewey maintained, mind is an integral part of its environment, there is no adaptation to the environment that does not involve its modification.[10]

Though it may not be immediately apparent that there is a relationship between controversies about Dewey's historicization of the self and his Hegelianism, it is noteworthy that polemics about Hegel's thought have revolved around many of the same types of issues as debates about Dewey's. Like Dewey, Hegel has been accused of naïvely believing in the inevitable progress of human society, going so far as to write progress into the very nature of reality, which evolves according to an inexorable dialectical law. Also like Dewey, Hegel's historicism has been blamed for a debilitating moral relativism, despite Hegel's absolutism, and the charge that he was an apologist for the reactionary, and increasingly bureaucratic, Prussian state is legendary. Many have feared that Hegel's statism inevitably leads to the sacrifice of the individual for the good of the whole. Finally, like Dewey, Hegel has been accused of undermining the traditional notion of truth by denying the principle of contradiction, espousing instead a coherence theory of truth according to which our beliefs are true as long as they are consistent with one another. Moreover, Hegel rejected the Cartesian dualism of mind and body, as did Dewey, dramatically undermining traditional philosophical dichotomies such as subject and object, relative and absolute truth, and the individual and society. An extreme interpretation might even compare Dewey's ultimate support of the American war effort in 1917 to Hegel's alleged glorification of war.[11]

Dewey and Hegel are accused of the same types of errors because they held a common conception of philosophy, one that is at odds with the mainstream western philosophical tradition, dating back to Kant's "critical turn." In *Kant, Herder, and the Birth of Anthropology,* John Zammito has recently identified and defined two rival German conceptions of philosophy during the time, and in the place, that the research university was first conceived. Herder advocated *Popularphilosophie,* and Kant, after his critical turn, advocated a new type of *Schulphilosophie.* According to Herder, philosophy must take the social and historical context of ideas seriously and serve as "a new ethical and sociopolitical agency for change and progress." Like the Renaissance humanists, Herder and other advocates of *Popularphilosophie* believed that the proper study of man is man. Thus Herder sought to supplant *Schulphilosophie* with philosophical anthropology. The critical Kant, on the other hand, subordinated anthropology to metaphysics, and it is crucial to bear in mind that Kant reduced metaphysics to transcendental logic, that is, to the study of what must be the case for us to be able to make the sort of truth claims we make about reality. The conception of philosophy Kant developed during the 1770s, as Zammito describes it, values "theoretical knowledge and its certainty." Zammito asserts that the conception of *Popularphilosophie* Herder defended in opposition to Kant carried "forward from Herder to Wilhelm von Humboldt and G.W.F. Hegel, to Friedrich Schleiermacher . . . to the Left Hegelians . . . and Wilhelm Dilthey: the tradition of hermeneutics and historicism."[12]

I agree with Zammito that Hegel embraced Herder's conception of philosophy, as well as elements of the closely related German neo-humanist tradition that began with Goethe. Because of these influences, philosophy, for Hegel, was *Bildung,* which, for now, I will define simply as an organic model of education as growth. Although by 1800 Hegel modified the concept he inherited to include a reconstruction of systematic philosophy, he never abandoned Herder's and Goethe's goals, individual and cultural renewal. During the middle of the nineteenth century, the *Bildung* conception of philosophy was embraced by many American intellectuals, most prominently the transcendentalists, but more importantly to the story of Dewey's intellectual development, the St. Louis

Hegelians. Through their publications, their *Journal of Speculative Philosophy,* and their work in social and political reform, the St. Louis Hegelians worked diligently to initiate a Hegelian *Bildung* tradition in American philosophy.

In *Philosophy and the Mirror of Nature,* Richard Rorty encouraged philosophers to abandon epistemology-centered philosophy in favor of edifying philosophy, noting that Gadamer had achieved the shift "by substituting the notion of *Bildung* (education, self-formation) for that of 'knowledge' as the goal of thinking." It is ironic that Rorty preferred the notion of edification to *Bildung* because the latter sounds "a bit too foreign."[13] Rorty's words bear witness to the fact that, despite the assiduous efforts of the St. Louis Hegelians, the *Bildung* tradition in American philosophy has been lost.

Shortly after the American Philosophical Association was founded around the turn of the twentieth century, a three-way battle ensued between pragmatists, idealists, and realists; by 1910 the realists had effectively won.[14] As American philosophy professionalized throughout the course of the century, realists rejected both pragmatism and idealism and embraced Kant's conception of philosophy, valuing epistemology and logic over the pursuit of practical wisdom. The Kantian conception of philosophy flourished in the new research universities because it concedes ground to academic disciplinization by placing limits upon the topics philosophers can justifiably examine as philosophers. For most of the twentieth century, American philosophers embraced the model of the mind as a mirror that reflects reality and sought to play border guard over other academic disciplines, ruling on what they can and cannot logically say.

By way of contrast, according to the American *Bildung* tradition, philosophy is the most practical of all endeavors. Although it might be described as "edifying philosophy," it is more robust than Rorty's conception of philosophy as an endeavor to simply "continue the conversation" of our culture.[15] In the American *Bildung* tradition, philosophical thinking is persistent critical examination of one's ideals, as well as the ideals of one's society, toward the goal of exposing ways in which actual practices fall short of those ideals. The philosopher should not only labor to expose contradictions; she should also offer practical solutions and actively work to implement them. The American *Bildung* tradition is based upon an inherently expansive conception of philosophy because it requires its practitioners to be broadly educated, across academic disciplines, to better understand their society's ideals, practices, and institutions. Moreover, it demands that philosophers keep one foot firmly planted in their social and historical context and one in their study. More theoretically, the American *Bildung* tradition rejects mechanistic, static views of reality in favor of an organic and historical model according to which individual persons and objects are interrelated within a dynamic process. Rather than assume the Cartesian notion that knowledge is gained by reducing complex wholes to their constituent parts, the *Bildung* tradition maintains that knowledge of the part comes from attending to the ways it is related to other parts and the way it functions within a larger whole.[16] In the following pages I argue that the most significant Hegelian deposit in Dewey's mature thought is the *Bildung* model of philosophy.[17] I hasten to concede, however, that Dewey rejected Hegel's systematic efforts, although I argue that those efforts are properly understood to be far more modest, and not as contrary to Dewey's mature thought, than at first meets the eye.

Although the content of Dewey's Hegelian deposit and the timing of his transition from idealism to instrumentalism are presumably rational issues, a more emotional subtext lurks behind them. At times, Dewey scholars seem to have a knee-jerk reaction against the prospect that there is a significant Hegelian deposit in Dewey's mature thought because they view Hegel as an embarrassment to Dewey.[18] This may be due to the fact that many contemporary Dewey scholars have studied with analytic philosophers who view Hegel's system as a prime example of philosophy gone dangerously awry. Further, intellectuals now have a post-1917 and post-Holocaust perspective on German culture, and may lose sight of the pre-1917 view of Germany as a progressive nation. I hope to counter this less rational subtext by carefully examining the way Dewey came to read Hegel during the 1880s and 1890s. Recent humanistic/historicist readings of Hegel suggest that Dewey's mature thought is more accurately seen as a deeper understanding of Hegel's most original philosophical insights.[19] In a similar spirit, I argue that although Dewey's increasingly critical stance toward metaphysics entailed a rejection of a particular British variant of Hegelianism, it was not a wholesale rejection of Hegel.

Many acknowledge Dewey's debt to the British neo-Hegelians (especially Thomas Hill Green, of whom Dewey did speak highly) but neglect his place within a distinctively American Hegelian tradition that sought to democratize Hegel and translate his ideas into a distinctive American idealism. On both sides of the Atlantic, late-nineteenth-century Hegelians were concerned about issues of social reform, and were particularly critical of the materialism, agnosticism, and atomistic individualism of British empiricism. Although many of the British neo-Hegelians were on the political left in their home country, and many were concerned with issues of social reform, their thought propagated the theological/metaphysical reading of Hegel that Dewey imbibed during the earliest years of his academic career. The most influential members of the British neo-Hegelian movement were Bernard Bosanquet, F. H. Bradley, Edward Caird, and Green. Although it is dangerous to generalize about their thought, it is safe to say that all accepted Hegel's critique of the British empiricist notion of isolated sense impressions, which made it difficult to explain how the mind logically associates individual impressions into complex ideas that correspond to the complex entities we encounter in experience. They sought to "rescue" Hegel from the charge of historical relativism by depicting his absolute as a transcendent God that also serves as a Kantian noumenal realm and provides a guarantee of eternal logical categories. There is order behind the flux of experience, according to the neo-Hegelians, because reality is a system of ordered mutual relations and this system implies the existence of an eternally complete consciousness or absolute mind. Individual minds are able to associate ideas because everything somehow participates in the divine mind. The British neo-Hegelians tended to neglect the *Phenomenology of Spirit,* emphasizing instead Hegel's

Science of Logic, which they read as a grand metaphysical deduction of the categories of reality rather than categories according to which we experience reality.[20]

Recently, John Shook has contributed greatly to our understanding of Dewey's relationship to the British neo-Hegelians and the timing of stages in his intellectual development. I agree with Shook that Dewey abandoned the notion of an absolute mind from 1887 to 1891 and that he developed his functionalist psychology from 1884 to 1896. I supplement Shook's work, however, by distinguishing Hegel from the neo-Hegelians and focusing on Dewey's place within the American Hegelian tradition.[21] I believe this enables me to be more precise as I argue that he found resources for a humanistic reading of Hegel in the American Hegelian tradition, and that he abandoned neo-Hegelianism from 1887 to 1891 as he began to combine the humanistic reading of Hegel with a historicist reading. I also agree with Shook that Dewey developed his instrumental logic from 1891 to 1903, but argue that his humanistic/historicist reading of Hegel provided him with critical resources for his instrumental logic.

Despite the fact that there were many varieties of Hegelianism by the time Dewey came along, scholarship on his Hegelian deposit tenaciously avoids clear definition of "Hegelianism" or "idealism" as well as thorough discussion of Hegel's writings. For the most part, Dewey scholars examine the deposit by looking exclusively at his relationship to the metaphysical/theological Hegel of the neo-Hegelians. When Dewey scholars look solely for evidence of the metaphysical/theological Hegel in his mature thought, they rightly conclude that there is little evidence of it, though they often refer to it simply as "Hegelianism" or "idealism." A far more interesting question is the extent to which we can find the humanistic/historicist Hegel in Dewey's mature thought. Working on the assumption that readers of this book may be unfamiliar with current Hegel scholarship, I articulate a humanistic/historicist reading of Hegel in chapter one, paying particular attention to his conception of philosophy. I do not assume that this is the true reading of Hegel, only that it is well supported by current scholarship and that it places Dewey's Hegelian deposit in a more revealing context.

In chapter two I examine the American Hegelian tradition that powerfully shaped Dewey's philosophical development. Unlike many Anglo-American philosophers today, the American Hegelians with whom Dewey associated emphasized Hegel's place within the German neo-humanist tradition and were attracted to him because they read him as an exceptionally practical and politically liberal philosopher.[22] Although these philosophers, centered in St. Louis, have been characterized as right wing, they are more accurately labeled center Hegelians because they rejected the revolutionary thought of the left Hegelians but were also critical of the Prussian reaction against liberal thought.[23] The St. Louis Hegelians were certainly aware of the British neo-Hegelians, but they were willing to undertake difficult philological work, insisting on studying the entire Hegelian corpus and on reading it in the original language. They also drew upon secondary sources written by some of Hegel's immediate followers in Germany who understood his neo-humanistic context.

In the aftermath of the Civil War, which the St. Louis Hegelians blamed on "brittle individualism," many American intellectuals were deeply concerned about the problems of cultural and national unification, an anxiety that was only heightened by the post-war influx of immigrants and the rapid growth of American cities and industry. The strength of American Hegelianism was its emphasis on the importance of well-founded institutions and man's interdependence during a period of rapid urbanization, specialization, and bureaucratization. Its weakness lay in its holism and seemingly metaphysical and theological nomenclature. Holism, which required that problems be analyzed socially, psychologically, and historically, as well as logically, made it difficult to reconcile Hegelianism with academic specialization, just as the social sciences separated from moral philosophy into distinct disciplines within the new research universities. The St. Louis Hegelians' talk of spirit as opposed to mind or brain made their thought seem "unprofessional" at a time when philosophers were at great pains to demonstrate that they were not being left behind with theology by the emergence of the social sciences. For these reasons American Hegelianism collapsed, ironically, for lack of institutional support.[24]

Dewey had close ties to the American Hegelian tradition, within which he occupied a left-wing position that has eluded scholarly recognition. The remainder of the book focuses on his emergence from that context and his intellectual development up to World War I, especially his reading and appropriation of Hegel. In the third chapter I examine the moderately romantic Burlington philosophy Dewey studied as an undergraduate at the University of Vermont, and the development of his thought at Johns Hopkins, where he worked with one of the most accomplished Hegel scholars in America, George Sylvester Morris. This chapter lays important groundwork for my consideration of why Dewey was attracted to Hegel, and the sort of Hegelianism he espoused during the early years of his professional career.

In chapter four I look at the development of Dewey's thought during the ten years he spent at the University of Michigan (1884–1894). Although he remained active in a local church, by the end of his tenure there, Dewey had worked out a humanistic religion, much like Hegel's, with no transcendent realities. I emphasize ways in which people who came into Dewey's life during these years—Alice Chipman, whom he soon married, Franklin Ford, and Thomas Davidson—influenced him to make his philosophy more practical. By the way he lived his life, Thomas Davidson, I contend, provided Dewey with a concrete example of philosophy as *Bildung.* I argue that Dewey's break with British neo-Hegelianism, after the publication of his *Psychology* in 1887, involved a growing emphasis on Hegel's *Phenomenology of Spirit,* at a time when the neo-Hegelians emphasized the *Science of Logic.* By 1891 Dewey rejected neo-Hegelianism by repudiating its commitment to a transcendent reality but, for Dewey, this did not include a rejection of Hegel. I demonstrate that Dewey combined the neo-humanistic reading of Hegel that the St. Louis Hegelians proffered with a historicist reading that he developed because of the influence of Darwinian biology and developments in psychology. In this way Dewey fashioned an interpretation of Hegel that is comparable to the one I outlined in chapter one and that was consistent with his emerging functionalist psychology, his philosophical method, and his ethics and political thought. Most importantly, I show that Dewey was moving toward a Hegelian conception of philosophy.[25] In an oft-quoted passage, in 1943 Morton White claimed that by 1894 Dewey could "out-James [William] James."[26] In this and the following chapter, I argue that Dewey was able to do so because he had out-Hegeled the neo-Hegelians.

I examine Dewey's ten years at the University of Chicago (1894-1904) in chapter five, tracing the development of his psychology, philosophy of education, and logic. But the centerpiece of this chapter is my analysis of an unpublished 1897 lecture on Hegel's philosophy of spirit, in which Dewey depicted Hegel as "the great actualist," rather than "the grand metaphysician." The lecture demonstrates that Dewey was still sympathetic to Hegel in 1897 and had an impressive knowledge of his life and thought. Most importantly, in the lecture Dewey offered to his graduate students a humanistic/historicist reading of Hegel that emphasized the practicality of Hegel's philosophy.

In chapter six, I argue that although Dewey spoke less of Hegel as he began to associate himself with the newly emerging pragmatist school of philosophy, his first definite, public break from Hegel occurred during World War I. I focus primarily on *German Philosophy and Politics* (1915), pointing out that much of the book is a Hegelian critique of Kant. I also argue that his criticisms of Hegel in that book are unsupported and indefensible. Thus Dewey's first, and only, real break from Hegel was ambiguous at best. I close the chapter and the book with a brief discussion of how Dewey's debt to Hegel's concept of philosophy as *Bildung* remains evident in his mature work. My hope is that now we can more soberly assess the relationship of the two philosophers and perhaps recover the American *Bildung* tradition.

I believe a clearer understanding of Dewey's continuing debt to Hegel clarifies important elements of his thought. Not only does it draw attention to his conception of philosophy as cultural criticism; it helps us better assess his relationship to the British empiricist tradition.[27] Many scholars have noted the influence of British empiricism on Dewey, and it is true that he applauded the empiricists' focus on everyday experience and their emphasis on consequences in ethics, but he consistently sought to balance those themes with an idealistic vision of what society might become. Because critics tend to identify the mature Dewey too closely with the British empiricist tradition, they treat his idealistic hopes as a lapse of rigor smuggled in because he did not have the strength of his positivistic and utilitarian convictions. Furthermore, when critics see elements of Hegelianism in Dewey's mature thought, they view it as an expression of nostalgia for the unfulfilled hopes and dreams of his youthful flirtation with Hegel.

Identifying Dewey with the British empiricist tradition misses the principal thrust of his thought. Dewey's critics often assume that his primary interest was epistemology and logic, but Dewey was influenced by Hegel to reverse a crucial hierarchy of post-Cartesian philosophy by making social and moral philosophy prior to epistemology. That Hoopes makes this very mistake is indicated by his claim that James's and Dewey's "notion of 'immediate experience' was not radical but grew out of the tradition of British empiricism in which the mind's knowledge of its ideas was considered immediate."[28] Such a claim completely misses Dewey's rejection of the Lockean way of ideas. Rather than a knowing consciousness, Hegel and Dewey viewed the self as an intentionally acting being, and self-knowledge (rather than knowledge of an external realm) as the key to the good life. As early as 1899 Dewey rejected "the entire epistemological industry" as a "Sisyphean" task, precisely because its commitment to mind/body dualism removed intelligence from the world and made the resolution of "philosophic problems so arbitrary that they are soluble only by arbitrarily wrenching scientific facts."[29]

Like Hegel, Dewey never viewed dualisms as the technical, logical problems of philosophers; rather, he saw them as manifestations of modern man's alienation from society, nature, and his highest ideals.[30] For Dewey, western philosophy's proclivity to set the mind off from the external world owed its appeal to the increasing depersonalization of the individual in large, bureaucratic organizations. His critique of mind/body dualism was fundamentally intertwined with morally laden functional distinctions between private and public, individual and society, the inward-looking professional philosopher and the more publicly focused amateur. In contrast to the isolated Cartesian self, an entity juxtaposed to its natural and social environment, Dewey consistently described the self as an integral part of its environment, enmeshed in a web of dialectical relationships within society and nature. Dewey was deeply concerned about the western propensity to divide fact and value, especially as manifested in the growing chasm between late-nineteenth-century social science research and philosophy. As early as 1891 Dewey told William James that "the question of the relation of intelligence to the objective world" is directly related to the issue of intellectuals' obligation to be actively engaged in efforts to resolve public problems.[31] As Thomas Bender notes, Dewey's rejection of a mentalistic view of experience "forced philosophy into the world."[32]

I arrive at conclusions that many Dewey scholars will find startling. On the humanistic/historicist reading of Hegel his absolute standpoint is analogous to Dewey's psychological standpoint because both remain truer to experience than British empiricism by rejecting Cartesian mind/body dualism and the notion that foundational realities exist beyond or behind experience. Because of their rejection of Cartesian dualism, both philosophers abandoned the correspondence theory of truth and emphasized the logical coherence of our beliefs, coupled with an existential requirement that true beliefs are those that foster inner harmony and wholeness by resolving specific practical problems. Dewey also believed that Hegel's dialectic resolved the problem of the one and the many by affirming the reality of the particular individual within an inclusive whole. Dewey modeled his theory of inquiry on Hegel's dialectic, according to which ideas are means to action and are always subject to further revision. Both Hegel and Dewey rejected faculty psychology, and depicted the mind as something that emerges through interaction with one's environment. This led Hegel to a rudimentary functional psychology that we see more fully developed in Dewey's mature thought, according to which the mind and its abilities are understood as functions of our interaction within the process of experience. Both philosophers embraced a romantic critique of the Enlightenment by viewing human experience as much more than cognitive, developing theories of learning rather than knowledge, and viewing cognitive success as synthetic rather than reductive. Dewey advocated a much more egalitarian political philosophy than Hegel, but both embraced a theory of positive freedom and viewed learning and education as a means to continual self-development within the context of one's society.[33] Finally, for both philosophers, we do not form societies in spite of our differences, but precisely because we are different and thus complementary to one another. On this model of society, diversity and cultural critique are essential to the health of society.

Notes

1. James Hoopes, *Community Denied: The Wrong Turn of Pragmatic Liberalism* (Ithaca: Cornell University Press, 1998), 2-3. Hoopes defines nominalism in a traditional way: general ideas do not exist, contra Platonism, rather they name general characteristics abstracted from the particulars of experience. Larry Hickman, *John Dewey's Pragmatic Technology* (Bloomington: Indiana University Press, 1990), 128; David Fott, *John Dewey: America's Philosopher of Democracy* (New York: Rowman and Littlefield, 1998), 54. Fott is not the first to state this criticism of Dewey. See, for example, George Santayana, "Dewey's Naturalistic Metaphysics" in *The Philosophy of John Dewey,* ed. Paul Arthur Schilpp and Lewis Hahn, 3rd ed. (Carbondale: Southern Illinois University Press, 1989), 245-261, esp. 247; Robert Wiebe, *The Search for Order, 1877-1920* (New York: Hill and Wang, 1967), 151; Horace M. Kallen, "Individuality, Individualism, and John Dewey," *Antioch Review* 19, no. 3 (Fall 1959): 299-314.

2. Dewey, "From Absolutism to Experimentalism" (1930), LW 5: 154.

3. On Dewey's historicism see Morton White, *Social Thought in America: The Revolt Against Formalism* (Boston: Beacon Press, 1970). By historicism, White means simply that Dewey and his peers (in addition to Dewey, White discusses Oliver Wendell Holmes, Jr., Thorstein Veblen, James Harvey Robinson, and Charles Beard) believed that knowledge was gained by the study of how a thing behaves through time, and that they therefore came to believe that all known, or experienced, reality is temporal (20-21). Throughout this study, when I apply the term "historicism" to Hegel, I mean it in the same way, although in that context, my primary emphasis is that Hegel's absolute spirit is not a reality that transcends the flux of history.

4. F.B.I. New York File No. 100-25838, New York, 29 April 1943 (copy at Center for Dewey Studies, Carbondale, IL). John A. Beineke, "The Investigation

of John Dewey by the F.B.I.," *Educational Theory* (Winter 1987): 43-52. For a fundamentalist attack see John A. Stormer, *None Dare Call it Treason* (Florissant, MO: The Liberty Bell Press, 1964), 99ff. For a Marxist attack see Harry K. Wells, *Pragmatism: Philosophy of Imperialism* (New York: International Publishers, 1954).

5. See Dewey's replies to Bertrand Russell in "Experience, Knowledge and Value: A Rejoinder" (1939), LW 14: 29-34; and "Pragmatic America" (1922), MW 13: 306-310. Reinhold Niebuhr, *Moral Man and Immoral Society: A Study in Ethics and Politics* (New York and London: C. Scribner's, 1932); Lewis Mumford, *The Golden Day: A Study in American Experience and Culture* (New York: Boni and Liveright, 1926); Randolph Bourne, "Twilight of Idols," in *The Radical Will: Randolph Bourne Selected Writings, 1911-1918,* ed. Olaf Hansen (Berkeley: University of California Press, 1977), 343; John Patrick Diggins, *The Promise of Pragmatism: Modernism and the Crisis of Knowledge and Authority* (Chicago: The University of Chicago Press, 1994); Brian Lloyd, *Left Out: Pragmatism, Exceptionalism, and the Poverty of American Marxism, 1890-1922* (Baltimore: Johns Hopkins University Press, 1997). Cf. Christopher Lasch, *The New Radicalism in America, 1889-1963: The Intellectual As a Social Type* (New York: Knopf, 1965); Christopher Lasch, *The True and Only Heaven: Progress and Its Critics* (New York: Norton, 1991).

6. Reinhold Niebuhr's biting attack is the classic example of this criticism of Dewey. Niebuhr, *Moral Man and Immoral Society.* Cf. Andrew Feffer, *The Chicago Pragmatists and American Progressivism* (Ithaca: Cornell University Press, 1993), 264-270. Even John McDermott, a sympathetic supporter of Dewey, has stated that Dewey "had an undeveloped doctrine of evil, the demonic, and the capacity of human beings en masse to commit heinous crimes against other human beings." McDermott, Introduction to LW 11: xxxi. Dewey, *The Poems of John Dewey,* ed. with an introduction by Jo Ann Boydston (Carbondale: Southern Illinois University Press, 1977). Boydston's introduction alone provides a wealth of insight into Dewey's poetry and personality. Steven Rockefeller takes good advantage of Dewey's correspondence and poetry, but his emphasis on Dewey's religiosity leads him to exaggerate existential crises and religious experiences in Dewey's life. Rockefeller, *John Dewey: Religious Faith and Democratic Humanism.* See my comments about Rockefeller in James A. Good, review of *Reading Dewey: Interpretations for a Postmodern Generation,* ed. Larry Hickman, *Transactions of the Charles S. Peirce Society* 35, no. 1 (Winter 1999): 245.

7. Lewis Feuer, Introduction to LW 15: xxxiii. Dorothy Ross mistakes Dewey's meliorism for unalloyed faith in science in Ross, *The Origins of American Social Science* (Cambridge: Cambridge University Press, 1991), 163-169. For an effective response to this error see Laura Westhoff, "The Popularization of Knowledge: John Dewey on Experts and American Democracy," *History of Education Quarterly* 35, no. 1 (Spring 1995): 27-47.

8. This criticism was particularly popular during the 1970s, but it continues to persist: Michael Katz, *Class, Bureaucracy and Schools: The Illusion of Edu-*

cational Change in America (New York: Praeger, 1971); Colin Greer, *The Great School Legend: A Revisionist Interpretation of American Public Education* (New York: Basic Books, 1972); Charles A. Tesconi, Jr. and Van Cleve Morris, *The Anti-Man Culture: Bureautechnocracy and the Schools* (Urbana: University of Illinois Press, 1972); Lloyd, *Left Out,* 49-50, 300-301. For effective rejoinders see Christopher J. Eisele, "John Dewey and the Immigrants," *History of Education Quarterly* 15, no. 1 (Spring 1975): 67-85; and Robert Westbrook, *John Dewey and American Democracy* (Ithaca: Cornell University Press, 1991), 178-189.

9. See Stanley Aronowitz, "Introduction" in Max Horkheimer, *Critical Theory: Selected Essays* (New York: Continuum, 1995), xvi. See also Dewey's response to Lewis Mumford in "The Pragmatic Acquiescence" (1927), LW 3: 145-151.

10. This is a crucial element of Dewey's understanding of experience, according to which, experience is always both active and passive. See Dewey, *Democracy and Education* (1916), MW 9: 146. "When we experience something we act upon it, we do something with it; then we suffer or undergo the consequences. We do something to the thing and then it does something to us in return." Intelligent action, for Dewey, always involves consideration of future consequences, of the ways our action will modify our environment and, in turn, how that modification will impact upon us.

11. For useful accounts and analyses of these charges against Hegel see Jon Stewart, ed., *The Hegel Myths and Legends* (Evanston, IL: Northwestern University Press, 1996). Brian Lloyd comes close to equating Dewey's support of World War I with Hegel's supposed fondness for war. Lloyd, *Left Out,* 8, 24-25, 50, 296-297, 298-301.

12. John Zammito, *Kant, Herder, and the Birth of Anthropology* (Chicago: University of Chicago Press, 2002), 7-9. Michael N. Forster has recently argued for Hegel's debt to Herder, at least in the *Phenomenology*. Forster, *Hegel's Idea of a* Phenomenology of Spirit (Chicago: University of Chicago Press, 1998).

13. Richard Rorty, *Philosophy and the Mirror of Nature* (Princeton: Princeton University Press, 1979), 359-360.

14. On this point, I am indebted to James Campbell's as yet unpublished history of the A.P.A., as well as conversations with him on this and other historical issues.

15. Rorty, *Philosophy and the Mirror of Nature,* 360, 373.

16. See the second rule of Descartes' *Discourse on Method,* a methodological manifesto of the Enlightenment. "The second [rule] was to divide each of the difficulties which I encountered into as many parts as possible, and as might be required for an easier solution." René Descartes, *Discourse on Method and Meditations,* trans. Laurence J. Lafleur (New York: Macmillan, 1960), 15. See also Steven B. Smith, *Hegel's Critique of Liberalism: Rights in Context* (Chicago: University of Chicago Press, 1989), 165-167.

17. Although he does not emphasize Dewey's debt to Hegel, or mention the concept of *Bildung,* I believe Philip Jackson captures Dewey's conception of

philosophy and the philosopher's task as well as any Dewey scholar I have read. Jackson, *John Dewey and the Philosopher's Task* (New York: Teacher's College Press, 2002), especially chs. 4-6.

18. See George Herbert Eastman's critique of Joseph Ratner's foreword to his edition of Dewey's writings. Eastman notes Ratner's need to show "that Hegelianism—and idealism in general—is an effete, a somehow suspect, if not dissolute philosophy from which Dewey wisely, and heroically, freed himself." Eastman, review of *John Dewey: Philosophy, Psychology and Social Practice, Studies in Philosophy and Education* 4 (1965): 95-104. See also Ratner's "Reply to George Eastman," ibid., 105-107. Similarly, in his description of Dewey's transition from idealism to instrumentalism, Morton White invokes the image of slavery when he writes that Dewey "continued to hammer away at his chains." White, *The Origin of Dewey's Instrumentalism* (New York: Columbia University Press, 1943), 106.

19. A convenient collection of essays that present Hegel in this way may be found in H. Tristram Engelhardt and Terry Pinkard, eds., *Hegel Reconsidered: Beyond Metaphysics and the Authoritarian State* (Boston: Kluwer Academic Publishers, 1994).

20. The British neo-Hegelians were very influenced by James Hutchison Stirling, who instigated the movement toward Hegel in British thought with his book *The Secret of Hegel* (1865). But Stirling tended to ignore the *Phenomenology*, and later British neo-Hegelians followed his lead on this point, viewing *The Science of Logic,* rather than the *Phenomenology,* as the beginning point of Hegel's system. See J. B. Baillie, Introduction to *The Phenomenology of Mind,* by Hegel, trans. J. B. Baillie (New York: Humanities Press, 1949).

21. John Shook, *Dewey's Empirical Theory of Knowledge and Reality* (Nashville: Vanderbilt University Press, 2000). Shook emphasizes the influence of Edward Caird, rather than T. H. Green, on Dewey's early thought.

22. Throughout this book, I use the "liberal" designation for Hegel, fully aware that he was highly critical of the British liberal tradition. In the context of this book, I call Hegel a liberal because he was committed to the ideals of the French Revolution—liberty, equality, and fraternity.

23. Many scholars have portrayed the St. Louis Hegelians as right-wing Hegelians. See John Watson, "Idealism and Social Theory: A Comparative Study of British and American Adaptations of Hegel, 1860-1914" (Ph.D. diss., University of Pennsylvania, 1975), 50; and Merle Curti, *Social Ideas of American Educators* (New York: Charles Scribner's Sons, 1935), 310-347.

24. Although the American *Bildung* tradition I have in mind virtually disappeared, Andrew Reck correctly argues that "the usual view that idealism died at the turn of the century and that pragmatism triumphed to dominate all subsequent thought in the United States proves to be patently false." Reck, *Recent American Philosophy: Studies of Ten Representative Thinkers* (New York: Pantheon Books, 1962), xvii. Cf. Reck, "Idealism in American Philosophy Since 1900," in *Contemporary Studies in Philosophical Idealism,* ed. John Howie and Thomas O. Buford (Cape Cod, MA: Claude Stark, 1975), 17-52.

25. Raymond Boisvert, *John Dewey: Rethinking Our Time* (Albany: State University of New York Press, 1998). I hope that the interpretation of Dewey that emerges in these pages will show that even Dewey's writings on logic and method, which Boisvert wants to de-emphasize, provide a rich vein of philosophical tools to promote individual and cultural growth.

26. White, *The Origin of Dewey's Instrumentalism,* 107.

27. Others have argued that Dewey was committed to cultural criticism. I hope that by grounding that claim within the context of the American *Bildung* tradition, I will add to its plausibility. In addition to Jackson, *John Dewey and the Philosopher's Task,* see: Westbrook, *John Dewey and American Democracy;* Richard Shusterman, *Practicing Philosophy: Pragmatism and the Philosophical Life* (New York: Routledge, 1997); Michael Eldridge, *Transforming Experience: John Dewey's Cultural Instrumentalism* (Nashville: Vanderbilt University Press, 1998); and, for a convenient collection of recent essays that generally support this reading of Dewey, see Larry A. Hickman, ed., *Reading Dewey: Interpretations for a Postmodern Generation* (Bloomington: Indiana University Press, 1998). See also my review of that book in *Transactions of the Charles S. Peirce Society* 35, no. 1 (Winter 1999): 240-247. Raymond Boisvert depicts Dewey's conception of philosophy in a similar way. Boisvert, *John Dewey: Rethinking Our Time,* 161.

28. Hoopes, "Objectivity and Relativism Affirmed," *American Historical Review* 98, no. 5. (Dec. 1993): 1551. Cf. Robert J. Roth, *British Empiricism and American Pragmatism: New Directions and Neglected Arguments* (New York: Fordham University Press, 1993).

29. Dewey, "'Consciousness and Experience" (1899), MW 1: 22.

30. Lewis S. Feuer, "John Dewey and the Back to the People Movement in American Thought," *Journal of the History of Ideas* 20 (1959): 565. Feuer compares Dewey's analysis of the psychological effects of dualisms to Freud's views on the effects of dualism between the super-ego and the id.

31. Dewey to William James, 3 June 1891; Thomas Bender, *Intellect and Public Life: Essays on the Social History of Academic Intellectuals in the United States* (Baltimore and London: Johns Hopkins University Press, 1993), 127-145.

32. Thomas Bender, *New York Intellect: A History of Intellectual Life in New York City, From 1750 to the Beginnings of Our Own Time* (New York: Knopf, 1987), 311.

33. Daniel Savage has recently argued that the concept of "self-development" is central to Dewey's moral and political thought, but he assumes that Dewey got this concept from Darwinian biology rather than the German neo-Humanists, Hegel, and the St. Louis Hegelians. Although Savage correctly states that Dewey rejected fixed ends, he claims that Dewey's moral theory is a type of "perfectionism." Dewey never used that term to describe his moral theory, however, and I believe it invites misunderstanding of his thought. Savage, *John Dewey's Liberalism: Individual, Community, and Self-Development* (Carbondale: Southern Illinois University Press, 2002).

Chapter One

The Humanistic/Historicist Hegel

In the twentieth century, the recovery of Hegel's popular political writings, complemented by biographical study, shed light on the way he conceived his philosophical project.[1] Steven B. Smith captures the gist of this scholarship particularly well in *Hegel's Critique of Liberalism: Rights in Context* where he argues that, for Hegel, the primary purpose of philosophy was immanent cultural critique. More specifically, Hegel intended the dialectic as a method of cultural criticism that identifies the standards of rationality within an existing culture or system of thought and then criticizes practices that do not accord with those standards of rationality. This method is immanent critique in the sense that it criticizes a culture on its own terms, on the basis of its highest ideals, rather than some apodictic first principle or transcendent, abstract moral standards.[2] In this chapter I argue that this reading of Hegel is justified by evidence drawn from the early years of his intellectual development and throughout his writings. I look at biographical information about Hegel because it is important that both Hegel and Dewey had a pietistic background that made them averse to dogmatism, not only in theology, but also in philosophy. That religious background also led them to reject the fact/value dichotomy and to search for cultural rejuvenation in a way that combined religious and political issues or, perhaps more precisely, made political issues take on religious overtones. Hegel's life also undermines the mischaracterization of his thought as inherently conservative and authoritarian by demonstrating his lifelong desire to actualize the ideals of the French Revolution. In the course of articulating this reading of Hegel's philosophy, I elucidate philosophical themes that appear in the American Hegelian tradition in which Dewey was schooled and, more importantly, that appear in Dewey's life and thought.

In general, Hegel was concerned with the modern problematic as he defined it. The liberal political tradition with its emphasis on the rights and dignity of the individual was the strength of modernity. But the liberal tradition failed to effectively ground individual rights or to provide a rationale that would ensure their protection because it neglected the concrete historical context in which rights emerge, positing a mythical and purely abstract state of nature instead. The liberal tradition offered a merely "formal" or abstract justification for rights that ignored the way they are established through historical struggle. Further, by assuming that rights are grounded in an ahistorical human nature, the liberal tradition ignored the ways in which individual psychology and moral personality develop through time. Another way to say this is that Hegel believed the liberal tradition, founded on British empiricism, was not empirical enough. Individual rights, for Hegel, had to be grounded in the concrete conditions in which we actually live, and realized in our individual and social development. Hegel addressed the modern problematic by questioning the abstract/concrete distinction, placing mind and ideals in the world rather than a separate metaphysical realm, and emphasizing man's social and historical context.

The modern problematic also raised troubling existential issues, because the Cartesian dualism on which it was based alienated Western man from nature, society, and himself. Hence, alienation—what recent scholars have called "the divided self" or "the Cartesian Anxiety"—was the root problem of modernity, and it was the result of the Enlightenment dualisms of mind and body, public and private, the legal and the moral, and the practical and the theoretical.[3] Hegel believed philosophy could heal this cultural wound by providing the conceptual framework for a unified self in the context of a unified modern, liberal society.

In an early essay, "The Difference Between Fichte's and Schelling's System of Philosophy" (1801), Hegel explained that antitheses—"spirit and matter, soul and body, faith and intellect, freedom and necessity, etc."—arise naturally as we struggle to understand our existence. These antitheses emerge, Hegel explained, in particular places and times in response to particular problems but, "with the progress of culture," they lose their force because past problems are no longer our problems. Nevertheless, these antitheses are enshrined as indubitable "products of Reason" and, as such, the same lifeless antitheses seem to animate philosophy for time immemorial. For Hegel, "the sole interest of Reason is to suspend such rigid antitheses." Reason is not opposed, Hegel wrote, to oppositions, limitations and dichotomies, because "life eternally forms itself by setting up oppositions. . . . What Reason opposes, rather, is just the absolute fixity which the intellect gives to the dichotomy . . . " Hegel recognized that conceptual dualisms serve a legitimate function in everyday life, but believed that problems arise when we mistake these functional concepts for fixed, eternal truths. He believed philosophy should serve the practical purpose of resolving dualisms that have become reified with age and that set man against himself, his neighbor, and his natural environment. Philosophy succeeds when it demonstrates that these dichotomies are contingent, that is to say, relative to an "original identity" that is in a process of becoming. In Hegel's words, "When the might of union vanishes from the life of men and the antitheses lose their living connection and reciprocity and gain independence, the need for philosophy arises."[4] The primary goal of Hegel's philosophy was a quest for social unity, as well as the existential unity of the individual. Consequently, Hegel was principally concerned with the reconciliation of oppositions or dichotomies that created rifts in the social fabric and within the lives of individuals. An examination of Hegel's intellectual development casts valuable light on how he arrived at this conception of philosophy.

Intellectual Origins

Hegel's lifelong quest for unity may have been a natural response to the constant political and social turmoil in which he lived. Georg Wilhelm Friedrich Hegel was born in Stuttgart in the Duchy of Württemburg in 1770, a Protestant territory ruled by a Catholic duke.[5] The duke had absolutist political ambitions that precipitated a crisis in the religious and political loyalties of the state's predominantly Protestant population. Württemburg, which was much closer to France than Berlin, also had deep republican political sentiments. These sentiments were held particularly strongly in the face of the perceived threat from the duke. As Laurence Dickey explains, Württemburg was unique among the German states with a religio-political tradition that was grounded in the thought of "down-to-earth Pietists" and a commitment to the "Good Old Law" that Protestants used to justify their resistance to the duke's encroachments upon their religious rights. Consequently, in Württemburg, Pietists viewed the duke's political ambitions in a religious context, and described him as an "Antichrist-tyrant," intent on subverting Protestant Christianity and reversing the gains of the Reformation.[6]

As Dickey has shown, Württemburg's down-to-earth Pietists criticized the escapism of religion that emphasized life in a hereafter and bequeathed to Hegel a conviction that political activism was not antithetical to Christianity. Hegel embraced a pietistic concept of "Protestant civil piety," according to which "one of the basic functions of religion was to make man better by improving the ethical quality of civil life."[7] This combination of religion and politics has created much confusion in Hegel scholarship, particularly in efforts to understand his concept of *Geist,* which is properly understood as a religio-political concept. In Württemburg, Hegel also developed a pronounced prejudice against Catholicism and authoritarian government.[8] His deep-seated opposition to authoritarianism is apparent in his political allegiances throughout his life. In 1789 Hegel saw the French Revolution as the promise of a more republican future. He was disillusioned by the Reign of Terror (1793-1794), but was an enthusiastic defender of Napoleon as one who would disseminate liberal ideals throughout Europe, and a conscientious objector to German nationalism and the "Wars of Liberation."[9] He was visibly pleased by the French defeat of Prussia and the frustration of German nationalism. Like Herder and Goethe, he remained at most a cultural (never political) nationalist, using the German language and the new ideas of German idealism to further the enlightenment of the human spirit as a whole.[10]

Although the Enlightenment defined Hegel's gymnasium education in Stuttgart, it was neither the critical Enlightenment of Kant nor the radical Enlightenment of Rousseau and Voltaire, but the Jewish-German *Aufklärung* of Lessing and Mendelssohn and the *Popularphilosophie* of Christian Garve.[11] The German writers stressed practical wisdom and education as self-cultivation (*Bildung*), religious tolerance and the compatibility of religions in a way that stressed the importance of social unity. These writers' emphasis on what Hegel called "subjectivity" encouraged his disdain of "book-learning" and "dead-thinking." Even at the gymnasium Hegel preferred the "naïve" straightforwardness of ancient Greek culture, as he romanticized it, to the formal doctrines of Christianity.[12]

Hegel matriculated into the *Tübingenstift,* the Protestant seminary in Tübingen, in 1788. He never considered entering the ministry; he attended the *Stift* simply because the state paid for his education. Among his fellow students were Friedrich Schelling (1775-1854) and the poet Friedrich Hölderlin (1770-1843). The impressionable Schelling was five years younger than the other two. Hegel, the "old man" of the group, was distinctively less creative, still struggling for an intellectual identity. Hegel and his friends (particularly Hölderlin) were strongly drawn to the calling of a *Volkserzieher* or a popular philosopher—one whose purpose is to raise the moral consciousness of his countrymen by disseminating Enlightenment ideals through popular writings, as well as more artistic and mythopoeic devices, and thereby to promote cultural regeneration.[13] Schelling and Hölderlin were well known in German intellectual circles by 1800, the former as a philosophical prodigy, the latter as a poet, novelist, and dramatist of note. By contrast, Hegel was well into his thirties before he produced the sort of work for which he is remembered. Hegel and his friends hated their theological studies, but they read, studied, and steeped themselves in Enlightenment Lutheranism, *Sturm und Drang* literature, and the thought of Spinoza, Kant, and Fichte. The greatest influence on them at the time, however, was the French Revolution. They were keen partisans of the Revolution, devouring French newspapers and enthusiastically reading and discussing Rousseau and Voltaire. Hegel never lost his commitment to the principles of the Revolution, drinking a toast to the storming of the Bastille every fourteenth of July, but his hopes for the Revolution were dashed when, in 1793, it began to self-destruct in the Reign of Terror; from then on he identified with the Girondin, a moderate faction of the Revolution.[14] Intellectual problems raised by the Terror animated Hegel's thought for the rest of his life.

Hegel evidently read Kant's *Critique of Pure Reason* and the *Critique of Practical Reason* as early as 1790, but he believed Kant overemphasized man's rationality to the neglect of his moral passions.[15] Hegel approved of Kant's insight that the mind is active, but saw his philosophy as emblematic of modern alienation: Kant's noumenal/phenomenal dualism alienated man from nature and made science impossible because the thing-in-itself was unknowable. Man was alienated from himself because, according to Kant, the empirical self could not know the transcendental self, which ordered experience according to transcendental categories. Man was also alienated from his empirical needs and desires because he was required to fulfill his absolute duty to the categorical imperative regardless of his desires and regardless of considerations about the consequences of his actions. Hegel also believed that Kant's notion of transcendent duty would promote social division because it could be used to foster dangerous religious and political zealotry, a belief that was only strengthened by the Reign of Terror.[16]

Convinced that modern man's problems were more deeply rooted than he initially recognized, by 1800 Hegel decided that the goals of popular philosophy required a reconstruction of modern philosophy. This crucial transition in Hegel's development was motivated by what he perceived as the failures of the French Revolution and his reading of the Scottish economists—especially Adam Ferguson, Adam Smith, and James Steuart. From these Scottish thinkers, Hegel took the lesson that the French revolutionaries had erred by underestimating the degree to which long-standing socioeconomic and political forces would frustrate their efforts to transform society rapidly. He decided that Protestant civil piety alone was not enough to achieve the sort of religio-political reform he sought, because it belittled the interplay of human action with complex socioeconomic forces. Although the Scottish economists profoundly influenced Hegel, he believed they had a pernicious tendency to reduce man to a rational, economic being. Further, Friedrich von Schiller's *Letters on the Aesthetic Education of Man* alerted him to the dehumanizing effects of the emerging industrial order, which, through commodification and its demands for narrow specialization in the name of efficiency, fragmented society and the human spirit.[17] He resolved to develop a rational articulation of reality that would reunite reason and emotion within the individual in a harmonious whole, and the enlightened and unenlightened elements of society in a spiritual community. Hegel viewed Christianity as a resource for the symbols needed in such a philosophy, and began to speak of *Geist,* or spirit, as the vehicle of unification.[18] In this way Hegel took Christianity more seriously than the typical Enlightenment thinker, but he also sought to secularize it by incorporating its insights into philosophy.

Hegel never abandoned the goals of popular philosophy, individual and cultural regeneration, but he struggled to find the best way to realize them. By 1800, he began to question the methods of popular philosophy, as he embarked upon an academic career. After 1800, his writings became much more technical and complex.[19] By the time he published the *Science of Logic,* Hegel had fully embraced the technical apparatus of academic German philosophy, but even in that highly technical tome, he sought to promote cultural unification through immanent critique of Western philosophical concepts.

Hegel began to develop the dialectic to assess and promote the progress of theories and cultures. This method is evident not only in his logic, but in all of his major works. Smith perceptively points out three key features of Hegel's method. First, Hegel's dialectic "must be immanent or internal to its subject matter." There is no God's eye view or Archimedean point from which we can investigate a subject matter. We cannot legitimately ask if a theory accurately describes its subject matter, because to some degree a theory always creates the subject it seeks to explain. We can examine a theory's internal coherence, however, and ask whether it accomplishes the goal(s) it sets for itself. Second, Hegel's dialectic is "dialogical in character."[20] The dialectic does not take place within an internal, private mind, but is always a conversation between past, contemporaneous, and future interlocutors. For Hegel, all thinking is mediated by the intellectual tradition we have inherited from our predecessors. For this reason, his works generally have the character of a conversation with illustrious predecessors in which he recognizes their contribution to our current point of view. Rather than refute his opponents, Hegel engaged them in conversation.[21] Third, Hegel's dialectic is based on the assumption that all theory has a vitally important historical dimension. He accepted Kant's contention that the mind actively categorizes sense data, but historicized his categories. For Hegel, our conceptual structure is historically and culturally relative; all logical categories, even those that appear to be the most permanent, are subject to change. The historical relativism of Hegel's account of logical categories has always raised eyebrows. He sought to counter the charge of relativism by claiming that historical epochs fit into a larger narrative, mankind's continual search for greater freedom. For Hegel, history has a moral unity and every historical epoch fits into that unity in some way. The *Weltgeist,* or world-spirit, tirelessly moves in the direction of ever increasing human freedom.

Early in 1801 Hegel moved to Jena, the birthplace of German Romanticism. At Jena, he accepted the tutelage of Schelling, now a successful philosophy professor at the university. Although his purpose was to pursue an academic career, a letter Hegel wrote to Schelling shortly before he moved to Jena indicates that he had not forsaken the practical goals of popular philosophy: "In my own development which began with the most elementary needs of man, I was necessarily pushed towards science and the ideals of my youth necessarily became a form of reflection, transformed into a system. I ask myself now, while still engaged in this, how to find a way back to the lives of men."[22] The rate at which Hegel's philosophy developed in Jena is astonishing. Rather than analyze all of his writings during this period, I will concentrate on the culmination of his intellectual development in the *Phenomenology of Spirit.* Because Hegel conceived the purpose of the *Phenomenology* as laying the groundwork for proper philosophical thinking, an exercise in learning or clearing one's mind of the implicit foundational assumptions of the modern problematic, I will draw upon it to further elucidate his conception of philosophy.[23]

Phenomenology of Spirit

Jena Romanticism played an important but complex role in Hegel's philosophical development. Although his quest for unity may be romantic, there is much in Romanticism and its use of the philosophy of Fichte, which Hegel and Shelling derided as subjective idealism, that he rejected.[24] Emphasizing spontaneity and autonomy, Fichte claimed the "I" achieves its identity only in struggle against and conquest over the sphere of the "not-I" (everything outside of the self). Jena Romantics who hovered around Friedrich Schlegel appropriated this theme in Fichte's thought to argue that man's true vocation was to achieve ever fuller freedom and loyal devotion to one's own individual intuitions and spiritual ideals, transcending the moral claims made upon the individual by society. Believing with Fichte that speculative understanding is superior to Kant's principle of reflective understanding, Schlegel gave primacy to the creative fancy for which the world is simply an occasion to express itself in all its fullness. Individual fulfillment and freedom is achieved in artistic activity in which the artist becomes increasingly aware of himself as creator, and discovers his genius, the divine within himself.

For Hegel, on the other hand, freedom consists in fully reciprocal, mutual imposition of norms within society, not in the one-sided imposition of norms upon oneself, which he feared would soon lead to the one-sided imposition of norms upon others as one "discovered" his divinity.[25] Hegel believed that this celebration of the "I" led to the violence of the Reign of Terror, and would lead to a dangerous extremism in any society. In the *Phenomenology*, he argued that Romanticism degenerates into a "beauty of the soul," according to which the individual follows the dictates of his own conscience regardless of the judgments of others, or the consequences of their actions upon others. Furthermore, such a soul is beautiful because it is unified, but it cannot act in a fragmented world without tarnishing itself. Ultimately, the beautiful soul does not dare to act because it knows it will compromise its own purity. Ironically, the beautiful soul can identify what ought to be done in a particular situation, but must keep its distance from society. Thus, for Hegel, radical individualism will lead either to self-centered fanaticism or inactive quietism. He concluded that the only way to move beyond this predicament is to recognize that we must act on reasons that can be shared by all, and that these reasons are not "given," as were Kant's, but must be negotiated and struggled over.[26]

Hegel sought to strike a mean between the extremes of Enlightenment reason and romantic mysticism. This philosophical goal makes him seem like the consummate Enlightenment philosopher with an exaggerated faith in reason and systematic, scientific thought, and at the same time, the consummate romantic philosopher emphasizing spiritual unification within an organic, developmental vision of the whole of history and reality. As H. S. Harris explains, Hegel sought "the fusion of the ideal of rational enlightenment with the romantic ideal of direct experience and living intuition." This ultimately led him "to a different and far deeper conception of reason itself," which always included the emotions as well as discursive abilities.[27]

Although he embraced reason, rather than romantic intuition, Hegel retained a conviction that philosophy should demonstrate to modern man how to regain, to the extent possible in nation states, the unity that existed in the ancient Greek polis.[28] In the *Phenomenology,* he agreed with the Romantics that philosophy must not be confined to the study. Philosophy, argued Hegel, must ultimately demonstrate that its results do not pervert the "natural attitude," the certainty we all have in our everyday lives that we have access to reality and that our projects prosper or falter as we function within that reality. He sought to demonstrate that the absolute standpoint lies within the natural attitude, and thus to establish the natural attitude on firm philosophical ground by articulating what is latent (the absolute standpoint) within it. As Joseph Flay explains, the goal of the *Phenomenology* was "to establish the *unity* of the experience of the natural attitude with the experience instantiated within the absolute standpoint of absolute idealism." Hegel rejected the traditional notion that the philosophical attitude is "the esoteric possession of a few individuals," and believed that philosophy should be "completely determined." By determined, he meant that one should be able to explain and state reasons for one's philosophical beliefs. Such a philosophy would be "comprehensible, and capable of being learned and appropriated by all."[29]

Hegel defended the common-sense view that we have knowledge, but he criticized everyday "natural consciousness" that "takes itself to be real knowledge," only because it is naïvely certain. He implicitly praised Descartes for utilizing "the pathway of doubt" which provides "conscious insight into the untruth of phenomenal knowledge," but clearly his attack on traditional epistemology included Descartes. In contrast to Descartes, Hegel called his method "the way of despair" to emphasize that it is much more than an intellectual process of "shilly-shallying about this or that presumed truth, followed by a return to that truth again, after the doubt has been appropriately dispelled—so that at the end of the process the matter is taken to be what it was in the first place." What he had in mind was doubt that calls into question our very forms of life, not just isolated, subjective beliefs. The way of despair reveals the limitations of the natural consciousness but, rather than mere negation, it leads us to determinate negation, a more profound and inclusive standpoint. Through a series of determinate negations we discover the absolute standpoint within natural consciousness. In absolute knowing, "knowledge no longer needs to go beyond itself. . . . Notion corresponds to object and object to Notion."[30] Absolute knowing is not knowledge of eternal truth; it is knowledge that does not go beyond itself to posit a metaphysical foundation such as Descartes' cogito, Kant's noumenal realm, or Fichte's self-positing ego.

Hegel's talk of notion corresponding to object sounds like an expression of the correspondence theory of truth, but he rejected the inner/outer dichotomy upon which that theory is ordinarily based, asserting that "knowing is not an activity that deals with the content as something alien."[31] In a temporal process, consciousness compares its conception of the object to the object's actual behavior, which also occurs within consciousness, and continually modifies its conception in that light. This is a correspondence theory of truth, but one in which the object is always an object of consciousness and is always changed by our conception of it.[32] So correspondence is the goal of knowledge for Hegel but, contrary to any philosophy that accepts Cartesian dualism, he did not view consciousness as an internal realm, or correspondence as a relationship between two ontologically distinct entities. Robert Solomon claims that Hegel's "is a heavily *practical* conception of Truth with strong affinities to what has been defended in this century (by William James and others) as the 'pragmatic theory of truth.'"[33] Though perhaps surprising to many scholars, Solomon's claim has prima facie plausibility in light of Hegel's discussion of truth in the *Phenomenology*. According to Hegel, "'true' and 'false'" are incorrectly thought to be "inert and wholly separate essences, one here and one there, each standing fixed and isolated from the other, with which it has nothing in common." His point was that truth and falsity do not preexist our experience of the world and they are not unchanging, Platonic forms. Hence, "true" and "false" are not objects to which our ideas could correspond. "Dogmatism," according to Hegel, "is nothing else but the opinion that the True consists in a proposition which is a fixed result, or which is immediately known." In words that could have been penned by William James, Hegel wrote, "truth is not a minted coin that can be given and pocketed ready-made."[34] By way of comparison, James claimed, "The truth of an idea is not a stagnant property inherent in it. Truth *happens* to an idea. It *becomes* true, is *made* true by events."[35]

Hegel also rejected the view that "in every falsehood there is a grain of truth" on the grounds that this "is to treat the two like oil and water, which cannot be mixed and are only externally combined." It is just as fallacious, he claimed, to speak of "the *unity* of subject and object, of finite and infinite, of being and thought, etc." because as contraries these terms designate disunity; we can only speak of subject and object when "they are *outside* of their unity, and since in their unity they are not meant to be what their expression says they are, just so the false is no longer *qua* false, a moment of the truth."[36] We can only properly speak of true and false when there is a disunity of subject and object, when we encounter a contradiction or conflict of some sort.

Hegel claimed "Consciousness provides its own criterion from within itself, so that the investigation becomes a comparison of consciousness with itself." Rather than a static correspondence of thought and being, truth is a conceptual activity through which we conceive the world together with our recognition that our concepts shape the world we experience. There is no reality "in itself" beyond our experience. Truth is experience conceived through *Begriff,* the "concept." Although *Begriff* is generally translated as "concept" or "notion," Hegel scholars often object that this obscures its relationship to the verb *begreifen,* which comes from *greifen,* to grasp or seize. Thus *Begriff* is more than concept or notion because it implies that mind is activity, rather than substance, engaged in capturing, embracing, or encompassing its object within consciousness. The object realizes or actualizes the concept, while "idea," in Hegel's usage, is the successful union of the concept and its object. Further, the concept is more than a representation or empirical conception; for that, Hegel used *Vorstellung.*[37] Rather than a mental entity, the notion is a tool we craft for use within our dialectical interaction with the environment. This point becomes apparent in Hegel's theory of universals, to which I will return in a moment.

We comprehend our experience within the network of our concepts, the intelligibility of our concepts in the face of our actual experience, our overall sense of total comprehension. Truth involves correspondence of the object with its notion, the logical coherence of our ideas, but it is absolutely imperative to appreciate that, for Hegel, logical coherence is a sense of self-satisfaction. We seek to avoid being driven back to "the same barren ego."[38] The attainment of truth provides enrichment or deepening of our experience. It is this sense of personal inadequacy, rather than mere logical or epistemological demands, that provides, for Hegel, the ultimate criterion of truth.

The Absolute, Absolute Truth, Philosophy as Science, and *Geist*

My discussion of the *Phenomenology* thus far—particularly Hegel's concepts of the absolute standpoint and absolute knowing—will undoubtedly make Dewey scholars cringe with discomfort. In an effort to dispel this discomfort, I will now directly confront several Hegelian concepts—the absolute, absolute truth, philosophy as science, and *Geist*—that might seem completely at odds with Dewey's mature philosophy.

In the preface to the *Phenomenology*, Hegel asserted that philosophy is the presentation of philosophical or "absolute" truth. In Hegel's day, German philosophers, especially Schelling, often used "absolute" as a synonym for infinity. But these philosophers seldom, if ever, used "infinity" as a mathematical term. Rather, "infinity" was more akin to Anaximander's *apeiron:* the boundless, or the unlimited.[39] For the German idealists, "infinite" meant complete or self-contained, and the absolute meant the whole, that which is undivided or unqualified. In the *Science of Logic,* Hegel distinguished between the genuine and spurious infinite, or a bad infinity; the former was self-contained and autonomous, the latter simply goes on and on in an infinite regress. For Hegel, cognition that is limited by the senses, the forms of intuition, the categories of the understanding, or the dictates of transcendent obligation is necessary to quotidian human life, but is merely finite. In order for such knowledge or action fully to make sense, to be fully meaningful, it has to be understood within the whole of human experience. According to Hegel, any philosophy that renders reality or our experience of it into separate, finite segments is inherently incomplete and inadequate.[40]

Hegel criticized Romantics who insisted that "the Absolute is not supposed to be comprehended, it is to be felt and intuited; not the Notion of the absolute but the feeling and intuition of it."[41] In this passage, Hegel used "absolute" to mean all of reality, containing all relations, and thus not related to anything beyond itself. In this sense, Hegel's absolute was analogous to Kant's thing-in-itself, but for Hegel the thing-in-itself was knowable. And in contrast to the Romantics, Hegel maintained that knowledge of the absolute requires the "Notion"; it demands articulation and "reasons" (*Grunden*).

To advocates of the historicist reading of Hegel's absolute, the view that it is the final cause, or end, of history makes his philosophy radically inconsistent. Historicists emphasize Hegel's claim that idealism can make no presuppositions or admit merely postulated entities, and argue that he could not consistently assert that the absolute is an ontological principle. On the historicist reading, Hegel's absolute is an epistemological principle, and absolute knowledge is not knowledge that is beyond time. As Rockmore explains, the historicist reading of Hegel's absolute takes its cues from the perspectival nature of the types of knowledge he discussed in the *Phenomenology,* his notion of historical reason, and the sentiment expressed in *The Philosophy of Right* that "every individual is a *child of his time*; thus philosophy, too, is *its own time comprehended in thoughts.*"[42] At the end of the *Phenomenology,* Hegel did not describe absolute knowledge as the final and absolutely true perspective, but rather as a perspective that is unique because it is aware of its own conditions and limitations.[43] On this reading, Hegel's later historicist claim in *The Philosophy of Right* is not a change but a development of his position in the *Phenomenology*.[44] Similarly, in his logic, Hegel argued that the final philosophical perspective is simply one that is fully thought out in terms of concepts. If no one can transcend their historical epoch then, for Hegel, claims to know must be based on knowledge at its current state of development.

Hegel also used "absolute" to refer to the outcome of a dialectical inquiry. The absolute notion "contains all the earlier categories of thought merged in it."[45] The absolute standpoint, reached at the end of the *Phenomenology*, is the point from which we can begin philosophy in the *Science of Logic*. It is a return to the "natural attitude" devoid of the naïve certainty that Hegel noted at the beginning of the *Phenomenology*. When used in this way, the "absolute" is a theoretical standpoint achieved when we free ourselves from dogmatic assumptions—particularly the division of thought and being that lies at the heart of representational epistemology—and apprehend their unity. In the absolute standpoint we know that we have knowledge, just as we did in the "natural attitude," but now, rather than simply assert it dogmatically, we can rationally respond to skeptics who question that we do. From this standpoint, we can acknowledge and examine the limitations of, and inconsistencies within, our beliefs. For this reason, Hegel also claimed that the categorial scheme he laid out in the *Science of Logic* was absolute because it overcame the problematic of representational epistemology. His logical categories were not functions of the empirical subject (modes of representation), hence they could not be subjective; rather, similar to Aristotle, Hegel believed logical categories are in things as much as they are in thought. Hegel criticized Kant on this very point:

> Thoughts, according to Kant, although universal and necessary categories, are *only our* thoughts—separated by an impassible gulf from the thing, as it exists apart from our knowledge. But the true objectivity of thinking means that the thoughts, far from being merely ours, must at the same time be the real essence of the things, and of whatever is an object to us.[46]

Hegel's talk of essences is commonly misunderstood, however, because he believed, unlike Aristotle, that the object of experience is constructed in the knowing process. It is vital to observe that Hegel was speaking about the real essence of what "is an object to us." In the "Lesser Logic," he asserted, "though the categories, such as unity, or cause and effect, are strictly the property of thought, it by no means follows that they must be ours merely and not also characteristics of the objects."[47] On this reading, Hegel's theory is idealist but not phenomenalist because he did not posit something behind or beyond the things of experience or, in a more current idiom, bracket off questions about what might exist beyond experience.[48] Indeed, to accuse Hegel of phenomenalism or subjective idealism is to remain captive to the Cartesian conception of thought and its relationship to being. Hegel's dialectical method in the *Phenomenology* reveals not just phenomena, as opposed to noumena, but real objects as they occur within the process of experience.

Through the understanding (*Verstand*), Kant conceived of individual objects as discrete and independent, but Hegel claimed we must grasp their interrelatedness through reason (*Vernunft*). Hegel's "absolute idea," the final result of the dialectic, is an ultimate principle according to which we conceive of the structural unity revealed by reason and overcome all dichotomies. He transformed Kant's account of the abstract conditions of the possibility of knowledge to an account of how it occurs by introducing a historical dimension to the problem of knowledge. The knowing process, for Hegel, is a concrete historical process, mediated through our relationships with other human beings. He moved from the analysis of the conditions of experience to the analysis of experience, and thus moved the discussion from the a priori level to the a posteriori. Experience provides the concrete historical mediation of logical principles.[49]

In sum, on the historicist reading of Hegel, absolute knowledge is a mode of self-critical thought that abandons dogmatic foundations and only accepts rational defense as philosophical justification. Absolute truth is truth that has been thoroughly, rationally examined, and thus is independent of external authority. On this reading, Hegel is a radically anti-foundationalist philosopher. In the words of Klaus Hartmann, "The Hegelian proposal is to avoid the problem of a first stance by invoking circularity . . . in terms of a theory of categories whose justification is borne out by the result of the categorial doctrine itself." Agreeing with Hartman on this point, Rockmore claims "Hegel . . . proposes a new paradigm of systematic knowledge without foundations, with an obvious, but as yet largely unexplored relation to pragmatism."[50]

In the preface to the *Phenomenology,* Hegel also claimed that philosophical truth, as opposed to "random assertions and assurances," must be "systematic" and developmental in form. To be systematic, philosophy must be science, *Wissenschaft.* Of course, the conception of science that was prevalent in Hegel's day was largely outmoded by the time Dewey began his philosophical career in the late nineteenth century. Dewey and his contemporaries generally drew a sharper distinction between "science" and "philosophy" than Hegel and his contemporaries. And, for now, it is sufficient to note that Dewey conceived of "science" as ongoing experimentation in which conclusions are always subject to revision. By way of contrast, for Hegel and the other German idealists, "science" is the systematic organization of a field of study. But rather than a field among others, philosophy is the systematic organization of all fields. Philosophy attains the status of science when it conceptually articulates the whole truth and thus corrects the one-sided truth of previous philosophies. For Hegel, philosophy is "developmental," which means that it cannot work with isolated hypotheses, but must always respond to and develop other philosophical positions. Gustav Emil Mueller writes: "what [Hegel] means by science is simply a logical maturity beyond any 'isms,' including 'rationalism' or 'absolute idealism.'"[51] When Hegel wrote the *Phenomenology,* he believed the time had arrived for philosophy to become science. He spoke of a "sunburst," perhaps meaning the French Revolution or Enlightenment liberalism, both of which were profoundly impacting Germany at that time. But rather than specific historical events, the sunburst was a new way of thinking, an attitude that rejected provincial beliefs and authoritative religions.[52]

For Hegel, "science" is the relentless revelation of all unexamined assumptions, and the ordering of rationally defensible beliefs into a logically consistent system. Science seeks a general understanding of the various forms of human knowledge, including what we now think of as the empirical sciences, but also art, religion and philosophy. The dialectic, Hegel's perception of scientific method, always begins with a hypothesis in that it is always a position that is asserted provisionally, adapted, developed, and ultimately sublated (*Aufheben*), that is, incorporated without being eliminated, into a more inclusive understanding of the subject matter. Moreover, Hegel believed the systematization of truth is a never-ending affair; it requires a constant process of self-examination in which we continually seek, and are confronted by, inconsistencies in our beliefs and in our forms of life. Hence, Hegel actually began to undermine the prevalent conception of science, moving it in the direction that Dewey later embraced. Science, for Hegel, is a willing suspension of final conclusions in favor of a never-ending process of learning in which we continually rethink and reexamine our beliefs.[53]

Although Hegel's commitment to systematic philosophy signifies a difference between him and Dewey, the difference is subtler than scholars may recognize because Hegel rejected the notion of a final system that would be true for all time. According to Mueller, Hegel "says philosophy must be a *system*: But if you look closely, you find that system means the impossibility of any system; systematic philosophy is the thorough demolition of all and every system. His 'system' is a chain-reaction of exploded systems and standpoints."[54] Although Mueller's statement is substantially correct, "demolition" is too strong a word, because when Hegel criticized previous systems he always found some truth in them that he sought to preserve in his own system.[55] Another way to get at what he meant by system is to emphasize his conviction that philosophy is an activity we only learn by doing. Hegel sought to unite theory and practice and explicitly rejected the notion that philosophy is a body of knowledge or a set of conclusions. According to Robert Solomon, Hegel understood philosophy as a process, and though one must reach some conclusion, it is the thinking process, not that conclusion, that is the truth of philosophy. For Hegel, "the way to Science is itself already *Science*." Philosophy, science, is a method, not a body of final truths.[56]

In the preface to the *Phenomenology,* Hegel invoked the concept of *Geist*, or spirit. After the Enlightenment, he claimed, religious faith was passé, but in desperation people turned "away from the empty husks" of religion to philosophy, not for knowledge but for "the recovery . . . of that lost sense of solid and substantial being."[57] Building on a theme in his early theological writings that reflected his pietistic background, Hegel claimed that the loss of spirit is not due to the loss of religion but to the emptiness of a theology that had never given sufficient attention to the importance of community and concrete understanding rather than incomprehensible doctrines. In this way, he articulated the conception of spirit he had been working toward in his early writings, spirit as humanity rather than a divinity above or an elusive soul within.[58]

Hegel spoke of subjective, objective, and absolute spirit. Subjective spirit is the study of mind in its most inward and generic sense. In the *Philosophy of Mind,* his analysis of subjective spirit proceeds through anthropology, the study of soul; phenomenology, the study of consciousness; and psychology, the study of mind.[59] Soul, consciousness, and mind are not faculties; they are aspects of spirit, moments within the process of its self-development, the realization of freedom. This process moves from simple soul-life (responses to general environmental changes) to the highest level of mind that only humans possess. In the process of self-development each moment remains in the subsequent moment, so that even the free mind, which is able to know universals and is self-determining, contains the primordial natural soul. In his discussion of subjective spirit, Hegel is only concerned with universal features of mind—mind in its inwardness as purely subjective, without reference to its context of external objects and individual peculiarities. At this level of analysis, the self is an abstract universal because it is wrenched from its context.

Hegel ended his analysis of subjective spirit with "practical mind," the mind "as will," as "the author of its own conclusions, the origin of its self-fulfillment."[60] In willing, an individual seeks to actualize its ideals and transcend its own subjectivity. Something is done; something is completed, out there, exterior to the subject. This begins the transition to objective spirit, creations of subjective spirit that take on a life of their own. "The purposive action of" subjective spirit "is to realize its concept," freedom, in "externally objective aspects, making the latter a world moulded by the former, which in it is thus at home with itself."[61] Subjective spirit seeks to transform the objective world into a welcoming environment that is consistent with and actualizes its goal of freedom. Objective spirit is the world of artifacts, labor and property, rights and laws, associations of individuals, institutions, and the state.

Both subjective and objective spirit are essentially one-sided, each suffering from limitations. Subjective spirit remains in the realm of the universal, mere abstract identity. Objective spirit is this abstract subjectivity willed outwards in artifacts, routines, and institutions. Insofar as it exists only in the objective world, objective spirit is one-sided. Absolute spirit, the completed spirit, overcomes the limitations of both types of spirit by combining without eliminating them within itself. Absolute spirit is the domain of man knowing himself in and through the artifacts and traditions in which subjectivity is displayed. This self-awareness is reached in the areas of art, religion, and philosophy. In art, absolute spirit knows itself in the form of immediacy, which is the sensuous artifact. The art object is an object in which beauty shows itself. The various art forms are ways in which beauty reveals itself, and each has limits to what it can possibly reveal. In his *Aesthetics,* Hegel analyzed the particular art forms of architecture, sculpture, painting, music, and literature in their actual historical development.[62] Each form is capable of telling us something about ourselves, and something about absolute spirit. The second moment, religion, captures something art cannot capture, large-scale universal truths. But religion captures universal truths in a partly sensuous element, *Vorstellung denken*, or representational thinking. These representations arouse the various emotions and feelings (joy, gratitude, sorrow, etc.) that are the province of religion. The third moment of absolute spirit is philosophy. Philosophy is pure self-awareness, not limited by sensuous objects or representations. In philosophy, absolute spirit achieves its own realization and returns to itself through its own internal differentiations.

According to the historicist reading of Hegel, all three types of spirit are fundamentally conceptual, articulate, and exist only through their expression of themselves.[63] Each type of spirit is activity rather than substance. Absolute spirit is not an external providence directing historical action; it is the human race in the activities of its historical self-development. Thus when Hegel claimed that there is reason in history, he could not have meant that reason is an agent driving history. History is our record of the self-development of the human race, and we always choose to construct a historical narrative because we have some purpose in mind. Because we approach the data with a purpose, certain features in the historical record capture our attention, enabling us to provide a rational articulation of the events under our consideration. The historian looks for and discovers reason in the historical record, and constructs a narrative on the basis of what she has found. This is a prime example of what Hegel meant when he claimed that we apprehend reason in, rather than impose it upon, the subject matter. Reason is in the subject matter because we always approach it with a particular purpose in mind. Consequently, spirit as seen in human history is not a sequence of events but an understanding of them; thus there is a sense in which, to Hegel, there is no history until there is a historian, one who articulates the rational meaning of history. Nevertheless, the facts of history, the historical record, are there all along.[64]

Hegel's Critique of Modern Epistemology

In the introduction to the *Phenomenology,* Hegel addressed the tendency of modern philosophy to end in skepticism, which he considered an utterly absurd position. According to Hegel, the conundrums of epistemology were generated by the mistaken assumption "that there is a boundary between cognition and the Absolute that completely separates them." He undertook "an exposition of how knowledge makes its appearance" rather than an examination of whether or not knowledge is possible.[65] Rather than attempt a refutation of skepticism, Hegel turned to a diagnosis of the modern problematic. A prime example of his dialectical method, Hegel questioned the assumptions upon which modern epistemology was founded. Why have efforts to establish the grounds for knowledge repeatedly ended in skepticism about the very possibility of knowledge?

Hegel questioned the central project of modern philosophy, which was to begin with the search for the correct method for gaining knowledge. As he explained, philosophers have sought a method because they "fear[ed] . . . falling into error"; he contended that we should consider "whether this fear of error is not just the error itself."[66] Rather than seek a method, we should take knowledge as a phenomenon to be examined and try to understand, as did Kant, what kind of beings we would have to be in order to have knowledge. Rather than searching for a method by which to gain knowledge, Hegel claimed, we should plunge into the subject matter. One does not learn what knowledge is by developing a method with which to prove it, but by assuming, from the outset, that we do know something, that we are in contact with the absolute, the things of the world, and do not need a method to prove this. Indeed, the search for a method is precisely what made it appear, in previous philosophy, as if it is possible that we are not in immediate contact with the absolute, and therefore might not know reality at all. In this way Hegel attacked the very idea of a theory of knowledge. To him, the idea of knowing a theory that precedes knowledge itself is a manifest absurdity. As Hegel says in the "Lesser Logic," "to seek to know before we know is as absurd as the wise resolution of Scholasticus, not to venture into the water until he had learned to swim."[67] Like swimming, according to Hegel, in order to understand knowledge we must learn by doing.

Hegel distanced himself from Kant as he attacked traditional epistemology through an examination of the two metaphors upon which it is based. The first assumes that consciousness is active; it is an instrument for getting hold of the things themselves. The second is a more passive metaphor, that consciousness is a medium through which we can see the absolute.[68] Both metaphors lead to skepticism because the instrument or the medium would necessarily distort the things themselves, and even if they did not we would have no way of knowing this because we could not escape our inner reality. Both metaphors assume consciousness is one thing, and reality, the absolute, is something else. The assumption that thought and being, consciousness and physical reality, are ontologically distinct immediately raises the quandary of how consciousness ever reaches beyond itself to the absolute. The two metaphors are based upon a deeper one, "that there is a boundary between cognition and the absolute that completely separates them."[69] According to Hegel, once one accepts the idea of an inner/outer boundary, crossing that boundary while always remaining on the inside becomes impossible.

Hegel believed Kant's fundamental error was an uncritical acceptance of two modern philosophical premises: the Newtonian model of reality as an aggregate of discrete particles of matter in motion, and the Cartesian model of mind and world as two metaphysically distinct realities. Hegel was convinced that these assumptions made insoluble the problem of knowledge. If reality was composed of discrete objects, and knowledge is accurate judgment about how things are related, how could we have knowledge? And if mind and world are metaphysically distinct, how can mind connect with the world to gain knowledge?[70] Beginning with the Kantian assumption that we do in fact have knowledge, Hegel sought to articulate the sort of relationship we must have to the world in order for that to be the case. He postulated that the world is a whole (the absolute) in which all of the parts are interrelated, as are the parts of a living organism. Hegel went so far as to say that all objects of experience are relations rather than unchanging entities that somehow possess relations. On this model, relations are not just in the world; they are the world.[71] As Hegel stated it, "Being is Thought."[72] On a historicist reading of Hegel, the claim that being is thought is not an assertion of a monistic metaphysics; the claim means that thought deals strictly with relations, and the world of our experience is relations. Hegel believed that this move allowed him to completely abandon Cartesian dualism and depict the mind as having direct access to the world in all its relational glory because thought and world have something significant in common; both are composed of relations.

Hegel also rejected Kant's notion of intuition because, as a passive medium, it necessarily separated us from reality as it is in itself. If we have no control over intuition, we could never get beyond it to experience the world as it is. Hegel concluded that reason is not restricted to a realm metaphysically distinct from the world; it is in the world in that relations are in the world. At the same time he rejected Kant's theory that a noumenal realm serves as a limit to thought, claiming that Kant's noumenal realm is a posit of thought and thought cannot posit a limit to itself.[73] Critics have argued that Hegel's rejection of Kant's faculty of intuition and the thing-in-itself led him down the slippery slope to precritical, that is to say, pre-Kantian, metaphysical speculation about mind and world. Because it seems that he rejected the limits that Kant placed on thought, but embraced Kant's theory that the mind actively constructs experience, critics have concluded that he became a subjective idealist believing that thought creates the world.[74]

Because of his rejection of Kant's transcendent realm, other critics have claimed that Hegel was a relativist. In his critique of philosophical dualisms, Hegel rejected the transcendent because he feared that the notion of transcendent truth would only fan the flames of fanaticism, and instead argued that all of reality is within the flow of history. Critics have charged that if Hegel's historicism left nothing that was not subject to the vagaries of history, he landed in a complete historical relativism with no guarantee that we could rise above the phenomenal, but this charge assumes the dualism Hegel rejected.

Kant's notion of a critique of pure reason was based on the assumption that we can transcend history. According to Kant, we must separate ourselves from our cognitive functions and analyze them from a neutral vantage point, which is not itself an act of knowing, in order to discover how we gain knowledge. To Hegel, Kant's analyzing reason must be analyzed before it can be trusted as a faculty capable of a critique of reason. Moreover, Kant's epistemology assumes that it makes sense to assert that things as they are experienced are different from things as they really are while maintaining that we can have no knowledge of the noumenal world. Hegel's solution to this dilemma was to reject the appearance/reality distinction as well as the objective/subjective and absolute/relative distinctions. To accuse Hegel of relativism is to beg the question against him.

Hegel asserted that we can only know and comprehend what occurs in experience. Moreover, his commitment to experience ran deep. Later in the *Phenomenology,* he claimed that "nothing is *known* that is not in *experience,* or, as it is also expressed, that is not *felt to be true,* not given as an *inwardly revealed* eternal verity, as something sacred that is *believed,* or whatever other expressions have been used."[75] According to Solomon, to find a similar concept of experience, we would need to look at the "practical-minded writings of the American pragmatists William James and John Dewey."[76] Let us see why Solomon might make such a surprising claim.

Hegel explained that

> experience is the name we give to just this movement, in which the immediate, the unexperienced, i.e. the abstract, whether it be of sensuous [but still unsensed] being, or only thought of as simple, becomes alienated from itself and then returns to itself from this alienation.[77]

For Hegel, experience is, in effect, a field in which subject and object ordinarily exist in undifferentiated unity and harmony. But experience is not a static field because it is a process of learning and growth. In the learning process, the self encounters opposition (Hegel's "negation") or, in more ordinary language, a problem. When it encounters a problem, the self posits it as an other, thus alienating itself from itself, distinguishing subject from object (*Verstand*). The self seeks to recover its lost unity by altering both itself and the other (Hegel's "mediation"), reuniting them (*Vernunft*) in a more inclusive whole. When the self arrives at a solution (Hegel's concept of *Aufhebung*), it returns to its original harmony enriched by the learning experience. Rather than distinct realities then, self and object are stages or functions within a process.

Since self and object are reciprocally related within the process of experience, an increase or broadening of the understanding of an object through its dissolution by negation and mediation within consciousness implies a corresponding increase in "determinacy" or awareness of the self through a similar dissolution by negation and mediation. These two processes are actually one and the same. This growth in consciousness occurs in varying degrees in all self-conscious beings, and the different degrees of consciousness form a single objective order that is ultimately transcended in something that is not a version but the whole itself. This whole, which Hegel variously calls "truth," "spirit," or "absolute," is a living process; it is propelled by the energy of negation and mediation, in which both selves and their objects are continuously emerging and undergoing development and being replaced by higher forms of themselves.

This discussion of Hegel's commitment to experience reveals why scholars have rejected the rationalist appellation that is so often placed upon him. Although it is misleading to characterize Hegel as an empiricist because he rejected the mind/body dualism upon which it is based, Westphal argues that he is an epistemological realist because he rejects the epistemological distinction between appearance and reality and simultaneously claims that doing so need not conflate the world with our knowledge of it.[78] Moreover, Hegel's conception of knowledge is not antithetical to empiricism. Like Dewey, Hegel praised British empiricism for teaching that experience is amenable to rational understanding. In this way, empiricism redirected man's attention to the world, enabling him to feel at home again after the long period of medieval other-worldliness; it also reaffirmed the importance of the testimony of the senses in determining truth.

Rather than an empiricist, Hegel is frequently described as a rationalist largely because of a misreading of a controversial sentence in *The Philosophy of Right*: "What is rational is actual; and what is actual is rational."[79] Many scholars have argued that this statement demonstrates Hegel's commitment to rationalism, and his conservative political commitment to the status quo. I will address Hegel's alleged rationalism now, and discuss his politics a bit later. Hegel clarified this claim in the introduction to the "Lesser Logic," where he explained that

"The actuality of the rational stands opposed by the popular fancy that Ideas and ideals are nothing but chimeras, and philosophy a mere system of such phantasms" and "by the very different fancy that Ideas and ideals are something far too excellent to have actuality, or something too important to procure it for themselves."[80] In both of these passages, Hegel's meaning is somewhat obscured in English translation. Translators have used "actual" for *wirklich,* which means "effective" as much as "actual." In both statements, Hegel meant to convey that the rational is that which actually has effects in the world. He also meant to criticize philosophers' tendency to embrace lofty ideals that have no real import in actual life. Hegel made the same point in the *Encyclopedia of the Philosophical Sciences* when he wrote, "Philosophy . . . has nothing at all to do with mere abstractions or formal thoughts, but only with concrete thoughts."[81] In chapter four I argue that Dewey read Hegel's claim about the rationality of the actual as a commitment to realism, a commitment to that which actually is.

There is ample evidence for this reading of Hegel. For example, Hegel's realism is evident in his statement of the purpose of the *Phenomenology.* Hegel declared that the book was an effort to systematically describe experience with a view toward understanding why it must be the way it is, thus it could not legitimately go beyond or behind experience in order to explain it. As Josiah Royce explained in an apparent allusion to William James's *Varieties of Religious Experience,* the *Phenomenology* can be understood as a study of the varieties of "individual and social types."[82] It is not hard to find contemporary Hegel scholars who agree with Royce's assessment.[83]

Psychology and Philosophy of Education

Hegel's dynamic conception of experience required him to develop a social and functional psychology. After the introduction to the *Phenomenology,* Hegel critiqued three "shapes of consciousness," modes of epistemic justification, on their own terms. Hegel believed he undermined these shapes of consciousness by demonstrating that they failed to deliver what they promised because any mental content, even what seems immediate, contains concepts, or in Hegel's terminology, is mediated. In today's terms, we might express this point by saying that all experience is "theory-laden." Hegel's primary point is that there are no uninterpreted experiences and, even if there were, there could be no knowledge of them without concepts and interpretation. Knowledge requires concepts, which consciousness provides. Nothing "*originates in the sensuous.*"[84] What we perceive is not simply based upon, or inferred from, the data of the senses, but already presupposes understanding (the use of concepts). There are no "given" objects that we experience directly, or that determine the judgments we make about them. In our experience, we are always aware of things as particular things and particular types of things, taking things to be this way or that, and contributing meaning to our experience that it does not automatically have. In order to avoid the contradictions of these three shapes of consciousness, we must recognize that we are always self-conscious about what we are doing and the goals we are working toward in making the judgments we make. We establish cognitive norms and make judgments on the basis of these goals and seek reassurance that our cognitive norms, and hence our goals, are valid.

Perhaps an example will illustrate Hegel's conception of experience more thoroughly. Imagine an archaeologist who uses sonar to locate an anchor from a sunken ship on the ocean floor, receiving information about the anchor from its effects. One might say that the archaeologist observes shadows of the anchor, rather than the anchor itself. This does not imply that the anchor is an inaccessible thing-in-itself, however, only that the archaeologist's experience of it is mediated by sound waves traveling through the water. If the archaeologist goes to the anchor in a submarine or as a scuba diver, it is still mediated as she observes it through a window or a mask and by the water between her apparatus and the anchor. Even if the archaeologist hoists the anchor to the surface and sets it on the deck of her ship so that she can observe it more directly, what she sees is a manifestation of chemical processes occurring at the molecular level. And even this manifestation of chemical processes is mediated through her senses. This is true even when she touches the anchor, a seemingly immediate or "objective" experience of it. Her experience of the anchor is both immediate and mediated. In his characteristically obscure way, Hegel explains, "*Existence* is the immediately appearing unity of immediacy and mediation, of being and seeming to be, of essential and non-essential, of being unproblematic in being problematic."[85]

I have only scratched the surface of the ways in which the anchor is mediated in the archaeologist's experience of it. Observation of the anchor is mediated by the light waves through which she observes it and the atmosphere between her and the anchor. Hegel also places a heavy emphasis on the fact that the archaeologist's experience of the anchor is always mediated by her intellectual and emotional inheritance, a complex collection of past experiences and ideas, some of which may be her own, but most of which have been transmitted or handed down to her by her past and present colleagues in archaeology and other relevant sciences and by her culture at large. Furthermore, the archaeologist's experience of the anchor is mediated by the expectations she brought to the experience and her purpose for seeking it. Rather than a potential work of art for a museum, the archaeologist sees the anchor primarily as an artifact that may provide clues about human history. Because she has a certain purpose, the archaeologist will readily notice certain aspects of the anchor (e.g., clues about its age) and may notice others only secondarily (e.g., its beauty). To some degree, the anchor is a different object to her than it is to an art collector.

The notion that all experience is mediated is the crux of Hegel's idealism. By idealism he did not mean that reality exists only as an idea inside of some mind. According to Hegel, mind neither creates nor modifies reality. As J. N. Findlay writes, "Hegel does not hold that the mind alters its object, but that by altering the manner in which that object is given to it, it penetrates to its true, universal nature."[86] As the mind encounters objects, it creates the objects of experience by interpreting them according to categories, but Hegel never suggested that objects must be experienced in order to exist. The fact that the archaeologist's experience of the anchor is mediated, in a variety of complex ways, gives her no compelling reason to doubt its existence; she has abundant empirical evidence that it exists. Although she may never stop learning about its attributes and inner structure, even at the molecular level, she has no reason to posit an unknowable thing-in-itself behind her experience of the anchor. As Westphal explains, Hegel insisted "that the contents of our conceptions (when we have true knowledge, at least) and the structure of the world are the same."[87] Although all experience is mediated and subjective, according to Hegel, it is nonetheless as objective as the archaeologist's experience of the anchor.

> Consciousness knows and comprehends only what falls within its experience; for what is contained in this is nothing but spiritual substance, and this, too, as *object* of the self. But Spirit becomes object because it is just this movement of becoming an *other to itself,* i.e. becoming an *object to itself,* and of suspending this otherness.[88]

The object of experience is spiritual substance in that the subject creates it; in this process, the otherness of the object, which exists apart from the subject, is overcome. Further, for Hegel, the mediators (e.g., the sound waves used by the sonar) are as real as the objects they mediate. The object, the mediators, and the one who experiences the object are equally real. There is no impenetrable metaphysical divide between us and the objects we experience and no gradations of reality. Finally, what I have called effects in this example, are simply relations. Objects have effects on objects to which they are related.

The crucial point for Hegel's social psychology, however, is that our interpretations of experience are, to a great extent, a social inheritance and that we seek recognition from others that the norms according to which we interpret experience are valid.[89] This leads him to a critical transition in the *Phenomenology* to a discussion of objective spirit, beginning in the section entitled "Self-Consciousness." Hegel believed that his critique of the modern, epistemological problematic points to a need for self examination. Epistemology is transformed into an examination of self-consciousness through the study of how we interact with one another in our endeavor to find recognition that our cognitive norms are valid. The phenomenology of objective spirit examines culturally distinct patterns of social interaction in terms of the patterns of recognition they embody. On the historicist reading, Hegel's notion of objective spirit does not commit him to a transcendent, metaphysical reality; rather spirit is viewed as culture or humanity. Because we seek reassurance that our cognitive norms are correct, we demand recognition from others like ourselves, recognition that our norms, and thus our goals, are worthy. At this point, Hegel makes the crucial claim that "self-consciousness is *Desire* in general."[90] Like Kant, Hegel believed that, above all, we desire norms that all rational agents would affirm and follow. Our cognitive norms are based upon structures of mutual recognition among self-conscious agents. Hegel examined the history of patterns of recognition in order to demonstrate why they have foundered, and thus how we have come to our current pattern of recognition. For Hegel, only a historically, socially constructed philosophical account of these patterns can facilitate our understanding of the modern standpoint and its cognitive norms.

This transition in the *Phenomenology* is crucial to the humanistic/historicist interpretation and to an argument I make in chapter four that Dewey found functionalism in Hegel. As Robert Pippin explains, Hegel's transition to "Self-Consciousness" is based on a conviction that the problem of epistemic criteria is intimately connected to the satisfaction of desire: "the 'truth' is wholly relativized to pragmatic ends . . . what counts as a successful explanation depends on what practical problem we want solved." Furthermore, Pippin continues, "*which* desires a subject determines to pursue, which ends to satisfy, and indeed what counts as true satisfaction . . . are *results* of the collective, historical, social subject's self-determination and have no natural status."[91]

As Hegel examined patterns of recognition, beginning with the master/slave dialectic, he maintained that we have certain natural desires that cause us to seek goals, but those desires cannot fully determine the norms by which they are judged. When one self-conscious agent encounters another, they both seek recognition that their norms are commendable. In so doing each agent recognizes that it is his own self-conceived project for life that determines his hierarchy of norms. We become aware of what Hegel called our "negativity" as we realize that our projects are never fully determined by any particular desire, but are the result of a host of competing desires. When one person decides that his desire for recognition is more important than life itself he becomes willing to enter into a struggle to the death. When one agent surrenders to the other out of fear for his life, he enters into a master/slave relationship in which the master imposes his norms upon the slave. Ultimately the slave comes to see the master's norms as one perspective among many and recognizes the sheer contingency of the master's hold on him. The master realizes that the slave cannot give the recognition he sought because it is not freely given. Because the master/slave relationship could not sustain itself, Western man sought other avenues (e.g., Stoicism and skepticism) for self-mastery and independence, but these also failed. Yet throughout the medieval period, a time of universal servitude, Christianity prepared the way for an assertion of self-activity (*Selbsttätigkeit*) that was realized in the Protestant Reformation. In the following section of the *Phenomenology,* entitled "Reason," Hegel painted a series of obscure portraits of various ways that early modern European culture sought to ground its normative commitments, and how each undermined itself on its own terms. The conclusion of this section is that reason gains authority only when we see that its norms are embedded in a worthy way of life.

After the section on "Reason," Hegel explicitly discussed objective spirit or, on the historicist reading, culture. The historicist interpretation is supported by the fact that the second part of "Spirit" is entitled "Self-Alienated Spirit. Culture."[92] Hegel's discussion of Spirit leads to his moral and social philosophy, but I will analyze that part of his thought in the following section.

Geist, which can be legitimately translated into English as "mind" as well as "spirit," provides clues about Hegel's conception of mind. On the historicist reading, similar to spirit as a historical reality, what we call the human mind is a hypostatization, or a supposition of philosophers that demarcates human experience. Rather than an entity, the mind is activity, and it exists in its being recognized as such; it is a thing in the world only by way of an interpretation. For Hegel, "mind" is not an internal, nonspatial, nontemporal reality, but an instrument for referring to certain functions of intelligent organisms. The mind is not a preexisting entity with faculties that can oppose one another; it is a collection of functions of self-conscious beings.

Hegel rejected Kant's faculty psychology, instead presenting the different "faculties" of the mind as moments, stages, or functions within a process.[93] Hegel's functionalism is particularly apparent in his concept of reason. Hegel used *Verstand,* normally translated as "understanding," for the Enlightenment notion of reason. Hegel also spoke of common sense (*der gemeine Menschenverstand*), or ordinary thinking, which deals with presentations, or the mental images of objects (*Vorstellung denken*) that the understanding turns into thoughts (*Gedanken*) by ordering them into logical categories. *Verstand* is deductive; it produces clear analyses by separating and differentiating the parts of the whole according to the principle of identity, and provides abstract understanding of the subject matter. Understanding is essential to analysis, but because it dissects the whole into parts it deals with merely abstract qualities, never reaching the concrete. *Verstand* is a necessary stage of logic, but for Hegel, it is only a beginning. *Verstand* analyzes processes into their constituent parts but, historically, philosophers have confused the results of analysis with the state of affairs they analyzed, rather than moving beyond analysis to an understanding of the parts as they are interrelated within a larger whole.[94] Hegel's concept of *Vernunft,* which is translated as "reason," designates our ability to see implicit contradictions and ambiguities in the abstractions of the understanding; at this stage *Vernunft* is negative reason. When it reaches the level of speculative reason, *Vernunft* is able to derive positive results from the contradictions of the understanding and see the whole.[95]

Furthermore, because of Hegel's rejection of Kant's faculty psychology, which rigidly separated understanding from reflection, Lewis Hinchman argues that he preferred not to distinguish sharply between common sense, understanding, and reflection, because "he was profoundly aware of the continuity between ordinary consciousness and science. To Hegel, science and the grounds, explanations, and models it works with in its capacity as understanding or reflection signify an extension of common sense principles, not their reversal."[96] Hegel did not view science as something utterly different from common sense, but as a refinement of techniques we ordinarily use in everyday life.

Hegel's theory of freedom, to which I will return in a moment, rests upon his concept of the will, which is also not a separate faculty, distinct from reason, but an aspect, or mode, of reason. In *The Philosophy of Right* Hegel declared that

> It must not be imagined [*sich vorstellen*] that a human being thinks on the one hand and wills on the other, and that he has thought in one pocket and volition in the other, for this would be an empty representation [*Vorstellung*]. The distinction between thought and will is simply that between theoretical and practical attitudes. But they are not two separate faculties; on the contrary, the will is a particular way of thinking—

> thinking translating itself into existence [*Dasein*], thinking as the drive to give itself existence.

Later in the same passage, Hegel wrote, "The theoretical is . . . contained within the practical."[97] He viewed all cognition as "*purposive activity.*"[98]

Hegel's conception of reason is central to his critique of Enlightenment moral and political thought. Although the emergence of modern subjectivity was a great advance, he believed, it had contributed to a breakdown of community as Enlightenment thinkers indiscriminately devalued all traditional institutions and codes of conduct.[99] Drawing on Schiller and Goethe, Hegel believed community was best represented in the actual practices, or the ethical order (*Sittlichkeit*), of the ancient Greek polis. Modern subjectivity promoted philosophical reflection and individual critique of social mores, but philosophy had failed to reach the level of *Vernunft,* and thus failed to unite its results with practical life in a spiritually unified self and society. To overcome this social fragmentation, philosophy needed to unite modern subjectivity and the negativity of the Enlightenment, its critical aspect, with a positive reunion within the self, and of the self with society.

Because he rejected Cartesian dualism and developed a functionalist psychology, Hegel's theory of knowledge is more accurately described as a theory of learning or discovery. Hegel's theory of learning follows from the cryptic but crucial phrase, "everything turns on grasping and expressing the True, not only as *Substance*, but equally as *Subject.*" In this statement Hegel emphasized that there is no unbridgeable opposition between the knower and the known, and truth is the way the world is for subjects. "The living Substance . . . is in truth *Subject*"; that is to say, the acquisition of knowledge is a matter of spirit's self-expression as it sets up its own opposition (the other), and then recognizes that this opposition is of its own making. This characterization of learning was based upon a novel conception of the self and its relationship to the world.

To fully grasp this conception of the self, it is imperative to place Hegel in the context of the German neo-humanist tradition that included Herder, Goethe, Schiller, Fichte, Schelling, and Novalis.[100] The neo-humanists preferred organic metaphors to describe human life and the learning process. The most prominent metaphor in their writings is *Bildung,* which neo-humanists used to mean a certain type of education, emphasizing the cultivation of knowledge, experience, and consciousness as organic wholes, through various stages or "moments" in a process that, at any given point, might well seem as if it were complete in itself. Moreover, *Bildung* entailed *Selbsttätigkeit*—self-activity, self-development, and self-direction. Neo-humanists contrasted *Bildung* with *Erziehung,* which was merely passive education, and with *Gelehrsamkeit,* the mere "learnedness" characteristic of Enlightenment universities. According to the neo-humanists, *Bildung* involved the estrangement of the mind from its natural state through a study of the ancient world and its languages, followed by a return, or reconciliation, to its own culture and language.[101] This process, they believed, would provide the individual with insight into the ideals of his culture and enable him to realize his full potential.

Thus, for Hegel, the self does not begin with a definite essence. An individual's identity is revealed and defined as he interacts in the series of subject-object relationships of experience. In order for an individual to define and come to know himself, he must become alienated from himself. When a person plunges ahead into the seemingly alien social and natural world, he discovers, as he creates, his own identity. Introspection is a very limited route to self-knowledge because it neglects the extent to which we are formed by our relationships with the "other," and the ways in which our relating is historically contingent. All experience is alienation and as we realize this we appreciate the degree to which we need recognition from others. Moreover, we recognize that our social self is forever separate from our inner awareness of who and what we are. In Hegelian terms, spirit is not simply self-alienated; it can only know itself as such.

Subject and object, according to Hegel, imply one another equally; neither exists alone. Rather, both the object experienced and the experiencing consciousness are dependent on each other for their respective existence. The experienced object may be said to exist only as it is experienced by an individual consciousness, and the existence or "being" of the individual mind or consciousness, consisting as it does in experiencing an object and thereby becoming aware of itself, is inseparable from the experience of the "other." This interdependence of consciousness/mind and "other," subject and object, returns us to Hegel's principle that "Being is Thought."[102] Hegel replaced the traditional, Aristotelian notion of substance as a union of form and matter, a self-identical and enduring entity that does not itself change but that possesses changing properties or attributes. Hegel's was an utterly new metaphysic based on the primacy of experience or consciousness that did away with the notions of independence and unchanging self-subsistence. Independence is in no way applicable to experience/consciousness since it relies on the opposition of the experienced object to the experiencing subject. True self-consciousness, reason or rational self-consciousness, also denies unchanging self-subsistence in that it consists of a constant series of changes whereby the opposition between subject and object is removed, and oneness or identity is established. This reconciliation or unification of opposing entities is an example of the Hegelian dialectic.

Hegel believed *Bildung* was a prerequisite to independent, philosophical thought.[103] Hence the *Phenomenology* can be profitably read as the story of both Spirit's and the individual's *Bildung,* the goal of which is the development of the higher humanity within ourselves, which emerges as we strengthen our truly human powers and subjugate the inhuman, as we strive to become a complete human being. Like Goethe's *Wilhelm Meisters Lehrjahre* and Schiller's *Wilhelm Tell,* Hegel's *Phenomenology* is, on this reading, a *Bildungsroman,* in which the reader is shown the development of an open and intelligent mind in a complex society that lacks universally accepted values as the main character encounters a wide variety of experiences. But the center of interest in a *Bildungsroman* is not the protagonist's character, adventures, or accomplishments; rather, it is the links between his successive experiences and his gradual achievement of a fully rounded personality and well-tested philosophy of life.[104]

Hegel's concept of *Bildung* dovetails with his view that knowledge is gained only from experience, and it also requires us to seek, like the protagonist of a *Bildungsroman,* the widest variety of experience. Furthermore, on the *Bildung* model, learning involves activity. Hence Hegel rejected Locke's passive spectator theory of the mind, according to which we should restrain our passions in order to gain objective knowledge. For Hegel, learning requires a passionate search for truth; it is a matter of conscious self-development that requires arduous individual effort and responsibility. For Hegel, fulfillment must come in the activities of real life. Finally, Hegel was critical of the Enlightenment's fixation on a narrow conception of knowledge, arguing that *Bildung* requires self-knowledge, an accurate perception of one's talents and abilities.

In his writings on primary and secondary education, Hegel averred that moral instruction must be given gradually and indirectly, primarily through the study of what we now call the liberal arts.[105] With the help and support of his close friend Friedrich Immanuel Niethammer, Hegel sought to put this model of education into practice as rector of the Nuremburg *Gymnasium* from 1808 to 1815.[106] In Nuremburg, Hegel developed a philosophy of education that was opposed to past German models and the Enlightenment model of education, the latter of which he identified as "utilitarian." Hegel contended that alienation of the mind from its ordinary point of view is best accomplished through the study of the ancient world and its languages because they are sufficiently alien to separate us from our natural state, but sufficiently close to our own language and world for us to return to ourselves enlarged and transformed. In his first annual speech as rector of the *Gymnasium* (29 November 1809), Hegel extended this pattern of estrangement and reconciliation to every phase of childhood development. On a very practical level, Hegel opposed vocational education in the German *Gymnasia,* arguing that education should prepare students for life rather than merely for jobs, but he supported the teaching of religion for the secular rationale that it would link students to social customs and traditions. He also believed that students should be treated with respect, as ends in themselves, and at the *Gymnasium,* encouraged discussion in class, but would not tolerate giving students complete freedom in the schools.[107] The goal of education, for Hegel, was to help students realize the ideal of modernity, which is for the individual to become a self-directed, self-formed person.

Logic

Although Dewey never showed an interest in Hegel's system per se, in later chapters I will argue that he embraced Hegel's method, which is abundantly evident in all of Hegel's published writings but most explicitly developed in his logical writings. It is useful to note that many current Hegel scholars now interpret Hegel's logic in a way that is consistent with the humanistic/historicist interpretation I offer in this chapter. According to Klaus Hartmann, Hegel's logic is a theory of the concepts, or categories, necessary for the possibility of knowledge, rather than a theory of reality. In an effort to avoid confusion arising from the historical ambiguities of the term "metaphysics," Hartmann refers to Hegel's logic as a "hermeneutical ontology," explaining that it is an endeavor to derive the categories according to which we experience the world.[108] This reading is consistent with Hegel's claim that his "objective logic . . . takes the place . . . of formal *metaphysics* which was intended to be the scientific construction of the world in terms of *thoughts* alone."[109] Rather than a break from the project of the *Phenomenology,* Hegel's logic is its completion, and the *Bildung* motif is relevant there too.

It is commonly remarked that, for Hegel, contradiction drives logical thought, but his conception of contradiction is often misunderstood. As a philosopher who emphasized process and becoming, Hegel was concerned with the enduring metaphysical question of how something can change through time and yet remain the same thing. Hegel's response to this issue draws upon the organic *Bildung* metaphor. A human being is not an embryo or infant or adult at the same time, but is all three of these "moments" in its becoming. None of these moments are entirely true or false descriptions of a human; they are simply partial descriptions of a human as a whole. In the *Science of Logic,* Hegel explained that "in the proposition: *the rose is fragrant*, the predicate enunciates only *one* of the *many* properties of the rose"; that judgment may be correct, but it is not the truth of the rose because the rose is many other things besides fragrant, and it is not always fragrant. "The True is the whole."[110] Truth and falsity, where philosophical viewpoints are concerned, are not opposites; a philosophical doctrine is not literally false, because it is not an attempt to describe a state of affairs to which it does or does not actually correspond. Rather, it is a representation of the whole of reality, and its inadequacy is more likely to be that of being one-sided or not well thought out.[111]

Because of his concern with self-cultivation and cultural unification, Hegel was more interested in practical contradictions than the purely logical ones of mutually exclusive propositions. He believed practical and moral dilemmas frequently arise because we hold one-sided, inadequate conceptions of our world and ourselves. Contradictions were important to Hegel precisely because they demand resolution; we cannot tolerate incoherent conceptions of ourselves that make our decisions and actions pointless. Logical and practical contradictions were important to Hegel because he believed that to know is to be engaged in an activity. To arrive at a contradiction is to frustrate the realization of a practical goal.[112] Royce clearly explained this aspect of Hegel's sense of contradiction:

> What in [Hegel's] logical philosophy appears as a conflict of categories, of points of view, of theses and antitheses, will appear in human life as a conflict of moral and of social tendencies, of opinions for which men make sacrifices, upon which they stake their fortunes. The conflicts of philosophical ideas will thus appear as a kind of shadowy repetition, or representation, of the struggles of humanity for life and for light.[113]

According to Royce, Hegel used "the dialectical method" in "its pragmatic form."[114] As Royce read Hegel, his rejection of Cartesian dualism, and of the form/content distinction exemplified in Kant's theory of categories, made his logic necessarily a logic of life. By putting mind and thought into the world, Hegel made thinking an inherently practical activity. For that reason, he could not view logical contradictions as mere puzzles for philosophers to solve; for Hegel, logical contradictions become apparent, and are problematic, when they are impediments to the realization of practical goals. The contradictions Hegel was most concerned about in his writings were, to him, manifestations of deep-seated problems in western culture.

Hegel also combined the *Bildung* metaphor with the theme of systematicity. *Bildung* connoted an "inner necessity" for the scientific system of truth, an urge that lies in the very nature of consciousness itself for total comprehension. For Hegel, the only ultimately satisfying philosophy would be one that is systematic, all-comprehending and, in effect, a unification of the truths of all past philosophies.

Hegel's logic begins with the concept of being, because it is the purest thought. He defines being as "indeterminate immediacy . . . similar to itself alone," and claims that this conception of being is not susceptible to further analysis. He claims it is logically equivalent to the concept of pure nothing, however, because pure being lacks any specificity; it is indeterminate. But this cannot be right. If any two categories are distinct, they are the categories of being and nothing. The concepts of being and nothing are inherently unstable, and we find ourselves moving back and forth between them. The passage from being to nothing is "ceasing to be," while the passage from nothing to being is "coming-to-be."[115] This leads us, according to Hegel, to a more inclusive category, becoming. Becoming does not supersede being and nothing; it contains both within it. Being and nothing are poles within the process of becoming.

The beginning of Hegel's logic is paradigmatic for the way he handles all philosophical dilemmas. Two seemingly antithetical concepts are equated, yet the contrary assumption—if anything is true, then being is distinct from nothing—also seems true. Hegel argues that the passage of being into nothingness (and vice versa) is a specific conception of becoming. This conception of becoming does not solve the dilemma, however; it dissolves it by placing it within a context that reveals it is two ways of viewing the same thing. He believed we can articulate these dilemmas by proceeding to a more developed conception that places it in a more inclusive context. We posit a concept of being, and we then see what we must posit in order to avoid the contradictions that ensue from that initial posit. The concept of becoming leads us to a more concrete conception than pure being, determinate being (i.e., existence), which allows us to distinguish being from nothing. "It is only Determinate Being itself which contains the true distinction between Being and Nothing, namely Something and an Other."[116] The logic of pure being has passed over into pure nothing, through becoming, to determinate being. This does not bring the dialectic to a close, however. Determinate being leads to a new contradiction and the process continues.

Hegel proceeded in this way through the three parts of his logic, the logic of being, the logic of essence, and the logic of the concept. In the logic of the concept, he developed a theory of universals that is relevant to Dewey's instrumental logic. Hegel's theory of universals is consistent with his focus on practical problems because they are tools we craft to facilitate the resolution of problems.[117] When a problem arises, a relation within a previously undifferentiated whole stands out in relief and captures our attention. Because the relation stands out from its context, it becomes an "abstract universal." This is the level of *Verstand,* analysis of the problem into its constituent parts so that we can precisely locate the difficulty. As Timothy Huson explains, "it is understanding itself which creates its objects in creating its universals."[118] An abstract universal is not false, but we err when we conclude that it is external to the concrete object. We move to the level of *Vernunft,* at which we apprehend the whole, as we formulate an explanation of the abstract universal's function within the whole. If the explanation succeeds, the abstract universal becomes a "particular" because it now has a place in a theory about the whole; we now see it as a particular component of the whole. The relation of the abstract universal to its other, its context, constitutes its particularity. These two phases are moments in the development of "individuality." If our explanation works, we are able to fit the abstract universal back into its context, but now, rather than an abstract universal, it is an "individual" because we have an explanation for it. An individual is both universal and particular, but it is not an abstract identity of the two; it is an identity containing difference. If we are able to reunite universal and particular, our explanation is verified. Throughout Hegel's works, the dialectic moves from universal to particular to individual, what he called the "three . . . 'moments' or functional parts" within the concept.[119] When the problematic relation becomes an individual, our theory about the whole has enriched it; it has become more meaningful. As Hegel would say, the abstract universal has become a "concrete universal."[120]

Hence, I return to an issue I mentioned in the preface, Larry Hickman's point about Dewey's "novel solution" to the "traditional problem of 'universals'" that rejected both nominalism, which generally holds that universals (abstract classes such as "matter") are merely linguistic conventions, and realism, which generally holds that particulars somehow participate in universals that exist in a separate realm. Both Hegel and Dewey came closest to Aristotle's conceptualism, which is that we form conceptions of universals on the basis of properties that exist naturally within particulars.[121] But because both Hegel and Dewey rejected Cartesian dualism and the traditional Aristotelian doctrine of substance, those properties cannot exist in a static world that is separate from our experience of it. Rather, for both philosophers, we craft universals on the basis of our purposes in attending to certain particulars that occur within the dialectic of experience. We pick out features that enable us to classify particulars in ways that are useful given the project in which we are engaged. For both philosophers, universals are moments or stages within the process of our interaction with the world.[122]

Rather than examine the adequacy of the specific transitions in Hegel's logic, which many critics have argued are artificial, I wish to note underlying assumptions. Hegel sought to demonstrate the instability of abstract categories and to draw out what is latent within them, progressively moving from the abstract to the concrete, from the indeterminate to the determinate. In so doing, the dialectic purports to articulate what is contained in the starting point. Furthermore, it is important to note that Hegel always confronted philosophical dichotomies by showing that the two poles of the dichotomy are compatible rather than disproving either of the poles. For Hegel, all of the classical dualisms of philosophy turn out to be only apparent dualisms when we examine the ways in which opposing concepts function within the processes of thought. Concepts such as subject, object, universal, particular, and individual are instruments we use to solve practical problems.

Hegel's treatment of the dualism of cause and effect provides an example that will also be relevant to my discussion of Dewey in later chapters. The understanding insists that cause and effect are patently distinct and opposing poles, but reason reveals that "effect contains nothing whatever that cause does not contain. Conversely, cause contains nothing which is not in its effect."[123] For reason, cause and effect are equally real functions within an essentially homogeneous continuum, the process of experience. According to Hegel, we only perceive a cause after we see its effect and, in the same way, we only perceive an effect after we discover its cause: "Both cause and effect are thus one and the same content."[124] This goes beyond mere perception, however, because a cause is actual "*only in its effect.*"[125] Hegel observed that only when a cause produces an effect, does it become a cause and thus, in this sense, it is the cause of itself and also the effect of itself. The effect can also be viewed as a cause, because only when it occurs does the cause become a cause. In this way cause and effect reverse their roles, and are more fruitfully seen as reciprocal rather than linear relations. Hegel's notion of reciprocity is consistent with his distinction between a bad infinity, in which the antecedents of an effect regress indefinitely, and a true infinity, which is circular. For Hegel, this is a more complete picture of causation than one that elevates one element, cause or effect, means or ends, as somehow more real than the other.

It is often claimed that Hegel's dialectic undermines the reality of opposing terms, absorbing them into a voracious but undifferentiated absolute. But Hegel's criticisms of *Verstand* entail that he could not consistently valorize one principle over another. He must give all significant categories a place within his thought and cannot postulate a supersensible reality. In this regard, Hegel moved beyond metaphysics as it was traditionally understood—the examination of that which is beyond or behind the physical. Furthermore, paying close attention to Hegel's historical context illuminates the issue of his alleged monism. He and Schelling denounced Fichte for reducing reality to spirit or mind in a subjective idealism. In the *Phenomenology,* Hegel broke from his ally Schelling by declaring that his "Identity Philosophy" collapsed nature and spirit into a vague, undifferentiated absolute. Schelling's philosophy, he asserted, tried "to palm off its Absolute as the night in which . . . all cows are black—this is cognition naively reduced to vacuity," and in another passage, Hegel described it as "a monochromatic formalism." Monism is vacuous, according to Hegel, because it denies the reality of the "self-originating, self-differentiating wealth of shapes" that we encounter in experience.[126] Rather than deny the reality of the objects we experience by subsuming them under an a priori principle (i.e., the absolute) as either subject or object, Hegel denounced the reduction of reality to a single substance. He affirmed the necessity of unique individual objects to cognition, which must be able to differentiate the objects of experience from one another and can do so because they really are different and unique. For Hegel, all of the unique things we experience are real; although he never invoked the term himself, it is now common parlance to call this view pluralism. In his development of the dialectic, which had been used by both Fichte and Schelling, Hegel introduced the crucial concept of *Aufhebung*—sublation—precisely because it was imperative to him to affirm diversity within unity. Sublation is the final moment of the triadic dialectic and, although it achieves a unity of previously opposing terms, it does so without undermining their reality within the unity. The uniqueness of the previously opposing terms is preserved in the resulting synthesis, and the larger whole is accordingly shaped by those terms. Diversity depends on unity because their unique relations to one another within the larger whole differentiates individual things. At the same time, the identity or character of the unity is dependent upon the diversity of the unique individuals within it.[127] Hegel placed the same emphasis on the interrelationship of diversity and unity in his ethics and political philosophy.[128]

Ethics and Political Philosophy

In 1802 and 1803, when Hegel was still struggling to specify what he approved and disapproved of in the philosophies of Kant and Fichte, he published an essay, "Natural Law," in which he developed one of the most essential concepts of his ethical thought—*Sittlichkeit.*[129] Usually translated as "ethical life," *Sittlichkeit* is the matrix of customs, rituals, rules, and practices that make up a society and make each one of us a part of society.[130] It is not, as social contract theory suggests, an external package of laws that we voluntarily adopt, as if we were visitors in a strange land. It is the collection of behaviors through which we define ourselves and learn the difference between right and wrong. Distinguishing between our own individual autonomy and the set of practices of our society is a prelude to theoretical and, in the case of the French Revolution, actual disaster. Yet, according to Hegel, this is precisely what theories like the social contract do, and the result is a feeble depiction of the law on the one hand, and ourselves—as creatures devoid of a culture—on the other.

Both Kant and Fichte committed this error, Hegel argued, and thus their ethics is mere *Moralität*; it is based on abstract, formal rules, and despite their claims to the contrary, it is imposed upon us. For Hegel, ethics, *Sittlichkeit,* must be based upon the actual, concrete practices in which we are engaged. In his distinction between autonomy, practical self-legislation, and heteronomy—moral legislation imposed upon us—Kant introduced what Hegel believed was the philosophically fatal distinction between the self as a rational moral agent abstracted from its context and the communal framework and mores in which we are raised and that naturally become our preferences—our emotions, moods, and desires.[131] Kant supposed that the moral law was universally valid, as a matter of rational principle alone, apart from any particular culture and practices. For Hegel, this view dissolves the all-important connection between our sense of morals and our sense of belonging to a society, and once this is done we seem trapped in the Rousseauan feeling that we are corrupted by our society and indoctrinated by its laws, instead of created through and by that society and those laws. Thus we find ourselves perpetually at odds with the state.

Moreover, because *Moralität* is based on the artificial notion that we are isolated, asocial individuals who have duties in abstraction from our social roles, it posits a moral ideal that is inevitably unattainable. We cannot, in fact, utterly transcend the social context in which we are forced to grapple with our limitations and conflicting obligations. By remaining at the level of these abstractions, Hegel argued, neither Kant nor Fichte rose above the understanding to the see the whole, *Sittlichkeit,* through reason. And perhaps what was worst for Hegel, Kant's and Fichte's systems of *Moralität* depict our transcendent moral duties as absolutely binding and imply that our actual social and ethical relationships are merely contingent. This poses two grave dangers, according to Hegel. First, the notion of transcendent duty can lead to fanatical commitment to moral absolutes regardless of what other members of society believe is morally correct and regardless of the actual consequences of our actions. Second, transcendent duty feeds the alienation, in this case from society and from ethical ideals, that is at the heart of modern anxiety, making it impossible for us to ever feel at home in our own society. In Fichte, Hegel believed, *Moralität* reached its logical conclusion, the justification of a police state, "the harshest despotism," because of the rigid dichotomy it generates between the individual and society, the private and the public.[132] Obedience to the laws of the state can only be externally forced upon the individual.

By way of contrast, Hegel's concept of *Sittlichkeit* summarizes what he believed was the natural synthesis of our moral sense and our social sense. Properly understood, morality is not only a matter of rational principles but is also a matter of social practices and good upbringing. In this way, Hegel refused to rigidly separate the is from the ought, fact from value. If morality was founded upon abstract, transcendent principles or seemingly "interior," subjective principles, it would be easily undermined by philosophers like Hume who could contend that the standards are arbitrary because they are not empirically verifiable as objectively real. Hegel believed that any philosophy that rigidly separated fact and value would undermine morality and community by depicting value as less real than fact. He was convinced that universal moral principles must be based on the concrete practices of a community; values must be based on facts. For this reason, Hegel's ethical thought is inseparable from his social and political thought.

By the time he wrote *The Philosophy of Right,* which was published in 1821, Hegel found a way to preserve the truth of *Moralität* by arguing that it becomes meaningful within a *Sittlichkeit.* Explanation of this point can be facilitated by reference to the *Bildung* metaphor. In my previous discussion of *Bildung,* I emphasized that the moral goal for Hegel was self-development, but if the self is not a latent essential substance, what is it that Hegel believed is to be developed? For Hegel, the self is activity and is known only by its activity: "What the subject is, is the series of his actions."[133] It is only in self-expression, overt action, that the self becomes actual, and that its ideality or lack thereof can be assessed. There is no metaphysical dualism between the actual and ideal selves;

the ideal self to be expressed and actualized is a culturally and historically contingent ideal. Self-development is the actualization of the ideal by imagining the moral rules that might describe the behavior of an ideal person. In this way, moral rules are not foreign, but are always part of one's chosen and ongoing project of self-development.[134] Moreover, the ideal self to be developed is a moving target because it must be constantly revised as the self matures and thus achieves ever-fuller understanding of the ideal self and the implications of its ideals. For this reason, there is no final state of self-realization and the freedom to imagine and constantly work toward the actualization of the ideal self is essential to the good life. An education that enables individuals to imagine and assess different forms of life is also crucial to self-development. This places certain duties upon the state to provide a nurturing environment in which self-development can best occur.

The recent biographies upon which I have relied maintain that Hegel's political thought was motivated by his commitment to the ideals of the French Revolution. The most fully developed account of his political philosophy, *The Philosophy of Right,* is probably his most controversial book. Once more, the historical context of the book is crucial to understanding it and the controversy that has always surrounded it.

The tumult of Hegel's lifetime did not end with the Reign of Terror. Throughout the years 1793-1815 various political entities (e.g., the Holy Roman Empire, Prussia, Austria, Great Britain) were almost constantly at war with France; until Hegel's death in 1831, various localities in which he lived—Jena, Bamberg, Nuremberg, Heidelberg, and Berlin—experienced radical swings in which it seemed at one moment that liberal reform was imminent only to be crushed at the next moment by reactionary forces. Hegel published *The Philosophy of Right* in a politically toxic atmosphere at the height of a conservative backlash against liberal reforms in Prussia.[135] In 1819, German rulers issued the Karlsbad decrees, imposing censorship on academic publications and providing guidelines for the removal of subversives from the universities. In the preface to the book, Hegel imprudently continued his longtime professional and philosophical rivalry with Jakob Friedrich Fries, who had been recently dismissed from his university post at Jena as a subversive. Though a number of Hegel's students and assistants were also arrested as subversives, his critics, some of whom must not have read beyond the preface, raised suspicions about his political thought immediately after the book was published. Hegel's claim in the preface that "what is rational is actual; and what is actual is rational," was immediately interpreted as bestowing an unqualified blessing on the political status quo.[136]

During this time of far-reaching geopolitical and cultural change, Hegel's political sentiments were surprisingly constant. He was consistently critical of German political nationalism, championing Enlightenment cosmopolitanism instead, and when he opposed social and political reforms, including some advocated by liberals, it was because he was averse to bureaucratic reform from above as the imposition of one group's will upon the citizenry. Freedom of the press and public dialogue, he believed, would provide for transformation of local culture so that reforms would be meaningful; the press was to serve as a mediating institution. Hegel never embraced democracy, but he feared democracy for liberal reasons. He believed democracy could not protect the rights of minorities and advocated a constitutional, representative, monarchical government instead.[137] Today, many commentators contend that Hegel's liberalism can be seen in the preface to *The Philosophy of Right,* and if one goes beyond the preface, his liberalism is abundantly clear.[138]

Placing Hegel in the neo-humanist tradition significantly clarifies his political philosophy.[139] During the late eighteenth and early nineteenth centuries, *Bildung* was a highly contested term in the German states. Many Germans associated it with the Enlightenment, which was controversial enough, and some associated it with Jacobinism, which they construed as a desire to murder the aristocracy and the leaders of the church. Those who advocated *Bildung* did so as part of an effort to promote cultural nationalism, the cultural unification of the small German states through the development of the German language, literature, and philosophy. During the French Revolution, *Bildung* took on radical political implications. Hegel and other neo-humanists fused it with the ideals of the Revolution, depicting it as an education that would enable individuals to be critical of established authority. Education as *Bildung* would kindle the moral renewal that was necessary to true political reform in the German states. For Hegel, the French Revolution had turned to Terror because moral renewal had not preceded the revolution; the French people lacked liberal modes of thought and habits, and French society lacked liberal institutions. Only a people of *Bildung* could form a liberal social fabric (*Sittlichkeit*) in which the necessary social and political institutions could be built and sustained.[140] As elements of this, Hegel believed that a stable, progressive society required its own art and civic religion to help individual members internalize the society's moral and political ideals. Unlike Robespierre's Festival of the Supreme Being of 1794, however, Hegel's civic religion had to be grounded in long-standing traditions.

Because self-development through the process of *Bildung* requires that the individual be able to gain perspective on his own particular interests, as well as his particular community, and to appreciate universal moral ideals, like other neo-humanists, Hegel sought to promote a unified German culture that was consistent with Enlightenment cosmopolitanism because it did not in any way imply a single national German state. He rejected Fichte's efforts during the Wars of Liberation to transform cultural nationalism into a movement for political unification. Hegel's emphatically cosmopolitan outlook led him to oppose, and even ridicule, efforts to promote German political unification.[141]

Under the influence of the neo-humanists, Hegel emphasized personal growth through self-alienation and return as the way to rise above one's narrow natural inclinations; under the influence of Kant, he emphasized that the educated person should seek to follow universal norms of conduct. For Hegel, the ideal of *Bildung* was that one would become not only a man of learning, but also a man of good taste, combining the study of the latest research with the appreciation of literature and the fine arts, thus uniting head and heart, thought and feeling. Advocating the revolutionary sentiment that "careers should be open to talent," Hegel believed that the moral and spiritual renewal of the German people would be realized through the establishment of a new elite of educated and cultivated leaders who would replace the corrupt, undereducated aristocracy, who held their positions simply by virtue of their birth.[142] Although, from our twenty-first-century perspective, it may appear that Hegel sought to replace one elite with another, this was a liberal sentiment in his time and place. For Hegel and other early-nineteenth-century German intellectuals, it was difficult to conceive that unrefined German peasants should be allowed to participate in their government.

Bildung is a central motif in *The Philosophy of Right,* in which Hegel illuminated the concept by repeating the advice of a Pythagorean philosopher to a father about the best way to educate his son: "Make him the *citizen of a state with good laws.*"[143] Thus *The Philosophy of Right* builds on the political connotations of the neo-humanistic conception of *Bildung. Bildung* requires a well-ordered society in which the individual has the freedom, and even luxury, to develop his unique talents and abilities. *Bildung* also requires a society in which there is scope for all kinds of complementary individuals and activities because exposure to different kinds of people and experimentation with different types of lives is crucial to the sort of moral development Hegel had in mind. He made it apparent throughout *The Philosophy of Right* that *Bildung* should begin in the family, continue more systematically in school, and be taken to a higher level in the university. After formal schooling is completed, in civil society the individual should achieve the final stage of *Bildung,* recognition of the rational basis of his society's institutions. The final stage of *Bildung* does not require acquiescence to the status quo. On the contrary, the man of *Bildung* is capable of independent thought and is thus exceptionally well prepared to engage in immanent critique of his society's practices. That is to say, he is able to criticize his society on its own terms, to appraise the extent to which it measures up to its rational basis, its highest ideals. Yet because Hegel believed true political reform had to be preceded by gradual cultural reform, he was never a radical. He rejected the revolutionary notion that society could be rapidly transformed.

Recognition played such a crucial role in Hegel's analysis of human experience, it is no surprise that in his political thought it is central to his conception of the relation of individuals to each other and to society as a whole. In my previous discussion of the master/slave dialectic, I focused exclusively on its epistemological implications, but of course many philosophers and activists have been inspired by it in other ways. According to Rockmore, the master/slave dialectic demonstrates that "Hegel's reputation as a social liberal is justified." Rockmore explains further that "Hegel's description here of social inequality can be read as a powerful call to social change, even as an encoded revolutionary manifesto, recommending the rise of social consciousness as the indispensable precondition for basic social change."[144] Perhaps the most important implications of the master/slave dialectic are that those who are oppressed will prevail over their condition of subjugation as their oppressors stagnate, and that fully developed social consciousness, which is essential to knowledge, requires social equality. Another important aspect of Hegel's concept of recognition is apparent in his discussion of contracts. Hegel argued that a contractual exchange of commodities between two individuals requires each person's recognition that the other is a proprietor of the inalienable value that is attached to their alienable possessions.

If and when this proprietorship is denied, the resulting exchange is fraud or theft. The difference between property and mere possession is that the former is grounded in a relation of reciprocal recognition between two willing subjects. In reciprocal recognition individual subjects rise above their particular arbitrary wills to share a common will. But whereas Rousseau believed that the common will exists *despite* the fact that particular wills have different ends in mind, Hegel argued that the common will exists *because* particular wills have different ends in mind. Individuals enter into contracts, which require mutual recognition, precisely because they want something different from the exchange. Identity of will is achieved because of coexisting difference.[145] This is how Hegel avoided what he is so often accused of, the absorption of the individual into the larger social and political whole.[146]

Because of the destructive modern dichotomy between the community and the individual, what Hegel called "universality" and "particularity," he sought to articulate an ethical and political theory that preserved modern subjectivity without undermining community. He based his theory on a concept of the human good as self-development of the human spirit, and a belief that the essence of the human spirit is freedom. Hegel rejected the notion that freedom is merely the ability to act without constraints, articulating a theory of positive freedom, according to which freedom is the ability to act rationally. According to Hegel, a free act is not arbitrary; rather, it is one that is determined solely by the self, on the basis of reasons, to be one that rises above particularity to the universal.[147] Hegel's concept of freedom also countered atomistic individualism because he argued that, although humans are free to renounce their society, such an act is merely "abstract" or "negative freedom," a one-sided conception of freedom erroneously elevated by the understanding "to supreme status." Those who adhere to the concept of negative freedom alone are prone to fanaticism because they find all that is different from them to be incompatible with their goals. "This is why," Hegel explained, "the people during the French Revolution, destroyed once more the institutions they had themselves created, because all institutions are incompatible with the abstract self-consciousness of equality."[148]

Concrete freedom, on the other hand, is realized not by fleeing from the other but by relating to it in such a way that the other becomes integrated into one's projects. The other serves to complete and fulfill one's projects when the self successfully includes it as part of its action rather than opposing it. Hegel argued that this requires us to act in harmony with moral standards that would be accepted by all. The most important object of our action is harmonization with the ideals of our social order, the sphere of "objective spirit." Hegel concluded that freedom can only be actual, or concrete, in a *Sittlichkeit,* a rational society in which social institutions are felt and known by the people to be rationally consistent with their needs and desires. To the degree that those institutions are not rationally consistent with the society's ideals—and they always fall short in some ways—they must be reformed. In a *Sittlichkeit,* however, the demands of social life do not conflict with one's needs and desires; rather, they fulfill individuality. Self-interest is not at odds with the good of the whole, and rather than limiting freedom, the fulfillment of social duties actualizes it. If we are aware of this harmony, we come to be "with ourselves," that is, individually liberated by our duties to others.[149]

Although I have referred to Hegel as a liberal, liberalism that is based on atomistic individualism and the social contract is clearly at odds with his notion of freedom because it defines freedom as the ability to do as we please, regardless of the advisability of our actions. Although his theory is not based on that conception of freedom, it is not hostile to it. In *The Philosophy of Right,* Hegel argued that social institutions must provide considerable scope for arbitrary freedom. Modern man can only achieve actualization, Hegel claimed, if he has "abstract rights," rights that are defined in abstraction from the particular use a person may make of them. Because he is a "subject," modern man derives self-satisfaction from determining his own particular good or happiness. Modern man can only achieve actualization by leading a reflective life shaped by his own actions. Specifically, Hegel argued that the modern state must enable people to shape their own identity and direct their own life. The state must honor individual moral conscience and can only hold people responsible for actions that are expressions of their subjectivity, that is, actions that are based on free, rational choice.[150] Hegel's concept of freedom assumes that we should have the unhindered ability to do as we please, but that the ability to do as we please is only valuable when the actions we choose are conducive to self-development and the actualization of ideals; otherwise, such freedom is worthless, and possibly harmful to ourselves and to others.

Hegel believed that personal rights can only be understood within a system of law, and many have taken this as a philosophical acquiescence to the status quo. If our rights do not transcend the laws of our society, it is believed, then we cannot make claims against society. Yet, in agreement with the natural law tradition, Hegel argued that we are not required to obey unjust laws, and he provided examples of such laws in *The Philosophy of Right.* Hegel claimed that slavery and the denial of private property were unjust in the context of any system of law.[151] He did not reject individual rights; he simply believed that they are empty abstractions in need of content that can only be provided by a rational social order. Hegel had less fear of the state than he had of atomistic individualism because he believed that a state that violated individual rights was self-destructive, at odds with the source of its own power, and thus would not long endure. But if people insisted too stubbornly on their individual rights, withdrawing into their subjectivity, they would become alienated from the common social life. Outside of the common social life, Hegel believed, a person may have vast options, but they are empty and meaningless.

Hegel held that "civil society" made the modern state decisively distinct from earlier and less developed social orders. He defined civil society as the realm of the market economy, the realm in which individuals exist as owners and disposers of private property, and as agents who chose their own life-activity. In modern society, Hegel claimed, individuals can achieve actualization only when they depend on themselves for their own livelihood; thus he viewed a collectivized or state-run economy as a pre-modern institution incompatible with modern subjectivity. But Hegel's study of the Scottish economists convinced him that civil society requires more than self-interest because collective market behavior displays a collective, though unintended, rationality. According to this collective rationality, individuals are best able to support themselves through endeavors that benefit the whole. Hegel argued that this fact of the market economy entails that society has a responsibility to prevent its members from falling into poverty; to be poor in a civil society is to be socially wronged whether poverty is caused by lack of education or the contingencies of the marketplace. Ultimately, Hegel believed that civil society required a middle course between a state-run economy and laissez-faire liberalism, and the responsibility of overseeing the economy fell under the purview of the state's police power.[152]

Beyond economic security, however, Hegel believed modern man needs a determinate, concrete social identity, or social estate, which he viewed as a specific trade or profession. As a member of an estate, the individual receives needed recognition from peers, and his economic activity rises above mere economic self-seeking because he contributes to an estate that exists in order to make a determinate contribution to the whole. In a type of guild socialism, Hegel argued that civil society should be organized into "corporations," meaning professional associations or guilds.[153] Members of guilds have a collective responsibility to properly train new workers, set standards for the work done, and to look out for the welfare of members, providing assistance to those out of work without undermining their dignity in the way that private charity or public assistance tends to do. Hegel also believed that political representation should be based on these corporations rather than geographical districts. He was unconcerned about the fact that wage laborers were not eligible for corporation membership, and believed that the unreflective spirit of the rural population was unsuited to such organization. In essence, representation in Hegel's rational society was restricted to the male urban middle class. In the final analysis, he wanted power to rest neither in the monarch nor in the people, but in a class of educated, professional civil servants who would serve as the king's ministers. But Hegel insisted that the ministers must be bound to represent the majority decision of the legislature.[154]

Despite his limited egalitarianism, Hegel saw the extremes of wealth in modern civil society as a contradiction in the social order, but he offered no solution to the problem. In a competitive market economy, he explained, the wealthy believe it is in their interest to have a dependent working class so that they can keep wages low and profits high. Rather than blame the wealthy or the poor for this situation, Hegel viewed it as a shortcoming of modern society that tended to produce a discontented rabble among the poor. "Despite an *excess of wealth,* civil society is *not wealthy enough*—i.e. its own distinct resources are not sufficient—to prevent an excess of poverty and the formation of a rabble." The rabble, justifiably outraged by its exclusion from the benefits of society, loses self-respect, respect for the rights of others, and thus produces a criminal element. Hegel did not claim that the status quo is ever completely free of contradictions, and his concerns about the maldistribution of wealth in capitalist economies indicates that he did not expect any society to achieve complete consistency with its ideals. He argued that political instability could result from the exclusion of some citizens from the benefits of society, but he was not committed to the enfranchisement of all citizens because he believed that in the early-nineteenth-century German states only university-educated professionals were ready to have a voice in their government.[155]

Hegel also contended that civil society changed the nature of the family because it no longer serves an economic function. The purpose of the family in the modern state is to provide a safe haven for individuals from the harsh realities of civil society. He believed property should be held in common within the family, but only the husband and father should administer it because he alone exercises rights in civil society. The wife and mother is limited to the sphere of the family, and she and the children only exercise personal rights if the family is dissolved in divorce, the children leave to found new families, or the father dies.[156]

Hegel distinguished between the political state and the state in a broader sense, the community as a whole. The "state," as he generally used the term, is the articulated totality of human relations, including family, civil, and political spheres.[157] Although he wrote that it is the "*highest duty*" of the individual to be a member of the state in the latter sense, he denied that patriotism, "the political disposition," consists in self-sacrifice for one's country. According to Hegel, patriotism is simply the habit of trusting the institutions of one's society.[158] He viewed the state, understood as our broader community, as our universal end because of his aversion to merely abstract universals. The state is a concrete universal in which we can truly find actualization. Hegel also viewed the state as the vehicle of world history because he rejected theories that depicted history as driven by some abstract or supernatural force. For Hegel, we do not become cosmopolitan by committing ourselves to abstract universals, but by recognizing that our actions are historically and culturally situated, and thus that our deeds are expressions of the spirit of our time and state.

I conclude my examination of Hegel's moral and political thought with a consideration of his treatment of war because Alan Ryan has recently argued that Dewey was always adamantly opposed to Hegel on this issue. According to Ryan, Hegel believed "all good sprang from evil" and that "philosophy must not . . . flinch from the rough spectacle of war and death."[159] Regardless of the other virtues of his book, Ryan's characterization of Hegel on this and other issues is singularly inaccurate. While it is true that Hegel claimed that war is not an "absolute evil," that some war is inevitable, and that it may preserve "the ethical health of nations," he wrote that war has the nature of something "which ought to come to an end." War should "entail the determination of international law" and "preserve the possibility of peace."[160]

Philosophy of History

Hegel began his philosophy of history with the Oriental World, at the point that its people were able "to form abstract distinctions and assign abstract predicates." Only at that moment, can man create a state with laws and thus subjugate "mere arbitrary will"; everything prior to that, the "ante-historical," is unworthy of the philosophy of history. In the Oriental World freedom existed only for the despot, who imposed his will on the people externally and was able to act as arbitrarily as he chose. The ancient Greek Sophists introduced the principle of subjective freedom, fulfilled by Socrates, who followed his own internal voice rather than externally imposed sanctions, and in the Classical World many more individuals attained freedom: "Spirit became introspective, triumphed over particularity, and thereby emancipated itself." The strength of Greek society was its *Sittlichkeit,* which was based upon a strong sense of community, but life beyond the polis was inconceivable to the Greeks; citizens found fulfillment only in the accomplishments of their city. Although the ancient Greek polis was Hegel's model of social harmony, he argued that it had vanished because its moral order made insufficient room for the individual to rise above society and critique it for himself. Thus "great individuals" who sought to reform Greek society after the Peloponnesian War were "great tragic characters" because they were "unable to extirpate the evils in question . . . and perish[ed] in the struggle."[161] After the decline of the ancient Greek polis, along with its political and religious practices and beliefs, the Roman Empire instituted a purely formal, legal, or institutional conception of the individual.

As Christianity advanced in the Roman Empire, it offered a freedom to all men that transcended the social order because it taught that the individual has infinite value as a candidate for eternal salvation. Christianity also provided a conception of the individual not as an isolated unity, but as a part of God, who is the absolute unity of nature and history.[162] During the Middle Ages, the church became corrupt because of its "externality"; in its efforts to impose moral and spiritual ideals upon the people from on high, it lost touch with their needs and thwarted their self-development. "The Reformation resulted from the *corruption of the Church.*" The "essence of the Reformation," Hegel wrote, is that "Man is in his very nature destined to be free."[163] The Reformation advanced the potential unification of man with nature and history, and simultaneously subverted it, as modernity emerged from the Protestant Reformation. Luther's doctrine of justification by faith affirmed the individual's direct relationship to the divine, but Western man first understood this new principle in a subjective way, turning to minute introspection of the self, which resulted in spiritual agony. The Protestant Reformation sought to eliminate the dualism of the individual and formal institutions through the principle that the individual does not need an institution to guard the truth and dole out salvation.

The notion that all men have access to truth gave birth to experimental science, but Protestant individualism also led to eighteenth-century philosophy that subjected all traditions and institutions to individual judgment. Because no institutions could withstand such scrutiny, skepticism carried the day. Modernity had provided the concept of the individual—modern subjectivity—that could correct the incompleteness of Greek society, but had not provided a *Sittlichkeit* in which the individual could be grounded. On the contrary, modern subjectivity had proven corrosive of all social institutions and led to a compartmentalization and fragmentation of society. In the Enlightenment and in eighteenth and nineteenth-century religious sects (e.g., Pietism and Wesleyanism) man had ultimately withdrawn from society and retreated into his subjectivity, concluding that he could act according to his own conscience regardless of the effects of his actions on society. "The principle of the Freedom of the Will, therefore, asserted itself against existing Right."[164] This transcendent, subjective freedom was given philosophical expression in the Enlightenment, but the French Reign of Terror demonstrated that modern freedom was one-sided because it disregarded the value of well-founded social institutions. Philosophy must undertake the task of developing a *Sittlichkeit* that would preserve modern subjectivity.

There is much in Hegel's philosophy of history that is distasteful to our ears today. He was certainly Eurocentric, but perhaps even more disconcerting was his concept of the world historical individual (e.g., Alexander the Great, Julius Caesar, and Napoleon) who somehow seizes the day and by his actions advances either the destruction of the old or the emergence of the new. In his delusions of grandeur, such an individual freely violates ethical norms, and Hegel regarded this as justifiable in some sense. This raises the prospect that his philosophy of history makes allowances for the nefarious acts of prominent leaders. We can only see world historical individuals to be such in retrospect, however, and we will only judge them to be so if their actions furthered the advance of freedom. Joseph McCarney explains that their actions can and should be criticized during their time, but at a later date "the world's court of judgement" may reveal that they unintentionally furthered human development.[165] Many have also raised questions about the status of *Weltgeist* in Hegel's philosophy of history. Although he often personified *Weltgeist,*[166] because *Geist* is always an activity rather than a being, on the humanistic/historicist reading, the trend toward fuller understanding and realization of human freedom is the movement of *Weltgeist*; it is Hegel's collective term for all of the manifestations of the human race (e.g., art, religion, philosophy, nations, and institutions) in its historical development.[167] Similarly, Hegel also spoke of the *Volksgeist,* the spirit of a people, and the *Geist der Zeit,* the spirit of the age.

The notion that Hegel believed in an end of history was recently resurrected by Francis Fukuyama, first in his article "The End of History?" and in his subsequent book *The End of History and the Last Man.*[168] Though Hegel scholars were quick to refute Fukuyama's claim that he advocated a Hegelian notion of the end of history, their refutations were too academic to receive as much attention in the popular press as Fukuyama.[169] Thus the myth endures.

When Hegel spoke of the end of history, he meant its purpose, not its termination.[170] Hegel thought the purpose of history could be discerned through careful examination of its course. To claim that Hegel believed in a termination of history, however, is to allege that he supposed he knew the future to some degree. Of course such a claim is at odds with the historicist reading of Hegel that I have articulated in this chapter. This view is also at odds with Hegel's conception of philosophy, particularly as he expressed it in the preface to *The Philosophy of Right.* Hegel argued that philosophy cannot tell us what ought to be because "it always comes too late to perform this function." In a famous passage Hegel wrote

> When philosophy paints its grey in grey, a shape of life has grown old, and it cannot be rejuvenated, but only recognized, by the grey in grey of philosophy; the owl of Minerva begins its flight only with the onset of dusk.[171]

Advocates of the historicist reading of Hegel place great emphasis on the preface to *The Philosophy of Right* where he asserted that the task of philosophy is to understand what has been, not to predict what will be. Moreover, contrary to a common caricature of Hegel, they see great humility in his method. As an example, Terry Pinkard writes that, for Hegel, "Philosophy comes on the scene when very basic beliefs, all of which *seem* to be true, also *seem* to contradict or to be somehow incompatible with each other. It is the task of philosophy to offer up alternative explanations for how these beliefs can be possible."[172] This understanding of the dialectic leads Hinchman to assert, "The great lesson . . . that one learns from Hegel is humility and self-criticism." Hegel "makes us sensitive to the one-sidedness and blindness of [our] world-views, their tendency to inspire us to act on a flawed understanding of man and his situation."[173] As I have argued, the historicist reading depicts Hegel's philosophy as providing a method of cultural criticism, dialectical immanent critique, rather than as a philosophy that professes to know the future.[174]

Another myth about Hegel's philosophy of history is that he declared it had properly culminated in the creation of the conservative Prussian state of the 1820s. Though this second myth is still bandied about, it is easily refuted. In the *Philosophy of World History,* Hegel claimed that

> it is up to America to abandon the ground on which world history has hitherto been enacted. What has taken place there up to now has been but an echo of the Old World and the expression of an alien life; and as a country of the future, it is of no interest to us here, for prophesy is not the business of the philosopher.[175]

On the same note, in the *Philosophy of History,* Hegel wrote that "America is . . . the land of the future," but philosophers "have to do with that which (strictly speaking) is neither past nor future, but with that which *is* . . ."[176] Furthermore, given his persistent opposition to political nationalism, it is a mistake to think that Hegel had political entities in mind in his philosophy of history. Although he declared that "The German Spirit is the Spirit of the New World," he meant the people of Protestant Northern Europe more generally, and the spirit he had in mind was the culture of freedom, rather than imperialistic conquest.[177] Most importantly, for Hegel, as subjective individuals turn inward to reconceive social and political institutions, those reconstructed institutions always provide a new basis for individual self-development. As Huson writes, "The potential, then, is always present for a *new* turn within at a higher level of social development." He adds that, for Hegel, "the question of which stage [of history] is higher is dialectical; it depends on how one looks at it."[178]

How one reads Hegel's philosophy of history is critical; in chapter six I argue that, during World War I, Dewey abruptly reversed his reading of Hegel's philosophy of history, claiming that it assumed a final termination. Although Dewey provided scant justification for this reading, it marks his first public break with Hegel. Prior to the bewildering events of that war, philosophers of the American Hegelian tradition drew heavily upon Hegel's philosophy of history without claiming that it posited an end to the historical dialectic.

Notes

1. The most important recent biographical studies are H. S. Harris, *Hegel's Development: Toward the Sunlight, 1770-1801* (Oxford: Clarendon Press, 1972); John Toews, *Hegelianism* (Cambridge: Cambridge University Press, 1980); H. S. Harris, *Hegel's Development: Night Thoughts (Jena, 1801-1806)* (Oxford: Clarendon Press, 1983); Laurence Dickey, *Hegel: Religion, Economics, and the Politics of Spirit, 1770-1807* (Cambridge: Cambridge University Press, 1983); Terry Pinkard, *Hegel: A Biography* (Cambridge: Cambridge University Press, 2000); and Horst Althaus, *Hegel: An Intellectual Biography,* trans. Michael Tarsh (Cambridge: Polity Press, 2000). In the following discussion, all biographical material is drawn from these sources. All of these biographers have benefited from Wilhelm Dilthey's discovery of Hegel's early theological writings, which were initially published by Hermann Nohl in 1907. Hegel, *Hegels theologishe Jugendschriften,* ed. Nohl (Tubingen: Mohr/Siebeck, 1907). T. M. Knox translated these essays as *Hegel's Early Theological Writings* (Chicago: University of Chicago Press, 1948). Though he overstates his case, the fact that Walter Kaufmann designated these essays Hegel's "anti-theological writings," reveals how they might undermine the theological/metaphysical reading of Hegel. Kaufmann, "Hegel's Early Anti-Theological Phase," *Philosophical Review* 63, no. 1 (Jan. 1954): 3-18. H. S. Harris's reading of these essays, in *Hegel's Development: Toward the Sunlight,* provides a provocative contrast to Kaufmann. These biographers also benefited from study of Hegel's "minor" political writings, which were translated in 1964 by T. M. Knox. Hegel, *Hegel's Political Writings,* trans. T. M. Knox, with an introductory essay by Z. A. Pelczynsky (Oxford: Clarendon Press, 1964). According to Frederick G. Weiss, Pelczynsky's introductory essay "quietly embarrassed" the myth of "Hegel's reactionary conservatism . . . into silence." Weiss, "A Critical Survey of Hegel Scholarship in English: 1962-1969," in *The Legacy of Hegel: Proceedings of the Marquette Hegel Symposium, 1970,* J. J. O'Malley et al., eds. (The Hauge: Martinus Nijhoff, 1973), 27. More recently, three more of Hegel's early essays have been translated as Hegel, *Three Essays, 1793-95: The Tübingen Essay, Berne Fragments, The Life of Jesus*, ed. and trans. Peter Fuss and John Dobbins (Notre Dame: University of Notre Dame Press, 1984).

2. Steven B. Smith, *Hegel's Critique of Liberalism: Rights in Context* (Chicago: University of Chicago Press, 1989). Cf. Lewis Hinchman, *Hegel's Critique of the Enlightenment* (Gainesville and Tampa: University Presses of Florida, 1984); and William Maker, "The Science of Freedom: Hegel's Critical Theory," *Bulletin of the Hegel Society of Great Britain* 41-42 (2000): 1-17. On this note, in his *Science of Logic,* Hegel wrote, "refutation must not come from outside; that is, it must not proceed from assumptions lying outside the system in question and inconsistent with it. The system need only refuse to recognize those assumptions; the *defect* is a defect only for him who starts from the requirements and demands based on those assumptions. . . . The genuine refutation must penetrate the opponent's stronghold and meet him on his own ground; no advantage is gained by attacking him from somewhere else and meeting him where he is not." Hegel, *Hegel's Science of Logic,* trans. A. V. Miller (Atlantic Highlands, NJ: 1969), 580-581.

3. On "the divided self" see Smith, *Hegel's Critique of Liberalism,* 17-31. On "the Cartesian Anxiety" see Richard J. Bernstein, *Beyond Objectivism and Relativism: Science, Hermeneutics, and Praxis* (Philadelphia: University of Pennsylvania Press, 1988), 16-20.

4. Hegel, *The Difference between Fichte's and Schelling's System of Philosophy,* trans. H. S. Harris and Walter Cerf (Albany: State University of New York Press, 1977), 90-91. Many have characterized Hegel's quest for unity as a religious quest and have taken his talk of absolute spirit as confirmation of that reading. Although not speaking of Hegel specifically, Richard Bernstein is correct to note, "It would be a mistake to think that the Cartesian Anxiety is primarily a religious, metaphysical, epistemological, or moral anxiety. These are only several of the many forms it may assume." Bernstein recommends that we understand the Cartesian Anxiety, in Heideggerian terms, as "'ontological' rather than 'ontic,' for it seems to lie at the very center of our being in the world." Bernstein, *Beyond Objectivism and Relativism,* 19. Bernstein's analysis of this anxiety suggests that not all philosophers have viewed it as a problem exclusive to philosophy, nor have they responded with Descartes' quest for certainty. Hegel and Dewey, I will contend, viewed the Cartesian Anxiety as a deep-seated cultural and existential problem and eschewed the Cartesian quest for an apodictic philosophical foundation.

5. On Hegel's family background see Toews, *Hegelianism,* 13-14. Laurence Dickey has demonstrated the importance of the religious and political tensions in Württemburg on the development of Hegel's thought. Dickey, *Hegel,* 1-180.

6. Dickey, *Hegel,* 8.

7. Ibid.

8. Despite his bias against Catholicism, during his years as a tutor in Frankfurt (1797-1800), Hegel displayed a genuine interest in learning about the religion. Althaus, *Hegel,* 44-46; Pinkard, *Hegel,* 69-72, 85.

9. Though it might seem doubtful that Hegel's support of the self-proclaimed Emperor Napoleon was a sign of his liberalism, it is important to note what Napoleon did to bring the small German principalities into the modern era. When Napoleon conquered Prussia in 1806 and dissolved the Holy Roman Empire, many of the German principalities were still ruled by small-minded tyrants of varying degrees of competence and were, in essence, corrupt structures of feudal Germany. Napoleon consolidated a number of these principalities into a single "Confederation of the Rhine" that was based upon new and enlightened rules of government, the Napoleonic code of laws, and the Revolutionary promise of "liberty, equality, and fraternity." Nonetheless, Hegel did feel some ambivalence about Napoleon. Pinkard, *Hegel,* 195.

10. See H. S. Harris's discussion of Hegel's essay, "Constitution of the German Empire," in *Hegel's Development: Toward the Sunlight,* 446-477, esp. 450-452.

11. Ibid., 17f.

12. Ibid., 140.

13. Pinkard, *Hegel,* 12, 47. Literally, a *Volkserzieher* is an educator of the people.

14. Ibid., 52-53.

15. This is evident in Hegel's earliest known composition, the "Tubingen Essay," in Hegel, *Three Essays, 1793-95.*

16. Hegel had reasons to fear that the critical philosophy would lead to divisive fanaticism. A contemporary philosopher, Friedrich Heinrich Jacobi, argued that because Kant's system precluded cognitive access to the thing-in-itself, his belief in its existence was an expression of dogmatism rather than the conclusion of a rational proof. A fideist, Jacobi argued that faith, not reason, was the basis of human knowledge of objective reality. For Hegel, Jacobi's fideism was tantamount to holding that a person's beliefs were true as long as he was passionately committed to them. See Hegel's 1802 essay, "Faith and Knowledge." Hegel, *Faith and Knowledge,* trans. Walter Cerf and H. S. Harris (Albany: State University of New York, 1977). See also Frederick C. Beiser, *The Fate of Reason: German Philosophy from Kant to Fichte* (Cambridge, MA: Harvard University Press, 1987), 89-91.

17. Dickey, *Hegel,* 139-180, 183, 192.

18. Hegel first began to use *Geist* in a way consistent with the usage in his mature writings in "Fragment of a System" (1800). Richard Kroner in Hegel, *Early Theological Writings,* trans. T. M. Knox with an introduction and fragments translated by Richard Kroner (Chicago: University of Chicago Press, 1948), 309-319.

19. Pinkard, *Hegel,* 87-88.

20. Smith, *Hegel's Critique of Liberalism,* 167-168.

21. Whereas for Rorty, the conversation seems to be the goal of philosophy, for Hegel it is a means to the goal of individual and cultural renewal.

22. Hegel to Schelling, 2 November 1800. Quoted in Smith, *Hegel's Critique of Liberalism,* 56.

23. See Stephen Bungay's characterization of Hegel's project, in which he explains that, for Hegel, "philosophy will not tell us anything we did not already know, like a new fact about the world, but will tell about what we already know, by subjecting our knowledge to an examination." Bungay, "The Hegelian Project," in *Hegel Reconsidered: Beyond Metaphysics and the Authoritarian State,* ed. H. Tristram Engelhardt, Jr., and Terry Pinkard (Boston: Kluwer, 1994), 20.

24. Richard Kroner correctly explains that "Hegel was a Romantic in his longing for unity; he was anti-Romantic in the way he gratified this longing." Kroner, "Introduction" in Hegel, *Early Theological Writings,* 15.

25. See Hegel's discussion of stages in the development of the idea of free will. Hegel, *Elements of the Philosophy of Right,* ed. Allen Wood, trans. H. B. Nisbet (Cambridge: Cambridge University Press, 1991), §33.

26. Hegel, *Phenomenology of Spirit,* trans. A. V. Miller (Oxford: Oxford University Press, 1977), §§632-671. See Carl Schmitt, *Political Romanticism,* trans. Guy Oakes (Cambridge, MA: MIT Press, 1986); and Robert E. Norton, *The Beautiful Soul: Aesthetic Morality in the Eighteenth Century* (Ithaca: Cornell University Press, 1995).

27. H. S. Harris, *Toward the Sunlight,* 26. Cf. Hinchman, *Hegel's Critique of the Enlightenment,* 253-255. Charles Taylor provides a thorough and insightful account of Hegel's relationship to both the Enlightenment and Romanticism in *Hegel* (Cambridge: Cambridge University Press, 1975), 3-50.

28. See Abel Garza, Jr., on Hegel's adaptation of the Greek ideal to the realities of modern society. Garza, "Hegel's Critique of Liberalism and Natural Law: Reconstructing Ethical Life," *Law and Philosophy* (1991): 371-398.

29. Joseph C. Flay, *Hegel's Quest for Certainty* (Albany: State University of New York Press, 1984), 9; Hegel, *Phenomenology of Spirit,* §§13, 26. I agree with Tom Rockmore that Flay exaggerates Hegel's desire for certainty. See Rockmore, *On Hegel's Epistemology and Contemporary Philosophy* (Atlantic Highlands, NJ: Humanities Press International, 1996), 72, n85.

30. Hegel, *Phenomenology of Spirit,* §§78, 80.

31. See Kenneth R. Westphal's discussion of Hegel's conception of correspondence in his *Hegel's Epistemological Realism: A Study of the Aim and Method of Hegel's* Phenomenology of Spirit (Dorchrecht: Kluwer Academic Publishers, 1989), 112-114, quote is at 141. Hegel, *Phenomenology of Spirit,* §§80, 54. In his "Lesser Logic," Hegel states, "This principle of Experience [British empiricism] carries with it the unspeakably important condition that, in order to accept and believe any fact, we must be in contact with it; or, in more exact terms, that we must find the fact united and combined with the certainty of our own selves." Hegel, *The Logic of Hegel, Translated from* The Encyclopaedia of the Philosophical Sciences, 3rd edition, trans. William Wallace (Oxford: Oxford University Press, 1975), §7.

32. Rockmore, *Cognition: An Introduction to Hegel's* Phenomenology of Spirit (Berkeley: University of California Press, 1997), 31. Dewey claimed his "*type* of theory is the only one entitled to be called a correspondence theory of truth." The traditional corre-

spondence theory of truth is unworkable, he argued, because it requires the self to transcend experience in order to compare one part of experience to something outside of experience. By way of contrast, Dewey meant correspondence in the sense "of answering, as a key answers to conditions imposed by a lock, or as two correspondents 'answer' each other; or, in general, as a reply is an adequate answer to a question or a criticism—as, in short, a solution answers the requirements of a problem." Dewey, "Propositions, Warranted Assertibility, and Truth" (1941), LW 14: 179-180. Tom Burke explains Dewey's notion of correspondence as a "correspondence between expected consequences and actual consequences." Burke, *Dewey's New Logic: A Reply to Russell* (Chicago: University of Chicago Press, 1994), 243-244.

33. Robert C. Solomon, *In the Spirit of Hegel: A Study of G. W. F. Hegel's* Phenomenology of Spirit (New York: Oxford University Press, 1983), 176.

34. Hegel, *Phenomenology of Spirit,* §§39, 40.

35. William James, *Pragmatism: A New Name for Some Old Ways of Thinking* (Indianapolis: Hackett, 1981), 92. Cf. also, "To ask if a category is true or not, must sound strange to the ordinary mind: for a category apparently becomes true only when it is applied to a given object, and apart from this application it would seem meaningless to inquire into its truth." Hegel, *The Logic of Hegel,* §35.

36. Hegel, *Phenomenology of Spirit,* §39.

37. Ibid., §37; M. J. Inwood, *A Hegel Dictionary* (Oxford: Blackwell Publishers, 1992), 58-61.

38. Ibid., §§81, 84, 80.

39. Rockmore, *On Hegel's Epistemology and Contemporary Philosophy,* 49. As Rockmore notes, perhaps the fundamental difference between religious and secular readings of Hegel is that some commentators have interpreted the absolute as a supernatural God, while others have preferred secular interpretations. Ibid., 54. Recent examples of secular readings include Joseph Flay's claim that Hegel's absolute merely shows what knowledge is and how it is possible. Flay, *Hegel's Quest for Certainty,* 284. Errol Harris argues that Hegel's absolute is the highest, most adequate, form of knowledge. Harris, *An Interpretation of the Logic of Hegel* (Lanham, MD: University Press of America, 1983), 286. Robert Solomon claims that Hegel's absolute is God, but that his God is not supernatural; he is nothing more than reality. Solomon, *In the Spirit of Hegel,* 188.

40. Robert Pippin, *Hegel's Idealism: The Satisfactions of Self-Consciousness* (Cambridge: Cambridge University Press, 1989), 68-69. Cf. Hegel, *The Philosophy of Right,* §22.

41. Hegel, *Phenomenology of Spirit,* §6. On the Romanticism that Hegel had in mind, see Frederick C. Beiser's discussion of Jacobi. Beiser, *The Fate of Reason,* 89-91.

42. Rockmore, *On Hegel's Epistemology and Contemporary Philosophy,* 64-65. Hegel, *The Philosophy of Right,* 21 (emphasis in the original). See also Rockmore, *Cognition,* 210-212.

43. Cf. Dewey's claims about his method in *Experience and Nature:* "An empirical philosophy is in any case a kind of intellectual disrobing. We cannot permanently divest ourselves of the intellectual habits we take on and wear when we assimilate the culture of our own time and place. But intelligent furthering of culture demands that we take some of them off, that we inspect them critically to see what they are made of and what wearing them does to us. We cannot achieve recovery of primitive naïveté. But there is attainable a cultivated naïveté of eye, ear and thought, one that can be acquired only through the discipline of severe thought." Dewey, *Experience and Nature* (1925), LW 1: 40.

44. This reading of *The Philosophy of Right* and the *Phenomenology* draws strength from passages in the *Phenomenology* that appear to foreshadow the later claim that philosophy is its own time comprehended in thought. Hegel, *Phenomenology of Spirit,* §§800, 808.

45. Hegel, *The Logic of Hegel,* §160.

46. Ibid., §41. Similarly, Hegel wrote, "it may be held the highest and final aim of philosophic science to bring about, through the ascertainment of the harmony, a reconciliation of the self-conscious reason with the reason which *is* in the world—in other words, with actuality." Ibid., §6. Compare Hegel's discussion of content and form in Ibid., §133 and Hegel, *Science of Logic,* 455-456.

47. Hegel, *The Logic of Hegel,* §42.

48. Westphal, *Hegel's Epistemological Realism,* 140.

49. Rockmore, *On Hegel's Epistemology and Contemporary Philosophy,* 61-62.

50. Klaus Hartmann, "On Taking the Transcendental Turn," *Review of Metaphysics* 20 (December 1966): 238; and Rockmore, *On Hegel's Epistemology and Contemporary Philosophy,* 90. Although he agrees with Hartmann's reading of Hegel in principle, Rockmore disagrees with his terminology, arguing that "From a Hegelian perspective, what Hartmann calls 'non-metaphysical' should be called 'metaphysical.'" Ibid., 79. See also William Maker's argument that Hegel refuted metaphysical idealism in favor of a methodological idealism that is based on his conviction that "self-determining thought," thought that requires no external foundation, is "the only mode of philosophically justifiable cognition." Maker, "The Very Idea of the Idea of Nature, Or Why Hegel Is Not an Idealist" in *Hegel and the Philosophy of Nature,* ed. Stephen Houlgate (Albany: State University of New York Press, 1998), 4.

51. Gustav Emil Mueller, "Translator's Note" in Hegel, *Encyclopedia of Philosophy,* trans. Gustav Emil Mueller (New York: Philosophical Library, 1959), 5.

52. Hegel, *Phenomenology of Spirit,* §11.

53. Solomon, *In the Spirit of Hegel,* 24-25. Solomon writes that the goal of the *Phenomenology* "is to gain a single all-encompassing conception, which makes sense of everything at once. But though this may be the goal of the *Phenomenology,* it is not its result; there is no end to the process of understanding life, while we are still living it. Hegel began looking for the Absolute, but what he discovered was the richness of conceptual history." Ibid., 25.

54. Mueller, "Translator's Note" in Hegel, *Encyclopedia of Philosophy,* 5.

55. As Rockmore explains, for Hegel, "we cannot separate prior from present views of knowledge. The process of education consists in making our own what was already known by our predecessors." Rockmore, *Cognition,* 14.

56. Hegel, *Phenomenology of Spirit,* §56. Solomon, *In the Spirit of Hegel,* 15, 26, 158-160. Cf. Rockmore, *Cognition,* 9, 27.

57. Hegel, *Phenomenology of Spirit,* §7.

58. See for example, Hegel, *Three Essays*; and "The Positivity of the Christian Religion," and "The Spirit of Christianity and its Destiny" in *Early Theological Writings.*

59. Hegel, *Philosophy of Mind, Translated from* The Encyclopaedia of the Philosophical Sciences, trans. William Wallace and A. V. Miller (Oxford: Clarendon Press, 1971). Hegel used the term "soul" (*Gemüt*) to distinguish the emotional aspect of the self from the more intellectual and active *Geist.* Inwood, *A Hegel Dictionary,* 189ff.

60. Hegel, *Philosophy of Mind,* §469.

61. Ibid., §484.

62. Hegel, *Aesthetics: Lectures on Fine Art,* 2 vols., trans. T. M. Knox (Oxford: Clarendon Press, 1975).

63. Hegel, *Phenomenology of Spirit,* §10.

64. I believe my discussion of Hegel's concept of recognition (below) demonstrates that the historian's interpretation of history is constrained not only by the existing record, but also by her need for recognition from her peers. Moreover, the writing and rewriting of history is, for Hegel, an ongoing and, to some degree, self-correcting endeavor. On Hegel's account, these constraints are present in any pursuit of knowledge. Ideally, for

Hegel, the historian makes no dogmatic assumptions, but tries to take her purposes and biases into account as she constructs her narrative. Hegel, *The Philosophy of History,* trans. J. Sibree (New York: Dover, 1956), 8-11; and Hegel, *Philosophy of Mind,* §549.

65. Hegel, *Phenomenology of Spirit,* §§73, 74.

66. Ibid., §74.

67. Hegel, *The Logic of Hegel,* §10.

68. Kant, of course, combined these two metaphors: Understanding was an active instrument. Intuition was a passive medium.

69. Hegel, *Phenomenology of Spirit,* §73.

70. Hinchman, *Hegel's Critique of the Enlightenment,* 72-73, 87-88, 103-104, 185-186.

71. Westphal, *Hegel's Epistemological Realism,* 141.

72. Hegel, *Phenomenology of Spirit,* §54.

73. Cf. Kant's posit of a "supersensible substrate" in the *Critique of Judgement*: "There must therefore be a ground of the *unity* of the supersensible, which lies at the basis of nature, with that which the concept of freedom practically contains; and the concept of this ground, although it does not attain either theoretically or practically to a knowledge of the same, and hence has no peculiar realm, nevertheless makes possible the transition from the mode of thought according to the principles of the one to that according to the principles of the other." Kant was at pains to claim that the supersensible substratum was not a dogmatic posit, arguing that it only has practical validity. Immanuel Kant, *Critique of Judgement,* trans. with an introduction by J. H. Bernard (New York: Hafner Press, 1951), 12. As John Zammito explains, "The architectonic of [Kant's] critical philosophy came more and more to rest on its tangency with a 'supersensible substrate' until, in the *Third Critique,* that notion of a transcendent ground featured decisively in rounding his system to a close." Zammito, *The Genesis of Kant's* Critique of Judgment (Chicago: University of Chicago Press, 1992). To Hegel, Kant simply revealed that he had not overcome the Cartesian problematic that strained British empiricism. As an example, according to John Locke, although material substance is the source of our ideas, it was an idea "which we neither have, nor can have, by sensation or reflection." Locke claimed that we "signify nothing by the word substance, but only an uncertain supposition of we know not what, i.e. of some thing whereof we have no particular distinct positive idea, which we take to be the substratum, or support, of those ideas we do know." John Locke, *An Essay Concerning Human Understanding,* ed. Peter Nidditch (Oxford: Clarendon Press, 1988), 95. George Berkeley's subjective idealism sprang from his conviction that Locke's postulation of material substance as the cause of corporeal phenomena was an ad hoc fiction, not a *vera causa.* Compare Hegel's argument that both Kantian and Fichtean idealisms are dualisms because, by "explaining the world from the standpoint of the subject" they inevitably depicted the object as in opposition to the subject; hence they are "nothing more than an extension of Lockeanism." Hegel, *Faith and Knowledge,* 78.

74. See George Santayana's characterization of the post-Kantians in his *Lotze's System of Philosophy,* ed. Paul Grimley Kuntz (Bloomington: Indiana University Press, 1971), 134ff. Cf. Allen Hance, "Pragmatism as Naturalized Hegelianism: Overcoming Transcendental Philosophy?" in *Rorty and Pragmatism: The Philosopher Responds to His Critics,* ed. Herman J. Saatkamp, Jr. (Nashville: Vanderbilt University Press, 1995), 100-125. Hance criticizes Rorty's claim that pragmatism is "naturalized Hegelianism," demonstrating that Rorty incorrectly assumes that Hegel's rejection of Kant's thing-in-itself commits him to subjective idealism. Hance argues that Hegel rejected representational epistemology much more successfully than Rorty, but the question of Hegel's relationship to Dewey is beyond the scope of his argument. Further, Hance equates naturalism with the reduction of reality to efficient causes and that which is studied by the

natural sciences, a view at odds with Dewey's, and probably even Rorty's, naturalism. Hance does claim, however, "Hegel . . . was more of a pragmatist than is ordinarily granted" (113). On the error of viewing Hegel as a subjective idealist, including a discussion of Rorty's inaccuracy, see Pippin, *Hegel's Idealism,* 91, 277-278 n. 1.

75. Ibid., §802.

76. Solomon, *In the Spirit of Hegel,* 11.

77. Hegel, *Phenomenology of Spirit,* §36.

78. Westphal, *Hegel's Epistemological Realism,* 141. Westphal defines epistemological realism as the view that "there is a way the world is which does not depend on our cognitive or linguistic activity" and "we can know the way the world is." Ibid., x.

79. Hegel, *The Philosophy of Right,* 20.

80. Hegel, *The Logic of Hegel,* §6.

81. Hegel, *Encyclopedia of the Philosophical Sciences in Outline and Critical Writings,* ed. Ernst Behler, trans. Steven A. Taubeneck (New York: Continuum, 1990), 58. Cf. Hegel's claim in the *Science of Logic* that "what is actual can act." Hegel, *Science of Logic,* 546.

82. Josiah Royce, *Lectures on Modern Idealism,* ed. Jacob Loewenberg (New Haven: Yale University Press, 1964), 139.

83. See for example, Forster, *Hegel's Idea of a* Phenomenology of Spirit.

84. Hegel, *Phenomenology of Spirit,* §129.

85. Hegel, *Encyclopedia of Philosophy,* §82.

86. J. N. Findlay, "Foreword," in Hegel, *The Logic of Hegel,* ix. Hegel's dismissal of Berkeley's idealism as "incomprehensible" is instructive on this note. Hegel, *Medieval and Modern Philosophy,* vol. 3 of *Lectures on the History of Philosophy,* trans. E. S. Haldane and Frances H. Simson (Lincoln: University of Nebraska Press, 1995), 366.

87. Westphal, *Hegel's Epistemological Realism,* 141. Westphal also argues that, in his theory of truth, Hegel embraced fallibilism. Ibid., 2.

88. Hegel, *Phenomenology of Spirit,* §§17, 18, 36.

89. An excellent source on Hegel's concept of recognition is Robert R. Williams, *Hegel's Ethics of Recognition* (Berkeley: University of California Press, 1997). Against those who have claimed that Hegel's concept of recognition was limited to his Jena period, Williams persuasively argues that it is a central category throughout his philosophical development. Moreover, Williams argues that the master/slave relationship is replaced, and thus overcome, by an intersubjective recognition of equals, making Hegel's philosophy a solid foundation for a democratic state.

90. Hegel, *Phenomenology of Spirit,* §167 (emphasis in the original).

91. Pippin, *Hegel's Idealism,* 148-149 (emphasis in the original). Pippin suggests that Hegel's is more than a pragmatic theory of truth because it requires more than immediate satisfaction, or the solution to immediate problems, but this is also true for Dewey. To imply that Hegel holds a pragmatic conception of truth is not to imply that he holds a shortsighted theory of truth. For both philosophers, truth is not limited to immediate satisfaction because the solution of specific problems is always rooted in a larger life project and a social context. For this reason, Dewey was not comfortable with James's formulation of the pragmatic theory of truth as "truth is what gives satisfaction." Dewey, "What Pragmatism Means By Practical" (1908), MW 4: 109. See also Burke, *Dewey's New Logic,* 12-14.

92. Hegel, *Phenomenology of Spirit,* §§484-671.

93. Pinkard, *Hegel,* 163ff. Cf. Hegel's claim that "Even our own sense of the mind's living unity naturally protests against any attempt to break it up into different faculties, forces, or, what comes to the same thing, activities, conceived as independent of each other." Hegel, *Hegel's Philosophy of Mine,* §379, cf. §§378, 440, 442, 445, 451. This is a

recurring theme in Hegel's writings: *Phenomenology of Spirit,* §§303, 304; Hegel, *The Logic of Hegel,* §§20, 24, 130, 135, 136, 195.

94. As I will discuss at length in later chapters, Dewey frequently deployed this same strategy to undermine philosophical abstractions and dualisms, calling them, in his early writings, products of "the historical fallacy." As Dewey explained it, philosophers make this mistake when they assume that terms they created in analysis refer to realities that existed before analysis. Cf. this statement in Hegel's "Lesser Logic": "And it is not unusual to draw such a distinction between a notion of understanding and a notion of reason. The distinction however does not mean that notions are of two kinds. It means that our own action often stops short at the mere negative and abstract form of the notion, when we might also have proceeded to apprehend the notion in its true nature, as at once positive and concrete." Hegel, *The Logic of Hegel,* §182.

95. Hegel, *Phenomenology of Spirit,* §§59, 61.

96. Hinchman, *Hegel's Critique of the Enlightenment,* 75.

97. Hegel, *The Philosophy of Right,* §4.

98. Hegel, *Phenomenology of Spirit,* §22 (emphasis in the original). Cf. Hegel's claim that "The difficulty for the logical intellect consists in throwing off the separation it has arbitrarily imposed between the several faculties of feeling and thinking mind, and coming to see that in the human body there is only *one* reason, in feeling, volition, and thought." Hegel, *Philosophy of Mind,* §471 (emphasis in the original).

99. See Hinchman, *Hegel's Critique of the Enlightenment,* 80. At times, Hegel criticized liberal reformers in Prussia and France precisely because he believed their atomistic individualism would undermine liberal reforms. Pinkard, *Hegel,* 608-609.

100. For a good study of this tradition see W. H. Bruford, *The German Tradition of Self-Cultivation: "Bildung" from Humboldt to Thomas Mann* (Cambridge: Cambridge University Press, 1975). On Hegel's concept of *Bildung,* I am indebted to John H. Smith, *The Spirit and Its Letter: Traces of Rhetoric in Hegel's Philosophy of* Bildung (Ithaca: Cornell University Press, 1988).

101. On Hegel's views on teaching of the Classics, see Michael George and Andrew Vincent, "Introduction" to Hegel, *The Philosophical Propadeutic,* trans. A. V. Miller, ed. Michael George and Andrew Vincent (Oxford: Basil Blackwell, 1986), xvi-xvii.

102. Hegel, *Phenomenology of Spirit,* §54.

103. Hegel, "Liberal Education: Preparation for Philosophy," in *Encyclopedia of Philosophy,* trans. Gustav Emil Mueller (New York: Philosophical Library, 1959), 43-53.

104. Josiah Royce is generally credited as the first English-speaking scholar to articulate this reading of the *Phenomenology* in his *Lectures on Modern Idealism,* originally published in 1919).

105. Hegel, *The Philosophical Propadeutic*; and Hegel, "Liberal Education: Preparation for Philosophy," 43-53.

106. In 1808, Niethammer was appointed to a high governmental position in Munich, *Zentralschul und Oberkirchenrat,* Central Commissioner of Education and Consistory, and immediately set to work reforming Bavarian education. Niethammer appointed Hegel to his position in Nuremburg to help an old friend, but also because the two agreed on the *Bildung* model of education. Terry Pinkard groups Niethammer, and by implication Hegel, in the "neo-humanist" tradition along with Wilhelm von Humboldt. Pinkard, *Hegel,* 269ff.

107. Pinkard, *Hegel,* 288-290, 304-307, 324-326, 504-505.

108. Klaus Hartmann, "Hegel: A Non-Metaphysical View," in *Hegel: A Collection of Critical Essays,* ed. A. MacIntyre (Garden City, NY: Doubleday, 1972), 101-124. See also Stephen Bungay, "The Hegelian Project," in *Hegel Reconsidered,* 23-24. Kant rejected metaphysics as the science of being on the grounds that it went beyond the bounds of possible experience. Hence with Kant, the term "metaphysics" became even more

ambiguous than it already was because he closely associated it with epistemology by redefining it as the study of the concepts necessary for the possibility of knowledge. Thus Kant spoke of "the schema for the completeness of a metaphysical system, whether of nature in general or of corporeal nature in particular, [as] the table of the categories." Kant, *Metaphysical Foundations of Natural Science,* trans. J. Ellington (Indianapolis: Bobbs-Merrill, 1970), 11. For a concise discussion of the historical ambiguities of the term "metaphysics," Kant's transformation of the term, and Hegel's understanding of metaphysics see H. Tristram Engelhardt, Jr., Introduction to *Hegel Reconsidered,* 2-4. Hegel's conception of metaphysics is elaborated in Tom Rockmore, "Hegel's Metaphysics, or the Categorial Approach to Knowledge of Experience," in *Hegel Reconsidered,* 43-55; and George Khusf, "The Meta-Ontological Option: On Taking the Existential Turn," in *Hegel Reconsidered,* 119-142.

109. Hegel, *Science of Logic,* 63.

110. Ibid., 633. Hegel, *Phenomenology of Spirit,* §§20, 39ff.

111. Hegel, *Phenomenology of Spirit,* §2.

112. Solomon, *In the Spirit of Hegel,* 317.

113. Royce, *Lectures on Modern Idealism,* 144.

114. Ibid.

115. Hegel, *Science of Logic,* 94, 103.

116. Ibid, 100.

117. The idea that universals are tools, for Hegel, was suggested to me by Jim Garrison in "Dewey's Philosophy and the Experience of Working: Labor, Tools and Language," *Synthese* 105 (1995): 87-114, esp. 90-94. In this article, Garrison argues, contra Rorty, that Dewey is "Hegelian all the way" by comparing Hegel's early philosophy of work and experience to Dewey's epistemology and metaphysics. Although I disagree with certain details of Garrison's characterization of Hegel, I believe the overall thrust of his argument, which is that significant similarities between Hegel and Dewey stem from their effort to make philosophy practical, is consistent with my claim that they share a common conception of philosophy.

118. Timothy Huson, "Hegel's Concept of the Self-Standing Individual as an Essential Moment of the Community," *International Studies in Philosophy* 32 (2000): 52-53.

119. Hegel, *The Logic of Hegel,* §163.

120. Hegel, *Philosophy of Right,* §251; Hegel, *The Logic of Hegel,* §§177, 210.

121. Larry Hickman, *John Dewey's Pragmatic Technology* (Bloomington: Indiana University Press, 1990), 128. On the proximity of Hegel's conception of universals to conceptualism see Rockmore, *Cognition,* 39-45; Ferrarin, *Hegel and Aristotle,* 297; and Huson, "Hegel's Concept of the Self-Standing Individual as an Essential Moment of the Community," 47-66.

122. Hegel, *The Logic of Hegel,* §§163, 227-231. Dewey, *Logic: The Theory of Inquiry* (1938), LW 12: 265.

123. Hegel, *Science of Logic,* 559.

124. Hegel, *The Logic of Hegel,* §153.

125. Hegel, *Science of Logic,* 559 (emphasis in the original).

126. Hegel, *Phenomenology of Spirit,* §§15, 16. Thomas C. Dalton describes Hegel as a proponent of *Naturphilosophie,* but this label for Hegel is misleading. Distinguishing his thought from Fichte's subjective idealism, Schelling argued that philosophy must include *Naturphilosophie.* Although Hegel agreed with Schelling on that point and included the philosophy of nature as a component of his system, the term *Naturphilosophie* came to be associated with Schelling and Romanticism. Thus Hegel distinguished his thought from the *Naturphilosophie* movement. Dalton, *Becoming John Dewey: Dilemmas of a Philosopher and Naturalist* (Bloomington: Indiana University Press, 2002), 9-11. Pinkard, *Hegel,* 564-566, 610.

127. Hegel, *Science of Logic,* 106-108.

128. Huson, "Hegel's Concept of the Self-Standing Individual as an Essential Moment of the Community," 47-66; Williams, *Hegel's Ethics of Recognition,* 266; and Paul Redding, *Hegel's Hermeneutics* (Ithaca: Cornell University Press, 1996). Redding makes a strong case for seeing a linkage between Hegel's maintenance of opposing perspectives in the dialectical progression of his logic with a demand for recognition and respect of differing perspectives in his social and political thought.

129. The full title of the essay is "On the Scientific Ways of Treating Natural Law, on its Place in Practical Philosophy, and its Relations to the Positive Sciences of Right." The essay was published in two parts in Schelling's and Hegel's *Critical Journal of Philosophy* between December 1802 and May 1803, and is available in Hegel, *Political Writings,* trans. H. B. Nisbet (Cambridge: Cambridge University Press, 1999), 102-180.

130. Inwood, *A Hegel Dictionary,* 91-93. My discussion of *Sittlichkeit* is indebted to Allen W. Wood, *Hegel's Ethical Thought* (Cambridge: Cambridge University Press, 1990), 131-133.

131. On Kant's distinctions between autonomy and heteronomy, see Immanuel Kant, *Groundwork for the Metaphysics of Morals,* trans. James W. Ellington (Indianapolis: Hackett, 1981), 44-46, 440-442.

132. Hegel, *Political Writings,* 171.

133. Hegel, *The Philosophy of Right,* §124.

134. It is imperative to emphasize that the moral ideal must be chosen. For Hegel, the modern individual must not only do what is right, but must do so with insight into why it is right. Hegel, *The Philosophy of Right,* §§129-132.

135. *The Philosophy of Right* is a development of the section on objective spirit in the initial version of the *Encyclopedia.* For a more detailed discussion of the political climate in which Hegel published *The Philosophy of Right* and the way it was received see Pinkard, *Hegel,* 418-468.

136. Hegel, *The Philosophy of Right,* §§15, 20. Of Hegel's students and assistants, Gustav Asverus, Friedrich Wilhelm Carové, Friedrich Christoph Förster, and Leopold Von Henning were arrested. Hegel attempted to intervene on his students' behalf, even posting almost three months' pay for Asverus's bail. Despite Hegel's efforts, Asverus was held for seven years. Hegel had a great deal of concern for his own position and for the fate of *The Philosophy of Right* at the hands of the censors; thus he may have hoped that the perpetuation of his vendetta against Fries in the preface would reassure censors that the book was not subversive.

137. Pinkard, *Hegel,* 54, 247, 252-254, 286-287, 451. On Hegel's cosmopolitanism, compare Steven V. Hicks, *International Law and the Possibility of a Just World Order: An Essay on Hegel's Universalism* (Amsterdam: Rodopi, 1999).

138. Allen Wood, "Editor's Introduction" to *Elements of the Philosophy of Right,* xxvi, n10. See also Smith, *Hegel's Critique of Liberalism.*

139. James Sheehan, *German History: 1770-1866* (Oxford: Oxford University Press, 1989), 215.

140. Huson, "Hegel's Concept of the Self-Standing Individual As an Essential Moment of the Community," 47-66.

141. Though Hegel's cosmopolitanism led him to oppose political unification of the German states, it also made him critical of their excessive localism. These are prominent themes in Pinkard, *Hegel.*

142. See Terry Pinkard's and Lewis Hinchman's discussions of *Bildung.* Pinkard, *Hegel,* 288ff; and Hinchman, *Hegel's Critique of the Enlightenment,* 104ff.

143. Hegel, *The Philosophy of Right,* §153 (emphasis in the original). Hegel also quoted this advice in his *Natural Law* essay. Hegel, *Natural Law,* 115.

144. Rockmore, *Cognition,* 67.

145. Hegel, *The Philosophy of Right,* §§73-78, 82.

146. A prime example of the accusation to which I refer appears in Ernest Barker, "Introduction" in Otto Gierke's *Natural Law and the Theory of Society, 1500 to 1800,* trans. E. Barker (Cambridge: The University Press, 1950), xvii. For a clear defense of the view that, despite his emphasis on *Sittlichkeit,* Hegel successfully preserved individual judgment and criticism, see Robert M. Wallace, "Hegel on 'Ethical Life' and Social Criticism," *Journal of Philosophical Research* 26 (January 2000): 571-591.

147. Hegel, *The Philosophy of Right,* §§11, 15, 23.

148. Ibid., §5.

149. Ibid., §268.

150. Ibid., §§105-106, 115-120, 121-123, 137, 185-206.

151. Ibid., §§145, 209-213, 258.

152. Ibid., §§158, 182-184, 189-190, 231, 235-236, 238-240.

153. Alan Ryan has argued that Dewey was a guild socialist as well; unfortunately that topic goes beyond the scope of this book. Ryan, *John Dewey and the High Tide of American Liberalism* (New York: W. W. Norton, 1995).

154. Ibid., §§250-255, 301-303, 310-311.

155. Ibid., §§241-245.

156. Ibid., §§166, 170-178.

157. See Hegel's description of the state as the "actuality of the ethical Idea—the ethical spirit as substantial will." Hegel also argued that "it is only through being a member of a state that the individual himself has objectivity, truth and ethical life." Hegel, *The Philosophy of Right,* §§257, 258.

158. Ibid., §§258, 267-268.

159. Alan Ryan, *John Dewey and the High Tide of American Liberalism*, 85, cf. 96, 157. Ryan's claims about Hegel's glorification of war and his views on international relations directly contradict the bulk of recent scholarship, which depicts Hegel's glorification of war as one of the myriad of Hegel myths. Cf. Shlomo Avineri, "The Problem of War in Hegel's Thought"; D. P. Verene, "Hegel's Account of War"; Errol E. Harris, "Hegel's Theory of Sovereignty, International Relations, and War"; Steven Walt, "Hegel on War: Another Look" in *The Hegel Myths and Legends,* ed. Jon Stewart (Evanston: Northwestern University Press, 1996), 131-182. Perhaps Ryan's claim that "Hegel's *Philosophy of Right* is not in the least difficult" provides a clue to why he misunderstands it so badly. Quoted in Paul Franco, *Hegel's Philosophy of Freedom* (New Haven: Yale University Press, 1999), xi.

160. Hegel, *The Philosophy of Right,* §§331, 338, 344.

161. Hegel, *The Philosophy of History,* 111, 222, 276.

162. Hegel wrote that "the unity of Man with God is posited in the Christian Religion. . . . [but] Man . . . is God only in so far as he annuls the merely Natural and Limited in his Spirit and elevates himself to God." Ibid., 324.

163. Ibid., 412, 417.

164. Ibid., 440, 446.

165. Joseph McCarney, *Hegel on History* (London: Routledge, 2000), 113-19.

166. For example, when speaking in general terms about the historical development of philosophy, Hegel wrote: "For these thousands of years the same Architect has directed the work: and that Architect is the one living Mind whose nature is to think, to bring to self-consciousness what it is, and, with its being thus set as object before it, to be at the same time raised above it, and so to reach a higher stage of its own being." Hegel, *The Logic of Hegel,* §13.

167. According to Josiah Royce, "'world-spirit' is explicitly allegorical. It refers to the self, viewed as the subject to whom historical or other human events and processes occur, so that it is as if this world-spirit lived its life by means of, or suffered and enjoyed

its personal fortunes through these historical and individual processes. The world-spirit, then, is the self viewed metaphorically as the wanderer through the course of human history. . . . The term is never a technically philosophical term." Royce, *Lectures on Modern idealism,* ed. Jacob Loewenberg (New Haven: Yale University Press, 1919), 149-150.

168. Francis Fukuyama, "The End of History," *The National Interest* 16 (Summer 1989): 3-18; and Fukuyama, *The End of History and the Last Man* (New York: Free Press, 1992).

169. For a devastating attack on Fukuyama's claim to be Hegelian see Philip T. Grier, "The End of History, and the Return of History," *The Owl of Minerva* 21, no. 2 (Spring 1990): 131-144. Reprinted in Jon Stewart, ed. *The Hegel Myths and Legends,* 183-198.

170. For a thorough refutation of the view that Hegel believed in an end of history, and thus an end of the dialectic, see Ibid.

171. Hegel, *The Philosophy of Right*, 23.

172. Terry Pinkard, *Hegel's Dialectic: The Explanation of Possibility* (Philadelphia: Temple University Press, 1988), 4.

173. Hinchman, *Hegel's Critique of the Enlightenment,* x.

174. Cf. Grier, "The End of History, and the Return of History," in *The Hegel Myths and Legends,* 192ff.

175. Hegel, *Lectures on the Philosophy of World History,* trans. H. B. Nisbet with an introduction by Duncan Forbes (Cambridge: Cambridge University Press, 1975), 170-171.

176. Hegel, *The Philosophy of History,* 86.

177. Ibid., 341.

178. Huson, "Hegel's Concept of the Self-Standing Individual as an Essential Moment of the Community," 56, 60.

Chapter Two

American Hegelianism, 1830–1900

Hegel's philosophy achieved an extraordinary intellectual ascendancy over the German intellectual world in the 1820s, largely because of his association with the University of Berlin, the first modern, and the most culturally progressive, German university. Nevertheless, Hegel's popularity declined rapidly after his death in 1831. His followers quickly fell into warring factions, first over theology (c. 1830-1841) and then over the political implications of his thought (c. 1839-1848). In 1841, Hegel's former friend Schelling, who had grown increasingly conservative in his later years, was summoned by authorities to "stamp out the dragon seed of Hegelian pantheism in Berlin," because of their concerns about liberal elements in Hegel's thought.[1] Schelling portrayed Hegel as a pre-Kantian metaphysical thinker, trapped in the realm of pure thought to the neglect of empirical existence. Propitiously, Søren Kierkegaard, Mikhail Bakunin, and Friedrich Engels attended Schelling's inaugural lecture at the University of Berlin in 1841. By mid-century Hegel's legacy had fallen into complete oblivion in Germany. He was viewed as the philosopher of the conservative Prussian state and peripherally approved of or vilified in consequence.[2] Hegel, many claimed, sought to restore the pre-Kantian, pre-French Revolution sociopolitical order by resurrecting "the old metaphysics, the dogmas of the church, and the substantial content of the moral powers."[3] Ultimately, this caricature of Hegel was codified in Rudolf Haym's 1857 biography of the philosopher.[4] Late-nineteenth-century American intellectuals, many of whom pursued advanced studies in Germany, were well aware of Hegel's status in his native land, and a few were influenced by the rebellion against Hegel to reject his thought. In order to elucidate the environment in which Dewey studied Hegel, in this chapter I focus on nineteenth-century American intellectuals who rejected the Schellingian caricature of his thought.

The Early American Reception of German Idealism

At the dawn of the nineteenth century, American intellectuals generally had two philosophical alternatives available to them—British empiricism and Scottish common sense realism, or intuitionism.[5] British empiricism was increasingly suspect because of its materialistic tendencies, David Hume's epistemological skepticism, and his criticisms of traditional religion. Intuitionism had dominated American colleges since the arrival of John Witherspoon at Princeton in 1768, but the thought of Sir William Hamilton, its most able mid-nineteenth-century defender, did not long survive the devastating attack rendered by John Stuart Mill in his *Examination of Sir William Hamilton's Philosophy* (1865). Intuitionism was in decline by mid-century. By 1890, if not much sooner, intuitionism was effectively dead, largely because it was committed to a static, unchanging reality that was difficult to defend against Darwinian biology and the palpable evidence of mutability forced into view by rapid urbanization and industrialization.[6] Gradually, a growing number of American intellectuals looked to German idealism as a distinct philosophical alternative.

German philosophy began to seep into American culture as early as the late eighteenth century, primarily through correspondence between American and German intellectuals.[7] Aware of the ongoing German cultural revolution, American intellectuals were fascinated with the reform of the German system of education and German idealism. It is no accident that Americans associated idealism with German educational reform. The idealist movement began at the dawn of the revolution in German education and was the first philosophy to dominate the new German universities.[8] Like many of their German counterparts, American intellectuals viewed German idealism and German education as vehicles to preserve and promote liberal values.

Two French intellectuals initiated American interest in German education before the Civil War. Madame de Staël's account of German society and culture, *De l'Allemagne,* appeared in the United States in 1814. Shortly afterwards, Americans began traveling to Prussia to pursue studies in the most advanced universities in the world and to observe the public school system. In 1835, Victor Cousin released a report on Prussia's public schools that led to the establishment of France's first national elementary school system and rekindled the American interest in German education. As a result, the state of Ohio commissioned Calvin Stowe to travel to Prussia to study the schools in Cousin's report. Upon returning to the United States in 1837, Stowe released a report in which he enumerated characteristics of the Prussian system that he felt the United States should adopt. The most notable of his suggestions were the recognition of the duty of every citizen to educate his children, formal teacher training, and the comprehensive and systematic instruction of all children. The state of Ohio printed ten thousand copies of Stowe's report and distributed them to every school district in the state. Massachusetts, North Carolina, and Pennsylvania all published his report as well, furthering America's knowledge of the Prussian school system.[9]

During mid-century, American exposure to German culture was facilitated by the numerous German expatriates who came to the United States after the revolution of 1848, many of whom were politically liberal, well-educated left-Hegelians. Because the "48ers" tended to remain aloof from American society, however, the increasing number of Americans who went abroad to study at German universities did far more to bring German idealism to America.[10] By the early 1870s, the infiltration of German idealism was so pronounced that Walt Whitman declared in his personal notes that, "Only Hegel is fit for America—is large enough and free enough."[11]

German idealism was initially introduced to the broader community of American literati through a Vermont intellectual, James Marsh.[12] Studying theology with Moses Stuart at Andover Seminary in the early 1820s, Marsh sought a Christian theology that would "keep alive the heart in the head."[13] Stuart encouraged Marsh to read Coleridge's *Biographia Literaria* and to study German philosophy, especially Kant and Herder. Proficient in philosophical German, by 1822 Marsh was probably the most widely read American-born student of German thought in the country. In 1825 he published the first American edition of Coleridge's *Aids to Reflection* with a fifty-five page exposition of the poet's philosophy and its German origins. The following year Marsh was elected president of the University of Vermont, located in Burlington, and, in his inaugural address, produced what has been described as "the first published utterance of the transcendentalists in America."[14] Immediately thereafter, Marsh set to work transforming the university from a struggling provincial college into the first American sanctuary of transcendentalism. Acting on his faith in public education as the great equalizer for all classes of people, Marsh secured the admission of part-time students to the university to allow working men to attend. In order to ensure that education at the university would promote free but critical thought, he introduced an elective system, allowing students greater flexibility to pursue their interests.[15] Marsh remained at the university as president or Professor of Moral and Intellectual Philosophy until his death in 1842. Philosophically, Marsh was, like Coleridge, persistently critical of Locke's empiricism, claiming that it bred materialism, determinism, and atheism. Because he did not admit of the existence of transcendent realities, argued Marsh, Locke could not distinguish between the natural and the spiritual or provide grounds for moral obligation. As materialists, Lockeans sought to explain all events in terms of causal law and thus could not account for free will. According to Marsh, conscience revealed the moral law to us, but materialism "subverts the authority of conscience."[16] In the following chapter I argue that elements of Marsh's "Burlington philosophy," to which he was exposed as an undergraduate at the University of Vermont, were vital to Dewey's intellectual development.

The Burlington tradition continued, largely in isolation from the rest of the country, under Joseph Torrey, a thoroughgoing transcendentalist and close student of Kant, Schelling, and Hegel. Torrey's knowledge of German is evidenced by his translation of J. A. W. Neander's four-volume *General History of the Christian Religion and Church,* but he was particularly known for his developmental aesthetics. Torrey was the first in the United States to offer a course in aesthetics and his lectures on the subject were edited and published posthumously by his daughter in 1874 as *A Theory of Fine Art.* In the lectures, Torrey applauded Coleridge's and Schelling's appreciation of nature and integration of fact and value, proclaiming that Schelling was "undoubtedly the philosopher to whom we are more indebted than any other individual in modern times for something like a rational hypothesis covering the whole ground of the subject now before us." He also drew upon Kant and Hegel, especially the latter, for his theory that art progressively developed through historical epochs—although, he believed, his present era was one of artistic decline.[17] According to his colleague Matthew Buckham, the concept of development furnished "the key to [Torrey's] whole philosophy."[18] When Torrey died in 1867, his nephew H. A. P. Torrey became the new herald of the Burlington philosophy and, from 1875 to 1882, Dewey's first philosophical mentor. I will discuss H. A. P. Torrey further in the next chapter, but for now affirm that he continued in Marsh's and his uncle's footsteps.

Some scholars have argued that Americans were drawn to German idealism as a bulwark for Christian theology against British empiricism, which by the mid-nineteenth century had led to the development of increasingly positivistic philosophy.[19] To be sure, after the publication of Darwin's *The Origin of Species* in 1859, British thought became hostile to orthodox theology as Herbert Spencer and T. H. Huxley described the theory of evolution as a final step on man's road to the elimination of metaphysical and theological language from his descriptions of nature.[20] Though developments in British thought certainly encouraged the Torreys to engage German idealism, positivism arose three decades after Stuart's and Marsh's initial interest in German thought. Stuart and Marsh, it would seem, were drawn to German idealism as a resource to counter the rationalism of Unitarians, such as William Ellery Channing, who sought to explain away miracles and the paradoxes of the trinity by subjecting Christian doctrine to the tribunal of reason.[21] Stuart and Marsh found in Kant's transcendentalism, mediated by Coleridge, a way to defend the notion that the most important truths are apprehended through intuition.

Aside from debates about the origins of early American interest in German idealism, it is essential to summarize the Burlington philosophy in which Dewey was schooled. Marsh and the Torreys emphasized intense study of German thought in the original language, a deep appreciation of natural beauty, individual religious experience combined with an unceasing criticism of the divisive social implications of Locke's "atomistic individualism," an opposition to the separation of "knowledge from action," and facts from values, as "formal, cold, and barren," and an insistence on a union of Kant's pure and practical reason through religious and aesthetic experience.[22] Though dressed in the garb of scientific naturalism, these philosophical themes are apparent throughout Dewey's oeuvre.[23]

As early as the 1820s and 1830s, many American intellectuals referred to Hegel's thought or began to make his views known to a broader community of American intellectuals. Several of the early American assessments of Hegel were negative, however. George Bancroft, one of the first of a group of Americans to study in Germany, attended Hegel's lectures at the University of Berlin for part of a term. In his journal and a letter of 1820 he described Hegel as "sluggish" and explained that he stopped attending the lectures because Hegel's vocabulary was unintelligible.[24] In 1831, the year of Hegel's death, German-American Francis Lieber's *Encyclopedia Americana* was the first source on Hegel available in English in the United States. The article merely referred the reader to the general treatment of philosophy in a later volume, gave the titles of a number of his works, and provided a brief note on his life and place among German thinkers.[25]

Frederich Augustus Rauch, president of the Mercersburg Seminary and Marshall College in Pennsylvania, was apparently the first enthusiastic Hegelian in the United States.[26] A native of Germany, Rauch arrived in the United States in 1831, having received the Doctorate in Philosophy at Marburg in 1827 after which he studied Hegel at the University of Heidelberg for one year. In 1840 he published *Psychology; or a view of the Human Soul; including Anthropology*, the first statement of Hegelian psychology to appear in English. Even after Rauch's untimely death in 1841, Mercersburg Seminary and Marshall College remained centers of German idealist thought for many years under the leadership of Philip Schaff and John Niven.

In 1838, Henry Boynton Smith, who would later strongly influence Dewey's early mentors, traveled to Germany, where he studied first with Friedrich Tholuck at the University of Halle and then studied Hegel with Friedrich A. Trendelenburg in Berlin. Smith was particularly impressed with Trendelenburg's critique of both Kant and Hegel, as well as his knowledge of Aristotle.[27] By the time he returned to the United States in 1840, Smith had mastered the theology of Friedrich Schleiermacher and Neander. In 1845 Smith published "A Sketch of German Philosophy" in the *Bilbliotheca Sacra* and prepared several translations of German theological treatises for the same journal. This work earned him a position as a professor of philosophy at Amherst in 1847, and in 1850 he moved to the Union Theological Seminary, where he remained until 1874. At Union, Smith encouraged several of his students to follow his path of study in Germany, most notably George Sylvester Morris and G. Stanley Hall, who were both important influences upon the development of Dewey's thought during his graduate years at Johns Hopkins.[28]

Frederic Henry Hedge was the first intellectual to introduce German idealism to Boston-area transcendentalists.[29] Hedge was the son of Levi Hedge, Professor of Logic, Ethics, and Metaphysics at Harvard. At the age of twelve, Hedge passed Harvard's entrance exam, but his father decided to send him with his personal tutor, George Bancroft, to Germany to gain a more complete education before he entered Harvard. Hedge's education in Germany was a crucial component of his intellectual development. By 1830 Hedge was one of the few New England intellectuals who could speak authoritatively on German philosophy. Known in his hometown of Cambridge, Massachusetts as "Germanicus Hedge," in the mid-1820s he befriended Ralph Waldo Emerson while the two were students at the Harvard Divinity School. Hedge was the first translator of Hegel in America; his *Prose Writers of Germany,* which contained translations of works by Kant, Fichte, Schelling, and Hegel, among others, made a strong impression on Emerson and other American transcendentalists, going through five editions from 1847 to 1870.

The philosophical work of Marsh and Hedge introduced Emerson, Bronson Alcott, and Theodore Parker, to German idealism. But Marsh's transcendentalism was relatively conservative; careful to characterize his philosophy in traditional theistic terms, Marsh steadfastly resisted the pantheism of the Concord transcendentalists.[30] Because of Hedge's influence, however, in the 1840s the transcendentalists took an interest in Schelling, whose philosophy encouraged their emphasis on feeling over reason and spiritual intuition over scientific knowledge. Further, Schelling's identification of the absolute with nature reinforced the Emersonian notion of the world soul. Like other versions of Romanticism, Concord transcendentalism sought to reunite man with God through an emotionally charged and spiritualized nature, a "natural supernaturalism."[31] The American transcendentalists also embraced Schelling's emphasis on individual genius, leading many of them to a libertarian political philosophy: established governments did little good for mankind, and civil society had a generally corruptive influence on the individual personality. According to Emerson and Henry David Thoreau, the truly free and enlightened individual would be wise to isolate himself from society and its institutions as much as possible.[32]

Led by Parker, America's foremost expositor of German higher criticism, the transcendentalists also studied and accepted D. F. Strauss's characterization of true Christianity as a matter of piety rather than an adherence to dogma and ritual. In 1840 Parker published a scandalously sympathetic examination of Strauss's *Das Leben Jesu* (1835), in which he criticized Strauss for reducing the orthodox biblical view of Christianity to pure myth with no basis in fact, but accepted Strauss's Hegelian historicization as a valid method for biblical studies. In 1841 Parker delivered a divisive sermon, "The Transient and Permanent in Christianity," a title taken from one of Strauss's essays. Like Strauss, Parker rejected the divine inspiration of the Bible and grouped miracles, prophecies, and the life of Jesus among the transient elements of Christianity, and its moral teachings as the permanent.[33] At the urging of Hedge and the St. Louis Hegelians, whom I will discuss shortly, in the 1850s the transcendentalists began to take a greater interest in Hegel and, after 1859, they sought to combine Hegel's historical dialectic with Darwinian evolution.[34]

In 1848 John B. Stallo of Canton, Ohio, published an extensive exposition and interpretation of Hegel's writings in his *General Principles of the Philoso-*

phy of Nature. Stallo, primarily a philosopher of science and politics, was one of the four individuals who have become known as the "Ohio Hegelians."[35] Emigrating from Germany with his family around 1820, Peter Kaufmann organized utopian socialist communities in Pennsylvania and Ohio, drawing upon Hegel's dialectical view of truth and knowledge to formulate a philosophy of social reform and moral perfectionism. An industrializing city, Cincinnati attracted a number of left-wing Hegelians, including many German socialists who were exiled after the failed revolution of 1848. Most notable among the "48ers" was August Willich, who, after the revolution of 1848 and a rupture with Marx and Engels in London, landed in Cincinnati where he edited the *Republikaner,* an adamantly pro-labor and abolitionist newspaper. During the Civil War Willich raised his own regiment, which fought heroically for the Union army.[36] Moncure Conway, a close associate of Emerson and Parker, arrived in Cincinnati in 1856 to accept a Congregationalist pulpit after being dismissed from a Unitarian church in Washington D.C. for his opposition to slavery.[37] Conway had already accepted Strauss's criticisms of miracles and the supernatural; his exposure to Willich in Cincinnati further radicalized his political beliefs. Both pacifist and abolitionist, Conway traveled to London during the Civil War and engaged an ill-conceived effort to negotiate a settlement with the Confederacy that would end the war immediately if the South freed its slaves. Roundly condemned by his abolitionist allies, Conway remained in London where he was appointed minister of the city's most radical, free-thought religious institution, South Place Chapel, and encouraged British socialists to study American transcendentalism.

In the 1850s and 1860s, German idealism began to appeal to a greater number of English-speaking intellectuals, and German educational theory and practice began to have a far more profound impact on American education. After the Civil War, the trickle of American intellectuals who traveled to Germany became a torrent, partly because of the unification of the German states, which was completed in 1870. Americans viewed unification as a liberal advance that seemed to parallel the unification of the United States during and after the Civil War. Moreover, the fact that German-Americans who fought in the Civil War overwhelmingly chose to fight for the abolition of slavery associated Germanness with the advance of liberal politics in the minds of American intellectuals. A number of these German-Americans were trained Prussian military officers who had fled to the United States after the 1848 revolution; thus they were some of the best officers in the Union Army. After the war, many German-Americans won influential political positions as the spoils of war and were well situated to promote the influence of German culture in America.[38] For whatever reason a specific individual might have gone to Germany, Carol Gruber estimates that between 1820 and 1920, nearly nine thousand Americans studied at German universities.[39] When they returned, many of these intellectuals obtained positions at prestigious American universities and began to implement educational practices they had observed in Germany.

On a tangible level, German influences on American education led to the establishment of a nation-wide system of public kindergartens, more rigorous teacher training in newly founded normal schools, and state boards of education that set standards for teacher certification. At the university level, German influences on American education included the seminar-style course, the lecture course, laboratories, research libraries, university presses, learned societies, and academic journals.[40] But the furthest-reaching German contributions to American education were more theoretical. American educators studied the pedagogical theories and techniques of Johann Heinrich Pestalozzi (who was Swiss-German) and Friedrich Wilhelm August Froebel, both of whom advocated love and respect for the individuality of the child.[41] Higher education in America was dramatically transformed by the German concepts of *akademische Freiheit,* or academic freedom, *Lehrfreiheit,* or the freedom of professors to teach "what they believed to be the truth" without fear of dismissal, and *Lernfreiheit,* the freedom of students to choose the academic courses they took.[42] Because of its emphasis on respect for the individual and these freedoms, American intellectuals viewed German educational thought as a liberalizing influence on American universities. As these German concepts permeated higher education in America, a system of research universities rapidly replaced the system of denominational colleges that were designed to train ministers.

Many American intellectuals attributed the liberal tendency of German educational philosophy to its association with German idealism, especially the philosophy of Hegel, which the majority of American intellectuals viewed as politically liberal. This is particularly apparent in the writings of the St. Louis Hegelians, who did more to promote the American Hegelian tradition that was crucial to Dewey's early philosophy than any other group. For the St. Louis Hegelians, the philosophy of Hegel was first and foremost a philosophy of cultural criticism and social activism; their reading of Hegel is apparent in their writings, but also in their deeds.

The St. Louis Hegelians

In 1910, Morris Raphael Cohen, distinguished American philosopher at New York City College, divided the history of modern American philosophy into three periods. According to Cohen's scheme, the three periods corresponded to three philosophical journals, the *Journal of Speculative Philosophy* (JSP), established in St. Louis in 1867, the *Philosophical Review,* established at Cornell University in 1892, and the *Journal of Philosophy, Psychology, and Scientific Methods,* which was founded at Columbia University in 1904. Cohen labeled these three periods of modern American philosophy "the theologic, the metaphysical, and the scientific." Though I question the adequacy of Cohen's labels for these periods, he was certainly correct that American philosophy had become increasingly secular. Cohen suggested a better way to understand the first period when he noted that, unlike the latter two journals, the JSP was founded not by university professors but by "practical men who believed they had found [a] superior point of view, fruitful insight into the fields of religion, art, history, education, and even practical politics."[43]

It has not been easy for historians to accurately characterize the JSP, nor have they adequately understood the thought of the St. Louis Hegelians who founded and operated it for twenty-six years. This misunderstanding is due to the fact that the St. Louis Hegelians held a Hegelian conception of philosophy that is largely lost today. For the St. Louis Hegelians, philosophy not only addresses the technical problems of philosophers; it gives meaning to the lives of individuals and unity to society. Moreover, the philosopher must be active in social reform as well as intellectual pursuits.

Cohen provides us with an important example that will clarify this conception of philosophy. In 1899 Cohen encountered Thomas Davidson, a prominent St. Louis Hegelian, and his life was quite literally transformed, and perhaps even saved.[44] Just seven years before, Cohen's family had fled poverty and anti-Semitism in the ghetto of Minsk, Russia, to the impoverished Lower East Side of New York City. Though he considered America a "blessed land of opportunity," as a child in Minsk he had contemplated suicide. One day his friends in the Marx Circle at City College informed him that a charismatic speaker at the Educational Alliance, a nearby settlement house, was denouncing socialism in a defense of individualism. Cohen and his associates decided, on a lark really, to go hear the speaker, and if possible, to disrupt his lectures. Cohen explained,

> Completely convinced of my own premises, I took advantage of the question period following the lecture to heckle the speaker, which I continued to do in later lectures, on all possible and many impossible occasions. To my surprise Davidson did not resent my views or my manners but responded to my attacks in the friendliest way.[45]

Impressed with Cohen, Davidson took him under his wing. On the pretext of needing someone to chop wood at his Glenmore Summer School of the Culture Sciences, Davidson financed Cohen's travel to his unusual school on Mt. Hurricane in the Adirondack Mountains of northeastern New York. At Glenmore, Davidson instructed Cohen and many of his young friends in world history, philosophy, and literature and, quite the taskmaster, demanded that they read primary texts in the original language. They were also permitted to attend lectures by some of the most prominent intellectuals of the day, including William Torrey Harris, editor of the JSP, Dewey, then a young philosophy professor at the University of Michigan, and William James, an established philosophy professor at Harvard.

Davidson's work with Russian immigrants like Cohen was an expression of the conception of philosophy he shared with his friends in St. Louis, according to which philosophy could serve as an antidote to suicide because it gave meaning to life. And in this regard, the philosophy expressed by the very act of publication of the JSP was significantly different from the philosophy of the founders of the *Philosophical Review* and the *Journal of Philosophy, Psychology, and Scientific Methods.* After a brief introduction to the chief St. Louis Hegelians, I will discuss their conception of philosophy.

By the time Davidson, a Scottish immigrant, joined the St. Louis Hegelians in 1868, they had already coalesced into a coherent cluster of intellectuals. The group traced its beginning to Harris's chance encounter with an eccentric Pomeranian immigrant by the name of Henry Conrad Brokmeyer at the St. Louis Mercantile Library in 1858. Brokmeyer had become a proponent of the philosophy of Hegel, strangely enough, after he left Prussia at the age of sixteen. Working at a series of odd jobs, Brokmeyer made his way to Memphis, Tennessee, where he operated a successful tanning, currying, and shoemaking business, and saved enough money to enter the preparatory department of Georgetown College, Kentucky, in 1850. After two years of study, Brokmeyer was threatened with expulsion because of a theological dispute with the president and traveled east to attend Brown University for two years, engaging in frequent debate with President Wayland. Already a Goethe devotee, at Brown, Brokmeyer perused Hedge's *Prose Writers of Germany* and determined that Hegel was the greatest philosopher of all time.

Leaving Brown without a degree in 1854, Brokmeyer traveled west and took up residence in an abandoned cabin in Warren County, Missouri. Given to periods of seclusion from society under the influence of Thoreau, Brokmeyer studied philosophy in his cabin for two years. He then took a job in a St. Louis foundry, but continued to devote his evenings to philosophy, encountering Harris at a meeting of the St. Louis Philosophical and Literary Society. Harris, who had dropped out of Yale after two and a half years (1854-1857) because he was dissatisfied with its predictable orthodoxy founded upon Scottish common sense realism, was impressed by his new friend's knowledge of German philosophy. Succumbing to Harris's entreaties, Brokmeyer reluctantly agreed to tutor Harris and a few others, but soon escaped to the solitary life in Warren County. In 1858, Harris discovered Brokmeyer near death from "an attack of bilious fever," brought him back to St. Louis, nursed him to health, and joined with some friends to commission Brokmeyer to translate Hegel's *Science of Logic* into English.[46] Thus began Harris's lifelong efforts to "make Hegel talk English."[47] Though Brokmeyer's disdain for the grammatical and spelling conventions of the English language doomed to failure all efforts to publish his translation of Hegel's *Logic,* his mind was crucial to the coterie of writers, educators, and professional men and women who comprised "the St. Louis Movement."[48] According to Harris,

> [Brokmeyer] could flash into the questions of the day, or even into the questions of the moment, the highest insight of philosophy and solve their problems. Even the hunting of wild turkeys or squirrels was the occasion for the use of philosophy. Philosophy came to mean with us, therefore, the most practical of all species of knowledge. We used it to solve all problems concerned with school teaching and school management. We studied the "dialectic" of politics and political parties and understood how measures and men may be combined by its light.[49]

At the most practical level, Brokmeyer continually exhorted those who studied philosophy with him to develop a rational account of their talents and abilities and a plan for how to develop and harmonize them in order achieve rational life goals.

Denton Snider, the self-appointed historian of the group, is one of the most interesting founding members of the post-war Philosophical Society. Upon graduating from Oberlin College in 1862, Snider enlisted in the Union Army, where he rose to the rank of second lieutenant, and resigned after one year because of ill health. In March 1864, he began to teach Greek and Latin in the College of the Christian Brothers in St. Louis, where he soon fell in with Harris and Brokmeyer, purchased an eighteen-volume set of Hegel's writings, and devoted himself to an intensive six-year study of the German thinker. A neophyte philosopher at the time, in the fall of 1866 he joined Brokmeyer's law office, ostensibly to study law, but in reality to become "a pupil of the University Brokmeyer in person."[50] Conversant in five foreign languages—Greek, Latin, French, German, and Italian—as well as the classic texts of the western literary tradition, Snider's scholarship expanded the intellectual interests of the group beyond the confines of German philosophy.

These three men are generally described as the core of the group, but scholars have unduly neglected the fact that, according to Snider, Susan Blow was one of the four major figures.[51] Whereas Hegel showed little respect for women's intellectual abilities, the St. Louis Hegelians sought to curb elitist elements in his thought and, certainly in their attitudes toward women, they were more egalitarian than the German philosopher.[52] One of the few St. Louis natives of the group, Blow was the daughter of a prominent businessman and state politician. Blow drew upon the writings of Hegel, Karl Rosenkranz, and Freidrich Froebel to articulate a sophisticated philosophy of education that she also put into action. In 1873, she and Harris organized the first successful public kindergarten program in the United States as well as a normal school in 1874. Under Blow's leadership, the kindergarten movement grew rapidly, leading to the formation of the New York Kindergarten Association and an International Union.

Many other local professionals joined these four leaders of the group, remarkably few of whom were German-American, despite the fact that the city was crowded with German immigrants. Not all of the members of the society were followers of Hegel; the group contained its own negation. Davidson obstinately argued for the superiority of Aristotle to Hegel, and Adolph Kroeger consistently preferred Kant and Fichte to Hegel. George Holmes Howison, who later built the philosophy department at the University of California, was always dubious of Hegel's ability to account for the reality of the individual and thus drew upon Aristotle and Leibniz to develop his own version of the philosophy of personal idealism that was fairly widespread in British and American circles by the turn of the century.

Although the St. Louis Hegelians have been characterized as right-wing Hegelians, that designation obscures their thought. The appellations left- and right-wing Hegelian first emerged as Hegel's followers disagreed about the extent to which his thought supported or undermined orthodox Christianity. Although Harris defended the doctrine of the trinity on Hegelian grounds, this alone would not definitively associate him with the right-wing Hegelians because, unlike them, he was not concerned with the preservation of the entire Gospel story. Moreover, the St. Louis Hegelians' political philosophy can be compared to a group that Karl Löwith has more accurately characterized as the Hegelian center—Rosenkranz, Eduard Gans, Karl Ludwig Michelet, and Johannes Schulz—immediate followers of Hegel who opposed Prussian conservatism as well as the revolutionary thought of the Young Hegelians.[53] Rosenkranz was an auxiliary member of the St. Louis Philosophical Society, and the St. Louis Hegelians were diligent students of his writings. Rosenkranz corresponded with them frequently and praised Harris's theistic reading of Hegel in the pages of the JSP.[54] The St. Louis Hegelians referred to themselves as "58ers," not only to commemorate the founding of their pre-war philosophical society, but also to contrast themselves with their more liberal German-American counterparts in St. Louis, the "48ers." The St. Louis Hegelians criticized the 48ers and radical abolitionists such as John Brown in the same terms; neither group appreciated the importance of well-founded institutions.[55] After a brief discussion of the St. Louis Hegelians' interpretation of the Civil War, which provides an excellent example of the application of Hegel's method of immanent cultural criticism, I will examine their appropriation of Hegel's concept of *Bildung* and their philosophy of education.

The Dialectic of Civil War

Napoleon's invasions of the German states had forced Hegel to grapple with the unification of individual and social interests; the Civil War raised the same issues for the St. Louis Hegelians.[56] The St. Louis Hegelians drew explicitly upon Hegel's social and political thought to conclude that the violent conflict was the result of a peculiar American philosophy of "brittle individualism." Hegel's criticisms of radical French revolutionaries provided them with the conceptual tools to argue that the radical abolitionists suffered from a deficient understanding of the relationship of the individual to society. Radical abolitionists believed they could judge society on the basis of transcendent morality; they also accepted what Hegel called a negative or abstract theory of freedom, the notion that man is free and equal in the absence of social restraints. In good Hegelian fashion, the St. Louis Hegelians argued that this incomplete conception of freedom led the radical abolitionists to mistakenly conclude that the destruction of the institution of slavery, without more profound cultural reform, would fully emancipate American slaves. Hegel's analysis of the Reign of Terror convinced the St. Louis Hegelians that negative freedom would inevitably lead to the indiscriminate destruction of social, religious, and political institutions as the way to protect transcendent rights. As institutions were destroyed in the Terror, Hegel argued, restraints upon individuals were diminished, resulting in an accelerating frenzy of annihilation. In the same way, the St. Louis Hegelians feared that negative freedom would inevitably lead to "some sudden eruption . . . of madness and fury."[57]

To address these aporia in American thought, the St. Louis Hegelians embraced Hegel's organicism, the theory that each individual is an organic part of society and the condition of any one individual affects the condition of all. They argued that freedom only arises within the constraints of social relationships and can only be achieved in the face of opposition presented by those constraints. As Harris explained, "the individual . . . can not exist as human apart from the institutions of society."[58] To be free and rational, the individual must draw upon the resources of an organized and differentiated society and must be educated to do so. The educated individual's will is in harmony with the ideals of the various social groups by which he has been influenced and, in civilized societies, with the more complex ideals of the state. By embracing the highest ideals of his society, the individual achieves his own rational ends and becomes free. They also accepted Hegel's claims that only the state was rational and disinterested enough to simultaneously protect individual freedom and advance the general will. By "the state," however, they correctly understood Hegel to mean the totality of human relations—family, civil, and political—rather than just the government.

Taking seriously Hegel's proclamation that "America is . . . the land of the future," these St. Louis philosophers developed a Hegelian vision of the historical role of their nation, state, and city.[59] They explained the war between the states as a manifestation of a profound development in the world-spirit, a decisive advance in the movement of world history toward the actualization of positive freedom. Because of its internal contradictions and central location between North and South, East and West, Missouri was a focal point in the struggle. Though officially Unionist, Missouri was a slave state and a hotbed of proslavery sentiment. St. Louis, the focal point of the state, was poised to become a world-historical city, promoting the cause of freedom in the war and cultural advance on the cusp of the frontier.[60]

Though the St. Louis Hegelians' interpretation of the war and the role of their state and city may seem naïve in retrospect, one must bear in mind the chaos they witnessed during the sectional crisis. Whereas the transcendentalists lionized John Brown for his raid on the federal armory at Harper's Ferry, Virginia, in 1859, the St. Louis Hegelians saw Brown through the lens of Lawrence, Kansas, where in 1856 he and his sons hacked five pro-slavery settlers to death with broadswords.[61] On 9 May 1861, just four weeks after the war began at Fort Sumter, pro-Union Congressman Blair ordered Captain Lyon to muster German-American troops and oust pro-Confederate Governor Jackson's militia from Camp Jackson. As Lyon marched the captured militia through St. Louis, a raucous crowd shouting "Damn the Dutch" threw stones and bricks at the German-American soldiers. Soon a riot began and by the end of the day twenty-eight civilians and two soldiers lay dead or dying. Anarchy prevailed in St. Louis for the following five weeks as pro-Southern mobs roamed the city searching for lone German-Americans. But Lyon's victory at Boonville, Missouri, on 17 June

1861 permitted Union troops to take control of the city. Although the city remained in Union hands, for the following four years the violence of guerrilla terrorism in Missouri exceeded anything else in the war. Pro-Confederate "bushwackers" and pro-Union "Jayhawking" Kansans pillaged and plundered civilians with impunity.[62] These events made the Hegelian dialectic especially poignant to the St. Louis Hegelians, who compared them to Hegel's 1806 experience of completing the *Phenomenology of Spirit* in Jena as the city fell into Napoleon's hands. Snider compared the sectional crisis to the "European Teutonic Movement"—the Prussian subjugation of Schleswig-Holstein in 1864, the defeat of Austria in 1866, and the Franco-Prussian War of 1870.[63] The bloodshed in Missouri and seemingly parallel events in Germany led the St. Louis Hegelians to conclude that they had witnessed a decisive moment in what Hegel called "the slaughter-bench" of history.[64]

The war plunged Brokmeyer into the depths of an anguishing philosophical crisis in which he sought to reconcile his Thoreauean sense of personal liberty with his Hegelian sense of social obligation. Like most German-Americans, he ultimately committed himself to the Union cause because he abhorred slavery and detested slave owners' claim to a right of secession from the Union. Organizing a regiment, Brokmeyer served one year in the state militia before he was imprisoned for disloyalty. But in the political tumult of the times, six weeks later he was elected to the state legislature, where he served two years as a "War Democrat."[65] Since Brokmeyer published very little, I will focus on Harris's and Snider's writings about the war.

Originally from Connecticut, Harris was a staunch Unionist. Due to a childhood eye injury, he remained in St. Louis during the war, working as a schoolteacher and administrator and translating Hegel's *Philosophy of History,* which helped him formulate a philosophical interpretation of the war. In this effort, Harris also applied insights gleaned from Hegel's *Science of Logic* and *The Philosophy of Right.* In a letter to his uncle dated nine days after the Union victory at Boonville, Harris invoked Hegelian language to declare that the United States had "an idea posited at the basis of its consciousness" to "develop and bring out in all its forms." The war would bring the United States closer to actualizing the abstract idea of freedom upon which it was founded.[66] In October 1861, Harris penned a letter to the editor of the *Missouri Republican* in which he was much more specific. He traced the idea of freedom in American history, arguing that the Revolutionary War had established the form of freedom by liberating the American colonists from foreign domination, but unresolved tensions had hindered the substantiation of freedom in the new republic. Because of these internal tensions a period of social and economic dissatisfaction—manifested as greed and arguments over slavery—peaked in the three decades preceding the Civil War. Although Hegel had conjectured that "the burden of the World's History" would someday "reveal itself" in a struggle between the nations of North and South America, Harris asserted that the historical dialectic had instead resulted in the current conflict between the northern and southern states.[67] The Union represented industry, democracy, and self-determination for all. The Confederacy embodied aristocratic values—passivity and slavery—according to which freedom was maintained through the enslavement of a racial group, and a person's social class was determined hereditarily rather than on the basis of his talents. War would prepare the nation for a synthesis of these conflicting principles.[68]

In the midst of the terror in Missouri, Harris praised the heroic, but institutionally sanctioned, behavior of Lincoln. For Harris, Lincoln "mediated" between the world-spirit and the particular passions of individual Americans. He argued that Lincoln's pursuit of the war was truly legitimate, not because he catered to "public opinion," which could never grasp more than "one side of the subject and that generally the unessential," but because he fully understood the historical dialectic. Lincoln moved beyond mere opinion to "*knowing*," which "grasps both sides of the subject," and understood that the federal government's cause was consistent with the movement of the world-spirit. According to Harris, Union victory was inevitable and would mark a necessary reconciliation of interests because, as Lincoln declared, the nation could not survive half slave and half free. The war's conclusion would effect an enduring transformation of the concepts of liberty and freedom and be a fulfillment of American history up to that time.[69] After the war, Harris's friend Snider echoed his arguments by according Lincoln a prominent role in American politics and world history in his books *Abraham Lincoln*, *The State*, and *The Ten Years' War*.[70]

In *Ten Years' War*, Snider highlighted the importance of the western states in the war by articulating a Hegelian interpretation of conflict between free and slave systems, from the Missouri "border ruffians'" invasion of Kansas in 1855 to the ultimate northern victory of 1865, which marked "the elimination of the dualism introduced into the Union at its birth."[71] The Confederate cause represented adherence to the letter of the law, because the Constitution protected slavery as a form of property, while the Union cause represented commitment to the universalization of freedom.

Much like Harris, Snider described the march of history and presented Lincoln as the true genius of the era, the man who read "the Folk-Soul aright." Yet Snider depicted leaders as more passive vehicles of the world-spirit than did Harris. "World-Historical individuals," like Jesus, Napoleon, and Lincoln, "did not act for their own selfish interest, but at the command of a power higher than themselves." When he reminisced about Blair's accomplishment at Camp Jackson, "the First Great St. Louis Deed" on the world-historical stage, Snider proclaimed that "the cosmical energy . . . took possession of [Blair] and made him perform things which appear to ordinary life superhuman." But "Blair . . . was chosen just the one time by the Spirit of the Age to execute its supernal behest."[72] Snider depicted his heroes as men who, even in protest, upheld established institutions. The violent actions of John Brown, Snider asserted, were no better than the violence inflicted upon southern slaves by their masters or the violence committed by the insurrection of the southern states.[73]

Snider also developed a Hegelian interpretation of American slavery. In *The Philosophy of Right,* Hegel maintained that slavery was immoral and that the slave is not morally bound to obey his master, because he "can have no duties; only the free human being has these." Moreover, in the "Lordship and Bondage" section of the *Phenomenology,* Hegel argued that the relationship of master and servant inevitably leads to a subtle role reversal in which the master becomes dependent upon the slave for his material needs and, through his ability to produce goods, the slave gains a certain mastery over the physical world. For Hegel, the slave ultimately achieves a higher state of consciousness in this relationship, while the master remains stagnant.[74] In the same way, Snider argued that "the best and most liberal minds of the South [had] become . . . intolerant upon the subject of slavery" because the "spiritual effects of the . . . relation of master and slave" had stunted their psychological development. Snider argued, however, that the lack of slave rebellion before and during the war demonstrated that blacks were not "socially ready" for freedom; "it was really the white man," and the world-spirit, "who was ready for the abolition of slavery."[75] The Union army would free the ruling Southern oligarchy from its anti-democratic control of the region, allowing whites to progress toward a greater understanding of freedom and democracy.

Snider also drew upon Hegel to argue that the mere abolition of slavery would not emancipate slaves because they had to be "disciplined into the civilized order of the world." At one time slavery was justified because it was a way of including "the African . . . by nature a docile, submissive, clinging, parasitic, race" into the social organism. Slavery had "trained the African to steady labor—no small or unimportant task by the way." But according to Snider, "slavery was educative indirectly," and the world-spirit had now established that Americans should "train the backward races through . . . education directly." Proper education would lead to economic opportunity and, Snider asserted, "Political freedom . . . cannot even be real without economic freedom." The abolition of slavery would give southern blacks abstract, formal freedom; education and genuine economic opportunity would provide its substance by allowing them to participate in society. Despite his derogatory remarks about the African race, Snider declared that the institutionalization of "racial freedom" was America's rational purpose, "what the World-Spirit [had] enjoined upon the American Folk-Soul."[76]

After the war, the St. Louis Hegelians surely believed they found confirmation of their reading of American history by correspondence with Rosenkranz, as well as Franz Hoffman, whose son was killed at the battle of Wörth in 1870 fighting for the unification of Germany. In a letter that was published in the JSP, Hoffman averred that his son had died for "a great cause. . . . The restoration of the German Empire on a national basis makes an onward move in the history of the world. North America and United Germany will certainly approach each other." Hoffman went on to remark that he had "just finished an essay on Hegel's Philosophy in St. Louis, which I shall send to-day to Dr. Bergmann for the *Philosophische Monatshefte*."[77]

From "Brittle Individualism" to *Sittlichkeit*

The purpose of the postwar St. Louis Philosophical Society, organized by Harris and Brokmeyer in January 1866, was to study philosophy, but more importantly, to promote the development of a more inclusive and harmonious American *Sittlichkeit* that would counter the "brittle individualism" that led to the war. In all of this, the St. Louis Hegelians sought to pursue a Hegelian ethic of self-actualization of the human spirit, creating themselves through self-expression and simultaneously shaping their social environment. To be sure, the Philosophical Society engaged in intense study of Hegel's *Science of Logic,* which, according to Snider, was Brokmeyer's and Harris's "one book of the Universe, their real Bible, to which they always came back for recovery after any divagation."[78] But the St. Louis Hegelians also sought to promote the development of *Sittlichkeit* in a "St. Louis Movement" that included an art club, an Aristotle club, a Shakespeare society, the St. Louis Academy of Science, the St. Louis Philharmonic Society, and the Academy of Useful Science. All of these organizations were primarily composed of local professionals—public school teachers and administrators, judges and attorneys.[79] The St. Louis Hegelians also worked diligently in social reform movements, published on a wide range of topics, from the metaphysical to the practical, and founded the JSP as a vehicle to extend cultural reform beyond the confines of St. Louis. In the JSP, they sought to further their goals by promoting philosophical thought in America, laboring to disseminate German neo-humanism and idealism through translation, study, and exposition of the writings of both movements.[80] Unlike the academic philosophers who would soon replace them, the St. Louis Hegelians believed their involvement in politics and social reform was as important as their scholarly work. Embracing Hegel's claim that "an individual cannot know what he [really] is until he has made himself a reality through action," all of their activities were acts of self-expression that formed their individual identities.[81] For the St. Louis Hegelians, philosophy was a vocation, a practical activity, rather than a profession restricted to cloistered academics.

Brokmeyer opened a law practice in 1865 and continued to pursue his political career. He was elected to the Board of Aldermen of St. Louis in 1866. Four years later he was elected to the state Senate and in 1875, as a member of the constitutional convention, he took a leading part in shaping the state's constitution. He ultimately rose to the position of lieutenant governor, and in 1876-1877, acting governor during the illness of Governor Phelps. Ultimately disgusted by political wrangling, in 1882 Brokmeyer traveled to the town of Muskogee in the future state of Oklahoma, where he notoriously worked as legal counsel to the M. K. and T. Railroad, befriended the Creek Indians, and reworked his translation of Hegel's *Science of Logic* in "the realm of primal solitude." According to his son, Brokmeyer ultimately conceded that perhaps it was unrealistic to expect an infant nation to devote itself much to philosophy while it was "carving civilization out of wilderness."[82]

Unlike Brokmeyer, Harris continued to struggle with social issues until his death in 1909. He was unflaggingly devoted to public education, serving as superintendent of the St. Louis public schools from 1868 to 1880. Buoyed by the success of an experimental kindergarten program in 1873, Harris and Blow lobbied for its extension, arguing that the children of wealthier families would also benefit from kindergarten because they were pampered by their parents and left in the care of uneducated servants. In 1877 the nationwide railroad strike, which was aggravated by a socialist-led general strike in St. Louis, greatly assisted Harris and Blow in their efforts as they argued that union organizing, labor unrest, and political corruption resulted from the ease with which rabble-rousers could manipulate poorly educated immigrants.[83] By 1883 every St. Louis public school had a kindergarten, making the city a model for the nation.

In 1879 Harris and Snider began teaching at Bronson Alcott's Concord School of Philosophy, where Harris remained on the faculty for ten years. In 1872 Alcott confessed to his journal that philosophical discussion was superficial in Boston; "philosophy," he proclaimed, "is published in St. Louis."[84] Emerson facetiously referred to Harris and his "active propagandists" as atheists, and unlike the transcendentalists, many of whom were discontented Unitarian ministers, the Hegelians focused more on social and political thought than on theology. But Emerson formed a close friendship with Harris and welcomed the 58ers' philosophical rigor to New England. Harris and Snider viewed the Concord School as an extension of the St. Louis Movement, and they sought to introduce a genuinely distinct alternative to New England intellectuals. In Concord, Harris's speaking ability and philosophical expertise made a strong impression as he and Hiram Jones, a Platonist from Illinois, became the two primary attractions.[85] Alcott marveled at Harris's ability to command "unbroken attention and interest" as he spoke on abstruse philosophical topics, remarking that Harris's "audiences increase in numbers from day to day."[86]

Having gained national recognition for his supervision of the St. Louis schools, Harris left Concord when he was appointed United States Commissioner of Education by President Benjamin Harrison in 1889, in which position he gained international recognition.[87] In addition to publishing four philosophical books and countless articles on theoretical and practical aspects of public education, arguing that it should be based on social science research, Harris also engaged in highly philosophical polemics in the JSP. Alongside Rosenkranz, he defended Hegel against the charge of pantheism; additionally, he wrote a critical analysis of the thought of Herbert Spencer, articles on the freedom of the will, and one on "Nominalism *vs.* Realism."[88] Although he embraced Hegel's philosophy of history, by the end of his life Harris was still concerned about the nation's actualization of positive freedom. In a letter written to Snider in 1906, he described the Civil War as a "gigantic object lesson of the dialectic in human history." The war had furthered Americans' understanding of the nation's rational purpose, but "a long series of portents," such as labor unrest and giant corporations, "threaten[ed] the stability of democratic government," revealing that the historical dialectic was far from complete.[89]

Less enamored with New England than Harris, in 1884 Snider left the Concord School and returned to the Midwest, where he became increasingly active in social reform. Snider assisted Blow in the St. Louis kindergartens, taught in the Chicago Kindergarten College, and worked with Jane Addams at Hull House. He organized "free universities" in St. Louis, Chicago, and Milwaukee, where he spoke frequently and eloquently on Shakespeare, Goethe, and Greek drama. He also established the Communal University in Chicago (1887-1895) and St. Louis (after 1895), which met in private homes and public libraries and provided free lectures to the general public. Snider published more than forty books on literary, philosophical, and psychological topics. During the last years of his life, Snider lived in the St. Louis ghetto, sharing his knowledge of philosophy and classical literature with his neighbors until his death in 1925. The "Snider Association" met annually at his grave for many years.[90]

Wintering in New York City during the 1890s, Davidson devoted his time to reaching young immigrants like Cohen. His work provides a wonderfully tangible example of education through alienation and return. Each summer, for the last ten years of his life, Davidson took groups of these young men and women to Glenmore, in effect, alienating them from ghetto life, and gave them a vision, in the scenic beauty of Mt. Hurricane, of what society could be through study of the great works of the Western tradition. When these young men and women returned to their home in the ghetto at the end of the summer, they had been utterly transformed and many of them went on to lead various reform movements of the Progressive Era.[91] Elizabeth Flower and Murray Murphey correctly note that Davidson's "Students grew into professionals and teachers, and the list of those associated with the college reads like a *Who's Who* of the next generation's intelligentsia and reformers."[92]

Shortly after Davidson's death in 1900, however, American philosophy changed in ways that obscured the American *Bildung* tradition. After the founding of the American Philosophical Association in 1901, American philosophy focused on issues much more narrowly conceived than the meaning of life. Despite some important exceptions, philosophers in America no longer viewed philosophy as an antidote to suicide. The philosophers who were exceptions to this trend, for example, Morris Cohen and John Dewey, were old enough to have been profoundly influenced by the St. Louis Hegelians.

The St. Louis Hegelians' cultural criticism and influence on American thought has been greatly underappreciated. Many historians have documented the transcendentalist's transition from a prewar individualistic emphasis on inner spiritual renewal to a postwar support of social and political institutions. Yet few historians consider the possibility that the St. Louis Hegelians played a role in this intellectual transition.[93] Bronson Alcott met with the St. Louis Hegelians in 1859 and 1866. Although treated harshly by the abrasive Brokmeyer, at his first visit Alcott was persuaded to begin a study of Hegel's *Philosophy of History* and when it became available in 1865, he studied James Stirling's *The Secret of Hegel.* Ralph Waldo Emerson spoke before the Philosophical Society on three separate occasions in 1867 and became an "auxiliary" member.[94] Moreover, the

St. Louis Hegelians' JSP, the first journal in the English language devoted to serious philosophy without a specific theological agenda, was read widely by eastern intellectuals, many of whom, including Dewey and his mentors, used it as a vehicle for their first publications.[95] Particularly impressed with Harris, Emerson and Alcott introduced him to other transcendentalists such as Hedge and James Elliot Cabot. Finally, from 1879-1888, Harris and Snider made a profound impression on intellectuals at Alcott's Concord School of Philosophy as they sought to promote a philosophical rigor they found lacking among eastern intellectuals.[96] Thus an examination of the St. Louis Hegelians' social and political philosophy can deepen our understanding of the transition from individualism to institutionalism in postwar American thought and set the stage for the intellectual milieu in which Dewey's thought developed.

Profoundly affected by the violence of the sectional crisis, the St. Louis Hegelians expressed concerns about American transcendentalism that mirrored Hegel's concerns about Fichte's subjective idealism and Romanticism. For the St. Louis Hegelians, Emerson's conviction that "the only right is what is after my constitution; the only wrong what is against it," expressed the sort of sentiment that could easily be misappropriated by fanatics.[97]

In 1865 the St. Louis Hegelians believed the Civil War had prepared the nation for an era of social solidarity. Governmental institutions, such as the presidency, state legislative and administrative bodies, and the citizen militia had proved their utility and legitimacy. Their wartime experience inspired them to focus more on social action and practical solutions to specific problems. Above all, the war convinced them that greater cooperation between individuals and institutions was essential to the development of their nation. In the midst of the continuing social and economic unrest of the postwar era, they argued that a dialectical appreciation of institutional and individual claims was more necessary than ever to negotiate the changes the nation was experiencing. They continued to encourage intellectuals to pursue a life of political and social action, criticizing anti-institutional thinking, yet calling for active involvement in the gradual reform of institutions.

It is significant that the St. Louis Hegelians chose to translate and publish Rosenkranz's essay, "Hegel as Publicist."[98] The essay is based on Rosenkranz's study of Hegel's life and his short political writings, to which virtually no one except Rosenkranz had access at that time. Rosenkranz's thesis was that one could appreciate Hegel's practicality throughout all of his writings, if one is familiar with his political tracts, and the momentous political events of his lifetime, including his support of the French Revolution as a young man. The article effectively counters the myth that Hegel was an apologist for the reactionary Prussian state. Their exposure to these sources led the St. Louis Hegelians to embrace the historicist/humanistic reading of Hegel.

The St. Louis Hegelians agreed that Hegel's greatest philosophical insight was his conviction that the individual could overcome the opposition between subject and object, rendering knowledge a relation of the two rather than the power of one over the other. But like the Hegelian center, the St. Louis

Hegelians were not uncritical disciples of Hegel. Snider commented, "to be true to Hegel in the deepest sense, we are to unfold Hegel out of Hegel." In an expression of Manifest Destiny, he explained that Hegel could not have appreciated the United States' potential to bring underdeveloped peoples into the modern state, nor the nation's potential, fully realized only after the Civil War, to generate free states on its western frontier and beyond.[99] And as I have already noted, the St. Louis Hegelians also protested elitist tendencies in Hegel's thought, insisting that anyone with an inquiring mind could learn to apply speculative logic to practical problems. Yet their anti-elitism was limited by a conviction that western Europeans were at the forefront of the historical dialectic. Although Harris and Snider believed that other groups could and should be brought into the modern state, Harris even supporting American imperialism on those grounds, they framed this in terms of a benign concern for backward races.

Harris extolled the virtues of the caretaker state but believed individual self-cultivation was the source of excellence in society. He maintained that individual initiative could be nurtured by the guidance of strong, mediating institutions, such as well-administered public schools. The school was to mediate between the family and the world, facilitating the transition to an adult life of independence. Through his friendship with Rosenkranz, Harris developed an interest in Hegel's *The Philosophical Propadeutic,* a collection of writings Rosenkranz compiled after Hegel's death and Harris translated into English. In these writings, which he composed as rector of the Nuremberg *Gymnasium* (1808-1815), Hegel articulated his philosophy of education. All of the St. Louis Hegelians believed that free public education, available to everyone, should be founded upon the notion of *Bildung.* In this regard, once more, they were less elitist than Hegel.

Harris described Hegel's process of self-estrangement and return as "the process of the adoption of the social order in place of one's mere animal caprice."[100] Also like Hegel, Harris viewed the social order as the universal order discovered through the study of the knowledge and wisdom of the ages, rather than the particular circumstances of one's current social environment. Proper education would mediate between particular selves and "universal humanity in its eternal process." Moreover, for Harris, self-estrangement was not a sublimation of individual desires and talents; it was a realization of one's "identity with the social whole." If one "rebels against [the social order] it crushes him . . . if he obeys it implicitly and passively, it crushes him still."[101] Like Hegel, Harris believed that the strength of the modern state was the insights that only self-determining individuals are free and that concrete freedom consists in choosing to harmonize one's particular desires with the highest ideals of the social whole.[102]

In order to comprehend the social whole, Harris argued, children needed instruction in the "tool subjects," the "five windows of the soul"—grammar, literature and art, mathematics, geography, and history.[103] He opposed Johann H. Pestalozzi's theory about the importance of vocational education, claiming that his emphasis on tactile learning was based on a deficient sensationalistic epistemology that assumed "we derive all our knowledge from sense-perception." Like Hegel, Harris thought education should do much more than prepare students to hold jobs. Though he believed Hegelian philosophy supported Christianity, Harris denounced religious instruction in public schools because it was authoritative and claimed education should promote the independent verification of ideas. But Harris criticized the notion of self-government in the schools that Dewey would champion, claiming that education should teach children to respect authority.[104]

In his social thought, Harris accepted urbanization and industrialization, but worried about the ways these developments contradicted traditional cultural values. He defended private property, free competition, industrial capitalism, and the accumulation of immense fortunes, but accused the wealthy of self-indulgence. By analyzing social problems in terms of conflicting class interest, Harris argued, socialists merely aggravated those problems. Education as *Bildung,* on the other hand, would teach people to recognize their common interest. As the St. Louis ghettos swelled with Irish-American immigrants after the war, Harris argued that charity would undermine self-respect, but education would spiritually and morally elevate the poor.[105]

Harris's social thought was shaped by political struggles in St. Louis, as he worked to improve the public schools. During this period debates over the St. Louis schools divided citizens along ethnic, religious, and class lines, pitting recent Irish-American Catholic immigrants against more established Lutheran or freethinking German-Americans. John O'Connell, an Irish-American member of the school board, objected that Harris's policies favored the more established citizens. The long depression of the 1870s created an excess of teachers, as young women sought employment. Partly as a response to this situation, Harris championed the professionalization of public schoolteachers and administrators but, as O'Connell alleged, the demand for professional training effectively limited the number of Irish-American teachers because they could not afford to attend normal school. But Harris maintained that society must tolerate and respect the ethos of immigrant groups and advocated equal educational opportunity for all. He also criticized the notion that only an upper class should receive cultural education, because such a class would oppress those who "have to spin and dig for them." The ordinary man, argued Harris, was destined to partake of "the realized intelligence of all mankind."[106] During the Spanish-American war, Harris used similar reasoning to actively support American imperialism on paternalistic grounds, arguing that war was the result of the inevitable conflict of ideas. Convinced of the superiority of Western culture, Harris claimed cultural education would bring colonized peoples into the modern state and eventually make war obsolete.[107]

Because Harris believed that social unity can only be achieved through the opposition of diversity, he advocated equal education for African-Americans and coeducation of women, arguing that women should have equal access to cultural education and to the newly emerging professional schools.[108] According to Harris, diversity is such only through the one; they mutually delimit and thus define one another. Therefore neither can exist without the other. The one and the many are simply moments or complementary elements of society.[109] Because of Harris's commitment to diversity, under his supervision the St. Louis public schools had more women in administrative positions than any other city. He officially mandated that salaries be equal for men and women, and all teachers in the St. Louis schools were paid exceptionally well for the time. In opposition to O'Connell, Harris fought for women's right to continue working after they were married.

Harris worked closely with a number of women, most notably Blow and Anna Brackett, a schoolteacher originally from Boston. In their work on the St. Louis public kindergarten program, Harris and Blow invoked the pedagogical theories of Friedrich Froebel and Rosenkranz. Harris and Blow argued that kindergartens would improve children's personalities, helping them learn through properly structured and supervised play.[110] Harris compared the "history" of childhood to the early history of the United States. He claimed that "caprice and arbitrariness" reign in the preschool child because the "character," the "rationally consistent" basis of behavior, had not yet discovered itself.[111] Children from poor families, Harris claimed, should begin school before their character was ruined by ghetto life. Blow published five books on early childhood education, in which she also depicted education as a dialectical process. Through the adaptation of roles in play, Blow argued, the child learns by encountering opposition. By assuming various characters, the child is estranged from him or herself, and then returns to the original self, expanded and transformed by what he or she has learned of the other and his or her own abilities. Self-estrangement and return also appeared in the writings of Brackett, the first woman appointed principal of a secondary school and, during its first few years of operation, director of the St. Louis Normal School that Harris and Blow had established. Primarily interested in secondary education, Brackett postulated that older children could undergo the process of self-estrangement and return through the study of characters and different worlds in literature. The primary difference is that older children are much more conscious of the process than kindergarteners.[112]

Hegel in the New Research Universities

Although American intellectual historians have described the St. Louis Hegelians as amateurs left behind by the professionalization of philosophy, their focus on philosophy rather than theology, their high standards of scholarship, the JSP, and their efforts to refine philosophical thought in the East promoted the professionalization of American philosophy. The St. Louis Hegelians were critical of academic philosophy, but they were most critical of American philosophers' slavish obedience to Scottish intuitionism and their isolation from the problems of society. As the denominational colleges were transformed into research universities, many of the intellectuals who displaced Scottish thought published their earliest articles in the JSP, lectured at Davidson's summer school, and engaged the St. Louis Hegelians in philosophical debate.[113]

Perhaps most relevant to the study of Dewey, Harris engaged in a spirited debate about Friedrich Adolf Trendelenberg's critique of Hegel's logic. Rather than delve into the intricacies of this complex debate, which also involved A. E. Kroeger, one of the St. Louis group, the Italian Hegelian philosopher Augusto Vera, and Dewey's future graduate school mentors, G. S. Morris and G. Stanley Hall, I will simply note that Trendelenberg's primary objection to Hegel's logic was that the "dialectic of pure thought" could not address the realities of lived experience, the practical problems of everyday life.[114] The Hegelian dialectic, he argued, did violence to the facts of history and science by forcing them into a dialectical pattern rather than letting them speak for themselves. In Germany, the search for a "logic of life," as this new philosophical quest was often described, spawned some of the most important philosophical movements of the late nineteenth and twentieth centuries and paralleled the age of rebellion against Hegel, the age of Ludwig Feuerbach, Arnold Ruge, Max Stirner, and Karl Marx. In America, the quest for a "logic of life" was just as intense. Thirty-five years ago Gershon Rosenstock noted a remarkable and somewhat mysterious similarity between Dewey's mature thought and the philosophy of Trendelenburg. Though Rosenstock discussed the fact that Morris and Hall studied with Trendelenburg in Berlin, he overlooks the debate that took place among American intellectuals in the 1870s, buried primarily in the pages of the JSP.[115] Given this debate, coupled with the fact that Dewey spent many summers with several of the interlocutors at Davidson's Glenmore Summer School for the Culture Sciences, it is quite likely that Dewey knew a great deal about the thought of Trendelenberg.

A promising young charter member of the St. Louis Philosophical Society, George Holmes Howison, also had a significant impact on academic philosophy for many years. Howison participated in the Concord and Glenmore summer schools and studied for several years in Germany with Rudolf Lotze, Jules Michelet, and Friedrich Paulsen. He formed friendships with many other distinguished German scholars as well as British neo-Hegelians Edward and John Caird and James Stirling and the embattled British pragmatist F. C. S. Schiller. Frustrated in his efforts to obtain a position in the Harvard philosophy department, Howison taught at a series of universities, including one year at the University of Michigan—preceding Dewey there. Finally, in 1885 Howison was hired to build the philosophy department at the University of California at Berkeley, where he remained until his death in 1917. At Berkeley, Howison established the Philosophical Union, which, in the spirit of the St. Louis Philosophical Society, drew intellectuals from the broader San Francisco community into philosophical study. The Union focused on a philosophical topic for a year, with monthly meetings, ending the session with lectures from a celebrated philosopher and publication of the years' work. Josiah Royce spoke on the conception of God in 1896. William James introduced pragmatism in a lecture in 1898, and the following year Dewey spoke on "Psychology and Philosophic Method."[116] Howison also trained numerous Ph.D.'s, including Arthur O. Lovejoy, who went on to Johns Hopkins by way of Washington University in St. Louis, and Charles

Bakewell, philosophy professor at Yale for thirty years.[117] Much like Davidson, Howison ultimately embraced a pluralistic philosophy that came to be known as personal idealism.

Yet with the exception of Marshall College and Mercersburg Seminary, Hegelianism did not begin to take root in American higher education until the 1870s, and then primarily as a system of social thought. The transition toward German thought was promoted by the increasing number of Americans who studied at German universities, impressed by the German model of academic freedom and the division of moral philosophy into the emerging disciplines of history, political science, political economy, and sociology. Hegelian terminology, if not full-blown Hegelian philosophy, briefly spread to many of the newly emerging disciplines. John W. Burgess, who taught social and political thought at Amherst and Columbia, earned the sobriquet "*Weltgeist*" for his theory of the inherent rationality of the state. Richard T. Ely, an economist at Johns Hopkins, was inspired by Hegel to proclaim, "it is a grand thing to serve God in the State." And Albion Small, sociologist at the University of Chicago, applied the Hegelian dialectic to social and intellectual history, claiming that "Conventionality, [i.e., laissez-faire individualism] is the thesis, Socialism is the antithesis, Sociology is the synthesis."[118]

Hegelian metaphysics and epistemology appeared more gradually in philosophy departments. G. S. Morris propagated Hegelian philosophy at the University of Michigan from 1870 until his death in 1889, and at John Hopkins, where he trained Dewey from 1877 to 1884 as he alternated semesters between Hopkins and Michigan. In 1884, Morris's Hegelian philosophy was supplemented when Dewey was added to the faculty at Michigan and was continued at Michigan by Alfred H. Lloyd until 1927, Robert M. Wenley until 1929, and DeWitt Parker until 1949.[119] In 1880-1881 George Palmer offered the first seminar on Hegel at Harvard. William James attended the seminar and recalled that their copy of Hegel's *Logic* was translated "by an extraordinary Pomeranian immigrant, named Brokmeyer." Samuel H. Emery and his brother-in-law Edward McClure, associates of the St. Louis Hegelians and leaders of the Quincy, Illinois, Plato Club, brought the manuscript to Cambridge in 1879.[120] In 1882, American Hegelian philosopher Josiah Royce received a one-year appointment while James was on leave, and so impressed his colleagues that he was able to remain at Harvard until his death in 1916. Although all of these academic Hegelians studied German idealism by reading the JSP, all but Dewey traveled to Europe to study Hegel. Palmer studied Hegel with Edward Caird at Glasgow in 1879, Royce in Germany with Lotze and Wilhelm Wundt, and Morris in Germany with Hermann Ulrici and Trendelenburg.

In spite of the emergence of pragmatism in the 1890s and realism after the turn of the century, idealism never completely disappeared from American universities. Yet during the mid-1890s, Dewey's crucial transitional years, American idealism made the transition to personal idealism, which sought to emphasize the importance of the finite individual. This shift was prefigured in concerns raised by the Trendelenburg debate, and occurred in a rather dramatic fashion when Royce, undoubtedly the most respected absolute idealist in the country at the time, delivered his lectures at Howison's Philosophical Union in Berkeley. Howison vigorously criticized Royce for, in effect, emphasizing the absolute to the point that he denied the reality of the individual. Though Royce never admitted defeat, when he published *The World and the Individual* four years later, he had clearly changed his position, emphasizing the extent to which each individual is not merely a part of the absolute, but also a representation of the absolute.[121]

Royce never explicitly embraced personalism, but in addition to Howison, there were many personal idealists, quite a few of whom studied with Lotze in Germany. The first personal idealist was the British neo-Hegelian, Andrew Seth, who announced his break with his fellow Hegelians in 1887. In the United States, Blow and Mary Whiton Calkins, who studied with James and Royce at Harvard, were both personal idealists. At Boston University, Borden Parker Bowne started the Boston school of personalism that included Edgar Sheffield Brightman, Walter George Muelder, Albert Cornelius Knudson, Peter Anthony Bertocci, and W. Gordon Allport. James Creighton, first president of the American Philosophical Association in 1902, led a group of personal idealist philosophers at Cornell who were actively involved in the founding of the A.P.A. Other personal idealists included William Ernest Hocking at Harvard from 1914 to 1943, and John Elof Boodin, who taught at UCLA from 1928 to 1950. One of Bowne's students, Ralph Tyler Flewelling (1871-1960), directed the School of Philosophy at the University of Southern California, and founded *The Personalist: A Quarterly Journal of Philosophy, Theology, and Literature* which was published from 1920 to 1979.[122]

Ironically, Hegelian thought receded in importance as another German influence impacted American thought: the new scientific empiricism of the late-nineteenth-century social sciences (*Geisteswissenschaften*).[123] The rise of the social sciences meant the simultaneous division of philosophy into rigorously defined social science disciplines, taught by experts trained in empirical investigation that was to be conducted in laboratories.[124] Nonetheless, it would be difficult to overestimate the degree to which idealism left its mark on American philosophy, including pragmatism. Charles Sanders Peirce, who is often characterized as the founding father of American pragmatism, was well aware of the American Hegelian tradition. In 1868 and 1869 he published four articles in the JSP in which he began to elaborate a pragmatic theory of the mind, and at Johns Hopkins Peirce taught alongside G. S. Morris. Peirce was philosophically indebted to German idealism as well. He maintained that his philosophical career began when he read Schiller's *Letters on Aesthetic Education.* Peirce's debt to Kant was crucial; he himself referred to Kant as "the King of modern thought," and claimed that he knew the *Critique of Pure Reason* "almost by heart."[125] Many scholars have also claimed that Peirce's triadic metaphysics, with its principles of firstness, secondness, and thirdness, demonstrates a Hegelian influence on his thought. Frederic Young remarks that Peirce's "expressed opinion of Hegel is a rather fascinating compound of a thoroughgoing rejection of Hegel's specific doctrinal formulations, and an equally thorough sympathy with Hegel's objectives and methodology."[126] In 1893, Peirce stated that some of his principles bore "a close affinity with those of Hegel," and "perhaps are what Hegel's might have been had he been educated in a physical laboratory instead of in a theological seminary." The previous year Peirce claimed that his theory of tychism "must give birth to an evolutionary cosmology, in which all the regularities of nature and of mind are regarded as products of growth, and to a Schelling-fashioned idealism which holds matter to be mere specialized and partially deadened mind." Peirce also acknowledged the possibility that he might have picked up his idealism as a youth, "born and reared in the neighborhood of Concord . . . at the time when Emerson, Hedge, and their friends were disseminating the ideas that they had caught from Schelling." Harvard, Peirce claimed,

> held many an antiseptic against Concord transcendentalism; and I am not conscious of having contracted any of that virus. Nevertheless, it is probable that some cultured bacilli, some benignant form of the disease was implanted in my soul, unawares, and that now, after long incubation, it comes to the surface.[127]

Even William James, known for his sharp criticisms of Royce's "block universe" and his description of Hegel's system as "a mouse-trap, in which if you once pass the door you may be lost forever," made friendly overtures to Hegel's insight that all things are related to one another. In the mid-1880s James wrestled with an idealistic philosophy of his own, but abandoned it primarily on moral grounds. Like the personal idealists, James could not reconcile the notion of the absolute with the reality of the individual finite mind. According to Ralph Barton Perry, James "had a sneaking fondness for Hegel," but "he liked him in undress, stripped of his logical regalia." For James, there was "a homely insight" in Hegel: "the fact that things contaminate one another, thus becoming something other than themselves."[128] This homely Hegelian insight, perhaps most clearly expressed as the principle of continuity, suffused the pragmatism of Peirce, James, and Dewey.[129]

Notes

1. Quoted in Walter Kaufmann, *Hegel: A Reinterpretation* (Notre Dame: University of Notre Dame Press, 1965), 294.

2. Thomas E. Willey, *Back to Kant: The Revival of Kantianism in German Social and Historical Thought, 1860-1914* (Detroit: Wayne State University Press, 1978), 21-39.

3. Karl Löwith, *From Hegel to Nietzsche: The Revolution in Nineteenth Century Thought,* trans. David E. Green (Garden City, NY: Anchor Books, 1967), 62.

4. Wood, "Editor's Introduction" in *Hegel, Elements of the Philosophy of Right,* ed. Allen Wood, trans. H. B. Nisbet (Cambridge: Cambridge University Press, 1991) ix-xi.

Cf. Joachim Ritter's discussion of Rudolf Haym's *Vorlesungen über Hegel und seine Zeit* (1857). According to Haym, Hegel was "the philosophical dictator of Germany," who made philosophy "the scientific dwelling of the spirit of Prussian Restoration." Joachim Ritter, *Hegel and the French Revolution: Essays on the Philosophy of Right,* trans. with an introduction by Richard Dien Winfield (Cambridge, MA: MIT Press, 1982), 35.

5. See G. Stanley Hall's and Dewey's descriptions of philosophical instruction in American colleges. Hall, "Philosophy in the United States," *Mind* 4, no. 13 (Jan. 1879): 89-105; and Dewey, "Inventory of Philosophy Taught in American Colleges" (1886), EW 1: 116-21.

6. Intuitionism was taught at Princeton until 1888 by James McCosh, at Harvard until 1889 by Francis Bowen, and at Yale until 1892 by Noah Porter.

7. Alvin S. Haag, "Some German Influences in American Philosophical Thought from 1800 to 1850" (Ph.D. diss., Boston University, 1939), 96ff.

8. Randall Collins, "Intellectuals Take Control of their Base: The German University Revolution," in *The Sociology of Philosophies: A Global Theory of Intellectual Change* (Cambridge, MA: The Belknap Press of Harvard University Press, 1998), 618-687. Collins's summaries of philosophical positions tend to be rather superficial, but the basic premise of this chapter, that "Idealism was the intellectual counterpart of the academic revolution," is correct (618).

9. John A. Walz, *German Influences in American Education and Culture* (Philadelphia: Carl Shurz Memorial Foundation, 1936), 8-19. Many other important American educators, such as Horace Mann, traveled to Germany and published influential reports in the United States. Karl-Ernst Jeismann, "American Observations Concerning the Prussian Educational System in the Nineteenth Century" in *German Influences on Education in the United States to 1917,* eds. Henry Geitz, Jürgen Heideking, and Jurgen Herbst (Washington, D.C.: German Historical Institute, and Cambridge: Cambridge University Press, 1995), 21-42.

10. Jurgen Herbst, *The German Historical School in American Scholarship: A Study in the Transfer of Culture* (Ithaca: Cornell University Press, 1965); Carl Diehl, Americans and German Scholarship, 1770-1870 (New Haven: Yale University Press, 1978); Geitz, Heideking, and Herbst, eds., *German Influences on Education in the United States to 1917.*

11. Walt Whitman, *The Complete Writings of Walt Whitman* (New York: G. P. Putnam's Sons, 1902), 9: 170.

12. For a more detailed discussion of Marsh's thought and its influence on Dewey, see my introduction to James Marsh, *The Remains of the Rev. James Marsh, D.D.: Late President and Professor of Moral and Intellectual Philosophy, in the University of Vermont; with a Memoir of His Life,* ed. Joseph Torrey, vol. 2 of *The Early American Reception of German Idealism,* ed. James A. Good (1843; reprint, Bristol, England: Thoemmes Press, 2002).

13. Marsh, *The Remains of the Rev. James Marsh,* 43.

14. Henry Pochmann, *German Culture in America: Philosophical and Literary Influences, 1600–1900* (Madison: University Press of Wisconsin, 1957), 132. Marsh's publisher lived in Burlington and was his brother-in-law, Chauncey Goodrich. Goodrich also published Coleridge's *The Friend* and *The Statesman's Manual* in 1831 and 1832 respectively. Marsh's edition of the *Aids to Reflection* enjoyed continuous reprinting, and his "Preliminary Essay" also appeared in W. G. T. Shedd's 1853 collected edition of Coleridge's work, the standard American text of Coleridge for over a century. Lewis Feuer, "James Marsh and the Conservative Transcendentalist Philosophy: A Political Interpretation," *New England Quarterly* 31, no. 1 (March 1958): 13; and James Marsh, *Coleridge's*

American Disciples: The Selected Correspondence of James Marsh, ed., John J. Duffy (Amherst: University of Massachusetts Press, 1973), 4.

15. Julian I. Lindsey, "Coleridge and the University of Vermont," *Vermont Alumni Weekly* 15 (1936), nos. 13-15. Cf. Feuer, "James Marsh and the Conservative Transcendentalist Philosophy," 3-31.

16. Marsh, *Remains of James Marsh,* 415.

17. Joseph Torrey, *A Theory of Fine Art* (New York: Scribner, Armstrong, and Co., 1874), 275, 166-177, 258-265.

18. *Services in Remembrance of Rev. Joseph Torrey and of Geo. Wyllys Benedict, Professors in the University of Vermont* (Burlington: Free Press Steam Book and Job Office, 1874), 25.

19. According to Herbert Schneider, orthodox American ministers "turned to German idealism in the hope of finding comfort against English positivism and empiricism." Schneider, *History of American Philosophy,* 2nd ed. (New York: Columbia University Press, 1963), 376. For a good discussion of theories about early American interest in German idealism see Lawrence Dowler, "The New Idealism and the Quest for Culture in the Gilded Age" (Ph.D. diss., University of Maryland, 1974), 13-22. Dowler concludes that, after the Civil War, Americans were drawn to German idealism because of a "loss of faith in traditional cosmic explanations" brought on by developments in science and a decline of religion, and that they looked to idealism as a philosophy of cultural unification. In the following section I agree with Dowler's analysis, as long as it is understood that post-Civil War American idealists were not particularly concerned about the preservation of orthodox Christianity. Although post-Kantian idealism can certainly be viewed as a religious school of thought, it is crucial to bear in mind that it often led to exceptionally heterodox religion.

20. Spencer had actually begun to write about evolution in 1850, proposing a theory similar to Darwin's although with a strong Lamarckian bent. Herbert Spencer, *Social Statistics: Or, the Conditions Essential to Human Happiness Specified, and the First of them Developed* (London: John Chapman, 1851).

21. Bruce Kuklick, *Churchmen and Philosophers: From Jonathan Edwards to John Dewey* (New Haven: Yale University Press, 1985), 89, 124.

22. Marsh, *Remains of the Rev. James Marsh,* 42. Torrey, *A Theory of Fine Art,* esp. 37-44, 54-57, 138-139, 170-175, 275.

23. Cf. Thomas Alexander's study of Dewey's thought in which he emphasizes the continuity of his early and mature philosophy by arguing for the centrality of aesthetics. Alexander, *John Dewey's Theory of Art, Experience and Nature: The Horizons of Feeling* (Albany: State University of New York Press, 1987).

24. Quoted in Haag, "Some German Influences in American Philosophical Thought from 1800 to 1850," 194. Bancroft remained interested in German philosophy, and in 1825 he published "Writings of Herder" in the *North American Review.* Richard Arthur Firda, "German Philosophy of History and Literature in the *North American Review:* 1815-1860," *Journal of the History of Ideas* 32 (1971): 138.

25. Francis Lieber, ed., *Encyclopedia Americana* (Philadelphia: Lea and Blanchard, 1829-1833), 6: 218–219.

26. The most reliable source of biographical information on Rauch is Howard Ziegler, *Frederick Augustus Rauch: American Hegelian* (Lancaster, PA: Franklin and Marshall College, 1953). I discuss Rauch in greater detail in my introduction to Frederich Augustus Rauch, *Psychology; or a view of the Human Soul; including Anthropology,* vol. 1 of *The Early American Reception of German Idealism,* ed. James A. Good (1840; reprint, Bristol, England: Thoemmes Press, 2002).

27. Elizabeth Lee Smith, ed., *Henry Boynton Smith, His Life and Work* (New York: A. C. Armstrong and Son, 1881), 269.

28. Union Theological Seminary had another important but little known connection to Dewey. Lewis Feuer discovered that the University of Vermont was "a kind of training ground for the Union Theological Seminary." From 1864 to 1867, graduates of the University of Vermont were the fourth largest group among the seminary's students. The most noted professor at the seminary, W. G. T. Shedd, was a transcendentalist who had studied with Marsh at the University of Vermont. Dewey's undergraduate mentor, H. A. P. Torrey, studied with Shedd and graduated from Union in 1864. Feuer, "H. A. P. Torrey and John Dewey," *American Quarterly* 10 (1958): 36.

29. I discuss Hedge's thought and influence in greater depth in my introduction to Frederic Henry Hedge, *Prose Writers of Germany*, vol. 3 of *The Early American Reception of German Idealism*, ed. James A. Good (1847; reprint, Bristol, England: Thoemmes Press, 2002).

30. John Dewey, "James Marsh and American Philosophy" (from a lecture delivered in 1929, first published in 1941), LW 5: 178-196. Peter Carafiol, *Transcendent Reason: James Marsh and the Forms of Romantic Thought* (Tallahassee: University Presses of Florida, 1982).

31. Pochmann, *German Culture in America*, 197-198. See especially, Ralph Waldo Emerson, "Nature," *Selections from Ralph Waldo Emerson*, ed. Stephen E. Wheeler (Boston: Houghton Mifflin, 1957), 27-56. On the "natural supernaturalism" of Romantic thought see M. H. Abrams, *Natural Supernaturalism: Tradition and Revolution in Romantic Literature* (New York: W. W. Norton, 1971).

32. Howard Mumford Jones, *Revolution and Romanticism* (Cambridge, MA: Harvard University Press, 1974), chapters 8-10; George M. Fredrickson, *The Inner Civil War: Northern Intellectuals and the Crisis of the Union* (New York: Harper and Row, 1968), ch. 1.

33. Theodore Parker, "The Transient and Permanent in Christianity," *The Christian Examiner* 28 (1839): 272-313.

34. Pochmann, *German Culture in America*, 204.

35. The best source on the Ohio Hegelians is Lloyd D. Easton, *Hegel's First American Followers, the Ohio Hegelians: J. B. Stallo, Peter Kaufmann, Moncure Conway, August Willich* (Athens: Ohio University Press, 1966), 123-158. See also my introduction to *The Ohio Hegelians*, 3 vols., ed. James A. Good (Bristol, England: Thoemmes Press, 2005). Stallo's *General Principles* is the first book on Hegel in English listed in the extensive bibliography in J. J. O'Malley et al., eds., *The Legacy of Hegel: Proceedings of the Marquette Hegel Symposium, 1970* (The Hague: Martinus Nijhoff, 1973), 308.

36. Easton, *Hegel's First American Followers*, 159-203.

37. See my introduction to *Autobiography and Miscellaneous Writings by Moncure Daniel Conway*, 3 vols. (1904, 1909; reprint, Bristol, England: Thoemmes Press, 2003).

38. Perhaps the best example of this is Carl Schurz, an exiled "forty-eighter" who served as a Brigadier General in the Union Army and, after the war, was elected to the U.S. Senate by the state of Missouri. His fellow officers criticized Schurz during the war for being a "political general" because he owed his commission to his services to the Republican Party during the campaign of 1860 rather than to military experience or training. After the war Schurz rose to prominence in the liberal wing of the Republican Party. In the Senate he was known for his promotion of civil service reform and his willingness to criticize the corrupt Grant administration. He ultimately rose to the position of Secretary of the Interior in the Hayes administration. Schurz also had a lifelong interest in educational reform. In 1856, Schurz's wife, Margarethe Meyer, opened the first kindergarten

in the United States in Watertown, Wisconsin. Hans Louis Trefousse, *Carl Schurz: A Biography* (Knoxville: University of Tennessee Press, 1982).

39. Carol Gruber, *Mars and Minerva: World War I and the Uses of Higher Education in America* (Baton Rouge: Louisiana State University Press, 1975), 17. Cf. Jurgen Herbst, *The German Historical School in American Scholarship: A Study in the Transfer of Culture* (Ithaca: Cornell University Press, 1965); Carl Diehl, *Americans and German Scholarship, 1770-1870* (New Haven: Yale University Press, 1978); and Konrad H. Jarausch, "American Students in Germany, 1815-1914: The Structure of German and U.S. Matriculants at Göttingen University" in *German Influences on Education in the United States to 1917,* 195-212.

40. In 1871, University of Michigan professor Charles Kendall Adams probably held the first seminar at an American university. Walz, *German Influences in American Education and Culture,* 53.

41. Neith Headley, *The Kindergarten: Its Place in the Program of Education* (New York: Center for Applied Research in Education, 1965); and Carolyn R. Toth, *German-English Bilingual Schools in America* (New York: Peter Lang, 1990). Cf. Karl-Heinz Günther, "Interdependence between Democratic Pedagogy in Germany and the Development of Education in the United States in the Nineteenth Century" in *German Influences on Education in the United States to 1917,* 43-58.

42. Walz, *German Influences in American Education and Culture,* 51; and Richard Hofstadter and Walter P. Metzger, *The Development of Academic Freedom in the United States* (New York: Columbia University Press, 1955), 383-407.

43. Morris R. Cohen, "The Conception of Philosophy in Recent Discussion," *The Journal of Philosophy, Psychology, and Scientific Methods* 7, no. 5 (21 July 1910): 401.

44. For biographical information on Cohen, see Morris R. Cohen, *A Dreamer's Journey: The Autobiography of Morris Raphael Cohen* (Boston: Beacon Press, 1949); Leonora Cohen Rosenfield, *Portrait of a Philosopher: Morris R. Cohen in Life and Letters* (New York: Harcourt, Brace, and World, 1962); and David A. Hollinger, *Morris Cohen and the Scientific Ideal* (Cambridge, MA: MIT Press, 1975). Davidson wrote a brief "Autobiographical Sketch" that was published in the *Journal of the History of Ideas* 8 (1957): 531-536. That essay is supplemented by Albert Lataner's "Introduction to Davidson's 'Autobiographical Sketch,'" *Journal of the History of Ideas* 8 (1957): 529-531. There are many other short biographical sketches of Davidson. See Cohen, *Dreamer's Journey*; William Knight, ed. *Memorials of Thomas Davidson: The Wandering Scholar* (Boston: Ginn and Co., 1907); Rosenfield, *Portrait of a Philosopher;* and William James, "A Knight-Errant of the Intellectual Life," in *Memories and Studies* (New York: Longmans, Green, and Co., 1911); and James A. Good, "The Value of Thomas Davidson," *Transactions of the Charles S. Peirce Society* 40, no. 2 (Spring 2004): 289-318. I am also deeply indebted to Margaret Myers Byrne, Michael DeArmey and Jonathan Hooker for details about Thomas Davidson I have learned through correspondence and conversations with each of them. Margaret Byrne allowed me to read her unpublished manuscript, "Great Scot: The Life and Philosophical Communities of Thomas Davidson," and Jonathan Hooker gave me an extensive tour of Glenmore as it stands today and allowed me to peruse the remains of Davidson's library in his Glenmore cabin.

45. Cohen, *Dreamer's Journey,* 103.

46. William Schuyler, "German Philosophy in St. Louis," *The Bulletin of the Washington University Association,* no. 2 (23 April 1904): 68.

47. Denton Snider, *The St. Louis Movement in Philosophy, Literature, Education, Psychology, with Chapters of Autobiography* (St. Louis: Sigma Publishing Company, 1920), 279. Cf. William H. Goetzmann, ed., *The American Hegelians: An Intellectual*

Episode in the History of Western America (New York: Alfred A. Knopf, 1973), 3. The best sources for women in the group are Dorothy G. Rogers, "'Making Hegel Talk English': America's First Women Idealists" (Ph.D. diss., Boston University, 1998); Rogers, ed., *Women in the St. Louis Idealist Movement, 1860-1925*, 4 vols. (Bristol, England: Thoemmes Press, 2003); and Rogers, *America's First Women Philosophers: Transplanting Hegel, 1860-1925* (London: Continuum, 2005).

48. Many of the St. Louis Hegelians commented on Brokmeyer's contempt for the English language, even varying the way he spelled his name. Snider notes that Brokmeyer's translation of Hegel's *Science of Logic* "needed revision in the matter of orthography, of syntax, of general style." Snider, *A Writer of Books in His Genesis; Written for and Dedicated to His Pupil-friends Reaching Back in a Line of Fifty Years* (St. Louis: Sigma, 1910), 318, cf. 324-325.

49. W. T. Harris, *Hegel's Logic: A Book on the Genesis of the Categories of the Mind* (Chicago: S. C. Griggs, 1890), xiii. On the St. Louis Hegelians' commitment to philosophy as a practical endeavor see also Snider, *A Writer of Books*, 317.

50. Snider, *The St. Louis Movement*, 11.

51. Ibid., 301.

52. On the St. Louis Hegelians' anti-elitism as an Americanization of Hegel see Frances Harmon, *The Social Philosophy of the St. Louis Hegelians* (New York: Columbia University, 1943), esp. 97-105. Cf. Mary Forrest Dowling, "The St. Louis Movement: Reconstruction of the Individual and the Nation Through Speculative Philosophy" (Ph.D. diss., St. Louis University, 1972), 123-131. Hegel's belief that careers should be open to talent manifested itself in a concern, throughout his teaching career, for economically disadvantaged students. His sense of egalitarianism toward economically disadvantaged male students was not matched, however, by his attitudes toward women. Further, Hegel did not believe everyone was suited for *Bildung*, but that it was necessary for those who sought to pursue professional careers. On his views toward women see Terry Pinkard, *Hegel: A Biography* (Cambridge: Cambridge University Press, 2000), 112-113, 281-282, 290, 481-482, 636; Lewis Hinchman, *Hegel's Critique of the Enlightenment* (Gainesville: The University Presses of Florida, 1984), 104ff; Hegel, *The Philosophy of Right*, §§ 166-167; and Hegel, *Phenomenology of Spirit*, trans. A. V. Miller (Oxford: Clarendon Press, 1977), §§457-460. Although no women are listed in the membership roles of the St. Louis Philosophical Society, Harris, Snider, Davidson, and others were leaders in local efforts to obtain suffrage for women. Furthermore, as Superintendent of the St. Louis public schools, Harris treated women employees exceptionally well. Stephen L. McIntyre, "'Our Schools are Not Charitable Institutions': Class, Gender, Ethnicity, and the Teaching Profession in Nineteenth-Century St. Louis," *Missouri Historical Review* 92 (October 1997): 27-44. For membership in the society see Kurt Leidecker, ed., *The Record Book of the St. Louis Philosophical Society Founded February 1866* (Lewiston, NY: Edwin Mellen Press, 1990).

53. Other St. Louis Hegelians did not share Harris's concern about the doctrine of the trinity. According to Denton Snider, the group sought to overthrow traditional American religion in favor of one that was more universal. "We sought to win a fresh spiritual communion with the Divine Order and its Orderer, and to create for the same a new unborn expression. But to accomplish any such purpose we had to throw aside the old carcass of tradition . . . and to begin over." Snider, *The St. Louis Movement*, 24-26. Thomas Davidson was highly critical of Harris's concerns about orthodox doctrines. See Thomas Davidson to William Torrey Harris, 4 August 1884, William Torrey Harris Papers, Missouri Historical Society (hereafter MHS). For scholarship that characterizes the St. Louis Hegelians as right-wing see John Watson, "Idealism and Social Theory: A Comparative

Study of British and American Adaptations of Hegel, 1860-1914" (Ph.D. diss., University of Pennsylvania, 1975), 50; and Merle Curti, *Social Ideas of American Educators* (New York: Charles Scribner's Sons, 1935), 310-347. On the Hegelian center see John Toews, *Hegelianism: The Path Toward Dialectical Humanism, 1805-1841* (New York: Cambridge University Press, 1980), 71-154, 203-242. Arnold Ruge characterized Rosenkranz as "the most liberal of the all the Old Hegelians." Quoted in Karl Löwith, *From Hegel to Nietzsche: The Revolution in Nineteenth-Century Thought,* trans. David E. Green (New York: Columbia University Press, 1964), 54.

54. Karl Rosenkranz, "The Difference of Baader from Hegel," trans. W. T. Harris, JSP 2, no. 1 (1868): 55-56. Ludwig Feuerbach, theologically a left-Hegelian, and J. H. Fichte were also auxiliary members. For an extensive list of members of the St. Louis Philosophical Society see Schuyler, "German Philosophy in St. Louis," 72-73. One hundred twenty-nine pages in the JSP were devoted to translations of Rosenkranz's commentary on Hegel. In 1872 Rosenkranz protested the way he was criticized in an article by Professor Hoffman of Würzburg in the first volume of the JSP. See Hoffman, "Letter on the Philosophy of Baader," JSP 1, no. 3 (1867): 190-192. Hoffman and Rosenkranz continued the debate, which revolved around whether Rosenkranz was correct to argue that Hegel was properly understood as a theist rather than a pantheist, in the JSP and in the *Philosophische Monatshefte,* published in Berlin. In the course of this debate, Hoffman published "Die Hegelsche Philosophie in St. Louis in den vereinigten Staaten Nordamerika's," *Philosophische Monatshefte* (1871): 58-63, in which he criticized W. T. Harris for falling into Rosenkranz's error among other things. I translated Hoffman's *Philosophische Monatshefte* article as "The Hegelian Philosophy in St. Louis in the United States of North America" in Michael H. DeArmey and James A. Good, eds., *Origins, the Dialectic, and the Critique of Materialism,* vol. 1 of *The St. Louis Hegelians* (Bristol, England: Thoemmes Press, 2001), 92-96. See also "Correspondence," JSP 6, no. 2 (Apr. 1872): 175-184. An article published by E. Hartmann in the JSP also touched off a debate between him and C. L. Michelet in the *Philosophische Monatshefte* about Hegel's dialectic. "Correspondence," JSP 6, no. 2 (Apr. 1872): 175-181.

55. During his involvement in state and local politics, Brokmeyer opposed the "48ers," whom "he branded as negative—hostile to all positive thought and its institutions." Snider, *The St. Louis Movement,* 29.

56. On Hegel's quest for unity see H. S. Harris, *Hegel's Development: Toward the Sunlight, 1770-1801* (Oxford: Clarendon Press, 1972); José María Ripalda, *The Divided Nation, The Roots of a Bourgeois Thinker: G. W. F. Hegel,* trans. Fay Franklin and Maruja Tillman (Amsterdam: Van Gorcum, Assen, 1977); George Armstrong Kelly, *Hegel's Retreat from Eleusis: Studies in Political Thought* (Princeton: Princeton University Press, 1978); and Laurence Dickey, *Hegel: Religion, Economics, and the Politics of Spirit, 1770-1807* (Cambridge: Cambridge University Press, 1987).

57. W. T. Harris, *Psychologic Foundations: An Attempt to Show the Genesis of the Higher Faculties of the Mind* (New York: D. Appleton and Co., 1898), 287. Harris's discussions of the "spontaneous or formal will," and the "moral or rational will," closely follow Hegel's analyses of abstract and concrete freedom. Ibid., 120-134. Cf. Hegel, *The Phenomenology of Spirit,* "Absolute Freedom and Terror," §§582-595; as well as relevant sections of *The Philosophy of Right,* such as "Abstract Right," §§34-40.

58. Harris, *Psychologic Foundations,* 291.

59. Hegel, *The Philosophy of History,* trans. J. Sibree (New York: Dover Publications, 1956), 86. Snider discussed and critiqued Hegel's analysis of the state in *The State, Specially the American State, Psychologically Treated* (St. Louis: Sigma Publishing Co.,

1902), 485-496; and *Modern European Philosophy: The History of Modern Philosophy, Psychologically Treated* (St. Louis: Sigma Publishing Co., 1904), 806-809.

60. Snider ultimately conceded that they were caught up in the "Grand Illusion" propagated by St. Louis boosters, but claimed that their grounding in philosophy equipped them to rise above the particular passions of the moment, which were shattered when the 1880 census showed that Chicago had surpassed the city in size and economic importance. Snider, *St. Louis Movement*, 70-137.

61. Denton Snider, *The American Ten Years' War, 1855-1865* (St. Louis: Sigma Publishing Co., 1906), 219-243.

62. Michael Fellman, *Inside War: The Guerrilla Conflict in Missouri during the American Civil War* (New York: Oxford University Press, 1989).

63. Snider, *The St. Louis Movement*, 143-144; James A. Good, "A 'World-Historical Idea': The St. Louis Hegelians and the Civil War," *Journal of American Studies* 34, no. 1 (December 2000): 447-464.

64. Hegel, *The Philosophy of History*, 21. Snider discusses the *Phenomenology of Spirit* as Hegel's effort to understand the French Revolution and Napoleon in *Modern European Philosophy*, 681-683.

65. See Snider's account of this incident in *A Writer of Books*, 381-383. I provide more information about Brokmeyer's reaction to the war in Good, "A 'World-Historical Idea,'" 447-464.

66. W. T. Harris to Dr. Peckham, 26 June 1861, Box 10, W. T. Harris Papers, MHS.

67. Hegel, *The Philosophy of History*, 86.

68. W. T. Harris, "Philosophy of History," *Missouri Republican*, 8 October 1861. (Signed "H"; identified as Harris by Kurt F. Leidecker, *Yankee Teacher: The Life of William Torrey Harris* [New York: Philosophical Library, 1946], 204-206.)

69. Harris, "Philosophy of History" (emphasis in the original). Cf. Harris's journal entry for 20 July 1865, Journal, Box 10, W. T. Harris Papers, MHS.

70. Denton Snider, *Abraham Lincoln: An Interpretation in Biography* (St. Louis: Sigma, 1908); and Snider, *The State*.

71. Snider, *The American Ten Years' War*, 526. Snider's historical work was particularly prodigious: Snider, *The American State* (St. Louis: n.p., 1874). *The American State* was the republication of an 1867 article by the same title, which appeared in *The Western*, another journal associated with the St. Louis Hegelians. Cf. Snider, *Social Institutions in their Origin, Growth, and Interconnection, Psychologically Treated* (St. Louis: Sigma, 1901); Snider, *The State, Specially the American State, Psychologically Treated;* Snider, *The American Ten Years' War*; Snider, *Abraham Lincoln;* Snider, *Lincoln in the Black Hawk War, an Epos of the Northwest* (St. Louis: Sigma, 1910); Snider, *A Writer of Books;* Snider, *Lincoln and Ann Rutledge; an Idyllic Epos of the Early North-west. Souvenir of Abraham Lincoln's Birth-day, 1912* (St. Louis: Sigma, 1912); Snider, *Lincoln in the White House; a Dramatic Epos of the Civil War* (St. Louis: Sigma, 1913); Snider, *Lincoln at Richmond; a Dramatic Epos of the Civil War* (St. Louis: Sigma, 1914); and Snider, *The St. Louis Movement.* Lawrence Dowler is critical of the thesis that the St. Louis Hegelians were drawn to idealism primarily for political reasons, seeking to counter American individualistic political philosophies with an organic theory of the state. Instead, Dowler opts for the theory that the St. Louis Hegelians viewed the sectional crisis primarily as a spiritual conflict and that, therefore, they were drawn to idealism for spiritual reasons. His argument is based primarily on the premise that "evidence for the 'political' interpretation rests heavily on three books by Denton Snider," all of which were written after 1900, a time when Snider claimed he had moved beyond Hegel. The three books Dowler names are *Social Institutions, The State, and Ten Years' War.*

Dowler, "The New Idealism and the Quest for Culture in the Gilded Age," 19-20, n. 36. Dowler seems to have overlooked Snider's *The American State* which was originally published only two years after the war, and belittled the fact that although Snider does claim to have moved beyond Hegel to psychology, his books on American history draw heavily on Hegel's *Philosophy of History,* which I note in my discussions of Snider's interpretation of the war. Moreover, the above list demonstrates that there are many more than three books by Snider that provide Hegelian analyses of American history.

72. Snider, *Ten Years' War,* 187; Snider, *The State,* 492; Snider, *The St. Louis Movement,* 52, 59, 62. Cf. Hegel's claim that although World-Historical individuals have "no consciousness of the general Idea they [are] unfolding," they are "thinking men, who [have] an insight into the requirements of the time." When World-Historical individuals' purpose is fulfilled "they fall off like empty hulls from the kernel." Hegel, *The Philosophy of History,* 30-31.

73. Snider, *The American Ten Years' War,* 230; Snider, *Biography of Ralph Waldo Emerson* (St. Louis: W. H. Miner, 1921), 347-349. One might quibble with both Harris's and Snider's belief that Lincoln acted within the parameters of established institutions by noting his suspension of the writ of habeas corpus during the war.

74. Hegel, *Phenomenology of Spirit,* §§155, 178-196.

75. Snider, *The American Ten Years' War,* 373-374, 323. Snider seems not to have considered the fact that Hegel erroneously saw the American system of bondage through the lens of a very different model of slavery, that of ancient Greece and Rome, which was far less oppressive than that of the American South. Had he taken this point into consideration, Snider might have been able to explain the lack of slave rebellion in the South as a result of oppression rather than racial inferiority of African-Americans. This may simply reveal the extent to which Snider was conditioned by the racial prejudices of American culture. Snider's discussion of various races mirrors, to a large extent, that of Rosenkranz in his treatise on Hegel's philosophy of history, a small portion of which was translated by G. Stanley Hall for the JSP. Karl Rosenkranz, "Hegel's Philosophy of History," JSP 6, no. 4 (Oct. 1872): 340-50.

76. Snider, *The American Ten Years' War,* 316-317, 321-323.

77. Quoted in "Correspondence," JSP 6, no. 2 (Apr. 1872): 177. Hoffman, "The Hegelian Philosophy in St. Louis in the United States of North America" in *Origins, the Dialectic, and the Critique of Materialism,* 92-96. In 1868 Rosenkranz wrote that "the Union has just done in the reconstruction of its Constitution against the insurrection of the Southern States." Rosenkranz, "Difference of Baader from Hegel," 56.

78. Snider, *The St. Louis Movement,* 127.

79. Snider, *A Writer of Books,* 389. The best accounts of the founding of both St. Louis philosophical clubs are in Leidecker, *Yankee Teacher,* 316ff; and Denton Snider, *The St. Louis Movement,* 66ff, 138-212.

80. Snider, *The St. Louis Movement,* 279. Cf. Goetzmann, ed., *The American Hegelians: An Intellectual Episode in the History of Western America* (New York: Alfred A. Knopf, 1973), 3. In the preface to the first volume of the JSP, Harris wrote, in words reminiscent of Emerson, that they sought to disseminate European philosophy in America, in order to promote the development of a "true 'American' type of Speculative Philosophy." To this he added, "it is not 'American thought' so much as American thinkers that we want. To think, in the highest sense, is to transcend all natural limits—such, for example, as national peculiarities, defects in culture, distinctions in Race, habits and modes of living—to be universal, so that one can dissolve away the external hull and seize the substance itself." W. T. Harris, "Preface," JSP 1, no. 1 (1867), iii. Although there are obvious similarities between this statement and expressions of cultural national-

ism before the Civil War, of which the transcendentalists were a crucial part, the contents of the journal reveal the St. Louis Hegelians' commitment to far more rigorous philological and philosophical means toward their goals than were generally employed by the transcendentalists.

81. Hegel, *Phenomenology of Spirit,* §401. See Snider's discussion of the fictitious Sigma Publishing Company, which one might assume published virtually all of his books. Snider came to define himself as *A Writer of Books,* and emphasized that his books were acts of "self-publication" and self-expression. Snider, *The St. Louis Movement,* 479-486.

82. E. C. Brokmeyer to Charles M. Perry, 5 July 1929; and E. C. Brokmeyer to Cleon Forbes, 16 January 1929; both reprinted in Perry, ed., *The St. Louis Movement in Philosophy,* 48, 50.

83. W. T. Harris, "The Kindergarten as a Preparation for the Highest Civilization," *Atlantic Educational Journal* 6 (July-Aug. 1903): 35-36. Cf. Selwyn K. Troen, "Operation Headstart: The Beginnings of the Public School Kindergarten Movement," *Missouri Historical Review* 66, no. 2 (January 1972): 211-229. Although they were to the political left of Hegel, I believe the way in which Harris and Blow used the 1877 strike makes them more vulnerable to the charge of using public education for the purpose of bourgeois social control of the masses than Dewey.

84. Bronson Alcott, *The Journals of Bronson Alcott,* ed. Odell Shepard (Boston: Little, Brown, 1938), 444.

85. On Jones see Paul Russell Anderson, *Platonism in the Midwest* (Philadelphia: Temple University Publications, 1963).

86. Alcott, *The Journals of Bronson Alcott,* 499.

87. According to James Canfield, Harris was the most frequently quoted American, "not even excepting Horace Mann," in educational journals. Canfield, *American Review of Reviews* 34 (August 1906): 164-166. Cf. John Roberts' list of articles written in praise of Harris. Roberts, *William T. Harris: A Critical Study of His Educational and Related Philosophical Reviews* (Washington, D.C.: National Education Association, 1924), 349-350. Interestingly, Harris is an excellent example of Hegel's ideal civil servant, a man of *Bildung,* continually involved in ongoing self-education, who finds his own good by working for the good of society. Pinkard, *Hegel,* 537.

88. W. T. Harris, "The Definition of Social Science and the Classification of the Topics Belonging to its Several Provinces," *Journal of Social Science* 22 (June 1887): 1-7. A complete bibliography of Harris's publications comprises thirty-one pages. Henry Ridgley Evans, ed., "A List of the Writings of William Torrey Harris," *Report of the Commissioner of Education for 1907* (Washington D.C.: Government Printing Office, 1908), 37-72. On the pantheism debate see Franz Hoffman, "Letter on the Philosophy of Baader," JSP 1, no. 3 (1867): 190-192; Rosenkranz, "The Difference of Baader from Hegel," 55-56; Hoffman, "Die Hegelsche Philosophie in St. Louis in den vereinigten Staaten of Nordamerikas"; W. T. Harris, "Immortality of the Soul" JSP 4, no. 2 (1870): 97-111; Harris, "Theism and Pantheism," JSP 5, no. 1 (Jan. 1871): 86-94; Harris, ed., "Correspondence," JSP 6, no. 2 (Apr. 1872): 175-181; and Harris, "Defense of Hegel against the Charge of Pantheism as Made in Hickok's Logic of Reason," JSP 9, no. 3 (July 1876): 328-334.

89. W. T. Harris to Snider, 24 September 1906, Box 1, W. T. Harris Papers, MHS Collections.

90. Mrs. D. H. Harris, "The Early St. Louis Movement and the Communal University," in *A Brief Report of the Meeting Commemorative of the Early Saint Louis Movement in Philosophy, Psychology, Literature, Art and Education,* ed. D. H. Harris (St.

Louis: n.p., 1922), 31-47. Snider describes his association with Hull House, including actually living and working there for a few months in the fall of 1893, in *The St. Louis Movement,* 498-510. In addition to his own writings, on Snider's Communal Universities, see Henry A. Pochman, *New England Transcendentalist and St. Louis Hegelianism: Phases in the History of American Idealism* (Philadelphia: Carl Schurz Memorial Foundation, 1948), 135 n. 103.

91. Cohen captured this well when he wrote, "Glenmore gave me my first taste of what a traveler in the desert of life feels when he first comes to a green oasis." Cohen, *Dreamer's Journey,* 108.

92. Elizabeth Flower and Murray G. Murphey, *A History of Philosophy in America* (New York: Capricorn Books, 1977), 2: 486. Snider engaged in similar work in several midwestern cities. In addition to Snider's *St. Louis Movement* and *A Writer of Books,* see D. H. Harris, ed., *A Brief Report of the Meeting Commemorative of the Early Saint Louis Movement,* 31-47, 120-121. See George M. Fredrickson, *The Inner Civil War*; Stanley Elkins, *Slavery: A Problem in American Institutional and Intellectual Life,* 3rd ed., rev. (Chicago: University of Chicago Press, 1976); and Anne C. Rose, *Transcendentalism as a Social Movement, 1830-1850* (New Haven: Yale University Press, 1981). Although in the preface to the 1993 edition of *Inner Civil War* Fredrickson expresses embarrassment about his acceptance of an "elitist canon" that undergirded his and Elkins's exclusive focus on New England intellectuals, he continued to neglect the St. Louis Hegelians in that preface. Fredrickson, *Inner Civil War,* vii-xiv. A notable exception is Wilfred McClay, *The Masterless: Self and Society in Modern America* (Chapel Hill: University of North Carolina Press, 1994), 134-136. McClay discusses the appeal of German idealism to postwar American intellectuals, but says nothing about the St. Louis Hegelians' impact on eastern intellectuals. Eduard Gans, one of Hegel's most liberal students, played a similar role in German history during the 1830s. Walter Breckman argues that Gans supported the establishment of autonomous associations that would enrich civil society in much the same way that I believe the St. Louis Hegelians understood their "St. Louis Movement." According to Breckman, Gans moved to the left of Hegel in this because he "conceived associationism as the educator of political society" and "advocated a direct interaction between civil society and the political life of the state." This gave a larger political role to the public and to public opinion than Hegel was willing to allow. Not surprisingly perhaps, given their American context, the St. Louis Hegelians moved to the left of Hegel in the roles they sought for the associations they founded in St. Louis. Breckman, "Eduard Gans and the Crisis of Hegelianism," *Journal of the History of Ideas* 62, no. 3 (July 2001): 559.

94. Harris was publicly embarrassed by Brokmeyer's verbal assaults on Alcott. Pochmann, *German Culture in America,* 271-272. Cf. Alcott, *The Journals of Bronson Alcott,* 340; and Brokmeyer, *A Mechanic's Diary* (Washington, D.C.: E. C. Brokmeyer Publisher, 1910), 229-233. See Emerson's reflections on his meetings with the St. Louis Hegelians in Emerson, *The Letters of Ralph Waldo Emerson,* ed. Ralph L. Rusk (New York: Columbia University Press, 1939), 5: 421-422, 514, 521.

95. It is frequently said that the JSP was the first English language journal devoted exclusively to philosophy, but because of the St. Louis Hegelians' broad conception of philosophy and its cultural role, a significant portion of it was devoted to art, literature and religion. For a fuller discussion of this issue see Good, "Introduction," in JSP (1867; reprint, Bristol, England: Thoemmes Press, 2002), 1: v-xx.

96. Louis J. Block, "The Philosophic Schools of St. Louis, Jacksonville, Concord and Chicago," in *A Brief Report,* ed. D. H. Harris, 25. See also Austin Warren, "The Concord School of Philosophy," *New England Quarterly* 2 (April 1929): 199-233; and Henry A.

Pochmann, *New England Transcendentalism and St. Louis Hegelianism: Phases in the History of American Idealism* (Philadelphia: Carl Shurz Memorial Foundation, 1948); Leidecker, *Yankee Teacher,* 357-372, 403-421. For Harris's profound impact on Alcott see Teck-Young Kwon, "A. Bronson Alcott's Literary Apprenticeship to Emerson: The Role of Harris's Journal of Speculative Philosophy" (Ph.D. diss., University of Nebraska, Lincoln, 1980).

97. Ralph Waldo Emerson, "Self Reliance," in *Selections from Ralph Waldo Emerson,* ed. Stephen E. Whicher (Boston: Houghton Mifflin, 1957), 150.

98. Karl Rosenkranz, "Hegel as Publicist," trans. G. Stanley Hall, JSP 6, no. 3 (July 1872): 258-279.

99. Snider, *Modern European Philosophy,* 737. Cf. Snider's discussion of the "genetic or creative" state in *The American Ten Years' War,* 17.

100. Harris, *Psychologic Foundations,* 282; and Harris, "Analysis and Commentary [of Karl Rosenkranz's *Pädagogik als System*]," JSP 15, no. 1 (Jan. 1881): 52-62. Cf., Terry Pinkard, *Hegel,* 284.

101. Harris, *Psychologic Foundations,* 281, 287, 289.

102. W. T. Harris, "The Philosophic Aspects of History," *Proceedings of the American Historical Association* (1891): 247-254; and preface in Thomas Davidson, *The Education of the Greek People* (New York: D. Appleton, 1894).

103. W. T. Harris, "What Shall We Study?" *Journal of Education* 2 (September 1869): 1-3. Cf. Harris, "A Brief for Latin," *Educational Review* 17 (April 1899): 313-316.

104. W. T. Harris, "The Psychology of Manual Training," *Educational Review* 9 (May 1889): 571-582; Harris, "Religious Instruction in the Public Schools," *Independent* 55 (6 August 1903): 1841-1843; and Harris, "The School City," *School Bulletin* 32 (March 1906): 113-114.

105. W. T. Harris, "Education to Regenerate the Slums," *Brooklyn Eagle* (30 December 1900).

106. W. T. Harris, *A Statement of the Theory of Education in the United States by Many Leading Educators* (Washington, D.C., 1874), 34-35. Cf. Harris, "Do the Public Schools Educate Children Beyond the Position Which They Must Occupy in Life?" New Haven: Board of Education, Report (1882): 34-35. See Stephen McIntyre's discussion of Harris's debates with O'Connell. McIntyre, "'Our Schools are Not Charitable Institutions': Class, Gender, Ethnicity, and the Teaching Profession in Nineteenth-Century St. Louis," *Missouri Historical Review* 92 (October 1997): 27-44.

107. Harris's notion of "cultural education" clearly assumed the superiority of western culture. W. T. Harris, "An Educational Policy for Our New Possessions," *National Education Association Proceedings* (1898): 69-79.

108. Leidecker, *Yankee Teacher,* 173-174, 265-266; W. T. Harris, "The Relation of Women to the Trades and Professions," *Educational Review* 20 (October 1900): 217-29; Harris, "Co-education of the Sexes," *Report of the Commissioner of Education* 2 (1900-1901): 141-147; Harris, "Why Women Should Study the Law," *Ohio Educational Monthly* 50 (July 1901): 289-292. See also McIntyre's discussion of Harris's willingness to hire and promote women in the public schools. McIntyre, "'Our Schools are Not Charitable Institutions,'" 41-43.

109. See W. T. Harris, "Record Book," W. T. Harris Papers, MHS Collections, 9-12.

110. Harris, "Analysis and Commentary [of Rosenkranz's *Pädagogik als System*]," 52-62.

111. Harris, March 1877 notebook, Box 10, W. T. Harris Papers, MHS Collections. Cf. Harris, *Psychologic Foundations,* "The Psychology of Infancy," 295-321.

112. Unlike Blow, Brackett was a feminist, and applied her philosophy of education specifically to women and girls. Rogers, *America's First Women Philosophers.*

113. Both Dewey and Josiah Royce published their first article in the JSP. Dewey, "The Metaphysical Assumptions of Materialism," JSP 16, no. 2 (Apr. 1882), 208-213; Royce, "Schiller's Ethical Studies," JSP 12, no. 4 (Oct. 1878): 373-392. G. Stanley Hall published his second scholarly work in the JSP. Hall, "Anti-Materialism," JSP 6, no. 3 (July 1872): 216-222. According to Dewey, Peirce first began to lay out "the conclusion that all thought was in signs and required a time" from which he developed "his pragmaticism, his theory of signs, and his search for a functional logic" in a series of articles published in the JSP in 1868. Dewey and Arthur Bentley, *Knowing and the Known* (1949) LW 16: 238-239. Peirce's four articles are: Peirce, "Questions Concerning Certain Faculties Claimed for Man," JSP 2, no. 2 (1868): 103-114; Peirce, "Some Consequences of Four Incapacities," JSP 2, no. 3 (1868): 140-157; Peirce, "What Is Meant by 'Determined,'" JSP 2, no. 3 (1868): 190-191; and Peirce, "Grounds of the Validity of the Laws of Logic," JSP 2, no. 4 (1869): 193-208.

114. A. E. Kroeger, "The Difference between the Dialectic Method of Hegel and the Synthetic Method of Kant and Fichte," JSP 6, no. 2 (Apr. 1872): 184-187; Augusto Vera, "Trendelenburg as Opponent of Hegel," trans. Anna Brackett, JSP 7, no. 1 (Jan. 1873): 26-32; G. S. Morris, "Vera on Trendelenburg," JSP 8, no. 1 (Jan. 1874): 92-94; G. S. Morris, "Friedrich Adolf Trendelenburg," *The New Englander* 33 (1874): 287-336; W. T. Harris, "Trendelenburg and Hegel," JSP 9, no. 1 (Jan. 1875): 70-80; and G. Stanley Hall, "Notes on Hegel and his Critics," JSP 12, no. 1 (Jan. 1878): 93-103. Hegel seems to have anticipated Trendelenburg's critique in the *Phenomenology of Spirit:* "Of course, the triadic form must not be regarded as scientific when it is reduced to a lifeless schema, a mere shadow, and when scientific organization is degraded into a table of terms" (§50). This was in fact Hegel's criticism of Kant's categories, which, he claimed, were purely formal. Hegel also addressed this issue in criticisms of the form/content distinction in logic. Hegel, *The Logic of Hegel,* §162.

115. Gershon Rosenstock, *F. A. Trendelenburg: Forerunner to John Dewey* (Carbondale: Southern Illinois Press, 1964), 11, 36-62, 76-100. In his review of Rosenstock's book, Herbert Schneider, a colleague of Dewey's at Columbia and a noted expert on the history of American philosophy, claimed that the close parallels between Trendelenburg's and Dewey's logic and psychology, which Rosenstock correctly describes as being much more striking than anything in Morris [Dewey's graduate school mentor] seem to me still somewhat of a mystery. Schneider, review of *F. A. Trendelenburg: Forerunner to John Dewey,* by Gershon Rosenstock, in *Journal of the History of Philosophy* 4 (1966): 266. Schneider's puzzlement may be due to the fact that Dewey never acknowledged a debt to Trendelenberg despite their uncanny similarity. I can only address that issue by noting that Dewey and Trendelenberg were deeply influenced by German idealism, and both sought to modify idealism in the light of advances in science, especially Darwinian biology, without succumbing to a deterministic materialism.

116. Josiah Royce, Joseph LeConte, George Howison, and Sydney Edward Mezes, *The Conception of God: A Philosophical Discussion Concerning the Nature of the Divine Idea as a Demonstrable Reality* (New York: Macmillan, 1898). William James, "Philosophical Conceptions and Practical Results," *University Chronicle* 1 (1898): 287-310. Dewey's lecture was first published in the *University Chronicle* 2 (1899): 159-179. See "Textual Commentary," MW 1: 370.

117. Flower and Murphey, *A History of Philosophy in America,* 2: 483-90.

118. Thomas Le Duc, *Piety and Intellect at Amherst College, 1865-1912* (New York: Arno Press, 1946), 53; John W. Burgess, *Reminiscences of an American Scholar: The*

Beginnings of Columbia University (New York: AMS Press, 1966), 254; Burgess, *Political Science and Comparative Constitutional Law* (Boston: Ginn, 1896), 1: 57; Richard T. Ely, "Co-operation in Literature and the State," in William E. Barns, ed., *The Labor Problem* (New York: Arno Press, 1971), 41; Albion Small and George E. Vincent, *An Introduction to the Study of Society* (Dubuque, IA: Brown Reprints, 1971), 41; Herbst, *The German Historical School in American Scholarship,* 66-67.

119. Evelyn Shirk, "Alfred Henry Lloyd: Beyond Labels," *Transactions of the Charles S. Peirce Society* 15, no. 4 (Fall 1979): 269-282.

120. William James, *Memories and Studies,* 81-82. Anderson, *Platonism in the Midwest,* 142-150. In *Memories and Studies,* James indicates that he studied the *Logic* with Emery and McClure in 1872, but they did not arrive in Boston until 1879. Emery became a close friend of Bronson Alcott and was director of the Concord School of Philosophy. Leidecker, *Yankee Teacher,* 406, 408.

121. James McLachlan, "The Idealist Critique of Idealism: Bowne's Theistic Personalism and Howison's City of God," *The Personalist Forum* 13, no. 1 (Spring 1997): 89-106. Cf. John McDermott, "The Confrontation between Royce and Howison," *Transactions of the Charles S. Peirce Society* 30, no. 4 (Fall 1994): 779-790; and Ignas K. Skrupskelis, "The Royce-Howison Debate on the Conception of God," *Transactions of the Charles S. Peirce Society* 30, no. 4 (Fall 1994): 791-802.

122. Andrew Seth, *Hegelianism and Personality* (Edinburgh: William Blackwood and Sons, 1887); and Howison, *The Limits of Evolution, and Other Essays Illustrating the Metaphysical Theory of Personal Idealism* (New York: Macmillan, 1901). Martin Luther King Jr. studied with Brightman and Muelder at Boston University. In 1985 Thomas Buford founded *The Personalist Forum* at Furman University to take over where Flewelling's *The Personalist* left off. Buford, "What We are About," *The Personalist Forum* 1, no. 1 (1985): 1-4.

123. On American idealism after 1900, see Andrew Reck, *Recent American Philosophy: Studies of Ten Representative Thinkers* (New York: Pantheon Books, 1962); and Reck, "Idealism in American Philosophy Since 1900," in *Contemporary Studies in Philosophical Idealism,* ed. John Howie and Thomas O. Buford (Cape Cod, MA: Claude Stark and Co., 1975), 17-52.

124. Herbst, *The German Historical School in American Scholarship,* 68-71. Even historians spoke of the graduate seminar as the laboratory of the social sciences. Peter Novick, *That Noble Dream: The "Objectivity Question" and the American Historical Profession* (New York: Cambridge University Press, 1988), 31-33. Daniel Wilson, "Science and the Crisis of Confidence in American Philosophy," *Transactions of the Charles S. Peirce Society* 23, no. 2 (Spring 1987): 235-262; Wilson, *Science, Community, and the Transformation of American Philosophy, 1860-1930* (Chicago: University of Chicago Press, 1990).

125. C. S. Peirce, *Collected Papers of Charles S. Peirce,* 6 vols., eds. Charles Hartshorne and Paul Weiss (Cambridge, MA: Harvard University Press, 1931-1935), 1: 369.

126. Frederic H. Young, "Charles Sanders Peirce: 1839-1914," in *Studies in the Philosophy of Charles Sanders Peirce,* eds. Philip H. Wiener and Frederic H. Young (Cambridge, MA: Harvard University Press, 1952), 275. Cf. Harvey G. Townsend, "The Pragmatism of Peirce and Hegel," *The Philosophical Review* 37, no. 4 (July 1928): 297-303; and William Elton, "Peirce's Marginalia in W. T. Harris's *Hegel's Logic,*" *Journal of the History of Philosophy* 2, no. 1 (April 1964): 82-84; and Otto Pöggler, "Hegel Editing and Hegel Research," in O'Malley, *The Legacy of Hegel,* 9. Pöggler notes that Karl-Otto Apel sees Peirce's and Hegel's philosophical starting points as parallel. Max Fisch writes: "Peirce was best understood . . . not by other pragmatists at home or abroad, but

by Josiah Royce, the philosopher of his acquaintance who, after W. T. Harris, had studied Hegel most deeply." In *The Problem of Christianity* (1913), "Royce developed Peirce's 'doctrine of signs' at length, applied it to metaphysics, and stated its relation to Hegel in the most important paragraph so far written on 'Hegel and Peirce.'" Fisch, *Peirce, Semieotic, and Pragmatism: Essays by Max H. Fisch,* ed. Kenneth Laine Ketner and Christian J. W. Kloesel (Bloomington: Indiana University Press, 1986), 275.

127. Peirce, "The Law of Mind," *The Collected Papers of Charles Sanders Peirce,* 6: 102-118. Max O. Hocutt, "The Logical Foundations of Peirce's Aesthetics," *The Journal of Aesthetics and Art Criticism* 21 (1962): 157.

128. William James, "On Some Hegelisms," in *Pluralistic Universe: Hibbert Lectures on the Present Situation to Philosophy* (New York: Longmans, Green, and Co., 1909), 89-90, 109. Ralph Barton Perry, *The Thought and Character of William James,* 2 vols. (Boston: Little, Brown, 1935), 2: 584. On James's mid-1880s thought see ibid., 1: 577-578.

129. According to Dewey: "So far as I know, Mr. Charles S. Peirce was the first to call attention to this principle, and to insist upon its fundamental logical import (see *Monist,* Vol. II, 534-536, 549-556). Mr. Peirce states it as the principle of continuity: A past idea can operate only so far as it is psychically continuous with that upon which it operates. A general idea is simply a living and expanding feeling, and habit is a statement of the specific mode of operation of a given psychical continuum. I have reached the above conclusion along such diverse lines that, without in any way minimizing the priority of Mr. Peirce's statement, or its more generalized logical character, I feel that my own statement has something of the value of an independent confirmation." Dewey, "Logical Conditions of a Scientific Treatment of Morality" (1903), MW 3: 19-20.

Chapter Three

Dewey in Burlington and Baltimore, 1859–1884

It is frustrating to scholars that Dewey frequently spoke of philosophers' "habit of neglecting the indispensability of context," yet throughout his life he showed little interest in autobiographical reflection.[1] The historian of Dewey hopes to frame his intellectual development squarely within the context of his life and times, but is left to speculate about how events in his life might have affected his thought. Aside from a few scattered remarks, Dewey left only two brief autobiographical sources. When he was sixty years old he wrote an autobiographical essay, "From Absolutism to Experimentalism," and when he was eighty, his daughter Jane edited an essay written "by the daughters of its subject from material which he furnished." Dewey's daughters explained that "in the emphasis on varied influences and in the philosophical portions [the essay] may be regarded as an autobiography, but its subject is not responsible for the form nor for all the details."[2]

Nevertheless, in "From Absolutism to Experimentalism," Dewey provided useful clues about his interest in Hegelianism. He noted that "the 'eighties and 'nineties were a time of new ferment in English thought; the reaction against atomic individualism and sensationalistic empiricism was in full swing." This reaction was led by British and American Hegelians, and "was at the time the vital and constructive [movement] in philosophy." Dewey also tantalized would-be biographers when he remarked that, as a young man, "Hegel's thought . . . supplied a demand for unification that was doubtless an intense emotional craving, and yet was a hunger that only an intellectualized subject matter could satisfy." Hegelianism, he asserted, alleviated "a painful oppression," an "inward laceration," that stemmed from "a heritage of New England culture" with its "divisions by way of isolation of self from the world, of soul from body, of nature from God."[3]

Because Dewey wrote this reminiscence forty years after he left his hometown of Burlington, Vermont, it would be easy to place more interpretative weight on it than it can bear. The essay makes it apparent, however, that Dewey believed that New England religious thought tended to separate the natural from the supernatural, the physical from the spiritual, and that this led to psychologically unhealthy dualisms. This reading is reinforced by Dewey's daughters' claim that, "From a present-day point of view, too much moralistic emotional pressure was exerted by the religious atmosphere, evangelical rather than puritanic, which surrounded [John and his brothers]."[4] The only issues concerning the importance of religion in Dewey's complaint about this oppressive laceration is the extent to which it can fully explain the pain he described, and what it might reveal about his mature religious thought. Recently, Steven Rockefeller closely examined Dewey's comment within a detailed study of his life. Rockefeller concluded that a youthful religious angst profoundly shaped the trajectory of Dewey's mature thought, which was essentially religious. While there can be little doubt that Dewey's youthful anguish was partly religious, Rockefeller's larger agenda of depicting Dewey as a religious philosopher overpowered his evidence. Less well known, but published years before Rockefeller's book, is Lewis Feuer's supplementation of the religious hypothesis with a class-based account of Dewey's sense of oppression. While a philosophy professor at the University of Vermont during the 1950s, Feuer did a great deal of research on Dewey's youth and uncovered some evidence that he was painfully aware of class tensions in his hometown.[5] In conjunction, the religious and class-based hypotheses about Dewey's early development shed light on his angst, but ultimately, the available evidence leaves us with little more than speculation about his innermost psyche.[6] The evidence may, however, tell us a great deal about the sort of Hegelianism he espoused in the 1880s and 1890s, as well as ways that it may have survived in his mature thought.

My examination of Dewey's early life focuses on elements that provide evidence about his inward laceration, but my ultimate goal is to consider why Dewey may have been predisposed toward Hegelian thought. I begin this chapter with an examination of Dewey's youth in Burlington, through the time he graduated from the local university in 1882, focusing only on biographical issues that have a direct bearing on his intellectual development. From there I proceed to a discussion of his earliest publications and his early training in Hegelian thought at the Johns Hopkins University from 1882 to 1884. This will clarify the type of Hegelianism Dewey championed.

Burlington

Clearly, there was something about Vermont that bothered Dewey. Although in later years he praised Vermonters' commitment to democracy and their belief that government should adapt to the "developing needs of the human family" and "contribute to human welfare," Herbert Schneider claims Dewey "told me he left that God-forsaken country as soon as he could."[7] In point of fact, Dewey's attitude toward the state was widespread among Vermonters during the nineteenth century. Charles Morrissey reports that at least forty percent of Vermonters left the state during the second half of the nineteenth century; "no other state in the nation was losing such a large proportion of its natives."[8] Whereas we now view the state as a vacation paradise, when Dewey grew up there it was one of the poorest states in the nation. Whether Dewey fully realized it or not, his avoidance of his home state from the time he left in his early twenties until the end of his life at age ninety-three makes him part of a larger demographic movement. Perhaps it is also no surprise then that Dewey had no immediate family in Vermont after his parents went to live with him and his wife in Ann Arbor, Michigan, at the end of 1890, and he only returned three times after that, each time to attend brief ceremonies at the University of Vermont (1904, 1929, and 1949). Dewey's final visit to the university was to attend festivities in honor of his ninetieth birthday, during which he suddenly left town while a lecture was being delivered in his honor at the university chapel.[9] Regardless of nineteenth-century demographics, I will examine Dewey's boyhood family, community, and religion in search of clues about his interpretation of why he left Vermont.

Dewey was born in Burlington in 1859, just four days after John Brown and his men seized the armory at Harper's Ferry.[10] It was a particularly important year for intellectual history. In addition to Dewey, Henri Bergson and Edmund Husserl were born in 1859. By the 1890s Dewey was impressed with Bergson's emphasis upon process, specifically his notion that consciousness was a stream of thought rather than an association of discrete, atomistic ideas. And although the work of Husserl had no apparent influence on the development of Dewey's thought, both philosophers, as well as William James, would ultimately seek a via media between the horns of the late-nineteenth-century philosophical dilemma of materialistic empiricism versus neo-Hegelianism by emphasizing phenomenological immediacy.[11] It was also a year of historically important publications: John Stuart Mill published "On Liberty"; Karl Marx published the "Critique of Political Economy"; and Darwin published *On the Origin of Species by Natural Selection.* At one point or another all three of these intellectuals would figure prominently in the development of Dewey's thought, which can be seen as part of a secularizing, historicizing, and naturalistic trend in Western philosophy.[12]

Yet complex philosophical doctrines were far removed from the young John Dewey as he grew up in Burlington. Sydney Hook claimed that the Burlington of Dewey's childhood "was a community in which no great disparities in wealth or standards of living were to be found," but in fact class, ethnic and religious diversity marked the city.[13] Rather than a product of an idyllic small New England town, Dewey grew up in an industrializing city whose population doubled within five years after the end of the Civil War, as some Vermonters moved to the city and abandoned their rock-strewn farms. Burlington was the connecting rail link between the Canadian lumber industry and other New England cities, with a flourishing textile mill nearby. Social and political tensions developed as the city faced complex urban problems brought on by overcrowding and immigration. There was an old-stock New England bourgeoisie, the "aristocratic Old Americans," who advocated political and economic laissez-faire, resolutely opposed slavery, but also opposed all forms of political radicalism. There was also a growing working class composed primarily of Irish and French-Canadian immigrants living in battered tenements.[14] Dewey learned little about town-meeting democracy in Burlington, which was abolished by a new city charter in 1865, but a great deal about rapid urbanization and economic disparity. Like the St. Louis Hegelians, Dewey witnessed what Robert Wiebe has described as the erosion of "island communities" and the middle class search for a bureaucratic order in which people were identified more by their function in the economy and less by their reputation or family name.[15]

Dewey was the third of four sons; the first-born son died as a young child, but John grew up with two brothers, Davis Rich, who was one and a half years older, and Charles Miner, who was two years younger.[16] Davis went on to receive a doctorate in economics from Johns Hopkins University under the direction of Richard T. Ely and became a prominent economist at the Massachusetts Institute of Technology. Charles was a moderately successful businessman in California who, in his adult life, remained distant from the rest of the family, geographically and emotionally. Although Dewey's father, Archibald Sprague Dewey, was descended from a long line of Vermont farmers, as a young man he had moved to Burlington to become a grocer. The family was not wealthy, but they were comfortable. According to his granddaughters, Archibald directed little effort "toward advancing himself financially and he was said to sell more goods and collect fewer bills than any other man in town."[17] Archibald was known for his dry wit, his exceptional memory, and his literary interests. He enjoyed Shakespeare, Milton, Charles Lamb, Thackeray, and Burns, and regularly quoted Milton as he worked.

At age forty-four Archibald married Lucina Artemesia Rich, nearly twenty years his junior and from a more prosperous and educated family. Lucina was descended from seventeenth-century New England Puritan stock; her grandfather was a United States Congressman; her father, a highly respected local judge, served in the Vermont General Assembly. By the mid-nineteenth century the religion of Lucina's family had evolved to a rational Universalism, but in her late adolescence she went to Ohio to visit another branch of the family, where she attended revival meetings and was converted to evangelicalism. In contrast, Archibald Dewey was a liberal Congregationalist, but showed little interest in theology or religion, except for a dislike of the unconventional theology of the transcendentalists.[18] Feuer notes that Dewey's family associated with the old-stock bourgeoisie, because of Lucina's family connections, but they may have had a sense of social and economical inferiority within that group. When Dewey visited his boyhood friend John Buckham in 1921, Buckham's daughter recalls that Dewey described Burlington as the "cold pinnacle of aristocracy." Apparently Buckham felt injured by the remark, concluding that Dewey had not grown out of a feeling of social inferiority that stemmed from his father's vocation as the proprietor of a small shop.[19]

Though fifty years old when the Civil War began, Dewey's father sold his store and enthusiastically enlisted as a quartermaster in the First Vermont Cavalry. Promoted to captain in 1862, throughout the remainder of the war Archibald's regiment saw heavy action. By 1864 Dewey's mother could no longer bear separation from her husband and moved the family to the regimental headquarters in northern Virginia, where the boys surely saw and heard the effects of the war, which apparently made a deep impression on John. According to Hook, a close friend of Dewey in later life, memories of the Civil War greatly contributed to his later views on the senselessness of violence in the accomplishment of social reform.[20]

Dewey remembered his mother as a strict and pious woman. She took the boys to church regularly and, Dewey recalled, frequently asked them—sometimes publicly—whether they were "right with Jesus." Dewey reminisced that his mother's religious questioning produced "a sense of guilt" in her sons "and at the same time irritation because of the triviality of the occasions on which she questioned us."[21] To be sure, Lucina's demanding piety was burdensome at times, but she was also known for her generous philanthropic work among the poor of Burlington, and at the local University of Vermont she acquired a reputation as a caring counselor of young students.[22] And although Lucina's family connections gave her sons opportunities to associate with the Burlington elite, her work among the indigent exposed them to the abject poverty of the lakeshore industrial area.

Rockefeller speculates that Dewey's "lacerations" were exacerbated by a childhood sense of being abandoned by his father during the Civil War, claiming that "his father's absence may have left him angry, even if unconscious of the fact, and also unsure of his father's love."[23] He also notes that Dewey was reprimanded in college for helping lock an instructor in a classroom and for frequently being late for required weekly military drills, and suggests that this "probably reveals some rebellious attitudes toward his father." Rockefeller utilizes this analysis of Dewey's psyche to bolster his argument that Dewey suffered profound existential and religious crises that stemmed, in part, from his insecurity about his relationship with his father, but there is precious little evidence about their relationship one way or the other. There are a few extant letters between Dewey and his father, but they are rather light-hearted and about mundane events, such as the weather and Dewey's living accommodations in Baltimore while he attended graduate school at Johns Hopkins.[24] The only recorded disagreement Dewey had with his father occurred when he and Davis declared that they would vote for the democratic presidential candidate, Grover

Cleveland. To Archibald, who remained a committed Republican until his death in 1891, his sons' votes were a betrayal of the Union cause.[25] Dewey's daughters give the impression that this argument occurred after Dewey's parents had gone to live with him and his wife Alice in Ann Arbor, Michigan, in 1890. Archibald died in 1891, so Dewey might have regretted that the disagreement occurred so soon before his father's death, but it provides little, if any, insight into a deep-seated childhood resentment Dewey may have had toward his father, and thus Rockefeller's speculation on this issue is unpersuasive.[26]

Having returned to Burlington in 1867, Archibald went back into business as the proprietor of a cigar and tobacco shop, and the family returned to the White Street Congregational Church. In contrast to Lucina's evangelical religion, the church's pastor, Lewis Orsmond Brastow, preached a liberal orthodoxy. Brastow studied systematic theology at Bangor Seminary under the direction of Samuel Harris, an influential Congregationalist theologian, who was known for his concept of progressive revelation, which emphasized the historical "development of theology," and upon piety and religious experience over doctrinal orthodoxy. From Harris, Brastow received a conviction that religious experience and its transformative effects upon one's life was more important than intellectual articulation of faith. According to Brastow, Harris's was "preeminently a man-building theology, not a mere thought-directing theology."[27] Harris's thought influenced many of the leaders of a late-nineteenth-century liberal turn in Congregationalist theology known as Progressive Orthodoxy, or Andover Liberalism, for the seminary at which it was developed. Andover Liberalism ultimately evolved into the Social Gospel, which peaked in the first two decades of the twentieth century. More politically progressive than the theology of Brastow, the Social Gospel questioned the wisdom of laissez-faire economics in the face of tremendous labor unrest, and called for active involvement of Christians in social reform. By the 1880s Dewey came to share that interest in social reform, but at this time he merely picked up Brastow's emphases on piety rather than doctrine, on the historical development of thought, and on the practical problems individuals face in this life.

The Dewey boys were encouraged to read at home by parents who had acquired a considerable collection of books, so much so that Davis recalled that when he went to college he "chafed under the scrutiny and solicitude of the [University of Vermont] librarian, who seemed unnecessarily concerned about the quality of my reading."[28] Their love of romantic literature, especially Wordsworth and Whitman, may have afforded John and his brothers a deeper appreciation of the problems of the city of Burlington and the beauty of the surrounding countryside.[29] The boys hiked in the Adirondacks; camped on Mt. Mansfield, the highest peak in the Green Mountains; and explored Lake Champlain and Lake George. Dewey often spoke of the beauty of the region in his letters.[30] Their cousin John Rich, whom the Deweys raised, and James and John Buckham usually accompanied the Dewey brothers. James and John Buckham's father, Matthew Buckham, taught history, politics, and economics, and was president of the university. John and his older brother Davis began attending the local public schools in the fall of 1867. By the time John finished high school in 1874, he could read Greek and Latin, was able to speak French with local French-Canadians, and had completed two years of French grammar and composition. After graduating from high school at the ages of sixteen and fifteen, Davis and John Dewey moved on to the University of Vermont, where they gradually became aware of a wider world of American and European culture.

The Burlington Philosophy

At the University of Vermont, Dewey studied the curriculum developed by James Marsh. His first two years were given to Greek, Latin, ancient history, analytical geometry, and calculus. Contrary to the claims of some biographers, Dewey displayed an interest in philosophy, history, and political issues throughout his undergraduate years. The university's library records reveal that in his first three years he read a translation of Johann Peter Eckerman's *Conversations with Goethe*; Walter Bagehot's *Physics and Politics*, which sought to apply insights from Darwinian biology to political thought and institutions; Sir James MacKintosh's *History of the Revolution in England in 1688*; Alexis de Tocqueville's *Democracy in America*; and Richard Josiah Hinton's *English Radical Leaders*. During his sophomore year Dewey wrote an essay on municipal reform and he gave a commencement speech on the "Limits of Political Economy." Library records also demonstrate that Dewey was acquainted with the St. Louis Hegelians by 1875. The first journal he checked out of the library was the first volume of the JSP, and he later checked out volume twelve.[31] Moreover, Dewey's undergraduate mentor, H. A. P. Torrey, was a distant relative of W. T. Harris and the two had a cordial relationship.[32]

Nevertheless, Dewey experienced an intellectual awakening at the beginning of his junior year when he studied geology, zoology, and physiology under Dr. Perkins, who structured his lectures on the theory of evolution. Dewey read *Elements of Physiology* by T. H. Huxley, one of Darwin's earliest champions. He credited Huxley's text as the primary impetus to his intellectual awakening, which brought a new "sense of interdependence and interrelated unity that gave form to intellectual stirrings that had been previously inchoate, and created a type or model of a view of things to which material in any field ought to conform."[33] It is evident from the change in Dewey's reading that the theory of evolution provoked thought in the young student. In the fall of his junior year, he turned to Matthew Arnold's books as well as English reviews that were devoted to discussion of the issues of the age, most particularly the implications of science and evolution for traditional religion. He continued to read heavily during his senior year, concentrating on the novels of George Eliot, the social theory of Auguste Comte, and the writings of Herbert Spencer, whom he studied more than any other philosopher.[34] Dewey claimed he was not persuaded by Comte's arguments for a new religion or his three stages of the evolution of society, but that Comte gave him an appreciation for "the disorganized character of Western modern culture, due to a disintegrative 'individualism.'" Dewey was also impressed by Comte's proposal for a "synthesis of science that should be a regulative method of an organized social life."[35] He was not persuaded by Spencer's use of Darwin, but his study of the British philosopher prepared him for a critique of agnostic materialism that he would publish in the JSP. During these last two years at the University, Dewey was transformed into a serious student, graduating second in a class of eighteen and inducted into Phi Beta Kappa.[36]

The university's "senior year course" in moral philosophy, required for all students, reinforced Dewey's new interests in speculative and social philosophy. The course was a group of classes taught by Torrey, heir to the Burlington philosophy of James Marsh, and Buckham.[37] Buckham, who was known as a "fortress of conservatism," taught the seniors political economy and international law, and required that they read Francois Guizot's *History of Civilization.* In his own book, *The Very Elect,* Buckham displayed his elitism by denigrating the thought of the "common man," and like Dewey's pastor, Brastow, Buckham railed against the morally pernicious effects of unbridled individualism in the United States.[38] Though Dewey's later emphasis on community was consistent with the criticisms of individualism he heard as a youth, Buckham's elitism never appealed to Dewey. Torrey covered the history of philosophy, psychology, ethics, and philosophy of religion. He steadfastly required that the seniors read Coleridge's *Aids to Reflection*; the *Remains of James Marsh*; Joseph Butler's *Analogy of Religion*, which drew an analogy between God's governance of the natural world by laws and the laws of the moral universe; Plato's *Republic*; and the *Manual of Rhetoric* by the British empiricist, Alexander Bain. In Metaphysics, Torrey used *Elements of Intellectual Science* by the intuitionist, Noah Porter, and in Fine Art he used his uncle Joseph Torrey's *Theory of Fine Art.*[39]

Though in later years Dewey remembered Torrey as a Scottish intuitionist, he was most sympathetic to the heavily Kantianized intuitionism of Sir William Hamilton. Torrey was an earnest student of German idealism, having worked through Kant's three critiques in the German, but his philosophy was tailored primarily to a defense of a moderately liberal Congregational Christianity.[40] He employed Hamiltonian epistemology to argue that science, including Darwinian biology, dealt with mere phenomena, and that the noumenal truths of morality and religion could be immediately apprehended through intuition.[41] Like Kant and Hamilton, Torrey distinguished sharply between the natural and the supernatural, and man and nature. Like Marsh, Torrey was highly critical of Lockean epistemology because he held that its separation of faith and reason was subversive of religious orthodoxy, which correctly understood that faith and reason were complementary. True religion was philosophical; true philosophy was religious.[42] The Burlington philosophy, as taught by Torrey, had an abiding effect on Dewey. When Herbert Schneider and friends presented him a copy of Coleridge's *Aids to Reflection* at a birthday party late in life, Dewey recalled that the book "was our spiritual emancipation in Vermont." He added that "Coleridge's idea of the spirit came to us as a real relief, because we could be both liberal and pious; and this *Aids to Reflection* book, especially Marsh's edition, was my first Bible." When asked when he got over Coleridge, Dewey replied, "I never did. Coleridge represents pretty much my religious views still, but I quit talking about them because nobody else is interested in them."[43] As noted in the previous chapter, in Burlington Dewey imbibed a fascination with German thought and aesthetics, a developmental theory of art and beauty, a trenchant critique of Lockean individualism, a deep appreciation of nature, and an insistence on the practicality of philosophy.[44]

Graduating from the University of Vermont in 1879, Dewey spent an anxious summer looking for a teaching position. A cousin who was principal of the high school in South Oil City, Pennsylvania finally offered him a job. Dewey taught Latin, algebra, and natural science there for two years. Sixty years later he recalled that "one evening while he sat reading" in Oil City he had his one mystical experience. It came by way of "an answer to that question which still worried him: whether he really meant business when he prayed." Dewey reminisced, "It was not a very dramatic mystic experience. There was no vision, not even a definable emotion—just a supremely blissful feeling that [my] worries were over. . . . I've never had any doubts since then, nor any beliefs." This was a fairly typical religious experience for a person reared in the Burlington philosophy.[45] For Dewey, it led to a union of pure and practical reason, his philosophical and moral beliefs. He compared the experience to the poetic pantheism of Wordsworth and Whitman, claiming that he was left with a feeling that "everything that's here is here, and you can just lie back on it."[46]

In an effort to emphasize Dewey's commitment to liberal Congregationalism, Bruce Kuklick characterizes this experience as Dewey's "conversion." While it is true that Dewey remained active in the Congregational Church until 1894, he interpreted the experience primarily as a conversion to a philosophical pantheism, which went beyond the pale of liberal Congregationalism and even the Burlington philosophy, and a loss of a sense of guilt, rather than a conversion to a particular set of Christian doctrines. Dewey's description indicates that, by 1881, he believed that "any genuinely sound religious experience . . . should adapt itself to whatever beliefs one [finds] oneself intellectually entitled to hold." This mystical experience, as well as his budding interest in social issues and philosophy, is consistent with his later statement that "social interests and problems from an early period had . . . the intellectual appeal and provided the intellectual sustenance that many seem to have found primarily in religious questions."[47] In some ways Dewey's intellectual origins are reminiscent of Hegel's; both philosophers were predisposed to combine spiritual and social issues. As Neil Coughlan has said, Dewey was pious "not so much in the narrow sense of religious faith as in the broader meaning of faithfulness to an upbringing and a culture."[48] By 1890, he rejected the theological component of Burlington thought, but retained the "pragmatic perspective" that philosophy must be relevant to and tested by lived experience.[49] Because Dewey felt no compulsion to play the part of Christian apologist he may have already been considering pursuing a Ph.D. in philosophy rather than the traditional Doctor of Divinity degree.

In Oil City Dewey studied philosophy on his own and in May 1881 he sent an essay and a deferential letter to W. T. Harris, beginning a friendship that would last for almost thirty years.

> Enclosed you will find a short article on the Metaphysical Assumptions of Materialism, which I should be glad if you could make use of, in your Review. If you cannot, if you will be so kind as to inform me, stamps will be sent for its return. . . . An opinion as to whether you considered it to show ability enough of any kind to warrant my putting much of my time on that sort of subject would be thankfully received, and, as I am a young man in doubt as to how to employ my reading hours, might be of much advantage. I do not wish to ask too much of your time & attention however.
>
> Very truly yours,
>
> John Dewey[50]

Dewey finally received an apparently positive response from Harris five months later. The essay was directed against the philosophical materialism Dewey had seen defended in British journals and in the writings of Spencer. He argued that materialism was internally inconsistent; one had to adopt a covertly antimaterialistic stance in order to assert it at all. Materialism, ostensibly a monism, Dewey argued, requires one to posit the existence of material substance, which is known, and mental substance, which knows. Materialism thus smuggles in a nonmaterialistic reality and is actually a dualistic theory.

By the time the first article was published, Dewey had sent another one, "The Pantheism of Spinoza," to Harris, acknowledging that his "duties as head of the Concord Summer School must . . . keep [him] very busy," and offering to translate Rosenkranz's introduction to "Kirchmann's ed. of Hegel's Encyclopädie," which, he stated, he had "been reading recently," but it never appeared in the JSP.[51] The Spinoza article appeared in the JSP in 1882. Similarly to the previous article, Dewey argued that Spinoza's monistic pantheism was based on a concealed dualism that required him to posit the existence of finite being (particular objects) that could not be derived from "the perfect infinite and absolute being."[52]

There has been some disagreement about Dewey's philosophical commitment in these two essays. Dewey referred to the period in which they were written as his "theological and intuitional phase," and explained that the period had little, if any, "lasting influence upon my own development, except negatively."[53] Some scholars have accepted Dewey's claim that the articles displayed an allegiance to intuitionism. Others argue that Dewey was primarily Kantian in his first two publications.[54] It is difficult to reach a definitive conclusion about Dewey's philosophical allegiance from these articles because, all told, they comprised only thirteen pages in the JSP. Moreover, Dewey was not clear about whether his "theological and intuitional phase" was a Kantian or a Scottish intuitionism, or some combination thereof such as what he had seen in Torrey's

Hamiltonian intuitionism. In the latter article Dewey accused Spinoza of holding a "Dogmatic Philosophy" in the sense that Kant and Hegel used that term; Spinoza's absolute, Dewey argued, goes beyond our possible experience. The articles do demonstrate, however, that Dewey had already gained a thorough grounding in the texts and arguments of Hume, Berkeley, Spencer, Kant, and Spinoza. But as Dewey stated, the essays are "highly schematic and formal," in that they simply try to expose internal contradictions in materialism and Spinoza's monism.[55] It is interesting to note, however, Dewey's early interest in the subject of philosophical dualism, a theme that animated his writings for the next seventy years.

Dewey remarked that W. T. Harris's response to his articles "was so encouraging that it was a distinct factor in deciding me to try philosophy as a professional career." He moved back to Burlington, where he taught at Lake View Seminary during the 1881-1882 terms and spent his spare time studying classic philosophical texts and German with Torrey.[56] In 1882, Torrey adopted two new textbooks for his metaphysics course, John Watson's *Philosophy of Kant as Contained in Extracts from His Own Writings* and G. S. Morris's commentary on Kant's *Critique of Pure Reason.*[57] More than likely, Dewey studied these texts, among others, with Torrey throughout that year. Dewey remembered Torrey as "constitutionally timid," but Dewey's friend John Buckham described Torrey as a prudent thinker who refused to jump to any "unjustified inference." Dewey noted that in a conversation he had with Torrey in the mid-1880s, his mentor had commented, "pantheism is the most satisfactory form of metaphysics intellectually, but it goes counter to religious faith." Dewey speculated that Torrey's "remark told of an inner conflict that prevented his native capacity from coming to full fruition." Torrey was not as intellectually timid as Dewey remembered; in his later years, Torrey came to prefer the pessimistic philosophy of Schopenhauer.[58]

There can be little doubt that Dewey had found a knowledgeable tutor in Torrey, and although it may be true that his philosophy had not "satisf[ied] what [Dewey] was dimly reaching for," Torrey was an important influence in Dewey's philosophical development.[59] In later years Torrey adopted Dewey's neo-Hegelian *Psychology* as a textbook, but he was always critical of neo-Hegelianism, because it did "not do justice to [free] will." According to Torrey, just as scientific materialism inevitably led to determinism by accepting the necessity of physical causation, neo-Hegelianism erred by accepting the "necessity of thought."[60] In 1885 Torrey published a series of three articles on "The 'Theodicy of Leibniz,'" which show that he surely exposed Dewey to the search for a logic of life. Torrey's primary criticism of Leibniz in these articles is that his thought is too abstract to address the problems of everyday life, and that his treatment of evil as a metaphysical issue evades the more difficult concerns of the victims of evil. "Light comes more," asserted Torrey, "from living than from thinking."[61]

Dewey had reservations about dualisms he encountered in Torrey's philosophy. He believed reason and intuition can and should work together to confirm the validity of beliefs. Dewey sought a metaphysics that "would have the same properties as had the human organism in the picture of it derived from study of Huxley's treatment."[62] Although he was dissatisfied with the Burlington philosophy as articulated by Torrey, Dewey could not accept British materialistic agnosticism; he was not ready to reject the possibility of knowledge of the supernatural for almost ten more years, and he never rejected the ideal, at least as a potential to be realized. But historicist tendencies in the Burlington philosophy and emphasis on a pious life rather than Christian orthodoxy prepared Dewey for the German idealism he would embrace during his studies with Morris at Hopkins.

Baltimore

In "From Absolutism to Experimentalism," Dewey accurately noted that he took a significant risk by deciding to pursue philosophy as a career. His applications for a fellowship and a scholarship were denied; in order to finance his first year of study he borrowed five hundred dollars from an aunt.[63] Moreover, Dewey's job prospects with a Ph.D. in philosophy would be dubious at best; the majority of college philosophy professors were still ministers with seminary degrees. At Hopkins, Dewey was trained for a different type of higher education in which the disciplines were to be studied as ends in themselves rather than as means to buttress previously held beliefs. Hopkins opened in 1876 under the leadership of Daniel Coit Gilman, who took the opportunity to create the first research university in the United States, dedicated to both advanced study and path-breaking research. The realization of Gilman's plans at Hopkins revolutionized higher education in America, leading to the research university system as it exists today. Hopkins was designed, after the German model, primarily as a graduate school with specialists, emphasizing the scientific disciplines and dedicated to original research. According to C. S. Peirce, the new research university was an institution created primarily for study and research, not for instruction.[64]

The Johns Hopkins faculty was distinguished. Dewey had chosen Hopkins in order to work primarily with Morris.[65] In addition, he studied logic with Peirce, minored in history with Herbert Baxter Adams, and studied physiological psychology with Hall. Hall and Morris were both part-time lecturers at Hopkins and engaged, with Peirce, in a competitive struggle for the one full-time appointment President Gilman planned to make in philosophy. In January 1884, Dewey's second and final year, Gilman and the executive committee cancelled all part-time faculty positions, including that of Peirce and Morris, and then renewed all of them but Peirce's, apparently because of considerations based on Peirce's personal life and the committee's discomfort with his religious views.[66] At the end of the spring semester, Morris lost out to Hall because Gilman viewed Hall's psychology, unlike Morris's idealism, as more consistent with the scientific emphasis of the university, a portent of the impending decline of idealism. Though Peirce had already formulated the basis for his pragmatic method, which Dewey later regarded as brilliant, Peirce did not influence him at this time because "by Logic, Mr. Peirce means only an account of the methods of the physical sciences, put in mathematical form as far as possible." In Dewey's mind, the course was "more of a scientific, than philosophical course."[67] But Dewey was clearly influenced by the emphasis on science at Hopkins, evidenced in the work of Adams, but especially in the work of Hall.

Adams had studied with Wilhelm Roscher and Karl Knies at the University of Heidelberg.[68] Roscher is remembered as the founder of a school of thought that came to be known as the German historical school of economics. Knies was one of Roscher's early followers. Under the influence of Hegel, Roscher developed the early methodological approach of the group. He rejected the notion that there can be a universal, normative theory of economics, arguing that economic behavior was relative to historical, institutional, and cultural context. Consequently, he argued that the science of economics was inherently descriptive and interdisciplinary. Building on Hegel's philosophy of history, much of the work of the German historical school was framed in terms of stages of economic development through history. Like his German mentors, Adams advocated the scientific study of history and maintained that the disciplines of history, economics, and political science were inseparable. He envisioned his historical seminar as a "laboratory of scientific truth . . . where books are treated like mineralogical specimens, passed about from hand to hand, examined, and tested."[69] Adams also held the Teutonic-germ theory of American history. According to Adams, "the origin of the English Constitution . . . is found in the forests of Germany." "The German race," brought the ideas of freedom and democracy "to the shores of Britain" in the fifth and sixth centuries. After successfully exterminating the inferior Celtic Britons, the descendents of the Teutons carried the seed of liberal democracy to the fertile soil of New England in the seventeenth century, where it blossomed into the New England town meeting.[70]

In a letter to W. T. Harris, Dewey described his minor with Adams as lacking in "the philosophic side" of the subject. Dewey wrote that "The philosophy of history and of social ethics in its widest sense is untouched, & as long as it remains so, they don't get more than half the good of their own courses it seems to me."[71] Although he was surrounded by it, Dewey was less inclined to overt Eurocentrism than Hegel and the St. Louis Hegelians, having no patience with theories of Teutonic or Anglo-Saxon superiority. During his "Hegelian" phase, Dewey claimed that the theory of evolution provided no justification for "bald Anglo-Saxon" talk "about the goal of the process of evolution being a goal for man," because man is merely "one form through which the course of evolution passes." He remained critical of notions of Anglo-Saxon superiority throughout his entire life.[72] Nevertheless, Dewey was impressed by the notion of scientific history. In 1938 he maintained that "the first task in historical inquiry, as in any inquiry, is that of controlled observations . . . the collection of data and their confirmation as authentic." According to Dewey, scientific methodology was the strength of "modern historiography." Historians had learned to treat ideas and meanings "as hypotheses" just like any other "physical inquiry that leads to a definite conclusion."[73]

Hall's impact on Dewey was more profound than Adams's. Dewey took all of Hall's graduate courses and did laboratory research in psychology while at Hopkins.[74] Hall's lectures encouraged Dewey to study experimental psychology, and the publication of Dewey's *Psychology* in 1887 testifies to the depth of his knowledge in that field.[75] Hall had worked with Trendelenburg, but was influenced primarily by the German philosopher's respect for empirical study, particularly in the natural sciences and in psychology. Trendelenburg's emphasis on development and process led Hall into a temporary Hegelian period that confirmed his belief in the fundamental importance of historical process. His studies in Germany cut short by the outbreak of the Franco-Prussian War in 1870, Hall returned to the United States where he tried to form a relationship with W. T. Harris and the St. Louis Hegelians. Harris published portions of Hall's translation of Rosenkranz's commentary on Hegel in the JSP in 1872, 1873, and 1874, but soon thereafter Hall began to move away from idealism in favor of the evolutionary and positivist philosophies of Spencer, Comte, and Comte's American disciple, David Goodman Croly. Hall gradually became hostile to Hegelianism; Dorothy Ross reports that in 1894, he went so far as to tell Josiah Royce at a professional meeting that his Hegelianism was intellectual masturbation. Nevertheless, as late as 1884 Hall was willing to work with Harris on the national Committee on Pedagogics. But his study of Spencer's *Principles of Psychology* (1870) and Wilhelm Wundt's *Grundzuge der physiologischen Psychologie* (1874) in the mid-1870s encouraged Hall to look for physiological explanations of the development of human consciousness as a natural product of evolution.[76]

In 1876 Hall went to Harvard to pursue further graduate study in the new experimental psychology with assistant professor of physiology, William James. From James, Hall learned to view thought as functional and the mind as dynamic. At James's urging Hall returned to Germany in 1878. During this second sojourn he studied with Hermann von Helmholtz and Wundt. Helmholtz convinced Hall that psychology should be seen as a branch of physiology rather than philosophy because human behavior would eventually be explained solely by reference to physical-chemical processes. Hall also absorbed the ideals and methods of scientific research that pervaded German universities.[77] By the time Dewey arrived at Hopkins, Hall was widely recognized as a leading expert in educational and child psychology.

Morris alternated between teaching at the University of Michigan in the spring and at Hopkins during the fall. During his first semester at Hopkins, Dewey took three of Morris's courses—History of Philosophy in Great Britain, Philosophy of History, and Science of Knowledge Seminary—and he was certainly the primary influence on Dewey at this time, and for several years after, as they both taught philosophy at the University of Michigan. Morris had accepted idealism after a brief flirtation with British empiricism, even embracing materialism for a short while. By the mid-1870s Morris was an active member of the American Hegelian school of thought. He knew W. T. Harris well; the two corresponded from 1874 until Morris's death in 1889, and he lectured on Kant at the Concord Summer School in 1881. Harris published several of Morris's original contributions to philosophy in the JSP, printed reviews of his books, and in 1877 reported on his courses of lectures at Hopkins. In 1881 Morris became the general editor of the new S. C. Griggs's "German Philosophical Classics" series, which was "devoted to the critical exposition of some one masterpiece belonging to the history of German philosophy." The series included two volumes by Morris, one by Dewey, and one by Harris.[78]

As he studied with Trendelenburg, Morris began to develop his own version of Aristotelianized idealism, but it is crucial to point out that Morris was neither a disciple of Trendelenburg nor of Hegel. According to Dewey, Trendelenburg was greatly influenced by German idealism, especially "the ideas . . . of the correlation of thought and being, the idea of man as a self-realizing personality, [and] the notion of organized society as the objective reality of man." Morris also accepted these idealist doctrines. But as I noted in the previous chapter, Trendelenburg was very critical of Hegel. In the same vein, Dewey noted that Morris "used sometimes in later years to point out pages in his copy of Hegel which were marked 'nonsense,' etc., remarks made while he was a student in Germany." But Morris, Dewey explained, found "in Hegel (in his own words) 'the most profound and comprehensive of modern thinkers.'"[79]

R. M. Wenley, Morris's first biographer, depicted Morris as opposed to the application of science to philosophical issues, but in fact Trendelenburg convinced him that philosophical inquiry must be informed by the findings of science.[80] In a letter to Wenley, Dewey commented that Morris's "objective and ethical idealism" united Aristotle, Fichte, and Hegel. "From Hegel," Dewey wrote, "Morris derived his method," but the "purely technical aspects" of the dialectic did not interest him. Rather, Morris was attracted to Hegel's emphasis upon "the organic relationship of subject and object, intelligence and the world . . . the supreme instance of the union of opposites in a superior synthesis." From all three philosophers, Dewey explained, Morris derived an ethical idealism, the conviction that man's search for truth was a moral struggle for the actualization of ideals that required active intelligence. From Aristotle's realism, he learned to scorn "the problem of the existence of the external and physical world," believing that "the philosophical problem concerned its nature, not its existence." Interestingly, Morris could have learned all three of these lessons from Hegel. Rather than viewing "Kant as the source of the idealistic faith," Dewey continued, Morris "tended to treat him rather as a phenomenalist, an agnostic, and found the root of his unconquered subjectivism in his original 'mechanical' separation of subject and object." From Aristotle, Fichte, and Hegel together, Morris absorbed the conviction that reality was teleological in character.[81]

Dewey readily embraced Morris's Hegelianism. Hegel's vision of reality as an organic whole collapsed the dualisms Dewey was struggling with, allowing him to avoid the dichotomy between the natural and the supernatural in Torrey's philosophy, and to counter British empiricism's agnosticism about the ideal and infinite. Yet Dewey could not embrace fully Trendelenburg's naturalism at this time. More so than Trendelenburg, Morris and Dewey sought to maintain an image of a reality with a universal, spiritual purpose, rather than a "mere mechanical aggregate" of particular purposes.[82] Both men continued to maintain that everything that happened in the world was part of a dynamic developmental process. Morris illustrated the process by claiming, like Hegel, that the history of philosophy was not a succession of isolated systems of thought, but a continuum of the absolute spirit's self-development in which progress was made as more inclusive insights were articulated and proven. The emergence of science was an important demonstration of the absolute spirit's development toward full self-consciousness.[83]

In a letter to Torrey, written a month after the fall semester began, Dewey stated that Morris "is a pronounced idealist—and we have already heard of the 'universal self.'" Dewey elaborated on Morris's philosophy, as he understood it so far: Morris argued that philosophy must choose between "two starting points." The first "regards subject & object as in mechanical relation, relations in and of space & time, & the process of knowledge is simply impact of the object upon the subject with resulting sensations and impressions." Though this view may seem to account for knowledge, it cannot account for being, "since nothing exists for the subject except these impressions or states, nothing can be known of real being, and the result is scepticism, or subj. idealism, or agnosticism." The other starting point "takes the facts & endeavors to explain them—that is to show what is necessarily involved in knowledge, and results in the conclusion that subj. & object are in organic relations; neither having reality apart from the other."[84] As explained by Dewey, Morris's approach to the problems of epistemology was the same as Hegel's, who, in the introduction to the *Phenomenology of Spirit,* denied that they were exclusively theoretical problems. Morris also assumed that there was an existential and cultural dimension to these issues.

Morris's influence on Dewey is evident in a paper Dewey read to the University Metaphysical Club entitled "Knowledge and the Relativity of Feeling." The paper, inspired by Morris's course in British philosophy, was subsequently published in the January 1883 issue of the JSP. Dewey explained to W. T. Harris that in this paper he "attempted to apply to one of the phases of Sensationalism the same kind of argument which [he] used regarding Materialism."[85] Specifically, Dewey criticized contemporary theories of knowledge, which hold that all knowledge is relative, by focusing on the premise that feelings are relative. Dewey used the word "feelings" to denote all of the contents of consciousness, including sensations and thoughts. According to the theory of the relativity of knowledge, Dewey explained, external objects cause feelings, and feelings express the way sentient beings are affected by objects. Since feelings are the exclusive contents of consciousness, knowledge can only be derived from feelings, and feelings are relative to the subject. Because feelings are relative, all knowledge is relative. "Relative," Dewey explained, means conditioned, subjective, and phenomenal. That is to say, feelings are relative because they depend on the current state of the feeling subject in addition to the object of which they are an effect. Thus feelings can only provide information about phenomenal reality, reality as it is experienced rather than as it is in itself.[86]

Dewey noted that positivists who believed in historical relativism held the theory of the relativity of feeling, as did Hamilton and his followers, and "associationalists" like Hume, but that the theory of evolution had given it new force. Evolution, an established scientific theory, entailed the emergent theory of mind.[87] Consciousness emerged "from the lowest form of life, or from matter," and thus is not handed down to humanity from on high, but is "conditioned by the state and quality of the organism. . . . [Consciousness] is therefore relative to the subject."[88] Existence, as it is in itself, is unknowable because our apprehension of it is conditioned by our current state of evolutionary development. In this way the theory of evolution bolstered historical relativism by lending it the authority of science.

The crux of Dewey's argument is that the theory of the relativity of feeling fails because, although it purports to be a theory about human psychology, it is also an ontological theory that assumes that being is independent of thought. But if feeling and knowledge are relative, then those who believe in the relativity of feeling are barred from ontology. According to Dewey, it is logically "suicidal" to assert that feelings, and hence all knowledge claims, are relative, and the universal claim that thought and being are ontologically distinct or that all knowledge comes from sensations.[89] Dewey argued that we could only know if feelings are relative if we have knowledge of something that is not relative, an absolute. He quoted Spencer, who admitted that the theory depends on the notion of an absolute, which is, according to the theory, unknowable. Dewey agreed with empiricists that feelings are relative, but maintained that we can only know this if there is something beyond feeling in thought. Consciousness must somehow transcend feeling to an absolute. One reason this essay is useful is that it provides our first clue about what Dewey meant by the absolute, a key term in his early thought; it is that which is not relative, not conditioned by our feelings or our perceptions.

Not only did Dewey claim that the theory of the relativity of feeling requires an absolute object, but "that this object must be . . . specifically related to the content of consciousness," and we must know something about what that absolute object is.[90] Though relative, feeling must transcend itself to an absolute; otherwise we would not be able to know that it is relative. Feeling is within consciousness, and consciousness cannot get outside of itself to contact an absolute any more than "a man can stand on his own shoulders, or outstrip his shadow." Feeling is able to contact an absolute because the absolute is within consciousness. From this argument Dewey concluded that the theory of the relativity of feeling "is compatible only with a theory which admits the constitutive power of Thought, as itself ultimate Being, determining objects." Consciousness, according to Dewey, experiences both feelings and objective reality, compares them, and judges feelings to be relative. Thought is grounded in the absolute, a self-conscious, constitutive, ultimate being. Feelings are relative to the absolute, but all relations are internal to the absolute, thus it is not relative to anything else. As Dewey explained,

> And . . . since this self-consciousness is the ground and source of relations, it cannot be subject to them. It is itself the true Absolute, then. This does not mean that it is the Unrelated, but that it is not conditioned by those conditions which determine its objects.[91]

It is revealing to note that in this essay Dewey articulated a classic idealist argument against empiricism. The critical idealist assumption in Dewey's argument is that we can only account for knowledge if being has something in common with thought. In his previous essay, Dewey noted that Spinoza had attempted "to show the unity between the Absolute and the seeming relative by the hypothesis of the Absolute alone," but had failed to derive the existence of finite things.[92] Spinoza's "identity" philosophy had affirmed the unity of reality, but at the expense of the diversity we encounter in everyday experience.[93] In "Knowledge and the Relativity of Feeling," Dewey assumed finite things and feelings exist within the realm of absolute consciousness, thus they are related to one another because they are internal relations of absolute consciousness itself. The absolute is the union of thought and being. If thought and being have nothing in common, Dewey and other idealists have claimed, then there is no way to explain the existence of a world apart from thought. According to Berkeley, Locke had erred by positing the existence of material substance as the source of our ideas about the material world while claiming that it was impossible to know what it was because it was an "outer" reality removed from the "inner" reality of consciousness. Hegel voiced the same critique of Kant's postulation of the noumenal realm.[94] And just two years prior to Dewey's presentation of "Knowledge and the Relativity of Feeling," Morris employed the same argument in *British Thought and Thinkers.*

For Morris, empiricists from Locke through Spencer were all ontological agnostics because they believed that sense data originates in an unknowable realm, and that we can only know phenomena as modified by our perceptual apparatus. Morris rejected Berkeley's answer to Locke, however. Berkeley had "penetrate[d] the clouds which bounded Locke's mental horizon," and transformed them into "celestial forms of light" by denying the reality of matter and affirming a theological monism.[95] Like Spinoza, Berkeley had denied the reality of finite things. Morris argued that immaterial thought and material being could only come into relation through some middle or common term that accounts for the reality and uniqueness of both.

> Knowledge as the union of thought and being, can be possible only in virtue of something which belongs equally to these two, something in which each resembles the other. And since thought is essentially active, this element common to thought and being must be some form of activity.[96]

Morris preferred Hegel's idealism, which affirmed that material objects exist, but are related to thought within a larger whole. Moreover, Morris agreed with Hegel's conviction that the need for a factor common to both thought and being means material objects are not "petrified" as they are in British thought.[97] The primary error of British philosophy, declared Morris, carried into German thought by Kant but corrected by the post-Kantian idealists, was the conviction that thought and being are ontologically distinct, one living and one inert. Morris consistently maintained throughout his philosophical career that acceptance of this dualism led to "an inextricable maze of contradictions."[98]

Dewey's ready conversion to Morris's idealism, coupled with the fact that he was the only student majoring in the history of philosophy, established him as Morris's prize pupil. Before he left for Michigan that December, Morris managed to get Dewey appointed to teach the undergraduate course in the history of philosophy in the following spring semester. During the spring semester Dewey presented two papers to the Metaphysical Club. The first was "Hegel and the Theory of Categories," but it is lost and there is no evidence from Dewey's letters about its content. The second paper, prepared primarily for presentation to the committee administering graduate fellowships for the academic year 1883-84, was a Hegelian criticism of Kant titled, "Kant and Philosophic Method." The latter paper won Dewey the fellowship for which he applied and was published a year later in the JSP.

In "Kant and Philosophic Method," Dewey acknowledged that Kant's method was a revolutionary turning point in the history of philosophy, and argued that Hegel completed the revolution Kant began. Kant had combined the philosophical methods of rationalists like Descartes, "the method of 'intellectualism,'" and of British empiricism. The rationalists analyzed concepts according to the laws of formal logic—non-contradiction, excluded middle, and the law of identity. They sought to discover truth by analyzing problems "down to those simple elements which cannot be thought away, and reach a judgment whose predicate may be clearly and distinctly seen to be identical with its subject." Hume showed Kant, however, that formal logic could not explain causation, "how one thing should arise out of another, when it is not connected with it." Dewey described the analytic method of the rationalists as "the method for pure thought," and agreed "it does not give any means for passing from thought to existence." "Reality," Dewey affirmed, "is added to our notions from without, not evolved from them."[99]

Dewey argued that Kant correctly supplemented the method of rationalism with the empiricists' conviction that experience "adds reality or existence to our thoughts." Dewey described the method of empiricism as "Analysis of perceptions with agreement as criterion."[100] Rather than conceptions, empiricism begins with analysis of perceptions and examines their agreement with reality. But empiricists were immobilized, Dewey claimed, by the indirect theory of perception, which entailed that we never experience reality, but only our perceptions of reality. Consequently, the empiricists could not explain how we get beyond our perceptions to external reality, nor could they adequately define agreement. How does the mind connect perceptions with external reality; how does it associate simple ideas such as "solidity" and "shape" into complex ideas like "chair," and how does it examine the adequacy of these connections? How does the mind synthesize simple ideas into mental representations of the complex things of experience?

Kant's great insight, Dewey asserted, was that "knowledge is synthesis, and the explanation of knowledge or truth must be found in the explanation of synthesis." Kant proposed that "when applied to a material given it," thought becomes synthetic. Thought connects the rhapsody of particulars we encounter in our experience through its conceptual, categorial apparatus. Kant's project, then, was to show that the categories used by the mind to synthesize the particulars of experience were not merely subjective, but objective. Kant did this by arguing that the categories make experience and its objects possible.[101] To Hume's question of how we can experience causation, Kant answered that experience is impossible without synthetic notions such as causation.

In his examination of the system of categories, Kant argued that they are "functions of a higher unity which is subject to none of them," Kant's "synthetic unity of Apperception or . . . self-consciousness." We know the categories are true, or objectively valid, and that there is a unity of apperception, because experience would not be possible otherwise. Moreover, we judge whether or not particular experiences are true, or objective, by reference to the categories. Hence Kant's explanation of the categories and experience was circular, because "the relation of categories to experience is the relation of members of an organism to a whole." The categories and experience are inseparably related. After Kant's discovery, philosophic "Method will consist in making out a complete table of these categories in all their mutual relations."[102]

For Dewey, Hegel correctly understood that Kant erred by assuming that the categories constitute experience "out of a foreign material to which they bear a purely external relation." Although the categories make our experience possible, we have no compelling reason to believe that they bear a necessary connection to objective reality, the noumenal world. "It is, Hegel says, as if one ascribed correct insight to a person, and then added that he could see only into the untruth, not the truth." Hegel demonstrated that Kant led us to believe that we could know the categories and how they are organically related to self-consciousness, but in fact we cannot examine the transcendental unity of apperception as it is because it is in the noumenal realm, necessarily modified by our conceptual apparatus. "Hence, it appears that our picture of a method was doubly false," Dewey argued, because our conceptual apparatus makes the noumenal realm, the realm of absolute truth, unavailable, and because the self that we seek to understand is a noumenal reality.[103]

For Dewey, and Hegel, Kant had retained a crucial error of modern philosophy by assuming that thought operates "upon matter foreign to it." Dewey maintained that "to Reason itself, nothing is given in the sense of being foreign to it." The self and the things it experiences, Dewey continued, are both "constituted by the categories" within the "synthetic unity of apperception or self-consciousness" which "is the real subject, and the so-called subject and object are but the forms in which it expresses its own activity."[104]

Dewey concluded the essay with a brief account of Hegel's dialectic, "the completed Method of Philosophy."[105] According to Dewey's Hegelian theory of mind, "the relation of subject and object is . . . but the first form in which Reason manifests that it is both synthetic and analytic; that it separates itself from itself, that it may thereby reach higher unity with itself."[106] In the process of alienation and return, experience begins with analysis, during which reason differentiates or denies itself. That is to say, reason discovers internal contradictions, instabilities, within its current stage of development. Reason then seeks synthesis, apprehension of the other, the external object to be known, and brings the other into itself. All knowledge then is growth, the subject attaining higher unity by sublation of the other. And in this essay Dewey agreed with one of Hegel's most controversial claims, that in the dialectic, "each lower category is not destroyed, but retained—but retained at its proper value." Dewey believed, contra Trendelenburg and the personal idealists, that Hegel's dialectic maintained unity in diversity; it maintained the identity and value of the particulars of experience, while at the same time synthesizing them into higher unities.

Though his dissertation is lost, Dewey apparently chose to develop the previous paper on Kant.[107] He explained to W. T. Harris that he planned to analyze Kant's psychology,

> that is, his psychology of spirit (so far as he has any) or the subjective side of his theory of knowledge, in which besides giving a general acc't. of his theory of Sense, Imagination, etc., I hope to be able to point out that he had the conception of Reason or Spirit as the center and organic unity of the entire sphere of man's experience, and that in so far as he is true to this conception that he is the true founder of modern philosophic method, but that in so far as he was false to it he fell into his own defects, contradictions, etc.[108]

We can assume from this statement and from "Kant and Philosophic Method" that Dewey argued that Kant's defects were corrected by Hegel's vision of subject and object existing as moments within the dialectical development of organic unity. It is also noteworthy that, very early, Dewey expressed an interest in Hegel's philosophy of spirit, whereas the British neo-Hegelians focused on Hegel's logic and were inclined to view him as a grand metaphysician deducing the categories of reality rather than of experience. Within a few years, Dewey's regard for Hegel's philosophy of spirit led him to study the *Phenomenology of Spirit* for himself, and thus to become highly critical of the neo-Hegelian's willingness to posit a transcendent reality.

Though Hall certainly piqued Dewey's interest in psychology, the psychological positions he sought to articulate were more indebted to Morris than to Hall. When he first began to study the new psychology with Hall, Dewey wrote to H. A. P. Torrey: "I don't see any very close connection between it & Phil. but I suppose it will furnish grist for the mill, if nothing else." The further he proceeded into his studies with Hall, however, the more excited he became about the new psychology and its implications for philosophy.[109]

In November Dewey described to Torrey a paper on psychology that he presented to the Metaphysical Club. The paper was about "the relations of conscious and unconscious activities and the very great importance of the latter." Dewey vaguely explained that he had come to believe that "All our psychical activity . . . is based on activities which do not as such come into consciousness . . . and that our ethical nature is conditioned similarly." Interestingly, Dewey claimed that he was "surprised to see how [he] was led to conclusions essentially identical with those of 'transcendentalism.'" His conclusions were that "all 'states' of consciousness" are dependent upon

> a permanent identical self-consciousness, which as such doesn't exist in time, but which by its constant activities . . . is continually differentiating itself into 'states' or successive conscious*nesses;* and that on the other hand these successive states are the realization of this self consciousness so that it really has no existence except in and through them [emphasis in the original].

Moreover, Dewey asserted, "any state of consciousness contains in itself both subject and object." Consciousness "is all there is, and there is nothing beyond it or behind it." Dewey told Torrey that he intended to develop the paper into his Ph.D. thesis.[110] This letter supports the conclusion that Dewey's dissertation argued that Hegel completed Kant's method by emphasizing reason or spirit as the consciousness in which subject and object exist. This is also our first evidence that Dewey accepted the neo-Hegelians' transcendent absolute, a position he held until 1891.

In early March 1884, Dewey presented a paper entitled "The New Psychology" to the Metaphysical Club. An eloquent appraisal of the new developments in psychology, the essay was printed later that year in the *Andover Review*. The paper began with praise for the new psychology's willingness to spurn the "unity and simplicity" of the old, introspective psychology, and its embrace of the complexity of reality. Dewey particularly attacked the British empiricists for dissecting experience and oversimplifying mental life. The empiricists analyzed thought abstractly, dividing the flux of experience into isolated, atomic sensations, ideas, or autonomous faculties. These earlier psychologists reflected "the *Zeitgeist* of their age, the age of the eighteenth-century and the *Aufklärung,* which found nothing difficult, which hated mystery and complexity, which believed with all its heart in principles, the simpler and more abstract the better, and which had the passion of completion."[111]

But optimism is the keynote of the essay as Dewey outlined the characteristics of the new psychology. The "New Psychology," Dewey maintained, represented a shift away from abstract, clear principles toward "organized, systematic, tireless study into the secrets of nature, which, counting nothing common or unclean, thought no drudgery beneath it, or rather thought nothing drudgery."[112] The most important factor in the development of the new psychology, he suggested, was the growth of physiology and physiological psychology, both of which used the new method of experimentation to supplement and correct the old method of introspection. Another important influence, as he saw it, was that of biology and its twin explanatory conceptions of the organism and its environment. For Dewey, these concepts complemented the philosophical developments of Hegel and made it impossible to think of experience or the mind as "an individual, isolated thing developing in a vacuum."[113]

Once again, Dewey employed the concept of organism to defend idealism and attack mechanistic empiricism, but now he also used it to emphasize the importance of the social environment. The new psychology, Dewey maintained, acquired added scope and vitality from the growth of the social and historical sciences. Dynamic, vital, and realistic in its approach, the new psychology, declared Dewey, abandoned all preconceived abstract ideas, placed the organism in its environment, and threw itself upon experience, "believing that the mother which [had] born it would not betray it."[114] His commitment to organicism ultimately led Dewey to conclude that all psychology is social psychology. The conclusion of this essay combined Dewey's idealism with his excitement about the new psychology by claiming that the functionalism of the new psychology is "intensely ethical" in its tendencies, viewing life as an organism in which immanent ideals or purposes realize themselves and make possible for the first time an adequate account of man's religious nature and experience.

Neil Coughlan has argued that some of "The New Psychology" appears to have been inspired by the Andover Liberal theologian Newman Smyth. Kuklick seized Coughlan's lead, arguing that this similarity, coupled with evidence drawn from Dewey's next four publications, demonstrated that, during these years, Dewey sought to provide a philosophical foundation for liberal theology. But Coughlan offers no evidence that Dewey read Smyth's work and Rockefeller is correct to view Morris and Hall as the most likely sources for the ideas Dewey expressed in this essay. Westbrook also states that he is not persuaded by Coughlan's argument for Smyth's "direct influence" on Dewey.[115] The similarities between Smyth and Dewey's writings were most likely a result of their working in a similar intellectual milieu. Smyth and Dewey's Burlington pastor, Brastow, were both influenced by Samuel Harris's emphasis on religious experience over correct doctrine and the Andover Liberals were well versed in nineteenth-century German thought, both idealism and the new experimental psychology of Wundt and Helmholtz. Even Denton Snider, as I have noted, sought to merge the new psychology with Hegelian idealism. Dewey, Snider, and Smyth were all engaged in what many thought to be the most important philosophical task of the time, interpreting the findings of experimental psychology within a philosophical framework that would demonstrate their deeper significance.[116]

The papers Dewey published at Hopkins made his early project clear. He planned to combine idealism and the new psychology in an organic view of man and his environment that would make sensationalism and formalism obsolete and would retain a place for the spiritual, or moral, side of human experience. The Burlington philosophy, with its developmental aesthetics and opposition to British empiricism, had predisposed Dewey to post-Kantian idealism, which he readily embraced as a graduate student at Johns Hopkins. Moreover, Dewey's liberal religious beliefs, with emphasis on behavior rather than correct doctrine, made it easy for him to entertain a philosophy, such as Hegel's, that was closely associated with heterodox religion. Dewey's fascination with Comte's analysis of modernity, and his early critique of dualisms, reveals the problem that animated all of his philosophical work. Though Kuklick and Rockefeller see Dewey as an essentially religious thinker, his primary motivation was the healing of philosophical dichotomies and man's alienation from nature and from his fellow man. At Hopkins, however, Dewey took an interest in Hegel's philosophy of spirit and thus viewed Hegel's thought as a study of human experience rather than the categories of reality itself. In the following chapter I contend that, although Dewey had some initial allegiance to British neo-Hegelianism, he quickly broke with that tradition and came to read and appropriate Hegel more as a phenomenologist than as a metaphysician. This philosophical move allowed Dewey to successfully combine his idealism with the new psychology.

Notes

1. Dewey, "Context and Thought" (1931), LW 6: 7. Herbert Schneider comments that "We tried to get [Dewey] to reminisce. And it was very difficult. I think on principle Dewey wouldn't reminisce. He liked to look forward to the future, and he certainly liked to keep *au courant* with the present. But to get him to reminisce about his early days was very difficult." Corliss Lamont, ed., *Dialogue on John Dewey* (New York: Horizon Press, 1959), 15.

2. Jane Dewey, "Biography of John Dewey," in *The Philosophy of John Dewey,* ed. Paul Arthur Schilpp (Evanston, IL: Northwestern University Press, 1939), 3.

3. Dewey, "From Absolutism to Experimentalism" (1930), LW 5: 153.

4. Jane Dewey, "Biography of John Dewey," 7.

5. Feuer was at the University of Vermont from 1951-1957. See his interesting discussion of his fascination with the life of Dewey in "A Narrative of Personal Events and Ideas" in *Philosophy, History and Social Action: Essays in Honor of Lewis Feuer,* eds. Sydney Hook, William O'Neill, and Roger O'Toole (Boston: Kluwer, 1988), 35-37. Feuer was particularly intrigued with the psychological issue of why Dewey, ostensibly a staid Vermonter, should be such a progressive thinker and drawn all his life to flamboyant personalities.

6. Although much of his research is quite useful, Jay Martin tends to go beyond the available evidence in his speculation about Dewey's psychological struggles in *The Education of John Dewey: A Biography* (New York: Columbia University Press, 2002).

7. John Randall adds to Schneider's comment that Dewey told friends "I don't see why you fellows want to go back to summer places in Vermont, I got out as soon as I could." Lamont, ed. *Dialogue on John Dewey,* 89. Cf. Bob Pepperman Taylor, "John Dewey in Vermont: A Reconsideration," *Soundings* 75, no. 1 (Spring 1992): 175-198.

8. Charles T. Morrissey, *Vermont: A History* (New York: W. W. Norton, 1981), 123.

9. *The Vermont Cynic* 67 (1949): 2. Cf. Feuer's discussion in "H. A. P. Torrey and John Dewey," *American Quarterly* 10 (1958): 34-54.

10. The most important sources on Dewey's youth are Neil Coughlan, *Young John Dewey: An Essay in American Intellectual History* (Chicago: University of Chicago Press, 1973); Jane Dewey, "Biography of John Dewey"; George Dykhuizen, *The Life and Mind of John Dewey* (Carbondale: Southern Illinois University Press, 1973); and Robert B. Westbrook, *John Dewey and American Democracy* (Ithaca: Cornell University Press, 1991). Unless otherwise indicated, the factual material in the account of Dewey's boyhood is drawn from these sources.

11. See the comparison of Dewey to Husserl and Maurice Merleau-Ponty in Victor Kestenbaum, *The Phenomenological Sense of John Dewey* (Atlantic Heights, NJ: Humanities Press, 1977). Dewey's only mention of Husserl appears in "Syllabus: Types of Philosophic Thought" (1921), MW 13: 351.

12. James T. Kloppenberg, *Uncertain Victory: Social Democracy and Progressivism in European and American Thought, 1870-1920* (Oxford: Oxford University Press, 1986), 3-11.

13. Sydney Hook, *John Dewey: An Intellectual Portrait* (New York: Prometheus Books, 1995), 5. Dewey's daughters also idealized Burlington in their "Biography of John Dewey." For more accurate discussions of politics and society in Burlington see Lewis Feuer in "H. A. P. Torrey and John Dewey," 34-54; and Taylor, "John Dewey in Vermont: A Reconsideration," 175.

14. See Matthew Buckham's indignant defense of the "Old Americans'" aristocracy as homegrown, "not imported from Beacon Street or Fifth Avenue." Because these families "cleared the woods, raised the first corn, built the first houses, established the first churches and schools . . . drove out the Yorkers and kept out the Britishers" they were "entitled to have their names and achievements kept in remembrance as long as any family pride can perpetuate them." Buckham, "Burlington as a Place to Live In," *The Vermont Historical Gazeteer* 1, no. 8 (1867): 724. In 1870 Henry James was struck by the number of Catholic French Canadians in Burlington. Mary Jane Harvey, "Henry James Describes Vermont," *Vermont History* 23 (1955): 348.

15. Robert Wiebe, *The Search for Order, 1877-1920* (New York: Hill and Wang, 1967).

16. The first-born son, named John Archibald, died in a tragic accident at the age of two and half. After he had fallen backward into a pail of scalding water, his parents tried to treat his wounds "swathing him in 'sweet oil and cotton batting,'" but the dressing caught fire and the boy died the following morning as a consequence of his burns. Coughlan, *Young John Dewey*, 3. Nine months after this traumatic event John Dewey, the subject of this book, was born, presumably as a replacement child (although he had no middle name).

17. Jane Dewey, "Biography of John Dewey," 6. Davis received the A.B. from the University of Vermont in 1879, the same year as John, and his Ph.D. in 1886, two years after John. He quickly found employment at MIT where he was an instructor of history and political science from 1886 to 1888, professor of economics and statistics from 1888 to 1933, and chair of the Department of Economics from 1893 to 1933.

18. Coughlan, *The Young John Dewey*, 4. Jane Dewey, "Biography of John Dewey," 5.

19. Lewis S. Feuer, "Prefatory Note," to "A Vermont Boyhood" by John Wright Buckham, *Vermont History* 30, no. 3 (July 1962): 202.

20. Sidney Hook, *Education and the Taming of Power* (LaSalle, IL: Open Court, 1973), 141-142. Cf. Feuer, "H. A. P. Torrey and John Dewey," 51-52.

21. Sidney Hook, "Some Memories of John Dewey," *Commentary* 14 (September 1952): 246.

22. George Dykhuizen discovered that in an 1899 novel, Lucina Dewey was depicted as "Mrs. Carver," a "wise and understanding counselor of college youths" who was "as solicitous of their moral and spiritual good as of their academic welfare." Elvirton Wright, *Freshman and Senior* (Boston: Congregational Sunday-School and Publishing Society, 1899). Dykhuizen, *The Life and Mind of John Dewey*, 7.

23. Cf. Martin, *The Education of John Dewey*, 7ff.

24. Archibald Sprague Dewey and Lucina A. Rich Dewey to John Dewey, 22 September 1882; Archibald Sprague Dewey to John Dewey, 16 October 1882; Archibald Sprague Dewey to John Dewey, 2 May 1883; Archibald Sprague Dewey to John Dewey, 21 October 1885; Archibald Sprague Dewey to John Dewey, 6 January 1886.

25. See Hook, *Education and the Taming of Power*, 141; Jane Dewey, "Biography of John Dewey," 26; and Feuer "H. A. P. Torrey and John Dewey," 52.

26. Jane Dewey, "Biography of John Dewey," 26. Cf. Willinda Savage, "The Evolution of John Dewey's Philosophy of Experimentalism as Developed at the University of Michigan" (Ph.D. diss., University of Michigan, 1950), 25-26. Steven C. Rockefeller, *John Dewey: Religious Faith and Democratic Humanism* (New York: Columbia University Press, 1991), 34-35.

27. Quoted in Frank C. Porter, "Lewis Orsmond Brastow, D.D.," *Yale Divinity Quarterly* 9 (January 1913): 75. Cf. Frederick William Whittaker, *Samuel Harris: American Theologian* (New York: Vantage Press, 1982), 9; George Harris, "The Function of the Christian Consciousness," *Andover Review* 2 (October 1884): 343; and Daniel Day Williams, *The Rise of the Andover Liberals* (New York: Octagon Books, 1941; reprint, Dallas, TX: Taylor Publishing Co., 1970), 42. Thomas Dalton also overestimates the extent to which Calvinism oppressed Dewey in Burlington, because he neglects to examine Brastow and the possibility that he offset the evangelicalism of Dewey's mother. Dalton, *Becoming John Dewey: Dilemmas of a Philosopher and Naturalist* (Bloomington: Indiana University Press, 2002), 25-27.

28. Quoted in Feuer, "H. A. P. Torrey and John Dewey," 48.

29. Much to his credit, Steven Rockefeller has done a great deal to demonstrate the importance of romanticism to Dewey's intellectual development. Rockefeller, *John Dewey*, 29-75.

30. Dewey to Alice Chipman, 6 August 1885; Dewey to John Wright Buckham, 9 December 1929. Cf. Jane Dewey, "Biography of John Dewey," 8.

31. Lewis S. Feuer, "John Dewey's Reading at College," *Journal of the History of Ideas* 19, no. 3 (June 1958): 416.

32. Lewis S. Feuer, "Letters from the Past: Letters of H. A. P. Torrey to William T. Harris," *Vermont History* 25, no. 3 (July 1957): 215-219. Though only three letters of their correspondence remain, and all of those were written in the late 1890s, they give evidence of a longer friendship.

33. Dewey, "From Absolutism to Experimentalism" (1930), LW 5: 147.

34. Lewis S. Feuer, "John Dewey's Reading at College," 415-421.

35. Dewey, "From Absolutism to Experimentalism," (1930), LW 5: 154.

36. Feuer, "John Dewey's Reading at College," 415-421.

37. Dewey, "From Absolutism to Experimentalism" (1930), LW 5: 147.

38. Levi P. Smith, "A Masterpiece in Living," in Matthew Buckham, *The Very Elect* (Boston: Pilgrim Press, 1912), 5. Cf. Lewis O. Brastow, "Comments about a Divorce Reform Bill," *Burlington Free Press* (16 February 1884): 1. Guizot's history was published in English in 1867; a new edition was released in 1877, one year before Dewey

took the senior year course. Francois Pierre Guillaume Guizot, *General History of Civilization in Europe, from the Fall of the Roman Empire to the French Revolution* (New York: D. Appleton and Co., 1867, 1877).

39. *Catalogue of the University of Vermont, 1878-79,* 18. It is not clear if Dewey was exposed to Bain's *Senses and the Intellect* (1855) in which he articulated a pragmatic theory of action. Similar to the position Dewey would take in 1896 in "The Reflex Arc Concept in Psychology" (EW 5: 96-109), Bain argued that stimulus and response are not discrete events, but are inseparably connected; thought and action are one.

40. *In Memoriam Henry A. P. Torrey, LL.D.: Marsh Professor of Intellectual and Moral Philosophy in the University of Vermont,* Address at the Annual Meeting of the Associate Alumni, 23 June 1903 (Burlington: University of Vermont, 1903), 8.

41. John Wright Buckham, "A Group of American Idealists," *Personalist* 1 (April 1920): 18-31; Feuer, "H. A. P. Torrey and John Dewey," 34-54.

42. See Marsh, Introduction in *Aids to Reflection,* by Samuel Taylor Coleridge (Burlington, VT: Chauncey Goodrich, 1829), xiv, xx.

43. Dewey as quoted by Herbert Schneider in Lamont, ed., *Dialogue on John Dewey,* 15. Cf. Schneider, "Reminiscences About John Dewey at Columbia, 1913-1950," unpublished manuscript, Special Collections Research Center, Morris Library, Southern Illinois University Carbondale; and Dewey, "Coleridge, Marsh and the Spiritual Philosophy: An Address on James Marsh in Relation to the Romantic Movement," lecture delivered at the University of Vermont, 26 November 1929, as part of the celebration commemorating the one hundredth anniversary of the first American edition of Samuel Taylor Coleridge's *Aids to Reflection*, (first published as "James Marsh and American Philosophy" in the *Journal of the History of Ideas* 2 [April 1941]: 131-50. See Dewey, LW 5: 178); Herbert Schneider's Oral History Interview of John Dewey, 29 June 1967, Special Collections Research Center, Morris Library, Southern Illinois University Carbondale; and Schneider, "John Dewey: A Talk Delivered by Professor Herbert W. Schneider in the Ira Allen Chapel, the University of Vermont, on October 26, 1949, at the Celebration of John Dewey's Ninetieth Birthday Anniversary," unpublished manuscript, John Dewey Papers, Special Collections, University of Vermont Library, 5.

44. Similarly, Feuer notes that John Wright Buckham, Dewey's boyhood friend, "was something of a nature-mystic." He wrote many essays on mountain climbing and acted as president of the John Muir Association from 1938 until his death in 1945. Feuer, "Prefatory Note," 202.

45. Cf. H. A. P. Torrey's religious experience, as described by his pastor, G. C. Atkins. According to Atkins, Torrey always remembered "the moment of his illumination." Walking alone in the woods one spring day, "there came suddenly and definitely, a clear shining, in the light of which the things of the spirit came into vital and harmonious relation, and that light grew and did not pass." *In Memoriam Henry A.P. Torrey, L.L.D.,* 25-26.

46. Max Eastman, "John Dewey," *Atlantic Monthly* 168 (1941): 673. Bruce Kuklick, *Churchmen and Philosophers: From Jonathan Edwards to John Dewey* (New Haven: Yale University Press, 1985), 231.

47. Dewey, "From Absolutism to Experimentalism" (1930), LW 5: 153-54.

48. Coughlan, *The Young John Dewey*, 47. Cf. Paul Conkin's statement that Dewey "never repudiated most of the values of his childhood. Instead, he correlated them with a new knowledge of man and his environment, a knowledge never possessed by his forebears." Conkin, *Puritans and Pragmatists* (New York: Dodd, Mead, 1968), 346.

49. On the timing of Dewey's transition away from religious concerns see Coughlan, *The Young John Dewey,* 90; Kuklick, *Churchmen and Philosophers,* 238; and Rockefeller, *John Dewey,* 145-154.

50. Dewey to W. T. Harris, 17 May 1881.

51. Dewey to W. T. Harris, 1 July 1882. See also Dewey to W. T. Harris, 22 October 1881. Rosenkranz wrote two introductions to Hegel's *Encyklopädie der philosophischen Wissenschaften im grundrisse,* an 1845 edition published in Berlin by Duncter und Humblot, and an 1870 edition published in Berlin by L. Heimann. Jay Martin incorrectly states that Dewey's translation of Rosenkranz's introduction appeared in the July 1882 issue of the JSP, but it was never published. Martin, *The Education of John Dewey,* 57. No doubt Harris did not accept Dewey's offer because Thomas Davidson had already published a translation of the introduction in the JSP. Karl Rosenkranz, "Introduction to Hegel's *Encyclopedia of the Philosophical Sciences,*" trans. Thomas Davidson, JSP 5, no. 3 (July 1871): 234-250.

52. Dewey, "The Pantheism of Spinoza" (1882), EW 1: 17. Dewey's argument that Spinoza's philosophy could not adequately account for the finite is a long-standing, if not traditional, critique. See Wiep van Bunge, "Spinoza in English, 1700-1900," *Intellectual News* nos. 6-7 (Winter 2000): 69. Similarly, in the *Science of Logic,* Hegel argued that Spinoza's doctrine of substance requires a thinking subject that cannot explain its own existence according to that doctrine of substance. According to Hegel, this is the "sole and genuine refutation of Spinozism." Hegel, *Science of Logic,* trans. A. V. Miller (Atlantic Heights, NJ: Humanities Press International, 1969), 581.

53. Dewey, "From Absolutism to Experimentalism" (1930), 5: 149.

54. For the intuitionist reading see Morton White, *The Origins of Dewey's Instrumentalism* (New York: Octagon Books, 1942), 4; George Dykhuizen, "John Dewey at Johns Hopkins," *Journal of the History of Ideas* 22, no. 1 (Jan.-March 1961): 109. For examples of the Kantian reading see Osamu Kurita, "John Dewey's Philosophical Frame of Reference in His First Three Articles," *Educational Theory* 21 (Summer 1971): 338-346; and Boisvert, *Dewey's Metaphysics* (New York: Fordham University Press, 1988), 17-21. As will be clear in the following discussion, I disagree with Boisvert's claim that Dewey's dissertation at Johns Hopkins was a transitional text during his shift from Kantianism to Hegelianism. Throughout his discussion of these phases of Dewey's development, Boisvert seems to assume that Hegel was a pre-Kantian philosopher who posited a supernatural absolute spirit. To be sure, many have read Hegel in that way, but it is a mistake to assume the correctness of that reading without some defense. Consequently, when Boisvert claims that Trendelenburg Aristotelianized Hegel by naturalizing him, it is not clear to me that he has really distinguished Trendelenburg from Hegel at all. This assumed reading of Hegel also generates problems in his discussion of G. S. Morris's thought.

55. Dewey, "From Absolutism to Experimentalism" (1930), LW 5: 150.

56. Ibid. Lake View Seminary was located just south of Burlington in the town of Charlotte.

57. John Watson, *The Philosophy of Kant, in Extracts* (Kingston, Ontario: Bailie, 1882); George Sylvester Morris, *Kant's Critique of Pure Reason* (Chicago: S. C. Griggs and Company, 1882). See *Catalogue of the University of Vermont, 1878-79,* 18. For a bibliography of Watson's publications see *Philosophical Essays Presented to John Watson* (Kingston, Ontario: Queen's University, 1922), 343-346.

58. Dewey, "From Absolutism to Experimentalism" (1930), LW 5: 148; John Wright Buckham, "Professor Torrey as Thinker and Teacher," *In Memoriam Henry A. P. Torrey,* 30.

59. Dewey, "From Absolutism to Experimentalism" (1930), LW 5: 149; Jane Dewey, "Biography of John Dewey," 13; Cf. John Wright Buckham, "A Group of American Idealists," 22-25; and Feuer, "H. A. P. Torrey and John Dewey," 34-54.

60. *In Memoriam Henry A. P. Torrey,* 13. Cf. H. A. P. Torrey, Review of *Facts and Comments* by Herbert Spencer, *The Philosophical Review* 12, no. 2 (March 1903): 193-199.

61. H. A. P. Torrey, "The 'Theodicy of Leibniz,'" *Andover Review* 4 (Oct.-Dec. 1885): 511.

62. Dewey, "From Absolutism to Experimentalism" (1930), LW 5: 148.

63. Ibid., 150. Cf. Jane Dewey, "Biography of John Dewey," 14; Aunt Sarah to John Dewey, 7 September 1882; and Lucina A. Rich Dewey to John Dewey, December 1882 or 1883.

64. When Peirce wrote the definition of "university" for the 1891 *Century Dictionary,* the editors objected to his assertion that it was "an association of men for the purpose of study," claiming that they believed the university was an institution for instruction. Peirce replied that a university had nothing to do with instruction. For Peirce, "the function of a university is the production of knowledge, and . . . teaching is only a necessary means to that end." Quoted in Max H. Fisch and Jackson I. Cope, "Peirce at the Johns Hopkins University," in *Studies in the Philosophy of Charles Sanders Peirce,* eds. Philip H. Wiener and Frederic H. Young (Cambridge, MA: Harvard University Press, 1952), 277-278.

65. John Shook notes that "Morris was one of only a handful of American academics who taught neo-Kantian and neo-Hegelian doctrines," but doesn't acknowledge the importance of extra-academic American Hegelianism. He is quite correct, however, to emphasize that Hopkins provided a unique academic experience for Dewey because he was able to study with an idealist as well as someone who was trained in the new experimental psychology, G. Stanley Hall. Shook, *Dewey's Empirical Theory of Knowledge and Reality* (Nashville: Vanderbilt University Press, 2000), 42.

66. Fisch and Cope, "Pierce at the Johns Hopkins University," 306-309; Joseph Brent, *Charles Sanders Peirce: A Life,* revised and enlarged edition (Bloomington: Indiana University Press, 1998), 139-64; and Hugh Hawkins, *Pioneer: A History of the Johns Hopkins University, 1874-1889* (Ithaca: Cornell University Press, 1960), 195-197.

67. John Dewey to H. A. P. Torrey, 5 October 1882. Cf. Marc Edmund Jones, *George Sylvester Morris: His Philosophical Career and Theistic Idealism* (New York: Greenwood Press, 1968 [c1948]), 185-186. Dewey took Peirce's Advanced Logic and Philosophical Terminology in the fall semester of 1883. See the textual apparatus to Dewey to H. A. P. Torrey, 5 October 1882 in *The Correspondence of John Dewey (1871-1918),* ed. Larry Hickman (Charlottesville, VA: InteLex Corporation, 2001).

68. In addition to Adams, in the United States the German Historical School's influence extended to Richard T. Ely, also at Johns Hopkins, and Edwin Seligman at Columbia University. Jurgen Herbst, *The German Historical School in American Scholarship: A Study in the Transfer of Culture* (Ithaca: Cornell University Press, 1965).

69. Quoted in Peter Novick, *That Noble Dream: The "Objectivity Question" and the American Historical Profession* (Cambridge: Cambridge University Press, 1988), 33.

70. See Herbert Baxter Adams, "The Germanic Origin of New England Towns," *Johns Hopkins University Studies in Historical and Political Science,* vol. 1, *Local Institutions* (Baltimore: Johns Hopkins University Press, 1882), 10, 9.

71. Dewey to W. T. Harris, 17 January 1884.

72. Dewey, "Ethics and Physical Science" (1887), EW 1: 220. Dewey spoke little of Anglo-Saxon, and even less of Teutonic, peoples. In 1920, he commented that "an enthusiastic American teacher of the Chinese in Honolulu told [him] that when the Chinese

acquired Anglo-Saxon initiative they would be the greatest people in the world." Dewey claimed he wondered "whether even the Anglo-Saxons would have developed or retained initiative if they had lived for centuries under conditions that gave them no room to stir about, no relief from the unremitting surveillance of their fellows?" As this passage indicates, Dewey always explained human development in terms of social and environmental factors. Racism required an essentialist definition of man that Dewey could not consistently entertain within his mature philosophy. See Dewey, "Racial Prejudice and Friction" (1922), LW 13: 242. For other passages in which he was critical of notions of Anglo-Saxon superiority and imperialism see "Education by Henry Adams" (1921), LW 13: 273; "Imperialism Is Easy" (1927), LW 3: 158; "William James's Morals and Julien Benda's" (1948), LW 15: 22. Dewey did at times claim that Anglo-Saxon peoples have been more practical than other peoples: "The reason the Anglo-Saxon civilization is superior is that we have learned to get methods and so can get particular results when we want them." In that essay, he went on to agree with "the Latin races" that "the Anglo-Saxon is . . . without the delicate susceptibility to attend to the needs of others; . . . they set up their mark and go at it roughshod, regardless of the feelings of others." Dewey, "Educational Lectures before Brigham Young Academy" (1902), LW 17: 296, 343. Jonathan M. Hansen correctly characterizes Dewey's vision of national unity as resolutely cosmopolitan, rather than ethnic, nationalism. Hansen, *The Lost Promise of Patriotism: Debating American Identity, 1890-1920* (Chicago: University of Chicago Press, 2003).

73. Dewey, *Logic: The Theory of Inquiry* (1938), LW 12: 231-232. Cf. Joseph Blau, "John Dewey's Theory of History," *The Journal of Philosophy* 57 (4 February 1960): 98. Dewey took four of Adams's courses: Institutional History Seminary, Sources of English History, Comparative Constitutional History, and International Law.

74. John Dewey to H. A. P. Torrey, 14 February 1883.

75. Dewey's citations in *Psychology* demonstrate that he was thoroughly familiar with current scholarship in psychology; however, he was always interested in psychology strictly for the light it shed on philosophical issues. In a letter to Arthur Bentley, Dewey wrote "I do not pretend to be a psychologist anyway, and what I've written on that subject has been mostly for the sake of clearing up my own mind about something in either ethics or logic." Quoted in Sydney Ratner and Jules Altman, eds., *John Dewey and Arthur F. Bentley: A Philosophical Correspondence, 1932-1951* (New Brunswick, NJ: Rutgers University Press, 1964), 53.

76. See G. Stanley Hall to W. T. Harris, 7 October 1871, Harris Papers, MHS; and Hall to Harris, 13 October 1871, Harris Papers, MHS. Hall translated a section of Karl Rosenkranz, *Hegel als Deutscher Nationalphilosph* (Leipzig: Duncker und Humblot, 1870). His translations appeared in the JSP as "Hegel as the National Philosopher of Germany." Dorothy Ross suggests that Hall may have distanced himself from the St. Louis Hegelians after this time because he was intimidated by the prospect of trying to convince them of his expertise in Hegel studies. Ross, *G. Stanley Hall: The Psychologist as Prophet* (Chicago: University of Chicago Press, 1972), 38-41, 45-49, 56-57, 254, 129, 59. In 1880 Hall wrote to William James that Hegelianism was "unsurpassed for helping men easily and without agony or crisis over any part of the long way from Rome to reason, but to rest in it as a finality is arrested development, and to go back to it seems to me mystic and retrogressive." G. S. Hall to William James, 15 February 1880, quoted in Ralph Barton Perry, *The Thought and Character of William James*, 2 vols. (Boston: Little, Brown, 1935), 2: 21.

77. Ross, *G. Stanley Hall,* 62, 73-77, 80-87.

78. Advertisement in JSP 15 (1881): 323. Ten volumes were projected, eight were published: George Sylvester Morris, *Kant's Critique of Pure Reason* (1882); John Wat-

son, *Schelling's Transcendental Idealism: A Critical Exposition* (1882); Charles Everett, *Fichte's Science of Knowledge: A Critical Exposition* (1884); John Kedney, *Hegel's Æsthetics: A Critical Exposition* (1885); Noah Porter, *Kant's Ethics: A Critical Exposition* (1886); George Sylvester Morris, *Hegel's Philosophy of the State and of History: An Exposition* (1887); John Dewey, *Leibniz's New Essays Concerning the Human Understanding: A Critical Exposition* (1888); W. T. Harris, *Hegel's Logic: A Book on the Categories of the Mind: A Critical Exposition* (1890). Dewey took over the editorship when Morris died unexpectedly in 1889.

79. Dewey, "The Late Professor Morris" (1889), EW 3: 7.

80. R. M. Wenley, *The Life and Work of George Sylvester Morris: A Chapter in the History of American Thought in the Nineteenth Century* (New York: The Macmillan Company, 1917), 151. Morton White also depicts Morris as antiscientific because he accepted Wenley's account of Morris, at that time the only biography available. White, *The Origins of Dewey's Instrumentalism,* 9, 12-14. One of the primary themes of Marc Edmund Jones's biography of Morris is an extended criticism of Wenley's book, especially on the point of Morris's view of the relationship of philosophy to science. Jones also effectively defends Morris from Wenley's claim that he was a right-wing Hegelian. Jones, *George Sylvester Morris,* 161ff. Cf. Shook, *Dewey's Empirical Theory of Knowledge and Reality,* 194, 275ff.

81. Wenley, *Life and Work of George Sylvester Morris,* 316-318.

82. George Sylvester Morris, *Philosophy and Christianity* (New York: Robert Carter, 1883), 20. Cf. Hegel's denigration of anatomy as "an aggregate of information" rather than a study of the organic whole. Hegel, *The Phenomenology of Spirit,* trans. A.V. Miller (Oxford: Oxford University Press, 1977), §1. Although he implies that idealism denies the reality of the physical world, Boisvert also claims that Morris spoke of the "universal self" or "universal consciousness" in order to emphasize that "existence is meaningful." Boisvert, *Dewey's Metaphysics,* 25. On my reading of Hegel, his absolute spirit emphasized the meaningfulness of history for humanity.

83. Jones, *George Sylvester Morris,* 249-270.

84. Dewey to H. A. P. Torrey, 5 October 1882.

85. Dewey to W. T. Harris, 29 December 1882.

86. Dewey, "Knowledge and the Relativity of Feeling" (1883), EW 1: 21.

87. See Dewey's 1925 discussion of "what has come to be called the 'emergent' theory of mind" in *Experience and Nature,* LW 1: 207ff.

88. Dewey, "Knowledge and the Relativity of Feeling" (1883), EW 1: 20.

89. Ibid., 23.

90. Ibid., 27.

91. Ibid., 26, 33.

92. Dewey, "The Pantheism of Spinoza" (1882), EW 1: 10.

93. Dewey to W. T. Harris, 17 January 1884. In this letter Dewey indicated that any system of philosophy that collapsed all of reality into an undifferentiated absolute was to be disparaged as an "identity system."

94. Hegel, *Phenomenology of Spirit,* §54.

95. George Sylvester Morris, *British Thought and Thinkers: Introductory Studies, Critical, Biographical and Philosophical* (Chicago: S. C. Griggs, 1880), 197-198. Cf. Dewey, "Knowledge and the Relativity of Feeling" (1883), EW 1: 26.

96. George Sylvester Morris, "Friedrich Adolf Trendelenburg," *The New Englander* 32 (April 1874): 319ff.

97. Ibid., 318.

98. Morris, *British Thought and Thinkers,* 387. Cf. Morris, "Friedrich Adolf Trendelenburg," 303.

99. Dewey, "Kant and Philosophic Method" (1884), EW 1: 35.

100. Ibid., 35.

101. Ibid., 37.

102. Ibid., 38. Shook claims that Dewey asserted "a rudimentary statement of a coherence theory of truth," in his characterization of Kant's categories as circular. I believe it is misleading to claim Dewey espoused a coherence theory of truth because that theory may be understood as holding that our beliefs are true as long as they logically cohere with one another. In the following chapter, I argue that in his 1887 *Psychology,* Dewey, like Hegel, had more than logical coherence in mind; both philosophers believed that an indispensable criterion of truth is a certain existential, as well as logical, coherence.

103. Dewey, "Kant and Philosophic Method" (1884), EW 1: 39.

104. Ibid., 41.

105. Ibid., 42, 39, 44.

106. Ibid., 40.

107. "Now that I am writing I may mention the fact that the statement (in one of the general Reports if I mistake not) that my thesis was published in Journal Spec. Phil is an error. The article published there was in somewhat the same line & was presented to obtain the fellowship, but the doctorate thesis is quite another matter & has never been published. 'The Psychology of Kant' was its title." John Dewey to T. R. Ball, 28 May 1888, Daniel Coit Gilman Papers, Special Collections, The Johns Hopkins University.

108. Dewey to W. T. Harris, 17 January 1884.

109. Dewey to H. A. P. Torrey, 4 February 1883. White, Dykhuizen, and Coughlan believe Dewey was torn between an allegiance to the physiological psychology of Hall and the idealism of Morris, but there is little reason to believe Dewey considered these viewpoints antithetical. Jennifer Welchman, *Dewey's Ethical Thought* (Ithaca: Cornell University Press, 1995), 14-17.

110. Dewey to H. A. P. Torrey, 17 November 1883.

111. Dewey, "The New Psychology" (1884), EW 1: 50.

112. Ibid., 51.

113. Ibid., 56. Both Paul Tibbetts and Kenneth Chandler claim that the scientific spirit displayed in "The New Psychology" demonstrates that Dewey never embraced idealism. Tibbetts, "John Dewey and Contemporary Phenomenology on Experience and the Subject-Object Relation," *Philosophy Today* 15 (1971): 252-255; and Chandler, "Dewey's Phenomenology of Knowledge," *Philosophy Today* 21 (1977): 44. Frank Ryan correctly counters their claims by arguing that in his earliest essays Dewey regarded experimentalism as the "process by which absolute consciousness reveals *itself* to individual and social consciousness." Dewey also acknowledged his debt and continuing allegiance to absolute idealism in writings published after 1884. Ryan, "The Kantian Ground of Dewey's Functional Self," *Transactions of the Charles S. Peirce Society* 28, no. 1 (Winter 1992): 127. Cf. Jennifer Welchman, *Dewey's Ethical Thought*, 5-6.

114. Dewey, "The New Psychology" (1884), EW 1: 60.

115. Westbrook, *John Dewey and American Democracy,* 24.

116. Coughlan, *The Young John Dewey*, 43-53; Rockefeller, *John Dewey,* 577, n48; Westbrook, *John Dewey and American Democracy,* 24, n19; Williams, *The Andover Liberals,* 42; James Wayne Dye "Denton J. Snider's Interpretation of Hegel," *The Modern Schoolman* 46 (January 1970): 153-167.

Chapter Four

Dewey in Michigan, 1884–1894

Three months after he presented "The New Psychology" to the Metaphysical Club, Dewey received his doctorate from Hopkins in the spring of 1884. A few months prior to Dewey's graduation, G. S. Morris was appointed full-time lecturer in ethics at the University of Michigan. Soon thereafter George Holmes Howison, of St. Louis Hegelian fame, left Ann Arbor to build the philosophy department at the University of California. Morris took the opportunity to recommend his former graduate student for the open position. Two months after Dewey completed his graduate studies at the age of twenty-four, James B. Angell, the president of the University of Michigan and a close family friend from Burlington, appointed him instructor of philosophy.[1] At Michigan, Dewey remained in the midst of liberal German cultural influence, as it was the first university in the United States to adopt the German model of higher education.[2]

During his ten years in Ann Arbor, Dewey's thought was in gradual but constant transition. In "From Absolutism to Experimentalism," he remarked that during the first fifteen years after he left graduate school he "drifted away from Hegelianism," and explained that "the word 'drifting' expresses the slow and, for a long time, imperceptible character of the movement."[3] Dewey never attempted to specify the degree to which his drift was from Hegel or from Hegelianism, that is to say, what currently went under the name of Hegelianism. Dewey was well versed in the writings of American Hegelians and the British neo-Hegelians—Thomas Hill Green, William Wallace, Andrew Seth, Edward and John Caird, Bernard Bosanquet, F. H. Bradley, and John Watson. Dewey's disagreements with his contemporary Hegelians can be documented in his publications, but he devoted little attention to exegesis of Hegel's, or any other philosopher's, texts. As a result, many scholars have assumed that his criticisms of Hegelianism reveal his positions on Hegel. In this chapter I present the drift as a move away from what then passed for Hegelianism, reserving the question of Dewey's relationship to Hegel for chapter five.

John Shook has recently argued that this transition in Dewey's thought should be viewed as his effort to formulate a consistent idealism rather than a rejection of an ill-considered, youthful fascination with Hegel.[4] I intend to sustain Shook's thesis that by 1891 Dewey had severed his ties with the neo-Hegelians when he rejected their transcendent absolute, but that alone does not constitute a rejection of Hegel. I add to Shook's view, however, by showing that Dewey began to develop a humanistic/historicist reading of Hegel and continued to draw upon key Hegelian insights. I also argue that Dewey's effort to articulate a consistent idealism was integrally linked to his developing conception of the role of the philosopher. In a letter written to his friend James Rowland Angell in 1893, Dewey wrote, "metaphysics has had its day, and if the truths which Hegel saw cannot be stated as direct, practical truths, they are not true."[5] Dewey was convinced that philosophers should address "the problems of men," and live a life of social involvement.[6] Finally, I note that as Dewey paid more attention to social and political philosophy, he also became less involved in the organized church. Neil Coughlan correctly states that Dewey "was becoming self-consciously, even aggressively, a secular thinker."[7]

Though I will continue to examine Dewey's writings and those to which he responded, in order to understand developments in his ethical thought I take seriously his statement that "Upon the whole, the forces that have influenced me have come from persons and from situations more than from books."[8] Scholars often note the importance of Dewey's relationship with his new wife, Alice Chipman, and a friendship with a visionary newspaperman, Franklin Ford, but have underestimated the influence of the most charismatic person Dewey knew during these years, Thomas Davidson.[9] I seek to correct that imbalance by examining the influence of Davidson and his friends in the Ethical Culture movement on Dewey's ethics. Scholars have also emphasized the important influence of William James's *Principles of Psychology,* published in 1890, and the writings of T. H. Green on Dewey's thought. Though Dewey spoke highly of Green, he was also critical of his metaphysics, and several scholars have cast significant doubt on the influence of William James.[10]

I begin by examining Dewey's drift away from institutional religion, emphasizing how it relates to developments in his psychology and his continuing interest in philosophical method. In the second part of the chapter I examine how Alice Chipman, Ford, and Davidson stimulated his interest in social philosophy and social justice, and how Davidson in particular provided Dewey with a concrete model of philosophy as *Bildung.* My emphasis upon the importance of these people in Dewey's life provides an important platform from which to understand a transition in his ethics away from transcendent ethical demands and goals.

Religion, Psychology, and Philosophical Method

We can get a general sense of the contours of the transition that was occurring in Dewey's thought simply by looking at what and where he published during these years. Dewey immediately began his career-long prodigious output, publishing during the next ten years forty-six articles, numerous book reviews, one edited volume, and four monographs; thus from 1884 on I can only discuss a small sample of his writings. After "The New Psychology," he published three more articles in the *Andover Review*. Kuklick has argued that Dewey published these articles in the *Andover Review* because he sought to lend philosophical expression to Andover Liberalism, so much so that Andover Liberalism "permanently left its imprint on the structure of [Dewey's] thought."[11] But aside from one article published in *Bibliotheca Sacra,* these articles are the only ones Dewey published in theological journals and, in correspondence with Joseph Ratner in 1946, Dewey stated that he did not spend much time reading the *Andover Review* and that he "never had much interest in theology as such."[12] After 1889, except for a few book reviews and a commencement address, Dewey quit publishing in theological journals altogether and began to publish most of his articles in journals associated with the Ethical Culture movement: the *Ethical Record,* the *International Journal of Ethics,* the *Open Court,* and the *Monist.* Dewey's writings focused almost exclusively on ethics and education; his course offerings at Michigan also reflected this change.[13] Of his four monographs, one was on psychology (1887), one was a study of the life and thought of Leibniz for Morris's Griggs's Philosophical Classics Series (1888), and two were on ethics (1891 and 1894).[14] He continued to pursue his quest for individual and social unity, but increasingly he did so beyond the parameters of organized religion. By 1889 his sights were locked in on psychology, ethics rather than religion, and the philosophy of education. Moreover, his writings on ethics tended to emphasize a very practical, albeit philosophically sophisticated, approach to the subject, with a particular emphasis on democratic culture and education as an instrument of social reconstruction.

When Dewey first arrived in Ann Arbor, however, he was still a liberal Congregationalist. He quickly transferred his church membership to a local Congregationalist church at which he began teaching Sunday School. Dewey's first book, *Selections of the Writings of George MacDonald; or Helps for Weary Souls* (1885), was a compilation of selections from the writings of a religious author. The selections constantly referred to a supernatural, omnipotent, omnipresent God, and Dewey's writings of this time indicate that he still believed in such a God. Dewey's 1887 *Psychology* demonstrated that he was well versed in the work of Wundt and other experimental psychologists, but he also frequently spoke of the divinity of the human soul. And in 1886 his essay, "Soul and Body," examined ways to study the soul scientifically. Dewey wrote that physiological psychology could not explain behavior mechanistically because the experiments of researchers like Wundt had shown that nervous activity involves "purposive adaptation to the stimulus." The discovery of purposive adaptation, even in simple organisms like frogs, indicated that physiological psychology had to account for behavior as teleological, as psychical. Physiology, Dewey claimed, had demonstrated that the "the psychical is immanent in the physical," or more precisely, the body was "the organ of the soul."[15] His first semester at the University of Michigan Dewey also argued, in "The Obligation to Knowledge of God," that all people are morally required to seek knowledge of God. In Dewey's words, "to fail to meet this obligation is not to err intellectually, but to sin morally."[16]

But Dewey's psychological and religious thought developed along a path that began in his earliest essays. He had consistently criticized the British empiricists and Kant for attempting to explain experience by introducing elements that went beyond possible experience. This led to agnosticism because, as Dewey explained before, it assumes that thought and being are foreign to one another and thus we can never really know the source of our experience. In the same way, in his psychology Dewey initially appealed to the notion of a transcendent, "perfect Will or Personality," analogous to the "Absolute Spirit" in the thought of Morris and the British neo-Hegelians, to explain our particular, individual experience, but he gradually abandoned this transcendent personality because it went beyond possible experience.[17] Just like Locke's material and mental substances or Kant's thing-in-itself, Dewey believed that appeals to that which was unknowable explained nothing. Explanation required us to relate the unexplained to something we did understand. By 1891, Dewey had transformed the perfect Personality into a social, non-transcendent process and he had begun to search for and find more pedestrian language for Hegelian concepts.[18] Ernest Renan's *Future of Science,* Dewey averred, had helped him conceive of evolution as the "law of historic growth, not as the dialectic unfolding of the absolute."[19]

We can also see the continuing influence of a pietistic faith, such as that found in post-Kantian idealism and in the Burlington philosophy, in Dewey's psychology and religious thought. As he would in his mature thought, in 1886 Dewey claimed that knowledge could not be understood as apart from will. Belief only becomes knowledge when "the commands which it lays upon the will have been executed, and . . . knowledge cannot arise except as our feelings and desires are involved that enable us to grasp the Biblical statements as sober facts, hard as they seem."[20] Knowing and its verification, asserted Dewey, is inseparably connected with action, with doing. In other religious writings Dewey warned against the extremes of religious fanaticism and apathy, and emphasized that religiosity was primarily a matter of behavior rather than doctrine. One passage is particularly revealing because it brings to mind Dewey's description of his mother's queries about her sons' rightness with God:

> Religious feeling is unhealthy when it is watched and analyzed to see if it exists, if it is right, if it is growing. It is as fatal to be forever observing our religious moods and experiences, as it is to pull up a seed from the ground to see if it is growing.[21]

Rather than constant self-examination, Dewey assured his reader, healthy religion comes from focusing our attention less upon ourselves, and more on God. True religion, according to Dewey, requires the cultivation of "humility in the presence of the perfect and matchless character of Christ."[22]

As early as 1887, Dewey criticized Christian agnosticism for "divid[ing] the kingdom of reality into halves, and proclaim[ing] one supernatural and unknowable, the other natural and the realm of knowledge." In so doing Christians made the same error as, and ceded ground to, "physical philosophers" like Herbert Spencer who sought to reduce man to "earthly clay," and ethics to natural science.[23] In "Christianity and Democracy," published in 1892, Dewey proclaimed that true religion is not based on mysteries; it "must reveal," and "Revelation undertakes . . . not only to state that the truth of things is such and such, it undertakes to give the individual organs for the truth, organs by which he can get hold of, can see and feel, the truth."[24] When theologians depict religious truth as mysterious they fall into Dewey's dreaded agnosticism, because they attempt to treat supernatural facts in isolation from natural facts. Supernatural/natural dualism violated Dewey's Hegelian organicism and holism, which entailed that all truths are interrelated in a larger whole and that the truth is the whole.

Like the perfect Personality, Dewey brought the Christian God down to earth, claiming, in "Christianity and Democracy," that "The kingdom of God, as Christ said, is within us, or among us"; religious truth "is, and can be, only in intelligence." In this essay Dewey portrayed Christianity as an inclusive social consciousness, with no special truths of its own, and special doctrines, such as the notion of sin, permanently dropped out of his thought. The only important Christian doctrine, asserted Dewey, was that "God is truth; that as truth He is love and reveals Himself fully to man." Here Dewey demonstrated his sympathy with German higher criticism, claiming that God's truth is in man and not in historical events like the resurrection or in special theories. More and more, Dewey viewed Christianity as requiring only that people live lives of social sympathy and social action. He asserted that "It is man's social organization, the state in which he is expressing himself, which always has and always must set the form and sound the key-note to the understanding of Christianity." The only tests of Christian truth, according to Dewey, are "the tests of fact." And consistent with the doctrine of progressive revelation he had heard Brastow preach in Burlington, Dewey asserted that Christianity's "attempt to fix religious truth once for all, to hold it within certain rigid limits, to say this and just this is Christianity, is self-contradictory."[25] The revelation of Christian truth, Dewey claimed, was ongoing, and revelation was consistent with reason. In 1894 Dewey proclaimed that science now provides "the actual incarnation of truth in human experience and the necessity of giving heed to it."[26] Dewey encouraged his reader to develop faith "in the light of the most searching methods and known facts," and that method was exemplified in science. Dewey referred to the kingdom of God, but he no longer thought in terms of a supernatural God. The "Kingdom of God on earth" was simply free, democratic society.[27] Steven Rockefeller accurately concludes that by the late 1880s Dewey had rejected original sin, the absolute transcendence of God, adopted a neo-Hegelian panentheism, and channeled his quest for unity with God "into an active social and ethical life."[28]

Developments in Dewey's psychology paralleled changes in his religious thought. As he converted the perfect Personality into a social reality, his psychological writings focused increasingly on practical subjects such as education. W. T. Harris, Susan Blow, or Anna Brackett could have written most of the arguments and claims Dewey made in his earliest educational writings. In 1890 Dewey wrote that college education was not about learning facts, but about character formation. Though he did not use the term, Dewey's conception of education was consistent with Hegel's notion of *Bildung.* The college student, declared Dewey, "should have ingrained within him the subordination of all learning, of all the sciences and all the arts, to social relationships and sympathies." Free interaction and inquiry among students, both men and women, would "develop an ethical atmosphere, and this will secure, as far as it goes, a real intellectual training." Education, for Dewey, was the development of concrete morality, Hegel's notion of *Sittlichkeit.*[29]

Many have noted that in his psychological writings Dewey sought to give his idealistic metaphysics credibility by founding it on experimental psychology.[30] It is true that Dewey wanted, like Trendelenburg and Morris, to ground his philosophy on science, but this observation should be supplemented with Dewey's claim that "as my study and thinking progressed, I became more and more troubled by the intellectual scandal that seemed to me involved in the current (and traditional) dualism in logical standpoint and method between something called 'science' on the one hand and something called 'morals' on the other."[31] Dewey was equally concerned with eliminating what he viewed as a methodological dualism in neo-Hegelianism in the same way that he sought to eliminate the distinction between natural and supernatural truth in his religious thought.

Dewey's thoughts on philosophical method are most clearly expressed at this time in three articles he published in *Mind,* "The Psychological Standpoint," "Psychology as Philosophical Method," and "Illusory Psychology." In these articles Dewey tried to combine the best insights of British empiricism with the best insights of neo-Hegelianism. This effort pleased neither empiricists nor neo-Hegelians; thus Dewey had struck out on his own, formulating a via media between the two dominant philosophical options of his time. I will briefly discuss these articles in the order in which they were published.

Dewey first used the term "psychological standpoint," with a brief explanation, in a November 1883 letter to Torrey.[32] Whereas Hegelians used consciousness as the starting point of philosophy, the British empiricists began with the "psychological standpoint," individual experience. In his brief letter to Torrey, Dewey implied that if the psychological standpoint were used consistently one would be led to idealism. It will become increasingly apparent that this is because Dewey viewed idealism not so much as a metaphysical doctrine, but as a commitment to philosophizing only about what appears to consciousness; for this reason, he increasingly labored to excise metaphysical assumptions he discovered in neo-Hegelian thought. Relative to the neo-Hegelians, throughout the 1880s and 1890s Dewey moved in the direction of phenomenology. The neo-Hegelians, especially Green, had argued that the psychological standpoint was the core difference between British empiricism and idealism. The neo-Hegelians argued that the psychological standpoint prevented British empiricism from addressing the most philosophical of issues, those that dealt with universals; British empiricism, they argued, could not go from individual experience to the universal.[33] To some extent Dewey agreed with the neo-Hegelians, but searching for a more inclusive perspective, where they saw only difference, he saw an opportunity for rapprochement. If one replaces the neo-Hegelians' word "consciousness" with "experience," it is easier to see how Dewey thought empiricism and idealism could be reconciled.

In "The Psychological Standpoint" Dewey stridently argued that the psychological standpoint was in fact "what both sides have in common." He defined the psychological standpoint as the view that "the nature of all objects of philosophical inquiry is to be fixed by finding out what experience says about them." Dewey claimed that empiricists should not be criticized for beginning with the psychological standpoint, but rather for not being true to the standpoint. Empiricists always appealed to unknowable "things-in-themselves" (Locke's unknowable substances, Hume's sensations, etc.) in order to account for the origins of experience, thus abandoning the psychological standpoint and becoming "'ontologists' of the most pronounced character."[34] This error, Dewey explained, was recapitulated throughout the empiricist tradition, because empiricists made two ontological assumptions that are not supplied by the psychological standpoint; they assumed there was an ontological distinction between thought and being, and that experience is individual. If empiricists would drop these empirically unjustifiable ontological assumptions, they would be studying what the neo-Hegelians called consciousness.

Dewey approved of the psychological standpoint as the starting point of philosophy and explained what it meant for philosophical method: "nothing shall be admitted into philosophy which does not show itself in experience, and its nature, that is, its place in experience shall be fixed by an account of the process of knowledge—by Psychology." Dewey also agreed with empiricists that knowledge is derived from sensations, but questioned their assumption that sensations exist "prior to or apart from knowledge," because that would make sensations unknowable. Even Hume, who acknowledged that Locke's substances were unknowable, violated the psychological standpoint by assuming that sensations exist prior to experience. The basis of Dewey's argument is that philosophical notions like sensations are the results of our analysis of experience, but we have no justification for reading the results of our analysis into experience as though they were there all along. For Dewey, many philosophical puzzles have been created because philosophers fallaciously assumed that terms they created for analytical purposes actually refer to real, static objects rather than functions within a process. Dewey questioned "the correctness of the procedure which, discovering a certain element *in* knowledge to be necessary for knowledge, therefore concludes that this element has an existence prior to or apart from knowledge."[35] If these elements can be used to explain knowledge, then they must be known. The elements of experience are not discrete, independently existing objects; they are functions within "an organic whole." Throughout his career, Dewey continued to criticize empiricists in just this way; he always appealed to what he believed was a more thoroughgoing and unwavering analysis of experience; this reveals that he never thought of idealism as antithetical to empiricism. For Dewey, idealism took experience more seriously than empiricism. Further, the psychological standpoint remained an integral part of Dewey's thought, though by 1905 he transformed it into the "postulate of immediate empiricism."[36]

As Shook points out, in "The Psychological Standpoint" Dewey had worked out what James called the "psychologist's fallacy" four years prior to James. In his *Principles of Psychology,* published in 1890, James defined the fallacy as "the [psychologist's] *confusion of his own standpoint with that of the mental fact* about which he is making his report."[37] Though Dewey adopted James's appellation for this error, it is a mistake to conclude, as some have, that it provides evidence that Dewey was influenced by James to accept the view that sensations could not be prior to, or independent from, knowledge. Some have argued that before James's *Psychology* influenced him, Dewey was a neo-Kantian who held that sensations must be synthesized by the mind prior to knowledge, yet as we have seen Dewey never accepted this view.[38] In chapter one I showed that Dewey could have found the psychological fallacy in Hegel's *Phenomenology of Spirit,* as well as other writings.

As though his argument to this point was not controversial enough, in "The Psychological Standpoint," Dewey also argued that if empiricists remained true to the psychological standpoint they would discover that the only way to account for the "becoming," or development, of individual consciousness "is by the postulate of a universal consciousness." Experience, or consciousness, examined without ontological assumptions, revealed itself as an organic unity of object and subject, and of individual and universal consciousness. On this point, however, Dewey's reasoning is sketchy. He seems to claim that because all psychological description is description of what appears within consciousness, without the assumption that it is individual consciousness, then these descriptions must hold true for consciousness itself, or consciousness in general. For example, when a psychologist describes the origins of an infant's experience he is describing a known baby, a baby "which exists for consciousness," not "a baby thing-in-itself." Because individual consciousness can speculate about its own origin, as it does in the theory of evolution, for example, it shows that it can transcend itself, and individual consciousness can only transcend itself if it participates in a universal consciousness that is atemporal and unchanging.[39] But here, Dewey himself introduced an unacknowledged metaphysical assumption. If, as he maintained, we can examine consciousness itself, this does not necessarily prove that there is a transcendent consciousness. The examination of consciousness with no metaphysical assumptions whatsoever does not entail the metaphysical doctrine that all individual consciousnesses participate in a transcendent consciousness. If Dewey had consistently substituted the word "experience" for "consciousness," he might have been less tempted to reify what he was examining. Ultimately, Dewey seemed to realize that the Hegelian talk of consciousness was prone to this error, but at this time he continued to use it.

In the following article, "Psychology as Philosophic Method," Dewey argued that since, according to Hegelianism, philosophy deals with absolute self-consciousness and its contents, the method of philosophy should be psychology. Since psychology is the study of finite self-consciousness, its results could be generalized to give knowledge of the absolute self-consciousness. Dewey was not advocating that philosophers abandon their work and become psychologists; rather he was claiming that they should understand that they are already doing psychology because all analysis of reality is analysis of reality as it is discovered in consciousness. Once more, Dewey took a position that ran counter to that of leading British neo-Hegelians, specifically Green and Edward Caird, who maintained a sharp distinction between psychology and philosophy. Neo-Hegelians viewed philosophy as the science of absolute self-consciousness, which uses the method of logic; psychology, they claimed, studied phenomenal manifestations of the absolute self-consciousness, and therefore required no special methods other than simple empirical ones.[40] Because of his adamant opposition to dualisms, Dewey maintained that the absolute self-consciousness and its phenomenal manifestations are the same reality viewed from different angles; a single method, that of experimental psychology is all that is needed. If, as Dewey maintained in the previous article, psychologists must study consciousness without ontological commitments about whether it is individual or universal, it cannot be said that their investigations are limited to individual consciousness. Psychology, Dewey declared, is "the ultimate science of reality, because it declares what experience in its totality is; it fixes the worth and meaning of its various elements by showing their development and place within this whole. It is in short, *philosophic method*."[41]

If, as idealists had claimed, we only know the absolute self-consciousness as it reveals or manifests itself in individual self-consciousness, then psychology, the study of consciousness, was the only possible philosophic method. It is important to note that Dewey accused Green of being neo-Kantian because he elevated the absolute self into an unknowable thing-in-itself.[42] This indicates that Dewey believed a consistent Hegelian would not posit anything beyond consciousness. Green had surrendered to the temptation to posit something beyond experience to explain the causes of our experience but, as I noted in my discussion of "The Psychological Standpoint," Dewey did not always resist this temptation himself. In "Psychology as Philosophic Method," Dewey stated, rather awkwardly, that idealism entailed that "Philosophy can treat of absolute self-consciousness only in so far as it has become in a being like man, for otherwise it is not material for philosophy at all." But again Dewey seems to fall into the error of making his own unjustified metaphysical assumption by claiming that idealism must avoid "the error of regarding this realization in man as a time-conditioned product, which it is not."[43] Time is not outside of consciousness, "it is a form within it, one of the functions by which it organically constitutes its own experience." Here Dewey sided against most British neo-Hegelians by arguing that it made no sense to talk about the absolute self-consciousness realizing itself in history because the category of time existed within the absolute self-consciousness. At this point in his development, Dewey, who would ultimately become the consummate historicist, believed in an ahistorical reality; the absolute self-consciousness could only be atemporal.[44] Dewey's claim entailed a rejection of a key point of Caird's and Green's metaphysics because he insisted that the individual self cannot be distinguished from the absolute self without abandoning the psychological standpoint, but he had posited an atemporal reality beyond possible human experience.

Dewey also criticized the neo-Hegelians' emphasis on logic because we, as individuals, are temporal beings, who experience the absolute self-consciousness temporally, but logic is atemporal and thus cannot by itself be the science of the absolute self-consciousness. Dewey argued that "Logic cannot reach, however much it may point to, an actual individual" and cautioned his fellow idealists that "If we start from reason alone we shall never reach fact. If we start with fact, we shall find it revealing itself as reason."[45] One fruitful way to view this article is as Dewey's effort to save idealism from the Trendelenburgian critique. If idealism must begin with pure, a priori thought, Dewey in effect argued, then Trendelenburg is right to criticize it for its inability to address the particulars of lived experience. If, however, idealism begins with pure thought as it is discovered through the psychological study of consciousness, it is grounded in lived experience; pure thought is, in effect, a posteriori. Pure thought is simply thought without metaphysical assumptions. Dewey clearly preferred the latter option, and this indicates that, unlike the British neo-Hegelians, Dewey increasingly saw Hegel's *Phenomenology of Spirit* as the preface to the *Science of Logic.*[46] The neo-Hegelians had tended to disregard the *Phenomenology,* developing an ultra-logical view of Hegel in which his system was thought to be a deduction of reality. Dewey's shift allowed him to sidestep Trendelenburg's critique of Hegel and provides an important clue about how Dewey read Hegel.

Though "The Psychological Standpoint" and "Psychology as Philosophic Method" were the lead articles in two issues of *Mind,* they seem to have had little impact on British or American philosophy. An empiricist, Shadworth Hodgson, published a reply in which he explained that he was "at a loss to see either how Mr. Dewey justifies on experiential grounds the existence of a universal consciousness, or in what he imagines the relation between the individual consciousness and the universal one to consist." Hodgson concluded that psychology, as Dewey proposed it should be understood, "retains validity neither as philosophy nor yet as scientific psychology. By one stroke it substitutes psychology for philosophy and makes its psychology illusory."[47] In a private letter to Hodgson, William James acknowledged that he had read Hodgson's criticism of "poor Dewey, which I approve in the main."[48] Though Dewey published a reply to Hodgson in 1887, he made no effort to answer Hodgson's primary challenge, which was to demonstrate that he could prove the existence of a universal self from experience alone with no metaphysical presuppositions. He merely claimed that his point was that British empiricism had implicitly assumed the existence of a universal consciousness and that this postulate should be made explicit and examined. Though one might argue that the empiricists had illegitimately assumed certain universals, it was another thing altogether to demonstrate that they had assumed the existence of a universal self. On that point, the burden of proof remained on Dewey. His response to Hodgson did score some points, however, when he noted that Hodgson's talk of the "stream of consciousness" always assumed that experience shows the stream to be individual without responding to Dewey's challenge to empiricists to demonstrate that experience alone provides that ontological assumption. It is worth mentioning this point because it is an example of the difficulty Dewey would always have in getting philosophers to examine their Cartesian commitment to experience as individual, and also because it shows that Dewey was familiar with the concept of consciousness as a stream before James wrote about it in 1890.[49]

Dewey attempted to articulate his new, psychological approach to Hegelian philosophy in his 1887 textbook, *Psychology*. The book used the latest findings in psychology to examine human development, to defend a Hegelian ethic of self-development, and hence to demonstrate that human personality is perfected through identification with "the perfect Personality or Will." Although the book ended with the perfect Personality, in the preface he explained that he sought to avoid metaphysics, which "is out of place in a psychology." Dewey's stated purpose was to introduce students to scientific psychology and "develop the philosophic spirit" by raising psychological questions in a way "which is philosophic."[50] Because Dewey posited a transcendent self, however, it is accurate to view this book as Dewey's most neo-Hegelian, rather than Hegelian. This point should become clear as I proceed to discuss the criticisms of neo-Hegelianism that Dewey published after this book. For now, however, I will discuss the *Psychology* to lay the groundwork for my examination of what Dewey later rejected and retained from his earliest Hegelianism.

Dewey's Hegelian theory of the self is essential to the entire book. The self, or consciousness, is not a metaphysical substance; rather it is a self-determining teleological activity. "Self is, as we have so often seen, *activity*. It is not something *which* acts; it is activity."[51] In an essay published the same years as the *Psychology*, Dewey claimed that "if we could strip any psychical existence of all its qualities except bare existence, there would be nothing left, not even existence, for our intelligence."[52] We know the self by its qualities or relations, or perhaps stated more plainly, by its effects in the world. For Dewey, the essence of the self is will and the goal of the will is perfection, which is to be understood as self-realization or self-actualization. Will is both subjective and objective because it is the objective manifestation of the subjective self. As Dewey explained, "This real self, which the will by its very nature, as self-objectifying, holds before itself, is originally a bare form, an empty ideal without content."[53] Throughout life, the will seeks to give this empty form positive content, which is the actualization or realization of the self's potential. Dewey also referred to this as the "process of idealization."[54] The discoveries of physiological psychology, claimed Dewey, reveal how the actual self develops itself into the ideal self.

The *Psychology* explained the process of idealization, unification of the ideal and the actual, through a study of the development of human consciousness. Dewey organized the book according to a threefold scheme—knowledge, feeling, and will—which, he argued, corresponds to the elements of every state of consciousness. It must be understood, however, that for Dewey neither intellect, feeling, nor volition have real existence; they are analytical scaffolding used to understand aspects of the whole, which is the act. They are *functions* within action. Every act of consciousness involves awareness of, and some information about, an object, a feeling of the quality or value that this awareness has for the self, and every act of consciousness is the expression of purposeful activity. All acts of consciousness can be distinguished into subjective and objective elements, which correspond to feeling and knowledge, to the individual and the universal. The will, the principle of organic unity of these seemingly disparate elements, realizes itself by relating subject and object. These dualisms arise in consciousness, but they are not ontological distinctions; rather they are psychological divisions to be overcome through self-realization, an awareness of the original unity of the subjective and the objective.

In experience or consciousness, taken in its purest form, there is no distinction between self and world, self and "not-self." The individual self formulates the distinction between itself and the world through "an active process of experimentation, directed by the will." In Dewey's words,

> If, for example, I wish to decide whether a spot of red which I seem to see on the wall is really there, or is only an organic affection, I move my head and eyes. If the "spot" then changes with change of muscular sensation, we say that it is "in one's eyes." If it remains permanent, and is dissociated from the muscular sensation, it is referred to the object. Were there no will to originate these movements, there is no reason to believe that we should ever come to distinguish sensations as objective or referred to things, or as subjective, referred to the organism.[55]

This demonstrates that even in his most neo-Hegelian book, Dewey emphasized experimentation and overt action. Already, experience was the interchange between the subjective and the objective, rather than an affair that occurs exclusively in a subjective, mental realm. In knowledge, the subject seeks to relate itself to the objective world in an effort to reproduce that world within itself. Moreover, for Dewey, experience would always be dialectical in nature. Both sensations and the self are changed in the process of experience:

> perception or knowledge of particular things is not a passive operation of impression, but involves the active integration of various experiences. . . . [C]onsider the process of scientific observation. The mind does not wait for sensations to be forced upon it, but goes out in search of them, sup-

> plying by experiment all possible conditions in order to get new sensations and to modify the old by them. Secondly, such processes as imagination and thinking are not mechanically working upon percepts, but are their transformation and enrichment in accordance with the same law of a demand for the unified maximum of meaning. Thinking transforms perception by bringing out elements latent in it, thereby completing it.

Additionally, "The self, in its *specific* character . . . is changed by every experience through which it passes."[56] Further, when Dewey spoke of the transformation of experience by "bringing out elements latent within it," he described Hegel's conception of dialectical logic. For Hegel, the outcome of the dialectical process is the articulation of what is contained within the starting point.[57]

Feeling, Dewey explained, "signifies not a special class of psychical facts . . . but *one side of all mental phenomena*" (emphasis in the original). Feeling is "coextensive with mental life." On this theory of feeling, objectivity is not the subjugation of one's feelings in the acts of perception and knowledge, rather "all knowledge occurs in the medium of feeling." Feeling drives us toward the enlargement of our experience; it impels will, overt action, which is designed to achieve this goal. In perception and knowledge we choose, according to feelings, to focus our attention upon certain things because we seek self-realization through the attainment of truth. Moreover,

> The very fact . . . that we regard this knowledge as *our* knowledge, that we refer it to ourselves as subjects, shows that it is also feeling. There is no consciousness which exists as *wholly* objectified, that is, without connection with some individual. There is, in other words, no consciousness which is not feeling.[58]

Again, we find in Dewey's most neo-Hegelian phase, a theme that is found throughout his mature thought: all perception and knowledge involves feeling.

In the final section of the book, Dewey explained that will interrelates knowledge and feeling, the objective and subjective, as it develops the power of self-determination in moral and religious experience, culminating in self-realization, or perfection of the will and identification with the "perfect Will or Personality." By making the will central to all mental life, Dewey avoided the separation of intellectual and practical activities, theory and practice, which was prominent throughout the history of philosophy, especially in Kant's distinction between pure and practical reason. Instead, Dewey emphasized that there was a voluntaristic, and thus teleological, element in all mental action. The goal, or end, sought in experience, Dewey maintained, is "the self; all other ends are means."[59] Though Dewey did not invoke the German term, Hegel's notion of *Bildung* looms large in his discussion of the goal of all mental activity as the organic growth of the self, of experience. Much like Hegel, he employed the metaphor of a growing organism:

> As the tree is not merely passively affected by the elements of its environment—the substances of the earth, the surrounding moisture and

> gases—as it does not receive and keep them unaltered in itself, but reacts upon them and works them over into its living tissue . . . and thus grows, so the mind deals with its experiences. And as the substances thus organized into the living structure of the tree then act in the reception and elaboration of new material, thus insuring constant growth, so the factors taken into the mind constitute the ways by which the mind grows in apperceiving power.

There is one important difference between the tree and the mind, Dewey explained. "The mind . . . is conscious of, and can direct . . . [its] processes."[60]

Through its "tendency to connect[,] the mind realizes for itself the maximum of significance; it gets the fullest possible experience." The mind has an "instinct for a full unity" which "often leads it astray, but . . . is the secret also of all its successes." Dewey maintained that "The discovery of laws, the classification of facts, the formation of a unified mental world, are all outgrowths of the mind's hunger for the fullest experience possible." Ultimately, the self seeks "moral volition, or the control of the will for itself as the absolute obligatory end. It alone is absolute end. Every other group [of ends] is also means." The self-realized will realizes the ideals of "absolute truth, absolute beauty, and absolute goodness." Upon self-realization, the will makes these ideals "a fact of recognized validity in life."[61] The will gives content to, and thus makes definite, the forms of absolute truth, beauty, and goodness.

Throughout the book Dewey demonstrated a remarkable familiarity with the latest results of experimental psychology, in several languages, but he did not convince empiricists that he could prove the existence of the absolute self-consciousness on the basis of empirical evidence alone. He claimed that "Every concrete act of knowledge involves an intuition of God; for it involves a unity of the real and the ideal, of the objective and the subjective."[62] Dewey suggested that this claim followed from the idealist doctrine of internal relations, but not from evidence discovered in experimental psychology. Dewey defined the doctrine of internal relations in the following passage:

> Science is the attempt to reduce the world to a unity, by seeing all the factors of the world as members of one common system . . . expressed in the form of laws. . . . These laws must not remain isolated, but must be referred, as far as possible, to some more comprehensive law, and thus connected with each other as factors of one whole. The highest form of knowledge previously studied—reasoning—develops, as we saw, what had been implied in all previous knowledge—namely, the dependence of every fact of knowledge upon its relations to other facts. This presupposition of all knowing whatever, that all facts are related to each other as members of one system, science more consciously develops, explicitly setting forth the relations.[63]

Dewey admitted, however, that even the doctrine of internal relations did not fully prove the existence of a universal self. Despite his constant attacks upon all forms of agnosticism, he claimed that "There cannot be knowledge that the true reality for the individual self is the universal self, for knowledge has not in the individual compassed the universal." Knowledge of the universal self was based on "will or faith" which transcends knowledge but is "implied in all knowledge."[64] As Dewey had stated in *Psychology as Philosophic Method,* logic may assert the logical necessity of the universal self, but "it cannot give it as reality."[65]

The *Psychology* also yields a summary of the processes of gaining knowledge and of self-realization that will facilitate later discussion of the process of inquiry that was so central to Dewey's mature thought. First, objects or events enter "into our intellectual life as significant" when they are "connected in an orderly way with the rest of our experience." By contrast, "The meaningless is that which is out of harmony, which has no connection with other elements." As we seek greater meaning in our experience, we try to relate meaningless facts or events to meaningful ones. In so doing we create new experiences:

> The new experience will harmonize with some past experiences, and be incongruous with others. There will be on one hand a feeling of fitness, of satisfaction, which will lead the mind to be content with the connection, and on the other hand a feeling of unrest which will lead the mind to investigate the relations of the two.[66]

In a statement consistent with his later instrumentalism, Dewey explained that "Our past experiences decide along what lines the present activities of intelligence shall be directed." We learn through past experience ways to interpret what is presented in experience. "The artist interprets his new experiences in harmony with his æsthetic tastes; in the same object, the scientific man finds illustration of some law; while the moralist finds that with which to teach a lesson." The process of education consists in forming "apperceptive organs" that effectively help us process new experiences as they occur.

> If I interpret a shadowy form, seen in dim moonlight, as a tree, and the judgment is true, it is so because all other judgments which I can make about it will be in harmony with this one. Truth, in short, from a psychological standpoint, is agreement of relations; falsity, disagreement of relations. It follows from what has just been said that the mind always tests the truth of any supposed fact by comparing it to the acquired system of truth.[67]

Though this notion of truth might be characterized as a coherence theory, it is actually more than that because, like Hegel, Dewey was talking about more than logical coherence. For Dewey, coherence has existential implications because it provides satisfaction and incoherence produces unrest. We seek more than mere logical coherence; we seek experiential coherence.[68]

This process begins only when we are presented with specific problems, or are in pursuit of specific goals. In his discussion of attention, Dewey explained that it uses meanings to select materials from experience in order to pursue the self's interests, to solve problems, to expand meaning, and that attention deals only with specific, concrete problems. "The point to be borne in mind is that attention always selects with reference to some end which the mind has in view, some difficulty to be cleared up, some problem to be solved, some idea to be gained, or plan to be formed." When disharmonies or problems arise in experience the mind formulates a specific, concrete "end in view"—a term critical to Dewey's later thought—and the process of idealization begins. We immediately set to work, through overt actions and experiments, trying to bring harmony back to our experience. In so doing the self grows and achieves more meaningful experience. In his later theory of inquiry, the importance of doubt as the instigator of the process of inquiry would become prominent. In the *Psychology* Dewey said little about doubt; however, he made it clear that he already believed doubt only arises in response to real contradictions in our beliefs, thus universal doubt, global skepticism, is not possible.[69]

Dewey's *Psychology* contains a number of themes that are important throughout the development of his thought. The self is act, rather than a metaphysical substance. Feeling is essential to every act of consciousness. We are motivated to act by feeling, and feeling directs our attention; it guides the ways in which we act. Because "the unity of the self is the will," in his psychology Dewey emphasized overt action.[70] We develop and are known by our actions. He described experience as a process of the interchange between, and synthesis of, the subjective and the objective, rather than a purely subjective, internal process. And for Dewey, experience would always be dialectical because its two terms, the subjective and the objective, are always changed in and by the process. Finally, all action is goal-directed, and the goal is harmony within oneself and with the universal; thus all action is essentially moral action. This point refutes the charge that Dewey's instrumentalism is a celebration of amoral, bureaucratic efficiency. The charge completely misunderstands Dewey's theory of action according to which "amoral action" is an oxymoron. Finally, the theory of truth Dewey articulated, with the existential implications I noted, is quite similar to his later view that truth is that which resolves a felt difficulty, a problematic situation.

Dewey's *Psychology* reveals that many of the most important themes in his mature thought can be presented in Hegelian garb. Furthermore, it is critical to see that the neo-Hegelian concept contemporary Deweyans would find most objectionable in the *Psychology,* "the perfect Personality or Will," is utterly inessential to the theories presented in the book.[71] It is arrived at by faith at the end of the book, and one could just as easily choose not to believe in it, as Dewey soon did. Dewey ended the book by arguing that the moral will cannot "entirely overcome that dualism between the actual and the ideal selves." Though the moral will can be good in particular cases, and repeated good actions form good character, "this character never gets so formed that it can . . . eliminate the conflict of good and bad desires." Rather, "It is religious will which performs the act of identification once and for all."[72] If we jettison the notion that this harmony should ultimately be achieved once and for all, fully embracing a model of human development as a never-ending project, as Dewey soon did, there is no need to posit absolute ideals. As Dewey abandoned absolute ideals, he also began to substitute "organism" for "the individual self," "environment" for "the universal," "inquiry" for the "process of idealization," and he more consistently substituted "experience" for "consciousness." This should raise doubts either about the extent to which Dewey was Hegelian in 1887, or about the extent to which he was not Hegelian in his mature thought. By translating Hegelian philosophy into the language of fin de siécle biology and psychology, Dewey was completing the St. Louis Hegelians' project of "making Hegel talk English."

Andrew Reck examined Dewey's revisions to the third edition of the *Psychology,* published in 1891, one year after the publication of James's *Principles of Psychology,* in order to determine the ways and extent to which Dewey was influenced by James's *Psychology.*[73] In his "Note to the Third Edition," Dewey acknowledged that he was indebted to the work of James Ward, William James, and John Watson.[74] Reck concluded that Dewey was influenced by James to develop a functionalist account of conception, but Shook has correctly argued that in the first edition Dewey viewed "all aspects of mental activity as functionally distinct modes of thought."[75] Dewey was influenced by James's *Principles of Psychology,* but not in as substantive a way as Reck supposed. James showed Dewey ways to articulate functionalist psychology with biological metaphors, freeing him from Hegelian terminology.

In "The Development of American Pragmatism," published in 1925, Dewey credited James's *Principles of Psychology* with two important contributions to the pragmatic movement. First, James "denie[d] that sensations, images and ideas are discrete and . . . replace[d] them by a continuous stream which he call[ed] 'the stream of consciousness.'" Dewey always rejected British empiricism's description of mental activity as the association of discrete atoms, sensations, and ideas, and in the first edition of the *Psychology* he described mental activity as a "continuous substratum of sensation out of which . . . apparently distinct sensations . . . [are] differentiated."[76] At most then, James may have encouraged Dewey to continue in this direction, and it was surely important to Dewey that an American philosopher whom he greatly respected was working along similar lines. Second, Dewey noted that James contributed an interpretation of human psychology based upon Darwinian biology. Because James's Darwinian interpretation depicted all mental phenomena as functions within the human organisms' efforts to accomplish specific goals, it reinforced Dewey's emphasis upon the teleological nature of psychological phenomena, including conceptions. James also contributed the theory that perceptions and conceptions are "biological sports, spontaneous variations which are maintained because of their applicability to concrete experiences after once having been created." Conceptions, James argued, arise randomly, but are retained if and when they prove to have practical value. As Dewey stated, James articulated the view that the

> fundamental categories have been cumulatively extended and reinforced because of their value when applied to concrete instances and things of

> experience. It is therefore not the origin of a concept, it is its application which becomes the criterion of its value; and here we have the whole of pragmatism in embryo.[77]

Shook acutely argues that James encouraged Dewey to draw more heavily on Darwinian biology, but he did not provoke Dewey to dramatically alter his psychological theories.[78]

In other venues Dewey noted shortcomings in James's *Psychology.* In "From Absolutism to Experimentalism," Dewey spoke of "two unreconciled strains in the *Psychology.*" James adopted "the subjective tenor of prior psychological tradition," which posited "a realm of consciousness set off by itself." Dewey was most impressed by the other, objective, strain in the *Psychology,* which had "its roots in a return to the earlier biological conception of the psyche, but a return possessed of a new force and value due to the immense progress made by biology since the time of Aristotle."[79]

Dewey's reminiscence about what was most important to him in James's *Principles of Psychology* is borne out in a letter he wrote to James shortly after the work was published, in which he commented on a passage in the first volume. In the passage James described the stream of thought as one of "*Scious*ness pure and simple" rather than "*con*-sciousness." In the stream, James contended, there is no distinction between "me" and "not-me." Rather, we make these distinctions in a hypothetical way; "the Thinker . . . [is] given to us rather as a logical postulate than as that direct inner perception of spiritual activity which we naturally believe ourselves to have." Matter is postulated "as something behind physical phenomena."[80] Not surprisingly, Dewey wrote to James that "I cannot suppress my own secret longing that you had at least worked out the suggestion you throw out on Page 304 of vol I. If I understand at all what Hegel is driving at that is a much better statement of the real core of Hegel than what you criticize later on as Hegelianism."[81] It is also worth noting that Dewey showed in the letter that he viewed Hegel as a functionalist, and had a greater allegiance to Hegel at this time than to the neo-Hegelians. Dewey wrote:

> Take out your "*postulated*" 'matter' and 'thinker,' let 'matter' (i.e. the physical world) be the organization of the *content* of sciousness up to a certain point, & the thinker be a still further unified organization [*not* a uni*fy-ing* organ as per Green] and that is good enough Hegel for me. . . . I surrender Green to your tender mercies, but the unity of Hegel's self (& what Caird is driving at) is not a unity in the stream as such, but of the *function* of this stream, the unity of the world (content) which it bears or reports—It may seem strange to call this unity Self, but while Kant undoubtedly tried to make *an* agent out of this (and Green follows him). But Hegel's agent (or Self) is simply the universe doing business on its own account. . . . But Hegel seems to me intensely modern in his spirit, whatever his garb, and I don't like to see him dressed up as Scholasticus Redivious—although of course his friends, the professed Hegelians, are mainly responsible for that.[82]

Dewey also seems to have found in James's *Principles of Psychology* clearer ways to state ideas he found in Hegel. In the same letter to James, Dewey wrote:

> Would it horrify you, if I stated that your theory of emotions (where you seem to me to have completely made out your case) is good Hegelianism? Although, of course, Hegel gets at it in a very different way. But according to Hegel a man can't feel his own feelings unless they go around, as it were, through his body.[83]

And in "The Theory of Emotion," published in 1894 and 1895, Dewey stated in a footnote that

> In my *Psychology,* e.g., p. 19 and pp. 246-49 [EW 2: 21-22, 215-217], it is laid down, quite schematically, that feeling is the internalizing of activity or will. There is nothing novel in the doctrine; in a way it goes back to Plato and Aristotle. But what first fixed my especial attention, I believe, upon James's doctrine of emotion was that it furnishes this old idealistic conception of feeling, hitherto blank and unmediated, with a medium of translation into the terms of concrete phenomena. I mention this bit of personal history simply as an offset to those writers who have found Mr. James's conception so tainted with materialism. On the historical side, it may be worth noting that a crude anticipation of James's theory is found in Hegel's *Philosophie des Geistes,* §401.[84]

It appears that Dewey believed he found in James's work a more precise and concrete way to articulate Hegel's theory of feeling and emotion.[85]

Dewey's *Psychology* received many negative reviews. His former mentor, G. Stanley Hall, sarcastically wrote that the book "unfolds with the most charming and unreserved frankness and enthusiasm, the scheme of absolute idealism in a simple yet comprehensive way, well calculated to impress beginners in philosophy." The book was filled with facts, but "the facts are never allowed to speak out plainly for themselves or left to silence, but are always 'read into' the system which is far more important than they." According to Hall, "that the absolute idealism of Hegel could be so cleverly adapted to be 'read into' such a range of facts, new and old, is indeed a surprise as great as when geology and zoology are ingeniously subjected to the rubrics of the six days of creation." The book would be disappointing to mature minds looking for an accurate account of the latest results of psychological research, but popular with adolescents "inclined to immerse themselves in an ideal view of the world."[86] James read Dewey's Psychology the year it was published and wrote to George Croom Robertson that he was "quite 'enthused' at the first glance, hoping for something really fresh" but "sorely disappointed" because "It's no use trying to mediate between the bare miraculous self and the concrete particulars of individual mental lives"[87] Even Torrey, who was generally sympathetic to the book, admitted that it was as much metaphysics as psychology.[88] Nevertheless, Dewey's *Psychology* was remarkably successful, going through three editions and remaining in print until 1946.[89]

Though Dewey was increasingly critical of the neo-Hegelians, his continuing allegiance to Hegel is also revealed in his logical writings during this time. In "The Present Position of Logical Theory," Dewey claimed, contrary to popular opinion, that "it is Kant who does violence to science, while Hegel (I speak of his essential method and not of any particular result) is the quintessence of the scientific spirit." Dewey acknowledged that the secret of Hegel was lost in the "dialectical fireworks" of the "Hegelian régime." But he explained his claim about Hegel's scientific spirit in reasoning that bears directly on the Trendelenburg debate. Kant, Dewey maintained, began with the "scholastic conception of thought," the notion that "thought in itself exists apart from fact and occupies itself with fact given to it from without." Dewey referred to this view as scholastic because it depicts thought as something transcendent that must be imposed upon reality; it makes the mind "an external, supernatural Unrealit[y]." But one of the most important advances of science, Dewey believed, was the rejection of transcendent realities. In Hegel, on the other hand, "there is no such conception of thought . . . as is found in Kant."[90] Note that Dewey implied here that, for Hegel, the absolute was not transcendent as it was for the neo-Hegelians. For Kant, thought could become objective when it synthesizes a given sense manifold, but for Hegel thought is objective because it is never apart from an external world. And unlike Green, who mistakenly made a Kantian move by assuming that relations exist apart from the world, Hegel saw both relations and the world as existing within experience. In the following passage Dewey stated a position that bears directly on Trendelenburg's critique of Hegel:

> "Refutations" of Hegel . . . which attempt to show that "thought" in itself is empty, that it waits for content from experience . . . are . . . simply meaningless. Hegel begins where these arguers leave off. Accepting all that they can say, he goes one step further and denies that there is any such "thought" at all anywhere in existence.[91]

For Dewey, the Trendelenburgian critique of Hegel misses the point. Of course the dialectic of pure thought receives content from experience. For Hegel, thought, just like the world, is a component of experience. To undermine Hegel's dialectic, Dewey maintained, one would have to demonstrate that he was wrong to assert that the truth is the whole. In Dewey's words, Hegel's

> contention is not that "thought," in the scholastic sense, has ontological validity, but that fact, reality is significant. Even, then, were it shown that Hegel is pretty much all wrong as to the special meanings which he finds to make up the significance of reality, his main principle would be unimpeached until it is shown that fact has not a systematic, or interconnected, meaning, but is a mere hodgepodge of fragments.[92]

Hegel's philosophy was also an advance over Kant's because Hegel eliminated the distinction between thought and being. Mind/body dualism, Dewey believed, completely undercut science because it eliminated the possibility that the mind could be in direct contact with reality. Hegel did not reduce reality to thought, according to Dewey, but affirmed that thought is a fact among the world of facts, and that all facts are interconnected.[93] To clarify this, Dewey explained that for Kant the principle of causation is a priori because without it science would not be possible; and because thought is separate from the world it must, through its synthetic ability, impose the principle upon experience. For Hegel, however, causation, like all other relations, is in experience. It is not imposed upon experience as thought processes sensation; rather the principle of causation is one fact among all connected facts. Dewey defended Hegel from the charge of subjective idealism with the same line of reasoning, arguing that the charge stemmed from philosophers' mistaken assumption that when Hegel spoke of "objective thought and its relations," he held "the ordinary conception of thought (that is, of thought as a purely separate, and subjective faculty)," and was "trying to prove that this apart faculty has some mysterious power of evolving truth."[94] But when Hegel described thought as objective, Dewey maintained, he meant that it has the same metaphysical status as the material world we experience.

Dewey reiterated these themes in "Is Logic a Dualistic Science?" in which he criticized "the Newer Logic," particularly the work of John Venn. Dewey asserted that "there is but one world, the world of knowledge, not two, an inner and outer, a world of observation and a world of conception." Like Hegel, Dewey claimed that "this one world is everywhere logical."[95] This controversial claim becomes clearer in the companion piece to this article, "The Logic of Verification."

Because of his resolute rejection of dualisms Dewey never embraced the correspondence theory of truth, the view that a true idea is one that corresponds to an external state of affairs, or in language he frequently used, that corresponds to fact. His rejection of the traditional theory of truth made it incumbent upon Dewey to elaborate a theory of verification, or of truth, that was consistent with his rejection of dualistic metaphysics.[96] Dewey believed that there is "a single realm of knowledge, logical throughout" because he rejected the notion of "ready-made" perceptions, claiming that "logical processes enter into the structure of perceptions as well as of ideas." According to this view of the operation of the mind and its relationship to the world, ideas cannot be verified by comparison with pure, unadulterated perceptions or facts. Dewey acknowledged that "It seems upon this theory that the only criterion of truth is the consistency of ideas with themselves"; however, that is inadequate because "everyone knows that ideas may be self-consistent, and yet untrue."[97]

In order to articulate his theory of truth, Dewey explained his conceptions of fact and idea. He argued that we only form ideas, as something distinct from facts, when we encounter a problem that sets us in search of truth. Thus idea and fact are functions, or instruments, within the logical process, rather than manifestations of two distinct metaphysical realms. Ideas are hypotheses, or theories, we formulate when we discover contradictions within our beliefs, when we recognize that some of our ideas cannot be projected as undisputed facts. A fact is simply an idea which is not contradicted, is consistent with our current set of ideas, and "which allows the mind free play and economical movement." Ideas are facts "about which difficulties are felt, which opposes a barrier to the mind's movement. . . . The process of transforming the hypothesis, or idea entertained tentatively, into a fact, or idea held definitely, is verification."[98]

According to Dewey, apparent facts, ideas, are in flux as we subject them to modification, testing, and verification, but real facts are also enlarged, altered, and made significant by hypotheses. Dewey illustrated this claim through a discussion of the hypothesis of evolution. The theory of evolution is proven or disproven by facts, but if facts prove the theory, they are enlarged, given new significance.

> Suppose there is some animal of which absolutely no new observation has been made since the formation of the theory of evolution; our knowledge of that animal, the *facts* of the animal, have been, none the less, transformed, even revolutionized.[99]

The idea, the theory, is tentative, in need of proof, and should be modified to fit the facts. Facts, however, are "not rigid, but are elastic to the touch of the theory." Verification is not a matter of adjusting "mere mental states" to rigid facts, but is a process of "mutual adjustment, or organic interaction."[100]

Dewey outlined his theory of verification in the following passage:

> The mind attacks the mass of facts which it suspects not to be facts piecemeal. It picks out some one aspect or relation of these "facts," isolates it (technically the process of abstraction), and of this isolated relation it forms a hypothesis, which it then sets over against the facts from which this relation has been isolated. The isolated relation constitutes, technically, the universal; the background of mass of facts is the particular. The verification is the bringing together of this universal and particular: if the universal confronted with the particulars succeeds in filling out its own abstract or empty character by absorbing the particulars into itself as its own details, it is verified. And there is no other test of a theory than this, its ability to work, to organize "facts" into itself as specifications of its own nature.[101]

In this passage, Dewey articulated a rudimentary pragmatic theory of inquiry and of truth, as well as the beginnings of his instrumental logic, in a defense of Hegelian logic as he understood it. Hegel's dialectic, and Dewey's inquiry, begins when we discover a problem, a contradiction. In Hegel's terminology, we begin at the level of *Verstand,* analysis of the problem into its constituent parts so that we can precisely locate the difficulty. The difficulty is some problematic relation; it is an abstract universal because it is abstracted from the particulars of its context within a larger whole. We then view the problematic relation as an apparent, tentative fact. In Hegel's terms, the problematic relation becomes a particular. We move to the level of *Vernunft,* at which we apprehend the whole, as we formulate a hypothesis. If our hypothesis works, it verifies, makes concrete, the abstract universal by modifying it, or our perception of it, so that we see how to fit it into the context from which it was abstracted. As Hegel would say, the problematic relation becomes a concrete universal. In so doing, we fit the tentative fact to real facts, and at the same time, we transform those real facts by fitting them into the theory that is the hypothesis. "This continued process of breaking up and recombination by which knowledge detects, condemns, and transforms itself is verification."[102] Further, Dewey believed this description of verification was also a description of scientific method.

One might object that Dewey's later pragmatic theory of inquiry dealt with actual, particular problems that arise in everyday experience, while Hegel's dialectic was driven by logical contradictions that arise within the realm of pure thought. As I demonstrated in chapter one, however, that objection assumes the dualism Hegel rejected, making him a subjective idealist. Dewey clearly rejected that reading of Hegel. This point is apparent, once more, in "On Some Current Conceptions of the Term 'Self,'" in which Dewey wrote: "When Kant speaks of a logical unity of thought he means that thought is formal, not real; Hegel in speaking of a logical unity means that thought is real and not formal."[103] In this statement, Dewey did not intend to imply that, for Hegel, the world is nothing more than thought, but that thought and the objects we experience are equally real. I will develop this point further in the next chapter.

One last argument before I begin my examination of the influence of individuals on Dewey: In his analysis of "On Some Current Conceptions of the Term 'Self'" (1890), Frank Ryan correctly claims that Dewey's drift away from idealism was not a repudiation but "a rational *reconstruction* of idealism."[104] Because Ryan does not distinguish sharply between Hegel and British neo-Hegelianism, however, his analysis leaves unclear the question of whether, in this particular article, Dewey believed he was taking neo-Hegelianism in a more Hegelian direction or that he was taking Hegel in a Kantian direction as Ryan maintains. This is a crucial point because Ryan claims that Dewey believed Hegelians had incorrectly identified the sensible with the intellectual; however, Dewey believed the neo-Hegelians, and not Hegel, were guilty of that error. "On Some Current Conceptions of the Term 'Self'" was Dewey's criticism of Andrew Seth's *Hegelianism and Personality,* in which Seth broke with absolute idealism and became a personal idealist; thus Dewey's article was not a critique of Hegelianism per se.

Ryan also assumes that Dewey criticized Hegel's *Logic* for emphasizing only one element of Kant's project in the *Critique of Pure Reason.* Dewey did acknowledge that the two books had different purposes, Kant's being "the examination of knowledge" and Hegel's being the "examination of thought." Ryan concludes from this that Dewey believed Hegel "advances a logicism which ultimately attempts to reduce experience to thought." If this were true, then Dewey would have taken a position consistent with Trendelenburg's critique of Hegel, but we know from "The Present Position of Logical Theory" that Dewey rejected the notion that Hegel was a subjective idealist. Ryan misses the point that Hegel did not intend the *Logic* as an examination of all that can be experienced, but as an examination of what can be thought rationally. Moreover,

Dewey articulated this view of Hegel's *Logic* in the piece Ryan examines when he asserted that Hegel's logic "asks what are the forms or principles by which we must think the world; or from the other side, what the world must be to thought."[105] Ryan argues that because he wanted a theory of the self that accounts for all of experience, not just thought, Dewey resorted to a Kantian correction of Hegel's theory of the self, and that because this theory depicted the self as "a real activity," it formed the basis of Dewey's functional theory of the self. Ryan is correct to claim that Dewey arrived at the functional self through idealism rather than through the influence of James's *Psychology,* but Dewey's June 1891 letter to James, which I discussed above, shows that Dewey believed that Hegel held a functionalist theory of the self and that Kant, Green, and other neo-Hegelians mistakenly reified the self into a substantial agent. For Dewey, this is because Kantians (including the neo-Hegelians under this rubric) accepted the Cartesian dualism that Hegel had successfully overcome.[106]

Persons and Situations

Except for one year at the University of Minnesota (1888-1889), Dewey remained at Michigan until 1894. Upon Morris's untimely death in 1889, Dewey returned to the University of Michigan as head of the philosophy department. Dewey's eulogy for Morris reveals a great deal about why Morris had a more profound influence on him than Torrey, and provides another illustration of why Dewey disliked philosophical dualisms. In the eulogy Dewey paid Morris his highest compliment. In contrast to Torrey, who Dewey claimed had an "inner conflict," Morris's "religious faith and . . . philosophic knowledge . . . were one—vitally and indistinguishably one." Dewey continued,

> In this union . . . his intellectual and moral nature had its roots—a union which made him so complete a man and his life so integral. He was pre-eminently a man in whom those internal divisions, which eat into the heart of so much of contemporary spiritual life, and which rob the intellect of its faith in truth, and the will of its belief in the value of life, had been overcome. In the philosophical and religious conviction of the unity of man's spirit with the divine he had that rest which is energy. The wholeness of intelligence and will was the source of power, the inspiring power of his life.[107]

Dewey's description of Morris illustrates, once more, that his opposition to dualisms was much more than a formal, logical concern. He deeply believed that all humans long for unity, within themselves and with their society, and that this unity was best understood as organic. "The other personal quality which gave color to Professor Morris's thought," Dewey claimed,

> was his profound feeling of the organic relationships of life—of the family and the state. At one with himself, having no conflicts of his own nature to absorb him, he found the substance of his being in his vital con-

nections with others; in the home, in his friendships, in the political organization of society, in his church relations. It was his thorough realization in himself of the meaning of these relationships that gave substance and body to his theory of the organic unity of man with nature and with God.[108]

When Morris died, Dewey took over editorship of the Griggs's Philosophical Classics Series and, in a reversal of roles, began to press W. T. Harris to complete *Hegel's Logic* for the series, which was published in 1890. This book provides an important clue about a shift that occurred in the American Hegelian tradition during the 1880s and helps explain the ways Dewey was working to combine his Hegelianism with the new psychology by looking to Hegel's philosophy of spirit. Harris remained a committed Hegelian, ending the book with the "absolute person." But he emphasized the importance of the *Phenomenology of Spirit* as preparation for the *Logic,* devoting five chapters to "Hegel's Voyage of Discovery," and identified artificial transitions in the dialectic.[109] Around the time that the book appeared, Josiah Royce, C. S. Peirce, and Denton Snider all began developing a new interest in Hegel's *Phenomenology.* In *The Spirit of Modern Philosophy* (1892), Royce began an effort to displace the neo-Hegelian reading of Hegel by rehabilitating the *Phenomenology,* but he went beyond Harris by relegating the *Logic* and the *Encyclopedia* to secondary importance.[110] By reference to sources like Peirce's marginalia in Harris's book, several Peirce scholars have documented his newfound interest in the *Phenomenology.*[111]

Stimulated in part by three lectures James gave on psychology at the Concord Summer School in 1881, during the 1880s Snider had already concluded that the Americanization of Hegel consisted in making his abstractions practical.[112] Influenced by Harris's new book, Hegel's study of the self in the *Phenomenology,* and advances in psychology, in the mid-1890s he sought to replace Hegel's philosophy of the absolute with a science of the individual ego. Snider described Hegel as "the last European philosopher," and argued that philosophy should be replaced by psychology, the science of self-understanding. Like the pragmatists, Snider argued that theory was not the "speculative play of idle minds," but must always be harmonized with "the deed." He criticized Hegel for limiting the individual's potential to that of a philosopher rather than recognizing that no individual is complete until he has understood the absolute and then reproduced it in practical action.[113] Although I have seen no evidence that Snider influenced Dewey, I believe his argument that psychology is philosophic method and his psychological standpoint indicate that Dewey was also influenced by the *Phenomenology* to develop a historicist reading of Hegel. I provide more evidence of this in the following chapter.

By the time of Morris's death, however, other people had become important to Dewey's intellectual development; perhaps most important was his wife Alice. Dewey and Alice Chipman met in 1884, married two years later, and during his tenure at Michigan had three children. Her maternal grandparents, Frederick and Evalina Riggs, raised Alice in Fenton, Michigan. Frederick Riggs was an adopted member of the Chippewa tribe and an advocate of Indian rights. Riggs encouraged his granddaughter to be critical of her society and cultivate an independent, self-reliant character.[114] According to their daughters, one of Alice's primary influences on Dewey was her "critical attitude to social conditions and injustices." An active feminist, Alice was "undoubtedly largely responsible for the early widening of Dewey's philosophic interests from the commentative . . . to the field of contemporary life."[115] These claims are corroborated by Willinda Savage's interviews of people who knew the Deweys during these years and by correspondence between Dewey and Alice.[116]

Dewey was also influenced by Alice's religious views. Their daughters wrote that Alice had a "deeply religious nature" although, like her grandfather, she "never accepted any church dogma."[117] Dewey's interest in institutional religion steadily declined after their marriage, and in 1893 he declared that "the function of the church was to universalize itself, and thus pass out of existence."[118] The Deweys did not join a church when they moved to Chicago in 1894, and refused to send their children to Sunday school. This refusal angered Dewey's mother, who was still living with them, but Dewey and Alice stood firm, telling his mother that Dewey attended more than enough Sunday school in his youth to suffice for his entire family.[119]

In 1888 Franklin Ford, a former editor of *Bradstreet's*, a commercial newspaper in New York in the early 1880s, approached Dewey about joining him in a newspaper enterprise that would revolutionize the industry. Disgusted by the extent to which the newspaper business was controlled by moneyed interests, Ford proposed a newspaper, *Thought News*, that would solve the nation's ills by disseminating information to the public. The newspaper would be a journal "which shall report thought rather than dress it up in the garments of the past." An informed public was the answer to the nation's social problems. Once communication was enhanced, good government and relief from economic problems was inevitable. The utopian dreams of the proposed *Thought News* experiment caused Dewey no small amount of discomfort when the venture was announced to the public and he began to doubt the wisdom of the idea. The paper never appeared, and in later years Dewey would only say that Ford "turned out to be a scoundrel," but the encounter nourished his desire to make his philosophy practical, if not outright political.[120]

In June of 1891, Dewey wrote to James that Ford had been important to his ethical thought. In the letter Dewey explained that Ford had come to believe that "the social structure," especially economic class interests, "prevented freedom of inquiry," and "he identified the question of inquiry with, in philosophical terms, the question of the relation of intelligence to the objective world." In the preface to his *Outlines of a Critical Theory of Ethics*, Dewey acknowledged that Ford encouraged him to emphasize "the social bearings of science and art." In the letter, he told James that his experience with Ford had revealed "the true or practical bearing of idealism—that philosophy has been the assertion of this unity of intelligence & the external world in idea or subjectively, while if true in idea it must finally secure the conditions of its objective expression."[121]

Morton White claims that this letter, in conjunction with Dewey's *Outlines*, contains the first evidence of Dewey's movement away from idealism, despite Dewey's assertion that Ford had advanced his understanding of idealism. White draws this conclusion by explaining that Dewey's "admission that intelligence and the world are unified only in idea" reveals that he was beginning to doubt the idealist notion that the real is rational; however, White does not consider the possibility that, rather than rejecting that idealist doctrine, Dewey was beginning to understand it differently. In the next chapter I argue that Dewey came to understand this Hegelian doctrine, not as an admonition to passively accept the actual, the status quo, because it is rational, but as a critique of ethical theories that provide only abstract rules, empty ideals, as guides to action. Truly rational moral principles have actual effects in the world. So White is correct to argue that Ford had motivated Dewey to reconsider the relationship of intelligence to the world, but this consideration led him to conclude that if, as Hegel maintained, mind is not removed from the world, then intelligence, and by extension philosophy, is necessarily involved acting in the world. Dewey's rejection of the neo-Hegelian, transcendental absolute, in favor of Hegel's immanent absolute, led him to a new conception of the role of the public intellectual. Dewey also asserted, in the letter, that technology, specifically the telegraph and the printing press, had made the time ripe for a tremendous impending movement "when the intellectual forces which have been gathering since the Renascence & Reformation shall demand complete free movement."[122] Here it seems Dewey was anticipating a world-historical transformation, much like the St. Louis Hegelians' interpretation of the Civil War, and again it is difficult to understand how White could view the letter as evidence of Dewey's impending rejection of idealism.

According to Robert Westbrook, "Alice's direct, intimate urging of Dewey to bring his idealism down to earth was joined by the less direct influence of T. H. Green."[123] In 1886, Dewey expressed a "deep, almost reverential gratitude" toward Green.[124] Green taught that absolute idealism was chiefly a philosophy of citizenship and urged his students to make philosophy practical. R. G. Collingwood asserted that Green's pupils at Oxford "carried . . . the conviction that philosophy . . . was an important thing, and that their vocation was to put it into practice."[125] Westbrook is right to emphasize that Hegelianism was associated with progressive reform in England and in the United States, but he may have overemphasized the influence of Green on Dewey. Westbrook claims that Green's writings taught Dewey to be critical of laissez-faire social thought, but as we have seen Dewey had gotten that theme from the Burlington philosophy. Westbrook also claims that Green's influence on Dewey's social thought at this time "was testimony less to [Dewey's] cosmopolitanism than to his relative isolation, in the provinces of southern Michigan, from the social and ideological ferment of his own society," but in fact Dewey was involved with a variety of scholars through his friendship with Thomas Davidson.[126]

Dewey met Davidson in 1889, a critical year in his intellectual development. Through Davidson, Dewey befriended leaders of the Ethical Culture Society, Fabian socialists, as well as other leading American and European intellectuals, many of whom were moving away from American Transcendentalism or German idealism toward personal idealism or toward what was then called a "dynamic" or biological orientation in philosophy. Most importantly, Dewey witnessed Davidson's striking example of the philosophical life.

Davidson was born in poverty in Scotland, but he managed to win a scholarship to Aberdeen University, from which he graduated with honors in 1860. He traveled to Boston in 1867, where he attended meetings of the Radical Club organized by Bronson Alcott at Emerson's home in Concord, and where he was influenced by the German higher criticism of the Bible.[127] Upon Emerson's recommendation, in 1868 W. T. Harris hired Davidson to teach Latin and Greek in the St. Louis public schools. In St. Louis, Davidson rejected Emerson's model of "The American Scholar," who could only help the world by withdrawing from its corrupting influence, in favor of the St. Louis Hegelians' model of the philosopher as one was strenuously engaged in social action.[128] Though an active member of the St. Louis Philosophical Society, Davidson never embraced Hegelianism because he was convinced that it absorbed the individual into the absolute and was therefore unsuitable as a basis of ethical and practical action.[129] Davidson was also more critical of formal education than the Hegelians, claiming that it "stops with knowing and does not go on to living and doing," but he was vitally concerned with the problem of education in a democracy and embraced the Hegelian notion of education as *Bildung*.[130]

From 1878 to 1883 Davidson lived in Italy, where he studied the writings of the Italian philosopher-priest Antonio Rosmini-Serbati and, for eighteen months, lived at the Rosminian monastery where he wrote *The Philosophical System Of Antonio Rosmini-Serbati*.[131] He was particularly influenced by Rosmini's doctrine that "the soul has a faculty [Rosmini's "intuition"] which sees God, and that this faculty requires for its cultivation, so that it may live the New Life, a society of the nature of the church." And we can live it "only by establishing noble and wise social relations."[132] Davidson's philosophy developed into a version of personal idealism. Deeply influenced by the pluralism of Aristotle and Leibniz, Davidson believed Hegelian idealism had to be corrected with a pluralistic metaphysics in which each person was taken as a fundamental metaphysical reality, and God was portrayed as the sum total of persons.

Davidson argued that reality is composed of an infinite number of spiritual substances—monads—but these monads could only develop in societies. Reality, he claimed, is a *Göttergemeinschaft,* a society of gods.[133] Davidson's God was a potential, collective reality.[134] "God is the goal," he declared, "not the starting point of creation." "The gospel of the future," Davidson proclaimed, would be realized only upon the actualization of each individual's potential.[135] Davidson also espoused a moral perfectionism that called for the release of each individual's potential divinity through self-cultivation. He was convinced that this release would lead to the only true reform of human society; it was to this task that Davidson devoted the latter part of his life as he wrote about "American Democracy as a Religion" and worked for the participation of working-class people in the moral and spiritual riches of the human race.[136]

In 1883 Davidson founded "The Fellowship of the New Life" in London. The organization included among its members Havelock Ellis, Ramsay McDonald, Sydney and Beatrice Webb, H. G. Wells, and George Bernard Shaw.[137] The group pursued moral improvement through disciplined, communal, ethical life, and sought to bring culture to the laboring classes through public lectures and reading and art groups. Soon, politically minded members of the Fellowship criticized Davidson's principle of "the subordination of material things to spiritual" and formed the Fabian Society.[138]

In 1887 Davidson went to New York to establish a branch of the Fellowship.[139] That summer he lectured at Alcott's Concord Summer School of philosophy, and soon established his own school in Farmington, Connecticut, which met for three summers (1888-1890). Dewey lectured at Farmington in 1889 and 1890. The 1890 session presented a typical program: Among other participants were Percival Chubb, the founder of the St. Louis chapter of the Society for Ethical Culture; Davidson; Dewey; and Stephen Weston, editor of the *International Journal of Ethics*, who spoke on "The Philosophy of T. H. Green." Dewey, along with W. T. Harris, also contributed to a series of lectures on "The Relations of Church and State." Davidson spoke on "The Greek Moralists," and Chubb, Weston, and W. M. Salter, a founder of the Society for Ethical Culture, spoke on "Primary Concepts of Economic Science."[140] At the end of the 1890 session, Davidson moved his summer school to Mt. Hurricane in the Adirondacks and renamed it "The Glenmore Summer School for the Culture Sciences."[141] William James and Felix Adler, Columbia philosophy professor and another founder of the Society for Ethical Culture, both already owned property nearby and participated in the school. Prestonia Mann, a Fabian Socialist who had met Davidson in New York City, soon established "Summer Brook Farm" on Mt. Hurricane, and Dewey bought land across Gulf Brook from Glenmore, where he built a small cottage.[142] A standing joke was that Davidson and Dewey were separated by not only a physical, but also a pedagogical, gulf. Dewey objected to Davidson's rigid schedule for meals and study, as well as his efforts to guide and discipline the youth at Glenmore.[143] The list of distinguished lecturers and students at Glenmore is too long to recount, but they included Davidson, Dewey, William James, Josiah Royce, and W. T. Harris.[144] No doubt Davidson, Harris, Dewey, and Royce spent many evenings around the campfire at Glenmore discussing the intricacies of Hegel's *Phenomenology*. Davidson, a lifelong critic of Hegel, would have railed against the notion of a transcendent absolute spirit and demanded that philosophy go beyond the classroom and change individual lives. Harris, Dewey, and Royce would have readily agreed with Davidson's practical emphasis, but put more stress on the social rather than the individual.

During the winters of the 1890s, Davidson worked with young Jewish immigrants at the Educational Alliance, a settlement house on the Lower East Side of New York City. As I mentioned in chapter two, he frequently brought students, including Morris R. Cohen, to Glenmore during the summers. In 1898 Davidson organized the Breadwinners' College on the Lower East Side to raise laborers to a higher level of intellectual and spiritual power by exposing them to the best culture of the ages.[145]

Davidson died in 1900 and, according to Elizabeth Flower and Murray Murphey, Glenmore's lasting importance was the professional exchanges it promoted between Dewey, James, Royce, Cohen, and others. Herbert Schneider conjectured "that the Davidson summer schools were much more important than the Concord summer schools in giving American idealism a so-called 'dynamic' (biological) orientation," and as we have already noted, Dewey was influenced by James's biological emphasis during this time.[146] There can be no doubt that important friendships were formed and engaging intellectual exchanges took place, but as James noted, "the value of Thomas Davidson . . . lay in the example he set to us all, of how—even in the midst of this intensely worldly social system of ours, in which every interest is organized collectively and commercially—a single man may still be a knight-errant of the intellectual life."[147] Ford had stimulated Dewey's reconception of idealism, but Davidson provided him with a concrete model of how to be both a serious scholar and a practical, public intellectual. It is perhaps no accident that soon after he met Davidson, Dewey began giving lectures at Jane Addams's Hull House, and perhaps the influence of both Davidson and W. T. Harris, whom he now knew in person, influenced Dewey's decision to become directly involved in the problems of public education and educational theory, even establishing the University Elementary School at the University of Chicago in 1895.[148]

Political Philosophy and Ethics

Dewey was just beginning to turn his attention to political philosophy and ethics when he became involved with Davidson's summer schools and the influence of Davidson and the Ethical Culture movement can be seen in its development. As early as 1888, in response to Henry Maine's criticism of democracy as an inherently unstable form of government, Dewey articulated themes that were constants in his mature political thought. He critiqued Maine's reliance on atomistic individualism as an "exploded theory of society," and claimed that the newer organic theory of society was well supported by biology and anthropology.[149] He argued that democracy was the highest form of government because, at its best, it required the participation of every citizen; every part of the organism was utilized. Political instability, Dewey reasoned, came not from the inclusion of all citizens in the political process, as Maine contended, but from exclusion of some. Excluded individuals do not embody their society's values, and "Having no share in society, society has none in them. Such is the origin of that body of irreconcilables which Maine . . . attributes to democracy."[150]

Not only is democracy the most stable form of government, more importantly, Dewey agreed with Davidson that it is a religious ideal. Democracy was "such a development of man's nature as brings him into complete harmony with the universe of spiritual relations."[151] Democracy is the perfection of both the individual and social organism because it facilitates the full and harmonious development of each individual in the society. Furthermore, unlike other, more elitist forms of political organization, democracy allows each citizen to discover his ideal for himself. Self-realization, Dewey maintained, requires the freely willed actions of every member of society. Contra Rousseau, men could not be forced to be good or free.

Soon after he met Davidson, the humanistic influence of the Ethical Culture movement also began to surface in Dewey's ethical thought in his rejection of a transcendent, absolute self-consciousness. Yet there are key elements of Hegelianism that never disappeared from Dewey's philosophy. In the *Outlines of a Critical Theory of Ethics,* Dewey continued to defend an ethic of self-realization, but he based the theory on appeals to experience, never mentioning the absolute self-consciousness. Self-realization came to mean the ability to act freely, through interaction with others, rather than the manifestation of an ideal self as a metaphysical entity.[152] Dewey never embraced Davidson's moral perfectionism, but like Davidson and Adler, in his quest for a logic of life Dewey criticized neo-Hegelian moral theory for making moral ideals unattainable.[153]

In 1892 Dewey criticized Green's moral theory for two very pragmatic reasons. First, Green erected a sharp dualism between the ends that would satisfy the finite, individual self, and those that would satisfy the infinite, universal self. The ideal self was the goal of the moral life, but it was ultimately unattainable for the particular self. Dewey argued that Green left individuals striving for ideals they could never realize, making "the moral life . . . a self-contradiction." Poignantly, Dewey declared that "no thorough-going theory of total depravity ever made righteousness more impossible to the natural man than Green makes it to a human being by the very constitution of his being." Second, Dewey argued that ethical theories based upon standards of moral perfection were impractical because they remain "the bare thought of an ideal of perfection, having nothing in common with the special set of conditions or with the special desire of the moment."[154] Here Dewey is simply stating Hegel's critique of Kant's categorical imperative. As Hegel claimed of Kant's moral theory, Dewey's primary point was that the unattainable standard of Green's theory led to a paralysis of action. Joseph Flay correctly asserts that Dewey's rejection of the neo-Hegelian dualism between the present and ideal selves "exemplifies his 'return to Hegel,' circumventing neo-Hegelianism."[155]

Dewey still identified the moral ideal as a "unified self," but by the early 1890s that self was no longer metaphysically distinct from particular individuals. In "Self-Realization as the Moral Ideal," he claimed that Green had hypostasized the realized, partial self and the ideal, unified self into separate entities, when in fact these were simply two functional stages of moral insight. The first was a relatively narrow, limited conception of the self; the second was a "more adequate comprehension and treatment" of the self aiming at "the highest and fullest activity possible." Throughout the remainder of his career, Dewey would find the source of philosophical conundrums in philosophers' proclivity to hypostasize functions into metaphysical realities. Dewey proposed that the self be "conceived as a working practical self, carrying within the rhythm of its own process both 'realized' and 'ideal' self." He implied that this conception was incompatible with Green's "Neo-Fichtean" ethics, but not with Hegelianism properly understood. Green's theory was neo-Fichtean because, as Schelling and Hegel both argued, Fichte made the moral ideal unrealizable. Further, Dewey's notion of self-realization was changing. In this essay, self-realization did not mean "to fill up some presupposed ideal self," but "to act at the height of action, to realize its full meaning."[156]

In *Outlines of a Critical Theory of Ethics,* Dewey also battled with F. H. Bradley who, in his *Ethical Studies,* had eliminated Green's dualism between the individual and ideal selves by making the ideal one's actual self with all its latent potentialities and capacities. Though Dewey also sought to eliminate this dualism, he could not abide Bradley's view that the individual may not find adequate means for his self-realization. In his metaphysics, Bradley had written that "Goodness . . . must imply an attempt to reach perfection, and it is the nature of the finite to seek for that which nothing finite can satisfy. . . . Goodness, or the attainment of such an impossible end, is still self-contradictory."[157] For Bradley, all individuals seek the good, but again it is unattainable. From this paradox Bradley drew the conclusion that there could be no science of morals. Morality required an act of faith; in spite of an inherently contradictory moral world, we had to trust that our good deeds would be rewarded.[158] By arguing that psychology was philosophic method, Dewey had committed himself to the view that all philosophy, including ethics, could and should be scientific.

Dewey sought to explain his conception of the science of morals in "Moral Theory and Practice," published in 1891 in the Society for Ethical Culture's *International Journal of Ethics* in response to four articles published in 1890 in its first issue. Adler and Salter, founders of the Society and Dewey's colleagues at Farmington and Glenmore, published two of the articles, and British neo-Hegelians Bernard Bosanquet and Henry Sidgwick, who were involved in similar organizations, authored the other two.[159] Dewey's primary concern was to counter the belief that "moral theory is something other than, or something beyond, an analysis of conduct," or the notion that "there is no intrinsic connection between theory and practice." Dewey argued that moral theory is the same as moral insight, and that moral insight "consists simply in the every-day workings of the same ordinary intelligence that measures dry-goods, drives nails, sells wheat, and invents the telephone."[160] Dewey continued to use this reasoning throughout the development of his moral thought. Morality, he argued, could be approached scientifically because science was simply practical reason at its best. It is crucial to understand that Dewey was not reducing ethics to science, but utilizing an expansive definition of science as intelligent inquiry into all kinds of practical problems.

Moral theory, claimed Dewey, is the "construction of the act in thought" and "conduct is the executed insight." All conduct is based upon ideas or theories. Dewey argued that when a child learns to walk, through observation, reflection, and trial and error, the child develops a "theory" of walking. The theory becomes second nature as the child masters the skills involved in walking but, responding specifically to Adler, Dewey claimed that the practice of walking continues to depend upon theory in adult life, and "the observation of some patient suffering with complete cutaneous anæsthesia will serve to test the hypothesis."[161] Certainly moral action requires more theory than walking, but Dewey's central point was that both require the same intelligence. Theories about simpler and more complex actions are different in the "degree of analysis," but they are not different in kind. Moral theories have often seemed inapplicable, however, because they are very general and "Conduct is absolutely individualized." Dewey equated moral action with "intelligent practice," a move that is central to his mature ethical theory, indeed to all of his mature thought, which extols the virtues of the "method of intelligence" in all human practices.[162]

Moral theory provides formal moral rules, such as "I ought not to lie." These rules do not tell us exactly what to do in every situation, but are tools or instruments we use to resolve moral dilemmas as they arise. For Dewey then, moral rules are never mechanical; they have to be applied skillfully just as the farmer learns, through practice, how to apply theories about animal husbandry. Without skillful, intelligent application in specific situations, a moral rule tends to become "a cramped and cramping petrification," or "a merely speculative abstraction." Theories of ethics should provide a rationale for moral rules, and thus keep them "from fossilizing," but they must also be applied intelligently or they "slip away into sickly sentimentalism, or harden into rude militarism." Ultimately, moral rules that are proven through application "filter into the average consciousness, and their truth becomes . . . a part of the ordinary insight into life."[163] In other words, the truly moral individual is able to give content to abstract moral rules if, like the farmer who understands animal husbandry, he has been trained in a practice, a way of life. To restate this in Hegelian language, for Dewey, individuals can apply moral rules to concrete situations only if they have been acculturated in a *Sittlichkeit.*

Dewey ended the essay with a discussion of the relationship between "the ought" and "the is." Many philosophers, such as Hume, had argued that an ought can never be derived from an is. Knowing all the facts about a situation, the argument goes, never, in and of itself, tells us what we ought to do. Dewey adds to this insight that "the 'ought' is never its own justification."[164] What we ought to do always depends on the facts of the situation, and although we can distinguish between what is and what ought to be, this does not justify an assumption that the two are metaphysically distinct. Hume's insight about facts alone not telling us what we ought to do, for Dewey, only shows that "the is" and "the ought" cannot be rigidly separated. Again drawing upon Hegel's notion of *Sittlichkeit,* Dewey argued that "the ought" is found in the concrete "is." This does not mean that one must conform to what is, however. In the *Outlines of a Critical Theory of Ethics,* Dewey argued that the dialectical relationship between self and society does not require conformity to society as it is. Social reform comes from bringing "the ought" implicit in "the is" to full, consistent realization. In a clear statement of Hegel's method of immanent critique, Dewey explained,

> Reflective conscience must be *based* on the moral consciousness expressed in existing institutions, manners, and beliefs. Otherwise it is empty and arbitrary. But the existing moral status is never wholly self-consistent. It realizes ideals in one relation which it does not in another; it gives rights to aristocrats which it denies to low-born; to men, which it refuses to women; it exempts the rich from obligations which it imposes on the poor. Its institutions embody a common good which turns out to be good only to a privileged few, and thus existing in self-contradiction.[165]

To elaborate on the relationship of theory to practice, Dewey described "a scene of ceaseless movement," with "needs, relations, institutions ever moving on." An intelligent being appears on the scene, discovers "that its law is his law, because he is only as a member sharing in its needs, constituted by its relations and formed by its institutions." We know how to give content to abstract moral rules only if we have been socialized through our relations with others and the institutions of our society. Understanding this scene, Dewey claimed, is to know oneself because we are part and parcel of the scene. The moral agent "puts forth his grasp, his *Begriff,* and arrests the movement," seizing "a cross-section" in order to understand what is.[166] This cross-section is taken by what Hegel called *Verstand.* As the scene continues on, we observe its direction so that we can visualize what "ought to be." In order to observe the direction of the flow, we have to see it within a larger whole; for Hegel, we must rise to the level of *Vernunft.* Dewey explained that

> This, then, is the relation of moral theory and practice. Theory is the cross-section of the given state of action in order to know the conduct that should be; practice is the realization of the idea thus gained: it is theory in action.[167]

Other Hegelian themes are apparent in Dewey's *Outlines of a Critical Theory of Ethics.* Dewey also continued to depict society as a moral organism, and like W. T. Harris and Denton Snider he spoke of individual freedom as the positive, or actual, freedom to make the best of oneself, and not merely the negative, or formal, freedom from external restraint. Freedom is the ability to form ideals or conceptions of ends. Self-realization can only occur in the context of a well-ordered society, one that allows individual freedom and equal opportunity for all. Positive freedom also goes beyond negative freedom in that it requires not only that the individual choose ends for himself but also that he choose correctly. "Only that end which executed really effects greater energy and comprehensiveness of character makes for actual freedom. In a word, only the good man, the man who is truly realizing his individuality, is free, in the positive sense of that word."[168]

In the *Outlines*, Dewey also borrowed a comparative technique from Hegel that he would continue to use throughout his career, "comparing opposite one-sided views with the aim of discovering a theory apparently more adequate."[169]

Like Hegel, Dewey found value in each theory he discussed, but found each one lacking in some important way. Dewey also continued to believe that social institutions are the outward, objective manifestation of our moral theories and beliefs. He agreed with Bradley, and others, that our social institutions are often morally contradictory, and thus create moral ambiguity and contradictory moral demands upon us. Rather than conclude, like Bradley, that the moral world is inherently contradictory, however, Dewey concluded that the contradictions in our social institutions are manifestations of contradictions in our moral theories. Dewey's faith in the science of morality entailed the conviction that the moral world, just like the physical world, is not inherently contradictory. Whether or not the world is inherently rational is not a matter to be resolved by the special sciences, such as the science of morality; it is a matter for metaphysics. All the special sciences are based upon faith that the world they seek to describe is rational. Such a postulate, Dewey claimed, was the basis for any special science, and thus was essential to a science of morality.[170]

Also like Hegel, Dewey criticized both consequentialist theories like Utilitarianism and deontological theories like that of Kant. After examining both types of theories, Dewey concluded, "The end of action, or the good, is the realized will, the developed or satisfied self." Satisfaction comes neither from avoiding pain and seeking pleasure "through the satisfaction of desires just as they happen to arise," as hedonistic theories like Utilitarianism assume, nor from "obedience to law simply because it is law," as Kant assumed. Dewey sought to combine the insights of the two approaches to ethical theory by arguing that self-satisfaction is found "in *satisfaction of desires according to law*." He disagreed with Kant by claiming, "This law . . . is not something external to the desires, but is their own law."[171] In acting on our desires, Dewey believed, we discover and come to understand rules and principles that apply to specific kinds of moral situations; thus rather than being imposed upon desires, laws arise from acting on them.

By 1893, Dewey had rejected self-realization completely, replacing it with the notion of "self-expression," but I will discuss this shift in the following chapter.[172] During his tenure at Michigan, Dewey had begun the process of naturalizing both his religion and his idealism. He replaced both the transcendent God of Christianity and the absolute self-consciousness with the individual's social environment. Dewey began to articulate a functionalist psychology, but not because of James's influence. Rather he found functionalism in Hegel, and ways to express it with biological metaphors in James's *Principles of Psychology*. Although these developments may have required Dewey to criticize late-nineteenth-century neo-Hegelianism, they did not require him to reject Hegel. In fact, Dewey articulated many key elements of his mature thought in Hegelian dress, including the notions that the self is action rather than substance, feeling is essential to all cognition, and experience is dialectical. Dewey's primary objection to nineteenth-century neo-Hegelianisms was that they did not take experience seriously enough, but he made the same objection to British empiricism. Because of the influence of Alice, Ford, Davidson, and the Ethical Culture movement, Dewey sought to transform his idealism into a philosophy of social and political action, and from Davidson he received a clear example of a philosophical life that included active involvement in the continual reconstruction of the social organism. In his political and moral theory, Dewey defended a Hegelian theory of positive freedom, and argued, like Hegel, that abstract moral rules can only be given content by agents who have been socialized in a specific society. In the following chapter I outline how Dewey continued to develop his philosophy, ultimately into instrumentalism, along the trajectory he staked out in these early years. Finally, publicly acknowledging the transition occurring in his thought, in 1894, Dewey referred to his philosophy as "experimental idealism," emphasizing with that appellation that we come to know by actively constructing the object of knowledge, and that this construction does not occur in a private mental realm; it involves overt action, experimentation.[173] In the following chapter I show where Dewey discovered this conception of idealism.

Notes

1. R. M. Wenley, *The Life and Work of George Sylvester Morris* (New York: Macmillan, 1917), 146; Dewey to James B. Angell, 19 July 1884, James B. Angel Papers, Bentley Historical Library, University of Michigan; and George Dykhuizen, *The Life and Mind of John Dewey* (Carbondale: Southern Illinois University Press, 1973), 3. Angell had been president of the University of Vermont, but had come to Ann Arbor as president twelve years before he hired Dewey.

2. John A. Walz, *German Influences in American Education and Culture* (Philadelphia: Carl Shurz Memorial Foundation, 1936), 45-50.

3. Dewey, "From Absolutism to Experimentalism" (1930), LW 5: 154.

4. John Shook, *Dewey's Empirical Theory of Knowledge and Reality* (Nashville: Vanderbilt University Press, 2000), 5, 121-216. Frank Ryan makes a similar argument in "The Kantian Ground of Dewey's Functional Self," *Transactions of the Charles S. Peirce Society* 28, no. 1 (Winter 1992): 127-144.

5. Dewey to James Rowland Angell, 10 May 1893, James Rowland Angell Personal Papers, Manuscripts and Archives, Yale University Library. James R. Angell was the son of James B. Angell, the president of the University of Michigan. James R. Angell studied at the University of Michigan as an undergraduate student and joined Dewey as a colleague at the University of Chicago in 1894. At the time of this letter, Angell was in Germany, where he pursued graduate studies at the Universities of Halle and Berlin. Dykhuizen, *The Life and Mind of John Dewey*, 77.

6. "Philosophy recovers itself when it ceases to be a device for dealing with the problems of philosophers and becomes a method, cultivated by philosophers, for dealing with the problems of men." Dewey, "The Need for a Recovery of Philosophy" (1917), MW 10: 46.

7. Neil Coughlan, *The Young John Dewey: An Essay in American Intellectual History* (Chicago: University of Chicago Press, 1973), 90.

8. Dewey, "From Absolutism to Experimentalism" (1930), LW 5: 155.

9. Jane Dewey, "Biography of John Dewey," in Paul Arthur Schilpp, ed., *The Philosophy of John Dewey*, (Evanston, IL: Northwestern University Press, 1939), 21. Cf. Willinda Savage, "The Evolution of John Dewey's Philosophy of Experimentalism as Developed at the University of Michigan" (Ph.D. diss., University of Michigan, 1950), 13-16, 32-45. Robert B. Westbrook, *John Dewey and American Democracy* (Ithaca: Cornell University Press, 1991), 51-58. A real strength of Martin Jay's recent biography of Dewey is that it shows precisely how Alice and other women influenced Dewey's development as a person and a thinker. Jay, *The Education of John Dewey: A Biography* (New York: Columbia University Press, 2002).

10. The emphasis on James's and Green's importance dates back to Morton White, *The Origin of Dewey's Instrumentalism* (New York: Columbia University Press, 1943). Several recent publications have challenged this view: Ryan, "The Kantian Ground of Dewey's Functional Self," 128-129; Jennifer Welchman, "From Absolute Idealism to Instrumentalism: The Problem of Dewey's Early Philosophy," *Transactions of the Charles S. Peirce Society* 25, no. 4 (Fall 1989): 413; Welchman, *Dewey's Ethical Thought* (Ithaca: Cornell University Press, 1995), 51-55; and Shook, *Dewey's Empirical Theory of Knowledge and Reality,* 71-120.

11. Bruce Kuklick, *Churchmen and Philosophers: From Jonathan Edwards to John Dewey* (New Haven: Yale University Press, 1985), 238.

12. Dewey to Joseph Ratner, 2 October 1946.

13. Savage, "The Evolution of John Dewey's Philosophy of Experimentalism," 46-54.

14. Dewey had apparently mentioned a plan to write an undergraduate psychology textbook to G. Stanley Hall in 1883. See Dorothy Ross, *G. Stanley Hall: The Psychologist as Prophet* (Chicago: University of Chicago Press, 1972), 146.

15. Dewey, "Soul and Body" (1886), EW 1: 100, 108, 112.

16. Dewey, "The Obligation to Knowledge of God" (1884), EW 1: 61.

17. Dewey, *Psychology* (1887), EW 2: 361. At the height of his neo-Hegelian phase Dewey spoke of the absolute self-consciousness, but never the absolute spirit or self. However, the "perfect Will or Personality" he spoke of in his 1887 *Psychology* was clearly analogous to the neo-Hegelians' absolute spirit.

18. Shook, *Dewey's Empirical Theory of Knowledge and Reality*, 143-55.

19. Dewey, "Two Phases of Renan's Life: The Faith of 1850 and the Doubt of 1890" (1892), EW 3: 175. Whether or not Hegel could have embraced Darwinian biology without modification of his concept of process is open to debate. It is well known that Hegel condemned theories of biological evolution, but Errol E. Harris and Daniel O. Dahlstrom have both argued that Hegel correctly condemned the inadequate theories of biological development that were then available. According to Harris, "An acceptable theory of evolution which could satisfactorily explain the origin of species would have fitted well with his dialectical method; but no such theory was available to him. . . . [Hegel] provides a dialectical structure that does accommodate an evolutionary world-picture, and which in many important ways anticipates biological concepts of the present day." Dahlstrom, "Hegel's Appropriation of Kant's Account of Teleology in Nature" and Harris, "How Final Is Hegel's Rejection of Evolution?" in *Hegel and the Philosophy of Nature,* ed. Stephen Houlgate (Albany: State University of New York Press, 1998), 167-188, 189-208, quote at 197.

20. Dewey, "The Obligation to Knowledge of God" (1884), EW 1: 61.

21. Dewey, "The Place of Religious Emotion" (1886), EW 1: 91.

22. Ibid., 92.

23. Dewey, "Ethics and Physical Science" (1887), EW 1: 206, 211, 205.

24. Dewey, "Christianity and Democracy" (1892), EW 4: 6.

25. Ibid., 7, 5.

26. Dewey, "Reconstruction" (1894), EW 4: 103.

27. Steven Rockefeller has shown that Dewey's emphasis on religion keeping pace with scientific truth parallels themes in Hall's writings on religion, which were inspired by Feuerbach's *Essence of Christianity*. Rockefeller, *John Dewey: Religious Faith and Democratic Humanism* (New York: Columbia University Press, 1991), 90-93.

28. Ibid., 166. As I use the term here, panentheism, as opposed to pantheism, is the view that God is one with the universe, but that he also goes beyond, or transcends, the universe.

29. Dewey, "College Course: What Should I Expect from It?" (1890), EW 3: 53-54. Westbrook also notes the extent to which Dewey drew upon Hegel's concept of *Sittlichkeit*. Westbrook, *John Dewey and American Democracy*, 44.

30. See for example, Coughlan, *The Young John Dewey*, 57; and Welchman, *Dewey's Ethical Thought*, 5-8, 14-17.

31. Dewey, "From Absolutism to Experimentalism" (1930), LW 5: 157.

32. John Dewey to H. A. P. Torrey, 17 November 1883. Shook provides some further insight into the term "the psychological standpoint" by discussing its use in the mid-1880s. Shook, *Dewey's Empirical Theory of Knowledge and Reality*, 44-46.

33. Though Dewey praised Green for clarifying the difference between British empiricism and idealism, he disagreed with Green's most fundamental point, which is that the psychological standpoint is the core difference. Dewey, "The Psychological Standpoint" (1886), EW 1: 122-123. Cf. Shook, *Dewey's Empirical Theory of Knowledge and Reality*, 21.

34. Dewey, "The Psychological Standpoint" (1886), EW 1: 123, 125, 127.

35. Ibid., 124, 125.

36. Dewey, "The Postulate of Immediate Empiricism" (1905), MW 3: 158.

37. William James, *The Principles of Psychology* (New York: Dover Publications, 1950), 1: 196 (emphasis in the original).

38. Shook, *Dewey's Empirical Theory of Knowledge and Reality*, 49. On this point Shook takes issue with J. E. Tiles's claims about James's influence on Dewey. Cf. Tiles, *Dewey* (London: Routledge, 1988), 29.

39. Dewey, "The Psychological Standpoint" (1886), EW 1: 138, 128, 129, 141.

40. Coughlan, *The Young John Dewey*, 62-64.

41. Dewey, "Psychology as Philosophic Method" (1886), EW 1: 144. See Willinda Savage's discussion of the ways in which Dewey addressed the issue of the relationship of psychology to philosophy in the courses he offered at the University of Michigan. Savage, "The Evolution of John Dewey's Philosophy of Experimentalism as Developed at the University of Michigan," 46-54.

42. Many scholars would agree with Dewey's assessment of Green as more Kantian than Hegelian. See John Passmore, *A Hundred Years of Philosophy*, 2nd ed. (London: Duckworth, 1966), 55-56; Rudolf Metz, *A Hundred Years of British Philosophy* (New York: Macmillan, 1950), 272-73; Geoffrey Thomas, *The Moral Philosophy of T. H. Green* (Oxford: Clarendon Press, 1987), 40-41. Dewey continued this critique of the neo-Hegelians in logical writings of this time as well. See Dewey, "The Present Position of Logical Theory" (1891), EW 3: 125-141. Shook is correct to note that Dewey was, in some ways, moving in the direction of Caird's idealism because Caird also criticized Green for making the absolute transcendent. Yet Shook also points out that Dewey criticized Caird for retaining the view that psychology and philosophy required different methods. Shook, *Dewey's Empirical Theory of Knowledge and Reality*, 66-69.

43. Dewey, "Psychology as Philosophic Method" (1886), EW 1: 160.

44. See Welchman's discussion of Dewey's view of the temporality of the absolute. Welchman, *Dewey's Ethical Thought,* 53-54.

45. Dewey, "Psychology as Philosophic Method" (1886), EW 1: 161.

46. I specify Harris rather than lump the St. Louis Hegelians as a whole into this group because Denton Snider moved in the same direction as Dewey on this issue of Hegel interpretation. See James Wayne Dye, "Denton J. Snider's Interpretation of Hegel," *The Modern Schoolman* 46 (January 1970): 153-167. Though Dye does not make this point, it seems apparent from his examination of Snider's psychological writings, particularly in his claim that philosophy should become psychology.

47. Hodgson, "Illusory Psychology," *Mind* 11, no. 44. (Oct. 1886): 480, 494.

48. William James to Shadworth Hodgson, 15 March 1887 in *The Correspondence of William James,* vol. 6, ed. Ignas K. Skrupskelis and Elizabeth M. Berkeley (Charlottesville: University Press of Virginia, 1998), 208.

49. Dewey, "Illusory Psychology" (1887), EW 1: 170-71. According to Ralph Barton Perry, "Hodgson anticipated James in his emphasis on the continuity and fluidity of the conscious stream." Perry, ed., *The Thought and Character of William James* (Boston: Little, Brown and Co., 1935), 1: 615. Hodgson seems to have first used the phrase in print in his *The Philosophy of Reflection,* 2 vols. (London: Longmans, Green, 1878), 1: 101.

50. Dewey, *Psychology* (1887), EW 2: 4.

51. Ibid., 216.

52. Dewey, "Knowledge as Idealization" (1887), EW 1: 178.

53. Dewey, *Psychology* (1887), EW 2: 319.

54. Dewey, "Knowledge as Idealization" (1887), EW 1: 192.

55. Dewey, *Psychology* (1887), EW 2: 151.

56. Ibid., 138-39, lxxvi.

57. As Hegel explained in the *Science of Logic,* "the advance is a *retreat into the ground,* to what is *primary* and *true,* on which depends and, in fact, from which originates, that with which the beginning is made." Hegel, *Hegel's Science of Logic,* trans. A. V. Miller (Atlantic Heights, NJ: Humanities Press International, 1969), 71 (emphasis in the original).

58. Dewey, *Psychology* (1887), EW 2: 215.

59. Ibid., 361, 320.

60. Ibid., 132-133. For examples of Hegel's organic metaphors see the *Phenomenology of Spirit,* trans. A. V. Miller (Oxford: Clarendon Press, 1977), particularly at §§2, 12, 51.

61. Dewey, *Psychology* (1887), EW 2: 85, 320, 358.

62. Ibid., 212.

63. Ibid., 202. I believe Westbrook misunderstands the logic of internal relations when he claims that it is the theory that "all the relations of a particular thing were 'internal' to it, that is, they were all *essential* characteristics of that thing." It would be more accurate to state merely that the logic of internal relations entails that all relations are internal to a larger whole. The notion that all relations are essential because they are internal to a larger whole can be viewed as a theory of explanation, rather than a theory about the thing-in-itself. For example, if we move a book from a table to a chair, it becomes the-book-on-the-chair rather than the-book-on-the-table. Nothing about the book's metaphysical structure has changed, but we now think of the book differently. The book's location may well be essential to our understanding of it at any particular point in time (if its location happens to be relevant). Although neo-Hegelians used the doctrine of internal

relations to prove the existence of the absolute because they believed that all relations were metaphysically essential, I believe Dewey ultimately came to see it merely as a theory of explanation. Hence he did not have to reject the logic of relations in order to reject neo-Hegelianism. At this time, however, Dewey does seem to assume, with the neo-Hegelians, that the logic of internal relations implies (but does not prove, hence his reliance on faith) the necessity of a transcendent mind in which all relations exist. Westbrook, *John Dewey and American Democracy,* 18. On page 29 and following Westbrook implies that Dewey's ultimate rejection of neo-Hegelianism was the result of a rejection of the logic of internal relations rather than a reconception of it as I believe. Throughout his entire corpus, Dewey emphasized "the dependence of every fact of knowledge upon its relations to other facts."

64. Dewey, *Psychology* (1887), EW 2: 361.

65. Dewey, "Psychology as Philosophic Method" (1886), EW 1: 166.

66. Dewey, *Psychology* (1887), EW 2: 78, 110.

67. Ibid., 112, 190-191.

68. On this point I disagree with Jennifer Welchman, who claims that as late as 1894 Dewey held a correspondence theory of truth. To me it is not clear that Dewey ever held such a theory. According to Welchman, in 1891 Dewey "had not come round to Peirce's view of truth as that to which all men are fated to agree," but I doubt that Dewey ever accepted Peirce's theory of truth, especially the notion that truth is asymptotic. Welchman, *Dewey's Ethical Thought,* 73, see also 115. Further, I believe it is crucial to understand that, for Dewey, truth was more than logical coherence. In a time when Anglo-American philosophy is still dominated by linguistic analysis, it is easy to overlook this experiential element in Dewey's and Hegel's theories of truth.

69. Dewey, *Psychology* (1887), EW 2: 119, 191. See Shook, *Dewey's Empirical Theory of Knowledge and Reality,* 97-98.

70. Dewey, *Psychology* (1887), EW 2: 357.

71. Ibid., 357.

72. Ibid., 360.

73. Andrew J. Reck, "The Influence of William James on John Dewey in Psychology (1887)," *Transactions of the Charles S. Peirce Society* 20, no. 2 (Spring 1984): 87-118.

74. Dewey, "Note to the Third Edition" (1891), EW 2: 5.

75. Shook, *Dewey's Empirical Theory of Knowledge and Reality,* 103. Westbrook also claims that "James's book did not . . . offer Dewey much functional psychology that he did not already have." Westbrook, *John Dewey and American Democracy,* 66.

76. Dewey, *Psychology* (1887), EW 2: 35.

77. Dewey, "The Development of American Pragmatism" (1925), LW 2: 15-16.

78. Shook, *Dewey's Empirical Theory of Knowledge and Reality,* 102-106.

79. Dewey, "From Absolutism to Experimentalism" (1930), LW 5: 157. Cf. Dewey, "The Ego as Cause" (1894), EW 4: 95 n. 4; and Dewey, "The Vanishing Subject in the Psychology of William James" (1940), LW: 14: 155-168.

80. James, *The Principles of Psychology,* 1: 304. James's talk of "sciousness" was an effort to emphasize that thought and reality are not two ontologically distinct realms, but rather functional distinctions we make within experience.

81. Dewey to William James, 6 May 1891. Quoted by permission of the Houghton Library, Harvard University, call number bMS Am 1092.9 (128)-(144). Andrew Reck argues that James's *Principles of Psychology* was based upon an idealist metaphysics. Reck, "Idealist Metaphysics in William James's *Principles of Psychology (1887),*" *Idealistic Studies* 9 (1979): 214-221. It is because of Dewey's ability to resist the temptation, that James fell prey to, to posit a substantial consciousness, ontologically distinct from

the world, that Morton White claimed Dewey came to "out-James James," but this letter reveals that Dewey believed he found this conception of the self in Hegel, hence the claim in my Introduction that Dewey had gone beyond James because he "out-Hegeled the Hegelians."

82. Dewey to William James, 6 May 1891 (emphasis in the original). Cf. Dewey's claim, made in 1892, that experience is naturally a whole, but that it gets divided into self and not-self when conflicts arise within it. "This contradiction in the activity of the organism breaks up the existing vague unity of consciousness and sets the various factors over against each other. . . . At the same time, since the unity satisfies, while the divided activity does not, there arises a contrast between the unity or whole as 'ideal' and the separate factors as 'actual.' The unity, the complete activity is now identified with the Self. The distinguished elements or conditions, set over against one another and against the whole, are identified as the Not-self." Dewey, "Syllabus: Introduction to Philosophy" (1892), LW: 17: 155.

83. Dewey to William James, 6 May 1891.

84. Dewey, "The Theory of Emotion" (1894-1895), EW 4: 171.

85. In the section of the *Philosophy of Mind* to which Dewey referred, Hegel contemplates a "peculiar science" of "psychical physiology" that would study the way feelings express themselves as "specific bodily forms." Hegel, *Philosophy of Mind, Translated from* The Encyclopaedia of the Philosophical Sciences, trans. William Wallace and A. V. Miller (Oxford: Clarendon Press, 1971), §401.

86. G. Stanley Hall, review of *Psychology,* by John Dewey, *American Journal of Psychology* 1 (1888): 154-159. Cf. George Croom Robertson, review of *Psychology,* by John Dewey, *Mind* 12, no. 47 (July 1887): 439-443.

87. Quoted in Perry, *Thought and Character of William James,* 2: 516. James expressed similar sentiments to his close friend Thomas Davidson, writing, "Have you read Dewey's book? A great disappointment to me; for I thought, on first turning over the leaves, that here *was* something altogether fresh and original" (emphasis in the original). Cf. William James to Thomas Davidson, 12 January 1887; and William James to G. Stanley Hall, 30 January 1887 in *The Correspondence of William James,* 188-189, 197-198.

88. H. A. P. Torrey, review of *Psychology* by John Dewey, *Andover Review* 9 (1888): 437-441.

89. The last printing was probably in 1930, but the book remained on the American Book Company's textbook list until 1946. Jo Ann Boydston, "A Note on the Text," EW 2: lii.

90. Dewey, "The Present Position of Logical Theory" (1891), EW 3: 134, 135, 141, 136.

91. Ibid., 137.

92. Ibid., 134, 139.

93. I hope this point will dispel some of the Hegel mythology contained in Dewey scholarship. Although Bertrand Russell's misrepresentations of Dewey are legendary among Dewey scholars, Raymond Boisvert cites Russell to the effect that all German idealists denied the reality of the material world. Russell is at least as poor a commentator on Hegel as he is on Dewey, perhaps worse. Boisvert, *Dewey's Metaphysics* (New York: Fordham University Press, 1988), 41 n. 37. Thomas Baldwin explains that "One of the founding myths of analytic philosophy is that Moore and Russell refuted their idealist predecessors by deploying robust common sense and a new logic." Baldwin demythologizes this view in "Moore's Rejection of Idealism" in *Philosophy in History,* ed. Richard Rorty, J. B. Schneewind, and Quentin Skinner (Cambridge: Cambridge University Press, 1984), 357.

94. Ibid., 140.

95. Dewey, "Is Logic a Dualistic Science?" (1890), EW 3: 81.

96. It is not clear that Dewey was a monist at this time because, beyond rejecting dualistic metaphysics, he avoided asserting a metaphysical theory, preferring instead to deal only with what is experienced.

97. Dewey, "The Logic of Verification" (1890), EW 3: 83.

98. Ibid., 86.

99. Ibid., 87.

100. Ibid., 87. Cf. Dewey's discussion of concepts and percepts in "How Do Concepts Arise from Percepts?" (1891), EW 3: 142-146.

101. Dewey, "The Logic of Verification" (1890), EW 3: 87-88. Dewey's discussion of "universal" and "particular" in this passage is analogous to Hegel's claim that the dialectic moves from "universality" to "particularity," ending with "individuality." The individual is a union of universality and particularity. Hegel, *The Logic of Hegel, Translated from* The Encyclopaedia of the Philosophical Sciences, 3rd ed., trans. William Wallace (Oxford: Oxford University Press, 1975), §§163, 227-231. In Hegel's terminology, the individual is a concrete universal. Hegel, *The Science of Logic,* 739.

102. Dewey, "The Logic of Verification" (1890), EW 3: 89.

103. Dewey, "On Some Current Conceptions of the Term 'Self'" (1890), EW 3: 60.

104. Ryan, "The Kantian Ground of Dewey's Functional Self," 130 (emphasis in the original).

105. Dewey, "On Some Current Conceptions of the Term 'Self'" (1890), EW 3: 72.

106. Ryan's interpretation of this article also makes it difficult, if not impossible, to understand Dewey's 1905 complaint about the "purely Anglo-American habit" of "interpreting Hegel as a Neo-Kantian, a Kantian enlarged and purified." Dewey, "Beliefs and Existences" (read as an A.P.A. Presidential address in 1905 with the title "Beliefs and Realities," and published in 1906 in the *Philosophical Review*), EW 3: 97. As was noted above, Dewey criticized neo-Hegelians for actually being neo-Kantians, and praised Morris for coming to Kant through Hegel rather than vice versa; thus it is unlikely that he believed Hegel should be corrected by Kant.

107. Dewey, "The Late Professor Morris" (1889), EW 3: 9.

108. Ibid., 10.

109. W. T. Harris, *Hegel's Logic: A Book on the Categories of the Mind: A Critical Exposition* (Chicago: S. C. Griggs and Co., 1890), 400. On the St. Louis Hegelian's study of the *Phenomenology* see John Wright Buckham and George Stratton, "A Biographical Sketch" in *George Holmes Howison: A Selection of His Writings with a Biographical Sketch* (Berkeley: University of California Press, 1934), 49-50.

110. Josiah Royce, *The Spirit of Modern Philosophy: An Essay in the Form of Lectures* (Boston: Houghton, Mifflin, 1892). According to John Smith, Royce came to view "the Hegel of the *Phenomenology* [as] superior to the Hegel of the *Logic* . . . Royce saw very well how prominent a place Hegel gave to experience, to concrete life and the inner development of the self in that vast and mysterious odyssey of the mind called the *Phenomenology.* Royce even suggested a parallel in James' *Varieties of Religious Experience.* Much of the current renewal of interest in Hegel's thought is focused on his concern for the self and for the dialectic of experience stemming from the crucial fact of self-consciousness. [Royce's] *Lectures* anticipates this consequence and thus puts the reader squarely in the middle of current discussion." John Smith, "Foreword" in Royce, *Lectures on Modern Idealism,* ed. Jacob Loewenberg (New Haven: Yale University Press, 1964), viii.

111. William Elton, "Peirce's Marginalia in W. T. Harris's *Hegel's Logic*," *Journal of the History of Philosophy* 2, no. 1 (April 1964): 82-84. Cf. Frederic H. Young, "Charles Sanders Peirce: 1839-1914," in *Studies in the Philosophy of Charles Sanders Peirce,* eds. Philip H. Wiener and Frederic H. Young (Cambridge: Harvard University Press, 1952), 275; and Harvey G. Townsend, "The Pragmatism of Peirce and Hegel," *The Philosophical Review* 37, no. 4 (July 1928): 297-303.

112. Calvin Victor Huenemann, "Denton J. Snider: A Critial Study" (Ph.D. diss., University of Wisconsin, 1953), 27.

113. Denton Snider, *Modern European Philosophy: The History of Modern Philosophy, Psychologically Treated.* (St. Louis: Sigma, 1904), 788. On Snider's claim that philosophy should be replaced by psychology see Ibid., 690-691, 695. Cf. James Wayne Dye "Denton J. Snider's Interpretation of Hegel," 153-167. Snider published ten books on psychology between 1896 and 1905. Arthur E. Bostwick, "List of Books Written by Denton J. Snider, Litt. D., with Annotations," *St. Louis Public Library Monthly Bulletin* (August 1924): 1-8.

114. Judy Suratt, "Alice Chipman Dewey," *Notable American Women: A Biographical Dictionary,* ed. Edward T. James (Cambridge, MA: Harvard University Press, 1971), 1: 466-467.

115. Jane Dewey, "Biography of John Dewey," 21.

116. Savage, "The Evolution of John Dewey's Philosophy of Experimentalism as Developed at the University of Michigan," 13-16, 32-45, 164; and Dewey to Alice Chipman, 29 March 1886.

117. Jane Dewey, "Biography of John Dewey," 21.

118. John Dewey, "The Relation of Philosophy to Theology" (1893), EW 4: 367.

119. George Dykhuizen, "John Dewey in Chicago: Some Biographical Notes," *Journal of the History of Philosophy* 3, no. 2 (Oct. 1965): 218.

120. Quoted by Horace Kallen in Corliss Lamont, ed., *Dialogue on John Dewey* (New York: Horizon Press, 1959), 30.

121. John Dewey to William James, 3 June 1891. Quoted by permission of the Houghton Library, Harvard University, call number bMS Am 1092.9 (128)-(144). Dewey, *Outlines of a Critical Theory of Ethics* (1891), EW 3: 239.

122. Dewey to William James, 3 June 1891.

123. Westbrook, *John Dewey and American Democracy,* 36.

124. Dewey, "Psychology as Philosophic Method" (1886), EW 1: 153. See also Dewey, "The Philosophy of Thomas Hill Green" (1889), EW 3: 15-16.

125. Collingwood as quoted in John Passmore, *A Hundred Years of Philosophy*, 56.

126. Westbrook, *John Dewey and American Democracy*, 37.

127. Thomas Davidson, "Autobiographical Sketch," *Journal of the History of Ideas* 18, no. 4 (Oct. 1957): 532. Cf. Max H. Fisch, "Philosophical Clubs in Cambridge and Boston," *Coranto* 2, no. 1 and no. 2; 3, no. 1 (Fall and Spring 1964, Fall 1965): 16-18, 12-23, 16-29; and Henry A. Pochmann, *German Culture in America: Philosophical and Literary Influences, 1600–1900* (Madison: University Press of Wisconsin, 1957), 232.

128. See Wilfred McClay's discussion of Emerson in *The Masterless: Self and Society in Modern America* (Chapel Hill: University of North Carolina Press, 1994), 51-56.

129. Davidson grappled seriously with Hegel's writings, claiming, "I think I have read everything of Hegel's that was ever published." Davidson, "Autobiographical Sketch," 532. For Davidson's mature reflections on Hegel see Antonio Rosmini-Serbati, *The Philosophical System of Antonio Rosmini-Serbati,* trans., with a sketch of the author's life, bibliography, introduction, and notes by Thomas Davidson (London: Kegan Paul, Trench and Co., 1882), 104ff. On Davidson's reasons for rejecting Hegel see

Wyndham R. Dunstan, "Recollections by Wyndham R. Dunstan," in *Memorial of Thomas Davidson,* William Knight, ed., 123.

130. Quoted in Hugh MacDiarmid, *Scottish Eccentrics* (London: Routledge, 1936), 146. Cf. Morris Raphael Cohen, *Dreamer's Journey* (Boston: Beacon Press, 1949), 108; and Thomas Davidson, "American Democracy as a Religion," *International Journal of Ethics* 10 (Oct. 1899): 28.

131. Rosmini, *The Philosophical System Of Antonio Rosmini-Serbati.* William James reviewed the book for the *Nation* 35 (1882).

132. Davidson, "Autobiographical Sketch," 536, 534.

133. Thomas Davidson, "Noism," *The Index* (29 April 1886): 525. "Noism" is derived from *Nous,* and is used by Davidson as a synonym for Apeirotheism. For Davidson's views on pantheism see his discussion of the pitfalls of Buddhism in his letter to Havelock Ellis, 20 October 1883. Davidson, "Letters to Havelock Ellis," in *Memorials of Thomas Davidson: The Wandering Scholar,* ed. William Knight (Boston: Ginn, 1907), 41.

134. Charles Bakewell, "Thomas Davidson and his Philosophy," in Thomas Davidson, *The Education of the Wage-Earners: A Contribution Toward the Solution of the Educational Problem of Democracy* (Boston: Ginn, 1904), 13.

135. Thomas Davidson, "Antonio Rosmini," *The Fortnightly Review* 36 (1881): 553-584; and Davidson, *The Philosophy of Goethe's Faust,* ed. Charles M. Bakewell (New York: Haskell House, 1969), 157. Cf. Davidson, "Bruno's Thought: Its Sources, Character and Value" in Daniel G. Brinton and Thomas Davidson, *Giordano Bruno: Philosopher and Martyr* (Philadelphia: David McKay, 1890), 43-68.

136. Davidson, "American Democracy as a Religion," 21-41.

137. Wyndham R. Dunstan, "Recollections of Wyndham R. Dunstan," in *Memorials of Thomas Davidson,* 120.

138. Thomas Davidson, "Development of the Society," in *Memorials of Thomas Davidson,* 27.

139. Percival Chubb, "Thomas Davidson" in *A Brief Report of the Meeting Commemorative of the Early Saint Louis Movement in Philosophy, Psychology, Literature, Art,* ed. D. H. Harris (St. Louis: n.p., 1922), 60. Charles Bakewell, "Thomas Davidson," *Dictionary of American Biography* (New York: C. Scribner's Sons, 1928), 5: 96; and Joseph Blau, "Rosmini, Domodossola, and Thomas Davidson," *Journal of the History of Ideas* 18, no. 4 (Oct. 1957): 527.

140. William Knight, "The Summer Schools at Farmington and Glenmore," in *Memorials of Thomas Davidson,* 56-57.

141. For a detailed description of the location of Glenmore and the program for 1891 see J. Clark Murray, "A Summer School of Philosophy," *The Scottish Review* 19 (January and April 1892): 98-113.

142. See Charlotte Perkins Gilman, *The Living of Charlotte Perkins Gilman* (New York: Arno Press, 1972), 229-231. Gilman mentions going on an "excursion up Mt. Hurricane" with Prestonia Mann (later Prestonia Mann Martin). "That impressive man of learning, Professor Thomas Davidson, had a group of his own up there; we went to hear him," 231. Cf. Dewey to William James, 3 June 1891.

143. The Dewey family continued to vacation on Mt. Hurricane until 1910. Jane Dewey, "Biography of John Dewey," in *The Philosophy of John Dewey,* ed. Paul Schilpp (La Salle, IL: Open Court, 1939), 30; and George Dykhuizen, *The Life and Mind of John Dewey* (Carbondale: Southern Illinois University Press, 1973), 106-107, 151. See also Dewey to Thomas Davidson, 26 October 1890, Thomas Davidson Papers, Manuscripts and Archives, Yale University Library; Dewey to Thomas Davidson, 12 January 1891,

Thomas Davidson Papers, Manuscripts and Archives, Yale University Library; Dewey to Thomas Davidson, 8 March 1892, Thomas Davidson Papers, Manuscripts and Archives, Yale University Library; and Dewey to Thomas Davidson, 9 October 1892, Thomas Davidson Papers, Manuscripts and Archives, Yale University Library.

144. Kurt Leidecker, *Yankee Teacher: The Life of William Torrey Harris* (New York: Philosophical Library, 1946), 498. Dewey to Thomas Davidson, 8 March 1892, Manuscripts and Archives, Yale University Library.

145. Cohen, *Dreamer's Journey*, 118-122. After Davidson's death in 1900, the Breadwinner's College faithfully continued his original vision for eighteen years as the Davidson School under Cohen's direction.

146. Elizabeth Flower and Murray G. Murphey, *A History of Philosophy in America* (New York: G. P. Putnam's Sons, 1977), 2: 486. Quoted in Joe R. Burnett to Herbert Schneider, 10 June 1971 (Center for Dewey Studies file, "'Glenmore School for the Cultural Sciences,' 1892"). By the time of his death, Davidson knew thirteen languages, had published eight books (two more appeared posthumously) and at least three dozen scholarly articles. James A. Good, "The Value of Thomas Davidson," *Transactions of the Charles S. Peirce Society* 40, no. 2 (Spring 2004): 289-318; Michael DeArmey, "Thomas Davidson's Apeirotheism and Its Influence on William James and John Dewey," *Journal of the History of Ideas* 48 (Oct.-Dec. 1987): 707 n. 78; and Robert Calhoun, "An Introduction to the Philosophy of Thomas Davidson, with Illustrative Documents" (Ph.D. diss., Yale University, 1923), 265-267.

147. William James, "Professor William James's Reminiscences," in *Memorials of Thomas Davidson*, 118. Stories of Davidson's criticism of ivory tower intellectuals are legion. William James recounted an amusing anecdote about Davidson denouncing him one evening for the "musty and moldy and generally ignoble academicism of my character. . . . Never before or since, I fancy, has the air of the Adirondack wilderness vibrated more repugnantly to a vocable than it did that night to the word 'academicism.'" Ibid., 112. A few years after Davidson's death, James published his infamous essay "The Ph.D. Octopus," in which he spoke of the artificiality of the "three magical letters," Ph.D. James, "The Ph.D. Octopus," in *Memories and Studies* (New York: Longmans, Green, and Co., 1917), 331.

148. Dewey actually became involved with Hull House before he moved to Chicago in 1894 and was on the first board of directors. Denton Snider worked at Hull House for a few months in 1893, and he described a meeting in January 1889 at the home of Mary Wilmarth in Chicago at which Jane Addams described her plan for Hull House and apparently asked for advice. Snider explained that Thomas Davidson was present at the meeting, and when asked for his opinion, he "belittled the co-operative life of such a Settlement as clanish . . . and declared the entire scheme 'unnatural.'" Of course, this meeting occurred within a few years after the failure of Davidson's community in London. This may explain his critical attitude toward Jane Addams's proposal. Snider, *The St. Louis Movement in Philosophy, Literature, Education, Psychology, with Chapters of Autobiography* (St. Louis: Sigma, 1920), 499. Jane Addams also mentioned the encounter with Davidson, writing that the meeting "was attended by that renowned scholar, Thomas Davidson, and by a young Englishman who was a member of the then new Fabian society [most likely Percival Chubb] and to whom a peculiar glamour was attached because he had scoured knives all summer in a camp of high-minded philosophers in the Adirondacks. Our new little plan met with criticism, not to say disapproval, from Mr. Davidson, who, as nearly as I can remember called it "one of those unnatural attempts to understand life through cooperative living." Addams went on to explain that "fifteen years later Professor Davidson handsomely acknowledged that the advantages of a group far out-

weighed the weaknesses he had earlier pointed out. He was at that later moment sharing with a group of young men, on the East Side of New York, his ripest conclusions in philosophy and was much touched by their intelligent interest and absorbed devotion." Of course it could not have been a full fifteen years later because Davidson died eleven years after the meeting in Chicago. Jane Addams, *Twenty Years at Hull-House with Autobiographical Notes* (New York: Macmillan, 1920), 89-90.

149. Dewey, "Christianity and Democracy" (1892), EW 4: 9.

150. Dewey, "The Ethics of Democracy" (1888), EW 1: 237-238. Dewey's essay was a critique of Sir Henry Maine's *Popular Government* (1885).

151. Dewey, "The Ethics of Democracy" (1888), EW 1: 241.

152. See Dewey, "The Moral End Is the Realization of a Community of Wills" in *Outlines of a Critical Theory of Ethics* (1891), EW 3: 254, 314-317.

153. See Thomas Alexander's discussion of Dewey's search for a logic of life in the second chapter of *John Dewey's Theory of Art, Experience and Nature: The Horizons of Feeling* (Albany: State University of New York Press, 1987), 15-55, especially 43ff.

154. Dewey, "Green's Theory of the Moral Motive" (1892), EW 3: 163.

155. Joseph Charles Flay, "Hegel and Dewey and the Problem of Freedom" (Ph.D. diss., University of Southern California, 1965), 94. See also George Armstrong Kelley, *Idealism, Politics and History: Sources of Hegelian Thought* (Cambridge: Cambridge University Press, 1969), 302-309.

156. Dewey, "Self-Realization as the Moral Ideal" (1893), EW 4: 50-51, 53, 49.

157. F. H. Bradley, *Appearance and Reality* (London: Oxford University Press, 1969), 373.

158. Fichte made a similar move, ultimately arguing that all knowledge and action is based on faith. See J. G. Fichte, *The Vocation of Man,* trans. William Smith, introduction by E. Ritchie (Chicago: Open Court Publishing, 1906), 100. Hegel found this aspect of Fichte's thought very troubling, precisely because he feared that it could lead to the kind of irrational passions that had manifested in the French Reign of Terror. Hegel wrote that, according to Fichte, "The Will itself . . . requires that its End should not be realized." Hegel, *The Logic of Hegel,* §234. Dewey continued to critique Fichte in this way in his mature thought. See Dewey, *The Quest for Certainty* (1929), LW 4: 50.

159. Henry Sidgwick, "The Morality of Strife," *International Journal of Ethics* 1, no. 1 (Oct. 1890): 1-15; Felix Adler, "The Freedom of Ethical Fellowship," *International Journal of Ethics* 1, no. 1 (Oct. 1890): 16-30; Bernard Bosanquet, "The Communication of Moral Ideas as a Function of an Ethical Society," *International Journal of Ethics* 1, no. 1 (Oct. 1890): 79-97; and William M. Salter, "A Service of Ethics to Philosophy," *International Journal of Ethics* 1, no. 1 (Oct. 1890): 114-119.

160. Dewey, "Moral Theory and Practice" (1891), EW 3: 94-95.

161. Ibid., 96.

162. Ibid., 97-98.

163. Ibid., 100, 102-103.

164. Ibid., 105.

165. Dewey, *Outlines of a Critical Theory of Ethics* (1891), EW 3: 358-359.

166. It is interesting that Dewey understood the root meaning of *Begriff,* the verb *greifen,* to grasp or seize. This tells us something about his knowledge of German, but also his appreciation of Hegel's efforts to depict the mind as activity rather than as a passive receptacle.

167. Dewey, "Moral Theory and Practice" (1891), EW 3: 109-110.

168. Dewey, *Outlines of a Critical Theory of Ethics* (1891), EW 3: 343-344.

169. Ibid., 240.

170. Ibid., 323. On this point, Dewey's theory compares well to Hegel's view of science. In his *Philosophy of Nature,* Hegel argued that modern science is based on specific presuppositions about nature. Rather than discuss the details of the presuppositions Hegel delineated, we can simply say that the crucial point is that he believed our knowledge of nature cannot be based solely on experience; we must first have a perception of nature as a whole in order to proceed. See Terry Pinkard, *Hegel: A Biography* (Cambridge: Cambridge University Press, 2000), 564.

171. Dewey, *Outlines of a Critical Theory of Ethics* (1891), EW 3: 300.

172. See Dewey, "Self-Realization as the Moral Ideal" (1893), EW 4: 42-53; and Dewey, *The Study of Ethics: A Syllabus* (1894), EW 4: 221-362.

173. Dewey, *The Study of Ethics: A Syllabus* (1894), EW 4: 264. Cf. Dewey, *The Quest for Certainty* (1929), LW 4: 134.

Chapter Five

Dewey's Transitional Years, 1894–1904

Dewey claimed he shifted from absolutism to experimentalism during the period of 1894 to 1904. There is a complex debate about the exact timing of this shift, and Dewey never analyzed it himself. Some have argued, on the evidence of his criticisms of T. H. Green, that Dewey rejected idealism as early as 1891, but I have already argued that he mounted a Hegelian critique of Green.[1] Morton White, as I have previously noted, claims that Dewey first began to show signs of moving away from idealism in 1891 in his *Outlines of a Critical Theory of Ethics* and his letter to James about the influence of Franklin Ford, but I rejected that view as well. Because he does not clearly define neo-Hegelianism, White misinterprets Dewey's abandonment of a transcendent absolute, claiming that in 1894 Dewey's term "experimental idealism" shows that he was in a transitional phase in which he was trying to unite his idealism with his functionalism.[2] This transitional phase, White contends, lasted until 1903, when Dewey and his colleagues published the *Studies in Logical Theory.*[3] Robert Westbrook argues that Dewey broke with idealism late in the 1890s, but agrees that is was not announced by him until the publication of the *Studies.* Although Dewey used the phrase "from absolutism to experimentalism" and scholars have described Dewey's contributions to the *Studies* as a criticism of absolute idealism, the term never actually appears anywhere in the *Studies.* In fact, one of the biggest problems with analyzing this transition is Dewey himself, because in numerous writings that are relevant to this issue he is frustratingly vague when he speaks of "idealism."[4] Hence it is not difficult to see why scholars have been confused about the Hegelian deposit in Dewey's mature thought.

Until recently, however, the view that Dewey broke decisively from idealist ranks no later than the publication of the *Studies* in 1903 has been accepted unanimously. John Shook has tried to shift the debate, however, by maintaining that we need to ask a different question: Rather than ask when did Dewey abandon idealism, "The better question is when did Dewey abandon the absolutism of his idealism, develop a functionalist psychology, and establish an instrumentalist version of pragmatism?"[5] Shook, of course, concludes that Dewey never really abandoned idealism, but simply modified it. In answer to Shook's question, I would argue that it would be more precise to ask not when Dewey abandoned the absolutism of his idealism, but when he abandoned the neo-Hegelian transcendent absolute, and reaffirm that it disappeared from Dewey's thought by 1891. By then he sought a philosophy that addressed the problems of lived experience, having concluded that transcendent truth was inherently unavailing and even dangerous because it aimed at the impossible, thereby fostering a sense of moral hopelessness. The development of Dewey's functionalist psychology was an integral part of his rejection of transcendent metaphysics. Increasingly, Dewey eliminated metaphysics by explaining elements of experience as functions within a process rather than as substantial entities. As he explained to James, Dewey believed he found this functionalism in Hegel.[6] Dewey also began to develop his instrumentalist logic in essays published in 1890 and 1891, but he did so in the context of a defense of Hegelian logic; this is particularly apparent in "The Present Position of Logical Theory" (1891), in which Dewey argued that Hegel's logic was more consistent with the scientific spirit than Kant's. In general, in the previous chapter I agree with Shook's analysis of when these developments occurred, but in this chapter I complement it by demonstrating how Dewey could derive these radically secular, humanistic doctrines from the philosophy of "the grand metaphysician" himself.

University of Chicago

Dewey continued to attend meetings at Glenmore throughout the 1890s, and continued to associate with leaders of the Ethical Culture movement. But in 1894 he moved his family to Chicago as he accepted the offer of William Rainey Harper, president of the newly founded University of Chicago, to become chairman of the Department of Philosophy. Dewey was attracted by the opportunity to build the new department, to focus on research, and by Harper's agreement to include psychology and pedagogy in the department.[7] Dewey's desire to combine these disciplines within one department reveals a great deal about the sort of philosophy he wanted to develop. As Dewey's mature thought took shape, he was increasingly fascinated with the study of how humans grow intellectually, morally, and spiritually. Consequently, the development of philosophy, for Dewey, required research into psychology and education and, for the first time, he would work alongside experimental psychologists and be actively involved in the study of elementary education.

About eighteen months after arriving in Chicago, Dewey helped found the University Elementary School within the University's newly established Department of Pedagogy, both of which were run under his guidance and inspiration. His wife Alice served as principal of the elementary school from 1901 to 1904.[8] The Elementary School, or as it was commonly known, the Dewey School, was conceived in the spirit of experimentation as a place where one could test hypotheses and learn more about the psychology of the child. Under Dewey's leadership, teachers were to view the child as an active, dynamic being with his own impulses and interests. The primary job of the teacher was to cultivate the children's natural abilities and help direct their activities in ways that allowed them to learn through activity. Because, according to Dewey's psychology, ideas do not exist prior to activity, teachers were to work from the assumption "that ideas arise as the definition of activity, and serve to direct that activity in new expressions."[9] The children were expected to learn from problematic situations that would naturally arise as they pursued their interests. And because Dewey held that learning was a social matter, the children were encouraged to engage in group activities. Moreover, Dewey believed this social interaction facilitated the development of moral and social attitudes necessary in a democracy.

The Dewey School became famous and attracted numerous state and national organizations to the campus for their convention meetings. Many prominent educators came to observe the school and speak on pedagogical topics. The Dewey School and Dewey's writings on education brought considerable acclaim to the University of Chicago's program in education; by 1900 it was considered the best in the country.[10] From this time on, Dewey's writings on psychology were based on actual observation of children at the school and were much more empirical. At Chicago, Dewey's interest in experimental science and its application to philosophy, psychology, and the social sciences came to the forefront of his writings, furthering the trend in his thought toward increasingly practical philosophy, focused on the development of strategies that would facilitate the intelligent solution of specific human problems.[11]

Chicago provided Dewey ample opportunity to reflect on the practical, social import of the metaphysical issue of unity in diversity. The city was crowded with European immigrants, the most recent of whom had arrived since the Civil War and were primarily from southern and eastern Europe. This ethnic diversity naturally led to unprecedented cultural and intellectual diversity. By the time Dewey arrived in Chicago, it had grown to a city of over one million inhabitants. A world apart from Ann Arbor, the city was a hotbed of social activism. Dewey arrived in the city to look for a home for his growing family in the midst of the great Pullman strike of 1894. He wrote to Alice, enclosing editorials from *Harper's Weekly* that were critical of the strikers and Eugene Debs. Dewey adamantly disagreed with the editorials, writing,

> It is hard to keep one's balance; the only wonder is that when the "higher classes"—damn them—take such views there aren't more downright socialists. . . . It doesn't make any difference that I see what the facts are; that a representative journal of the upper classes—damn them again—can take the attitude of that Harper's weekly & in common with all other journals, think Debs is a simple lunatic or else doing all this to show his criminal control over the . . . criminal "lower classes"—well, it shows

> what it is to become a higher class. And I fear Chicago Univ. is a capitalistic institution—that is, it too belongs to the higher classes.[12]

In many ways Dewey's stay in Chicago facilitated his efforts to put the St. Louis Hegelian's notion of practical philosophy to good use, but his concerns about the university being a "capitalistic institution" may have tempered his enthusiasm for political action. Those concerns were soon confirmed when a colleague, Edward Bemis, was dismissed for his pro-labor stance.[13] Dewey noted ironically that at the University of Michigan, a state university, "there was freedom as to social questions, but some restraint on the religious side," while at the University of Chicago, a private "Baptist institution there is seemingly complete religious freedom, but . . . a good deal of constriction on the social side."[14] Like Thomas Davidson and the leaders of the Ethical Culture movement, however, Dewey's writings focused mainly, though not exclusively, on psychology, ethics, and education. He did not engage in the sort of controversial political activism for which he became famous in later years, perhaps because of concerns about job security, but given the administrative responsibilities he faced, it is difficult to imagine where he would have found the time.[15]

But when he first arrived, Dewey saw opportunity in the mayhem of Chicago, and he wanted the full experience of the city. "Chicago," he wrote to Alice, "is the place to make you appreciate at every turn the absolute opportunity which chaos affords—it is sheer Matter with no standards at all!" Dewey hoped his philosophy could ultimately provide direction for the chaos of matter in random motion that he experienced in one of the fastest-growing cities in the United States. A friend took Dewey on tours of the city, showing him "a salvation meeting out of doors, a 'happy gospel' meeting in doors, part of the show at the Park Theatre, the worst one in town, four or five wine rooms, where some of the street women hang around, a ten cent lodging house . . . two gambling places . . . & three houses of prostitution."[16]

Dewey also quickly connected with intellectuals in the city. During his first winter in Chicago he met Denton Snider of St. Louis Hegelian fame at the Chicago Kindergarten College, and at a meeting of an "Aristotleian Society" held at the home of Dr. Foster, whom he and Alice had met at Davidson's Glenmore. Dewey remarked that Snider was not the "long-bearded thing" he expected, but "looked quite a regular business man type."[17] Dewey read a paper at Foster's and was amused at the response he received. He spoke of "several bright women there" who "warmed up to my paper," while Snider, and other "strictly 'phil' gentlemen," criticized his contention that "philosophy must become experimental." Dewey explained that "Snider talked about 15 minutes on the limitations of physiological psychology, & said, amiably, (then apologizing still more amiably) that when the Zeitgeist went through the gates of the future the college professor would be left on the ground outside somewhere." Dewey joked "that after having been called a speculative Hegelian by the scientific brethren I finally had the pleasure of being set down by the orthodox Hegelians as a crass empiricist."[18] At this time, Dewey's philosophy did not fit neatly into any existing school of thought, nor did he demonstrate any concern about that fact.

Philosophically, Dewey had struck out in his own direction, and it was understandably difficult for his contemporaries to label his thought. And now Dewey began to apply his philosophical theories to social reform more earnestly than ever before. Before he arrived in Chicago, he was a member of the first board of trustees of Jane Addams's Hull House, which was founded in 1889 as a settlement house for social work among immigrant workingmen and women. Dewey had lectured at Hull House before he moved to Chicago but now he had more opportunity to meet workers and witness their daily problems. He was also exposed to liberals, socialists, anarchists, communists, and others who frequently met at Hull House to exchange ideas.[19] Dewey's exposure to workers and people with more radical views than his own sharpened his social thought and nourished his interest in real social problems.

Dewey's first task at the University of Chicago was to build the Department of Philosophy. James H. Tufts was already an associate professor of philosophy at Chicago, and Dewey quickly expanded the department by hiring James R. Angell and George Herbert Mead. Tufts, Angell, and Mead had all been affiliated with the University of Michigan and had all pursued graduate studies in Germany.[20] Addison W. Moore and Edward S. Ames were selected as teaching fellows in 1894, and both eventually became regular members of the department after completing their doctorates there. Moore was primarily interested in logic, and Ames in the psychology of religion. Dewey, Tufts, Angell, and Mead were particularly interested in developing a psychology that was consistent with the latest findings of evolutionary biology, and these four were founders of the school of functionalist psychology for which the University of Chicago became known.

Of these colleagues, Dewey claimed that George Herbert Mead had the greatest influence on him, but their development is so parallel that it is difficult to reconstruct his influence with any precision. In his eulogy for Mead, written in 1931, Dewey emphasized the importance of Mead's work "in social psychology, and in a social interpretation of life and the world." Dewey explained that Mead's social psychology

> worked a revolution in my own thinking though I was slow in grasping . . . its full implications. The individual mind, the conscious self, was to him the world of nature first taken up into social relations and then dissolved to form a new self which then went forth to recreate the world of nature and social institutions.[21]

As an instructor at Michigan, Mead was impressed by Dewey's version of Hegelianism. Mead claimed that his social treatment of self-consciousness was indebted to Hegel and, much like Dewey, he argued that "with Hegel, philosophy becomes a method of thought rather than a search for fundamental entities." Rejecting the metaphysical reading of Hegel, Mead asserted that the purpose of philosophy, for Hegel, was to articulate "the method by which the self in its full cognitive and social content meets and solves its difficulties." From the Hegelian dialectic, Mead took the theory that thought proceeds by negating objects of thought that have come into conflict and discovering a new synthesis in which the present difficulty is overcome and the problematic object of thought is reinterpreted or reconstructed. On this theory, the objects of thought are not "fixed presuppositions," but "means for the purpose of conduct."[22] Gary A. Cook explains that, although after 1903 he rarely invoked the name of Hegel in his writings, Mead always retained an emphasis on

> the reconstructive function of thought, and his conception of the intellectual method to be employed in the realization of this function never departed from the view he had set forth in his early Hegelian period: he simply stopped speaking of this method as Hegelian or dialectical and began referring to it instead as the method of reflective, scientific, or experimental intelligence.[23]

Cook's description of Mead's debt to Hegel is also true of Dewey. Both philosophers retained Hegel's emphasis on the social nature of consciousness, were particularly interested in Hegel's method, which they viewed as a general method of inquiry rather than a method of metaphysical inquiry, and reinterpreted the dialectic in naturalistic language they learned from biology and the new psychology. They were not the only American idealists who came to read Hegel in this way. In a discussion of the post-Kantian dialectic, Josiah Royce stated that "Our idealists were, one and all, in a very genuine sense what people now call pragmatists" because of their emphasis upon "the relation of truth to action, to practice, to the will."[24]

Mead ultimately rejected Hegel's term "absolute" because he believed that Darwinian biology's talk of organisms living in environments to which they must adapt in order to survive provided a more transparent nomenclature for an organic philosophy. Darwinian biology provided a way to articulate how qualitatively new forms of organisms could emerge from a natural process without connotations of an immutable or transcendent principle of teleology. Moreover, Mead believed that Hegel's dialectic was the fundamental structure of human reflection in its highest form, and that it described the procedure of the experimental sciences though Hegel did not fully appreciate it as such.[25] Once more, this description of the development of Mead's Hegelianism is also true of Dewey's.

The question arises, if Dewey and Mead found the intellectual tools they needed in Darwinian naturalism, why would they retain anything from Hegel? A bit later in this chapter I argue that Hegel's theory of causation, which was essentially rooted in his organic holism and dynamic view of reality, gave a peculiar twist to Dewey's naturalism. First, the holistic aspect of Hegel's view of causation convinced Dewey that scientific method must not be reductive; it must address and seek to account for the whole of experience, including elements that were often devalued by empiricist philosophers as merely subjective. Second, Hegel's dialectical account of causation inclined Dewey to view mechanistic, stimulus/response accounts of human behavior as simplistic or only partial explanations of a more complex process. Finally, Hegel's theory of causation prevented Dewey from succumbing to the scientific determinism that plagued late-nineteenth-century intellectuals such as William James and John Stuart Mill, according to which environmental causes seemed determinative of human behavior and denied free will.[26] Hegel showed Dewey that cause and effect are instruments we use to rationalize, make sense of, experience, and that it is a mistake to assume that those categories exist prior to experience. Another way to state this is that Hegel's dialectical theory of causation undercut the metaphysical and linear conception of causation, leading Dewey to view cause and effect as instrumental categories best understood as circular when we rise to the level of *Vernunft,* seeing the larger organic whole of which these relationships are a part. This allowed Dewey to avoid a narrow conception of instrumentalism as a mode of analysis that pursues ends efficiently, but without regard for the morality of the means employed or evaluation of the ends that *should* be sought.[27] Hegel's theory of causation places means and ends in a dialectical relationship, in which both constantly affect one another and thus must both be continuously evaluated and reevaluated. As we shall see, this theory of causation underlies Dewey's psychology and philosophy of education, and neither can be understood without recognizing this; later in this chapter I directly address Dewey's understanding of Hegel's theory of causation. In sum, Hegel not only gave Dewey a process philosophy, but the dialectic, which is evident in Hegel's theory of causation, gave him a very rich model of process. Nonetheless, Dewey continued to reconstruct Hegelian terminology for philosophical reasons. Increasingly, he spoke of experience rather than consciousness and intelligence rather than reason, in order to avoid the connotations of an internal mental reality.[28]

Psychology and Philosophy of Education

According to Angell, the primary goal of the Chicago psychologists was to develop, through experimentation, a model of the mind consistent with evolutionary biology. It was crucial that this theory of the mind "be shown to generate hypotheses and predictions that could be experimentally tested."[29] Because they sought an organic theory of the mind, the Chicago psychologists looked for ways to undermine mechanistic interpretations of the mountains of data being collected about conscious behavior by physiological psychologists. Their first target was a reinterpretation of the reflex arc theory of stimulus and response.

Though Dewey was not involved in experiments aimed at undermining the reflex arc hypothesis, his paper, "The Reflex Arc Concept in Psychology" (1896), came to be viewed as the foundation of functionalist psychology. The paper is also important to historians because it marks Dewey's first explicit use of James's "psychologist's fallacy." Jennifer Welchman claims that Dewey's use of this "Jamesian concept, together with adoption of the functionalists' goals for psychology . . . gradually transformed Dewey's theory of mind to such an extent that it was no longer compatible with idealism."[30] But as Shook points out, Dewey had worked out a version of the psychologist's fallacy ten years earlier in "The Psychological Standpoint." It is accurate to say, however, that in the mid-1890s Dewey and Mead found a way to replace the neo-Hegelian notion of a transcendent absolute with a naturalistic conception of process. As Dewey explained to James in 1903, "It may be the continued working of the Hegelian bacillus of reconciliation of contradictories in me that makes me feel as if the conception of process gives a basis for uniting the truths of pluralism and monism, and also of necessity and spontaneity." In the letter, Dewey made it clear that the realm of necessity corresponded to "the world of fact," and the realm of spontaneity corresponded to "the world of ideas." He understood the two realms to be "teleological and dynamic conceptions rather than ontological and static ones."[31] In other words, fact and idea, world and mind, refer to functions rather than static realities within the process of experience.

The significance of function can be clarified by examining "The Reflex Arc Concept in Psychology." In an effort to banish metaphysics from psychology, psychologists had sought to model their theories on the natural sciences, particularly Newtonian mechanics. Psychologists had postulated that mental and physical process emanated from ontologically different entities, and sought to discover mechanical principles of their interaction. The reflex arc, presupposed by psychologists, was a theory about the relation between the experimental subject and his or her environment, a relation all too neatly bounded in time and mechanical in character. In the article Dewey developed a position James articulated in his *Principles of Psychology,* even borrowing James's example of an infant reaching for a bright light that turns out to be a lit candle. According to the view Dewey was criticizing, the light stimulates the infant's mind, causing it to focus its attention on the light and form an attitude toward it (e.g., curiosity). At the same time the infant's body is stimulated to undertake an overt action based on its psychological response—reaching for the candle. Dewey complained that this interpretation made the stimulus/response process "a patchwork of disjointed parts, a mechanical conjunction of unallied processes" initiated by external sensory stimuli.[32]

Dewey attacked the reflex arc theory in the same way he had criticized the dualistic psychology of British empiricism for over ten years. He charged that the mechanistic theory of the reflex arc was not based on science but on unfounded metaphysical assumptions; it was just another species of mind/body dualism:

> We ought to be able to see that the ordinary conception of the reflex arc theory, instead of being a case of plain science, is a survival of the metaphysical dualism, first formulated by Plato, according to which the sensation is an ambiguous dweller on the border land of soul and body, the idea (or central process) is purely psychical, and the act (or movement) purely physical.[33]

Not only is there no scientific basis for this dualistic metaphysics, Dewey argued, it has no explanatory value. The theory merely assumes, without proof, that two unexplained entities behave in a particular way, and perpetuates a metaphysical puzzle that has never been successfully defended or resolved.

According to Dewey, the process did not begin with the external stimulus of the light from the candle, but with a "sensori-motor co-ordination," the child's act of seeing. When the act of seeing stimulates the act of reaching, both acts "fall within a larger co-ordination." Sensation/movement is not a fixed and bounded event; rather it is contained within a larger temporal process, the act. When the child is burned, once more the sensation from the flame is a component of the larger whole: "it is simply the completion, or fulfillment, of the previous eye-arm-hand co-ordination and not an entirely new occurrence." It is only because the entire process is a unit that the child is able to learn from the experience; learning is a process of comprehending relations, not discrete entities. For the child, seeing a lit candle becomes, "seeing-of-a-light-that-means-pain-when-contact-occurs." Stimulus and response are not distinct entities, but "distinctions of function . . . with reference to reaching or maintaining an end."[34]

Psychologists had misunderstood stimulus and response because they committed a version of James's "psychological fallacy." Dewey preferred to call the error the "historical fallacy" in order to emphasize that those who make this mistake do so because their analysis artificially truncates a temporal sequence or process. The fallacy occurs when

> A state of things characterizing an outcome is regarded as a true description of the events which led up to this outcome; when, as a matter of fact, if this outcome had already been in existence, there would have been no necessity for the process. Or, to make the application to the case in hand, considerations valid of an attained organization or co-ordination, the orderly sequence of minor acts in a comprehensive co-ordination, are used to describe a process, viz., the distinction of mere sensation as stimulus and of mere movement as response, which takes place only because such an attained organization is no longer at hand, but is in process of constitution.[35]

In this awkwardly worded passage, Dewey sought to make the point that psychologists had substituted their point of view for that of their subjects. More specifically, Dewey argued that actions seem mechanical when they are analyzed in a fragmentary manner. When we are sensitive to process, the mechanical events of "stimulus" and "response" appear as moments within a larger, more complex behavior. All acts proceed out of a prior coordination, a habit, in which we never distinguish between stimulus and response. We only become aware of stimulus and response when a problem arises that interrupts our usual coordinated interaction with our environment.[36] Dewey provided an example to clarify this point. If a child has had conflicting results when reaching for a bright light, sometimes agreeable sometimes painful, the child's response will be uncertain rather than habitual, and for the child the stimulus is uncertain. The child distinguishes between stimulus and response, examining the stimulus before constituting her response. In so doing the child constitutes a more intelligent, habitual way of acting. A stimulus is a phase within experience, not a separate existence.

For Dewey, the reflex process was not an arc, part of a circle, but a circuit, or a complete circle of action that had been temporarily disrupted by a problem. Noting that stimulus and response can be understood to stand for world and mind, it is apparent that Dewey was translating into the empirical and naturalistic language of his generation the dynamic process that Hegel called the dialectic. An original unity of stimulus and response, world and mind, which Dewey called habit, is disrupted by a problem or conflict of some kind. The self, or in biological language, the organism, takes steps to restore this unity. The self seeks knowledge in such a situation, but only as a means to the restoration of the integrity of its unified relationship with the world. In the following section I provide further evidence of the similarity between Dewey's description of this process and his understanding of Hegel's dialectic.

Scholars often point to the "Reflex Arc" essay as an important marker in Dewey's move away from Hegel, but the primary argument is itself a Hegelian critique of the reflex arc.[37] Dewey asserted that what we call the stimulus is always relative to the larger context of which it is a part, and the object as sensed is always a product of the experiential context in which it is sensed. To illustrate this, Dewey discussed the hearing of a loud noise. "If one is reading a book, if one is hunting, if one is watching in a dark place on a lonely night, if one is performing a chemical experiment, in each case, the noise has a very different psychical value; it is a different experience."[38] Dewey concluded that the stimulus should not be viewed as a static entity but a function that has meaning only within a specific activity. In essence, Dewey's claim was that, although not false, the reflex arc was a one-dimensional, artificially truncated theory of mental operation that obscured the fundamentally dialectical character of experience. If we always try to understand behavior as part of an ongoing dialectical process of interaction between the individual and the world, we will achieve a higher level of understanding.

Yet the essay also reveals that Dewey was modifying his idealism in a couple of ways. First, he had articulated a critique of the deepest of all the dualisms that had troubled him for years, mind and world, without appealing to a transcendent consciousness. Second, Dewey soon began to employ the historical fallacy in a critique of neo-Hegelian ethics. Neo-Hegelian, self-realization ethics had hypostasized an ideal reality that was latent or potential in the self, as in Bradley's theory, or metaphysically separate from the particular self, as in Green's theory. In 1902, Dewey argued that this was an example of the historical fallacy. In this context, the primary point Dewey sought to make with the historical fallacy was that it pinpointed cases in which philosophers discounted some part of experience as mere appearance, as less real than some other part. In self-realization ethics, Dewey argued, the later form of the self "is the reality of which the first form is simply the appearance."[39] This was an abandonment of the psychological standpoint because it assumed that part of our experience is mere appearance, not real. For Dewey, all experiences, including ones as ethereal as dreams or illusions, are equally real experiences.[40] We only distinguish between the real and the apparent when we discount the subjective and imagine that there is an ontologically distinct objective realm beyond experience. Ultimately, Dewey was motivated by a social and political concern. This becomes clearer in later writings, but Dewey worried that when we valorize one part of experience, we then conclude that there is ultimately one good, one truth, for all. This conclusion can then be used to devalue people who, it is believed, do not measure up to the one standard. After the turn of the century, as Dewey criticized moral theories that postulated one all-embracing and fixed end, he included self-realization ethics in his critique. Ultimately, Dewey argued that there is no one moral end, but that self-realization was a happy side effect of moral action.[41]

Westbrook claims that "The Reflex Arc" essay reveals Dewey's drift away from idealism to naturalism because he broke with idealism's tendency to equate experience with knowledge, instead subordinating knowledge to action.[42] In the next chapter, however, I note that in his 1905 Presidential Address to the American Philosophical Association, Dewey excluded Hegel from the philosophers who made this mistake. In her analysis of the "The Reflex Arc," Welchman emphasizes the importance of the historical fallacy as a signal of Dewey's drift away from idealism as he himself abandoned self-realization ethics, which entailed that the ultimate goal of the moral life was to liberate a self metaphysically more real than the apparent self. She also argues that Dewey may not have immediately seen the full implications of the historical fallacy for idealist ethics, because in another essay published in 1896, "Interest in Relation to the Training of the Will," Dewey described the goal of education as the encouragement of a child's "self-expression," the term Dewey began to use in place of "self-realization." The key premise of Welchman's argument seems to be that "There is no intimation in this paper that the self to be expressed is in any way altered through or as a result of the educative process."[43] If Dewey believed that there is an unchanging, ideal self to be manifested through education, Welchman contends, then he was guilty of the historical fallacy himself. Yet we have already seen that as early as his 1887 *Psychology,* Dewey claimed that "Self is, as we have so often seen, *activity*. It is not something *which* acts; it is activity."[44] This definition of the self demonstrates that he never believed in a substantial self, even at the height of his own self-realization ethics.

Moreover, Dewey continued to use the term "self-expression," which helped him distinguish his theory from neo-Hegelian ethics, in his mature thought, after his Hegelian phase as Welchman demarcates it. Dewey first used the term "self-expression" in his 1891 *Outline of a Critical Theory of Ethics,* and continued to use it in his 1894 *The Study of Ethics.* During the 1890s, however, the term appeared most in "Interest in Relation to Training of the Will." But even the term "self-expression" created some confusion. Dewey extensively revised the essay in 1899 and, in response to complaints from his critics about the vagueness of that term, in some places he substituted terms such as "growth," "direct experience," and "realization."[45] Beginning in *How We Think,* first published in 1910, Dewey criticized educational theorists who used "self-expression" to advocate spontaneous, unstructured activity for children in school; however, he used the term approvingly in 1915 and again in 1918.[46] Rather than a commission of the historical fallacy, Dewey's term "self-expression" simply meant the "development of powers" in which the impulse to action encounters a difficulty and is "checked and thrown back upon itself" (the process of alienation and return), prompting reflection.[47]

Thus Dewey's concept of self-expression is consistent with Hegel's concept of self-development, and it should be placed within the context of the American

Bildung tradition. Much like Hegel and the St. Louis Hegelians, in 1900 Dewey spoke of the goal of inquiry as

> the expansion of a given experience through suggestion, into a larger and richer whole. It consists in the capacity to see a whole in a part or to treat what is a whole in direct perception as if it were simply a part of a larger whole.[48]

The notions of the expansion and enriching of experience are constant themes throughout Dewey's mature thought. In 1916, Dewey claimed that "intellectual growth means constant expansion of horizons and consequent formation of new purposes and new responses."[49] Like Hegel and his American counterparts, Dewey was concerned with the learning process, rather than knowledge in the traditional sense, because it was the means to growth.

While I am on the topic of self-expression, I should note that Dewey was quick to criticize educational theorists who saw self-expression as an end in itself, rather than as a means to education, because their view was based on a partial understanding of freedom, what Hegel called negative freedom. Dewey did not see "self-expression" as the moral goal, but as a means to growth. And in response to educational theorists who believed that perplexing tasks had to be imposed arbitrarily on students in order to stimulate reflection, Dewey argued that "Every vital activity of any depth and range inevitably meets obstacles in the course of its effort to realize itself—a fact that renders the search for artificial or external problems quite superfluous." Like Hegel, in this passage and many others Dewey argued that the development of "genuine freedom," that is to say, Hegel's positive freedom, requires opposition.[50] His primary point in "Interest in Relation to Training of the Will," and in *How We Think,* was that educators must learn to use the self-expression that is generated by the child's natural interests to encourage reflection, problem-solving, and growth. Dewey made the same argument in 1895:

> The fundamental principle is that the child is always a being with activities of his own, which are present and urgent and do not require to be "induced," "drawn out," or "developed," etc.; that the work of the educator, whether parent or teacher, consists solely in ascertaining, and in connecting with, these activities, furnishing them appropriate opportunities and conditions.[51]

Dewey did disagree with one prominent Hegelian in "Interest in Relation to Training of the Will," however. W. T. Harris was a proponent of discipline, tradition, and the training of the will in the public schools, and he disapproved of Dewey's emphasis on working with the child's interest, claiming that it was not conducive to developing the will. To the Hegelian right of Dewey, Harris placed a greater emphasis on respect for authority, chosen rationally, and believed it was undermined by Dewey's principles.[52] Harris was one of those who believed educators should impose problematic situations on children without regard for their natural interests. This was Harris and Dewey's first public disagreement, but they remained close friends until Harris's death in 1909.

Because Dewey used a version of the historical fallacy in "The Psychological Standpoint," published ten years before "The Reflex Arc" essay, and because Hegel employed a very similar critique of past philosophies, it is not clear that his use of it in the latter essay signals a watershed in his philosophical development. It is significant, however, that Dewey used the historical fallacy in a critique of neo-Hegelian ethics and, in the following section, I argue that Dewey did not believe Hegel made the same mistake.

The "Great Actualist"

One of the difficulties of determining the nature of Dewey's indebtedness to Hegel is that, in his published work, he engaged in precious little exposition of Hegel's writings. There is one extant, unpublished source, however, in which Dewey dwelt at length on Hegel's philosophy. This source is a 103-page lecture, titled "Hegel's Philosophy of Spirit"; Dewey's graduate students hired a typist to type the lecture for a seminar he offered at the University of Chicago in 1897, one year after the publication of "The Reflex Arc" article. According to the University of Chicago "Annual Register," the course was titled "Seminar in the Philosophy of Hegel" and was described in the following way:

> Hegel's Lesser Logic and Philosophy of Mind, as translated by Wallace, will be made the basis of study. Points of connection with the thought of his predecessors, especially Kant and Spinoza, will be studied, and Hegel's own ideas will be further developed by reference to selected portions of the *Phenomenology*, the *Philosophy of Law*, and the *Æsthetics*. For graduate students.[53]

Clearly the lecture is not a polished draft. It has many typographical errors, paragraphs that should be broken into smaller ones, a number of awkward sentences, and there are no citations. Keeping the course description in mind, however, I will supply citations to Hegel's works to indicate the textual basis of the lecture. Despite its roughness, the lecture provides evidence that Dewey was still quite sympathetic to Hegel at this late date and that he had embraced a humanistic/historicist reading of the philosopher.[54] The unifying theme of the lecture is Dewey's claim that Hegel is a "great actualist" rather than a "grand metaphysician." Briefly, Dewey's reading of Hegel as a great actualist means that his idealism did not reduce reality to the thought processes of a transcendent thinker, but affirmed the reality, and objectivity, of thought. As I unpack this theme, my discussion will shed light on five issues important to my endeavor to analyze Dewey's permanent Hegelian deposit: Dewey's perception of Hegel's project, how Dewey found functionalist psychology in Hegel, Dewey's understanding of Hegel's method, whether or not Dewey believed Hegel committed the historical fallacy, and how Dewey interpreted Hegel's ethics and political philosophy. Careful examination of these themes demonstrates that, by 1897, Dewey's reading of Hegel was notably comparable to the one I offered in chapter one.

Hegel's Project

The lecture begins with a brief biographical section in which Dewey drew upon Karl Rosenkranz's biography of Hegel.[55] This fact alone is significant because at that time there were only two full-length biographies available, the one by Rosenkranz and Rudolf Haym's *Hegel und seine Zeit.*[56] The Rosenkranz biography emphasized that Hegel was motivated by the practical goal of actualizing the ideals of liberalism; Haym's book served to codify the myth of Hegel as the official philosopher of the Prussian restoration, a view that Dewey rejected in this lecture. I have already demonstrated that the St. Louis Hegelians read Hegel as a politically liberal and practical philosopher under the influence of center Hegelians like Karl Ludwig Michelet and Rosenkranz. I also noted that Dewey offered to translate Rosenkranz's introduction to "Kirchmann's ed. of Hegel's Encyclopädie" for the JSP, and can assume that he read the St. Louis Hegelians' numerous translations of Rosenkranz's work.[57] From this evidence it seems likely that Dewey's preference for Rosenkranz's characterization of Hegel's was an informed choice.

In the biographical section of the lecture, it is evident that Dewey was still sympathetic to Hegel in 1897, depicting him as an inherently humble thinker.

> [Hegel's boyhood studies] manifest at least one great trait of his philosophical method:—his attempt to get at the natural relations of his subject matter, unpreverted [sic] by his individual sentiments. Self effacement, Hegel held to be the first law of the intellect. In his discussion of the Pythagoreans, Hegel saw that the duty of silence is the essential condition of all culture and learning. We must begin with being able to apprehend the thoughts of others and this implies a disregarding of our own ideas.[58]

This insight into Hegel's personality, Dewey explained, provides the key to his entire philosophy. According to Dewey, Hegel's mature philosophical method was a theoretical articulation of his youthful modesty. Hegel's restraint, his reluctance to speak "in order that the fact may be heard . . . does not imply a low consеption [sic] of thought or reflection: it implies rather the highest conception of the value of thought." Dewey continued,

> It implies that thought is so real that it can be found only in the object and not in any subjective opinion. Nor does such a method imply that knowledge is passive, that the mind is to be merely receptive in knowing; on the contrary, it implies the most acute, the most intense mental energy. It is when mental energy is only partial that we indulge in opinions and arguments. We get part way into a subject and, lacking energy to pursue the quest for the real meaning of the fact, we come to a halt. Then the checked energy relapses into subjective reflection and disputation. The mind has not enough activity to break out of the weary treadmill of its own ideas; to make its way to the fact itself. The highest activity of thought is that which will make itself the pure expression of the facts.[59]

So, from the outset of the lecture, Dewey presented Hegel as a humble philosopher who rejected the passive spectator theory of the mind, and who held facts, rather than ungrounded speculation, in the highest esteem. This last point is consistent with what he had said about Hegel in "The Present Position of Logical Theory" (1891). As I noted before, in that essay Dewey claimed Hegel rejected the notion of thought as something that exists apart from the objects we experience. Moreover, in the passage above, Dewey claimed that Hegel's objection to one-sided, incomplete explanations is that they are the result of the arrested development of our thinking. Incomplete explanations arise at the level of *Verstand.* Appreciation of the whole truth, *Vernunft,* requires the hard work of freeing ourselves from our settled opinions and attending to the facts themselves.

Dewey explained that he emphasized this point because it is essential to understand that for Hegel "all thought is objective, that relations of thought are forms of the objective world; that the process of thinking is simply following the movement of the subject matter itself." He also wanted to defend Hegel from critics who so often mistakenly assume just the opposite:

> that thought as a special faculty of the mind has the power of evolving truth out of itself; that subjective ideas, by some magic, transform themselves into objective facts. But his real meaning is that there is no such thing as a faculty of thought separate from things: that thinking is simply the translation of fact into its real meaning; it is subjection of reality subjecting.[60]

Dewey continued to develop the implications of this point throughout the lecture. Like the St. Louis Hegelians, Dewey claimed Hegel was concerned with ideals only as they actually have effects and make a difference in the world. He asserted that, unlike his immediate predecessors, Hegel was first driven to philosophy by the social and political problems of real life; his interest in more technical issues of logic and metaphysics came second. Dewey's understanding of Hegel's primary interest sets the stage for the central argument of the lecture:

> Hegel was a great actualist. By this I mean that he has the greatest respect, both in his thought and in his practice, for what has actually amounted to something, actually succeeded in getting outward form. It was customary then, as now, to throw contempt upon the scientific, the artistic, the industrial and social life, as merely worldly in comparison with certain feelings and ideas which are regarded as specifically spiritual. Between the two, the secular, which after all *is* here and now, and the spiritual, which exists only in some far off region and which *ought* to be, Hegel had no difficulty in choosing. Hegel is never more hard in his speech, hard as steel is hard, than when dealing with mere ideals[,] vain opinions and sentiments which have not succeeded in connecting themselves with the actual world.[61]

In this passage, Dewey was surely thinking of Hegel's claim in *The Philosophy of Right* that "What is rational is actual; and what is actual is rational."[62] For Dewey, this was not an admonition to acquiesce to the status quo. On his reading, the aphorism meant that only ethical principles with which individuals can identify (i.e., view as rational) can serve as actual principles of ethical life; abstract, alien principles fail to motivate us to action because they do not connect with our real lives.[63] To have any effect in a person's life, ethical principles must somehow resonate with them. Dewey continued to depict Hegel in this way in his mature thought, writing in 1929 that "Hegel . . . is never weary of pouring contempt upon an Ideal that merely ought to be. 'The actual is the rational and the rational is the actual.'" To put it in another way, Dewey understood Hegel's pronouncement to mean that the actual, the efficacious, is the real that is rational, and what is rational is actual, or efficacious. This makes Hegel's claim a call to action, meaning that philosophers, cultural critics, should discover the rational in reality and work to advance it. Again, in 1929 Dewey wrote that, for Hegel, "The moral task of man is not to create a world in accord with the ideal but to appropriate intellectually and in the substance of personality the meanings and values already incarnate in an actual world."[64] Clearly, Dewey saw a pragmatic element in Hegel's controversial claim: principles are meaningful only to the extent that they are put to work and have actual effects in the world.

According to Dewey, the driving force behind all of Hegel's thought was the concrete realization of individual and social unity. In "From Absolutism to Experimentalism" Dewey explained that, "in [his] undergraduate days" he was influenced by Comte's "idea of the disorganized character of Western modern culture, due to a disintegrative 'individualism,' and his idea of a synthesis of science that should be a regulative method of an organized social life," and added that he "found . . . the same criticisms combined with a deeper and more far-reaching integration in Hegel."[65] This lecture demonstrates that Dewey viewed Hegel's philosophy as cultural criticism and as offering a solution to the problem of modernity, the breakdown of community and the concurrent atomization and isolation of individuals.

In the biographical section of the lecture, Dewey also examined the development of Hegel's philosophy of history, a topic to which he returned later in the lecture. Though Dewey discussed Hegel's philosophy of history in some detail, I will discuss this portion of the lecture only as it contributes to the question of how Dewey understood Hegel's project. Dewey traced Hegel's philosophy of history from the Oriental World to the French Revolution, emphasizing along the way that Hegel believed philosophy should help modern man regain the social harmony of the ancient polis without surrendering the advance of modern subjectivity and individual rights.

The Protestant Reformation led to the conviction that all men have access to truth, and this was the impetus that gave birth to modern science. Dewey claimed that Hegel learned from science that nature is neither one with man, nor is it an obstacle to him; nature is instead "so bound up with man's own life that he had to master its meaning in order to preserve his own mental integrity." But Protestant individualism also led to a pure negativism that indiscriminately undermined all traditions and institutions. Instead, Hegel advocated determinate negation that, in the course of cultural criticism, would lead to the articulation of realizable goals. The most important goal was the development of a *Sittlichkeit* that would foster the unification of the modern individual with society. As Dewey explained,

> All of Hegel's speculative work grew out of this practical problem, the problem of how a free natural life is possible; how a man can live as a whole, neither surrendering himself to a fixed external authority, nor in his desire to escape this external something, retiring into his own private feelings or into a region of intellectual abstractions.[66]

Dewey explained that a crucial element of the problem of disharmony, according to Hegel, was that Protestantism's rigid separation of church and state had created divisions within society and within individuals because it gave "the domain of the internal, the domain of conscience in the sense of subjective ideas and beliefs, wholly to the Church, to religion, while the outward forms of life and the actual points of contact between men should be reserved wholly for the State." In this way the inner, spiritual life was "deprived . . . of all concrete bases and ends, reducing it to an empty spirituality," and the outward life became "perfunctory and without any deep spiritual meaning."[67] Hegel valued the *Sittlichkeit* of the Greek polis, Dewey noted, because "there was no division, no divorce of the worldly and the spiritual, of piety and virtue. Man lived a single, concrete life in which science, art, religion and politics were as one."[68]

Furthermore, Dewey explained, Hegel rejected the rational religion of Enlightenment philosophers like Kant and Fichte because it perpetuated the Protestant error by confining religion to "intellectual abstractions." Rational religion "made of no value the feelings, the desires, or the sensuous side of man." Hegel believed religion should "unite the reason, avoiding all superstitions, with the positive course of history and the imagination and feelings." Individual religion needed to be situated within the context of history and grounded in the individual's social setting. Hegel's ideal was a culture that would unite "reason and feeling; the world of nature, of the individual and society."[69]

Hegel's critique of modern philosophy more generally, according to Dewey, was essentially the same. Modern epistemology erred because it facilitated the retreat into private feelings and intellectual abstractions by creating divisions within the self because it

> makes a thing out of matter and another thing out of the soul and then asks how it is possible that these two fixed and separate things should have any relation to each other. The question put, is, by its very nature, insoluble, and thus we have from the persons who put this problem long dissertations upon the incomprehensibility, upon the mysteriousness of the relations of the soul to matter.[70]

In the same way, modern social and political thought promoted alienation. Rousseau's exaltation of the individual denigrated every social institution—the family, civil society, the state, and even institutions of science, art, and religion. Radical individualism came at a great price because "The higher the individual was declared to be, the more he was cut off from all specific relations of life, and the more empty and thus apparently worthless he became."[71]

In Dewey's words, Hegel saw the French Reign of Terror as "the conflict of the private reason of the individual with the public reason embodied in law, institution and tradition." Subjective freedom—"the right of the particular subject . . . to get his own satisfaction and get it in his own way, not having to take either his ideals or his means from another person"—thus led to an anarchic individualism. As Dewey explained, "Seemingly all social ties, all objective institutions, all settled authority, had been dissolved in favor of an unstable liberty of the individual. The excess of the French revolution seemed to be the logical outcome of the [Enlightenment] principle of freedom." The Enlightenment disregarded the right of the other, or what Hegel called "the right of the object." The other, or the object, has the right "to be recognized in its own rationality." This is true when we seek knowledge of material objects, but also when we interact with other self-conscious beings. We have a duty to seek "the rationality of the subject matter."[72]

In this way, Dewey depicted the primary goal of Hegel's philosophy as not only cultural unity, but also cultural criticism. Because Hegel embraced modern subjectivity, unity and criticism went hand in hand. In the modern era, only a society that provided for the individualism necessary for penetrating critique of its practices and institutions could gain, to some degree at least, the sense of community of the Greek polis. The task of philosophy was to articulate a conception of the individual and society that would support the reconstruction of society along these lines, and provide for a blending of social and individual imperatives.

Several other avenues of interpretation follow from the notion that Hegel was the great actualist. The goal of Hegel's philosophy of spirit, Dewey explained, was self-knowledge, which should always be understood as including understanding of one's culture, because Hegel viewed reality as an organism that united in a totality reason and feeling, man and nature, and man and society. This organism was *Geist* or spirit and Dewey accepted the notion that Hegel's concept of spirit was a dynamic process rather than an unchanging substance: "spirit is only what it does." This is another strong indication that Dewey had embraced the humanistic/historicist reading of Hegel, according to which spirit is humanity in its development rather than a transcendent God. At one point in the lecture, Dewey put a Darwinian spin on *Geist,* describing it as "the process of evolution itself out of which every species of individual comes, and back into which it goes." He went on to write that "different human beings" can be seen "simply as so many accidents or qualities into which the one substantial process of life has differentiated itself during its evolution."[73]

In his discussion of spirit, Dewey defended Hegel from the oft-stated charge that he made history "purely *a priori,*" forcing events into a preconceived end to be realized. Dewey boldly declared that this charge "is absurd." Every history must be given some sort of unity, he explained, or it would not even be "a child's fairy tale, for children require a certain point in their stories." Dewey argued that this charge against Hegel would be correct if he had postulated the goal of history arbitrarily, but that he found the goal by taking the facts of history seriously and letting them speak for themselves. Dewey implied that Hegel was able to see reason in history because he had become "conscious of the end of the whole and identifie[d] himself with it"; consequently, Hegel "actively participate[d] in the whole."[74] Further, to the degree that a nation becomes conscious of, and identifies itself with, the end of history, it becomes both a means to the end and an end in itself. When Dewey spoke of the end of history in this lecture, it is apparent that he meant the goal of history rather than its conclusion.

Dewey's exposition of Hegel's philosophy of history indicates that it resonated with him and that we should expect to see elements of it in his thought. In the lecture, Dewey discussed Hegel's theories about the history of art in some detail, closely tracking the developmental aesthetics he had studied in Joseph Torrey's *A Theory of Fine Art* as an undergraduate at the University of Vermont.[75] And in 1897, the year of this lecture, Dewey began to discuss historical and social factors that, he believed, have affected the development of philosophers' thinking about epistemology and logic, specifically discussing how the ancient Greek search for self-knowledge and the modern search for scientific knowledge have shaped the field of epistemology. This type of historical, or genealogical, account of the problems of philosophy was a prominent feature of Dewey's mature thought.[76] Nevertheless, living in the age of Darwinian biology, Dewey never found the same degree of logical progression that Hegel saw in history; Dewey always left room for contingency.

Functional Psychology

Dewey's discussion of spirit also provides clues about his reading of Hegel's philosophical psychology. Dewey argued that, whereas British empiricism had hypostasized the abilities or functions of mind into faculties, and sense data into an external metaphysical realm, Hegel viewed the mind, mental faculties, and empirical data as "elements in the development of the active unity of spirit." Hegel rejected faculty psychology, Dewey maintained, because "it resolves the soul into an aggregate of independent powers which stand in mechanical relations to each other." Hegel's psychology, by contrast,

> shows that these so-called faculties of mind, and also all concrete empirical material, are simply elements in the development of the active unity of spirit. We understand spirit, then, not when we begin by supposing a substance which we term soul or by supposing a lot of separate mental faculties, but only when we trace the varied process by which spirit realizes itself. Our so-called faculties will then appear in their proper place as stages in its evolution. Thus the whole science becomes living, organic and systematic.[77]

Dewey also explained that, according to Hegel's actualism, the soul's "unity with nature" entailed that "it can feel its own qualities only so far as these find bodily expression," taking on an outward form.[78] In language reminiscent of his 1891 letter to James about the *Principles of Psychology,* Dewey wrote that, for Hegel, "a man cannot feel his own feelings except as they come in this roundabout way through his body. . . . That is to say, sadness or joy, scorn, hatred, courage, etc., are not felt directly and of themselves; they are felt only through the outward bodily expression."[79] According to Dewey, Hegel believed that "we only know our thoughts when we give them an objective form, when we . . . get them out into spoken sounds or written words." Only when thoughts and ideas are verbalized and shared do they gain a certain reality and universality. Thought that is inexpressible is simply confused, because clear thought "must objectify itself and get concrete form."[80] In the same way, in an 1896 essay on the teaching of artistic expression, Dewey criticized the notion that we can speak of an idea and its expression, because "the expression is more than a mode of conveying an already formed idea; it is part and parcel of its formation." Dewey elaborated on the implication of this view of thought for education: "Education, like philosophy, has suffered from the idea that thought is complete in itself, and that action, the expression of thought, is a physical thing." According to Dewey, recent psychology bolstered this view of thought by showing that "thought is thought only in and through action."[81] The pupil does not have a fully developed idea until she has acted on it, and learning truly consists in doing.

Dewey claimed Hegel's philosophical psychology grew out of his successful reconciliation of Fichte and Schelling, and heralded this accomplishment as a critical moment in Hegel's development. Dewey understood that Hegel rejected Fichte's subjective idealism and Schelling's identity philosophy as contrasting monisms, one valorizing spirit, and the other a vague, undifferentiated absolute. For Hegel, "subjectivity or spirit [is] the ultimate reality of the world," and nature is "a factor in the process of spirit itself." This may sound like a monism, but Dewey maintained that it is not because spirit is activity rather than substance; it "is simply a theoretical formulation of the idea of subjectivity, of individuality, of freedom, which has played so large a part in the modern consciousness."[82] Hegel surpassed his two predecessors

> by conceiving of spirit as an active unity in which all absolute oppositions are overcome but in which they are maintained as relative distinctions. Nature, for example, is neither swallowed up in spirit nor of equal value with it. It is a factor in the process of spirit itself and spirit maintains itself by means of the eternal maintaining of nature in existence.

Hegel reconciled Fichte and Schelling by developing a richer conception of process in which all moments are equally real and important to the whole. Hegel postulated the absolute as "a unity of *activity* to be realized in and through diversity and opposition." Further,

> The true absolute could be found only when this original identity had differentiated itself and when out of its differences it had reached a unity of life and of activity in which the subject and the object no longer expressed two parallel lines, but were themselves factors contributing to the higher unity of the spirit.[83]

This passage also demonstrates that Dewey believed there was room for diversity in Hegel's holism. As Dewey explained it, for Hegel, unity requires diversity.

Individual experience is an equally rich process in which the reality of individual mind and object are maintained in the dialectic of experience because they are distinct moments or functions within it. As I have already noted, Dewey articulated the same view in the "Reflex Arc" article and countless other writings. According to Hegel's and Dewey's rejection of faculty psychology, reason, feeling, and will can be logically distinguished as different activities of the self, but should not be viewed as separate agents or realities. The self is not an aggregate of independent parts, each of which exists and operates by itself, or which can oppose one another; rather they are simply different aspects of one self-conscious being and, ideally, all work together. According to this unitary notion of the self, it is misleading to suggest that the will or emotions must be subdued in order to allow reason to function properly. As Hegel would say, the self is a unity in difference. Further, epistemology and ethics are artificial separations of the subject matter of philosophy because the objects they investigate are intertwined within the self. Experience is a concrete whole in which the self-conscious subject is at once reasoning, feeling, and willing.[84] Finally, diversity is equally important to the development of the whole at the level of individual experience. Individual growth occurs best when an individual encounters the widest variety of experience, which requires a society in which there is scope for all kinds of complementary individuals and activities. Exposure to different kinds of people and experimentation with different types of lives is crucial to the sort of growth Hegel had in mind.

Dewey further elaborated on Hegel's philosophical psychology by claiming that all of the activities of mind or spirit are "ways by which the external is brought back to the internal, is made ideal":

> In sensation, in feeling, the soul is at one with the object. But when self-consciousness rises this unity breaks into two, the object is set over against the subject, the subject against the object. But this division makes a contradiction in spirit, whose very nature is to be an active unity. The subject, therefore, sets to work to subdue the object to itself.

According to Dewey, in Hegel's process of alienation and return, the internal and the external are not ontologically separate realms; the process of idealization is a restoration of the original unity of the internal and the external. As Dewey explained,

> All the activities of spirit, says Hegel, are only ways by which the external is brought back to the internal, is made ideal. Only through this process of restoration, through this idealizing or assimilating of the external does the spirit come to be.[85]

Rather than a static state of knowing, the focus is on an active process of growth in which spirit seeks unity within experience. Dewey repeated a position similar to the one he voiced in "Psychology as Philosophic Method." According to Hegel, he explained, when philosophy deals with spirit "man is not dealing with a material external to himself." Knowledge is not a process in which mind comes to know a reality external to itself, but "the process by which the reality comes to a consciousness of its own basis, meaning and bearings."[86]

Dewey also offered a functionalist account of Hegel's theory of the will. For Hegel, in the process of molding one's world, reason becomes will and rationalizes the individual's appetites and inclinations, organizing them "into unity with all the aims and ends of life." In other words, when the learning process is successful, it rationalizes the self, making it more consistent with the rationality it has discovered in the objective world. This process is the formation of good habits, which allow the individual to know, and master, his experiences. Dewey explained that the will spans the divide between the objective and the subjective because it gives outward, objective manifestation to ideas. "Will . . . is not merely an act of changing ideas into existences," however; "it is the activity which comprehends within itself as factors both an idea and an object."[87] Reason and the will translate objective and subjective particulars into universal, rational form.

Dewey also claimed that, for Hegel, the merely felt unity of body and soul is completed in habit by the activity of the soul.

> That unity of the body and the soul which merely *existed* in feeling is transformed in habit in a *made* unity, a unity which is the outcome of the soul's own activity. It thus forms also the transition between the soul and the whole outer world. It is getting the mastery of the body through habit that the soul gets the power to master the whole world.

In habit the soul masters the body, because it is able "to know its experiences instead of being lost in them," and thereby gains the power to master the world.[88] This is why Brokmeyer insisted that each member of the St. Louis Philosophical Society give a rational account of his life. As philosophers of the American *Bildung* tradition, Dewey and the St. Louis Hegelians believed that the purpose of personal growth is to seek harmony within the self and within the world. The formation of rational habits that are consistent with universal, humanistic ideals would lead to the realization of harmony by allowing a person to overcome contradictions, diremptions, or dualisms. According to this American Hegelian tradition then, knowledge, and in fact all life activity, should be directed at a practical goal because man is not an atomistic, knowledge-seeking being, but a social self, seeking psychological or spiritual integrity.[89]

This discussion of intelligence and habit clarifies what it meant for Hegel, and Dewey, to claim that the distinction between subject and object, soul and the world, "is not a fixed separation but . . . one stage in the process of spirit by which it ultimately affects its own particular unity and activity." The individual finds subjective unity through the formation of habit, and objective unity through the discovery of laws, or universals, in the objective world. In so doing the self "finds itself and thus becomes self-conscious." In discovering "a concrete universal or ideality manifested in differences, the self is elevated to universality." But according to Hegel, Dewey explained, the self is not a uniting activity, as it was for Kant; it *is* the unity of experience, and as the self comes to self-consciousness, "it realizes this unity which is forever involved in the constitution of the objective world."[90]

On Dewey's reading of Hegel's theory of desire, the self must become practical in order to get a clear sense of its power over nature.[91] Desire is a function of the requirement that self-consciousness have external objects for its survival, and yet finds itself limited by anything that is outside itself. Consumption of physical objects is the most rudimentary level of practicality because, in consuming, the self demonstrates its negative power over its environment. The self does not take things as they are, but changes them in accordance with its own needs. In consumption, self-consciousness expresses its desire for survival; self-consciousness appropriates realities foreign to itself, but then overcomes this foreignness and regains its integrity. But this integrity proves to be fleeting, Dewey noted, because once the object of desire is done away with as an independent object, self-consciousness will have "annihilate[d] the object which satisfied it."[92] Self-consciousness seems doomed to be permanently unsatisfied, in a perpetual state of desire. Because new desires arise endlessly, man never returns to a non-desiring, static self. In sum, the object constrains but also provides the context for the survival of self-consciousness.[93]

For this reason, man seeks an object that endures, "an object which is as permanent and universal as himself." Dewey explained that, for Hegel, the process of satisfying desire leads to self-consciousness because the individual recognizes that the self is not an object that is consumed, but an object that consumes, a universal. As Dewey described Hegel's theory, what man truly seeks is not knowledge per se, but a certain integrity within himself and with his environment. To achieve integrity man needs an other that can be negated without being consumed; thus Hegel's functionalist psychology is also a social psychology. The basic desire of human self-consciousness can only be fulfilled, therefore, by another self-consciousness. For this reason, man struggles for recognition from equivalent selves and finds himself surrounded by other individuals struggling for recognition. Initially, the individual responds to this situation "by giving battle to every other self," trying to reduce the other to a thing for his own satisfaction. The one who is victorious in the struggle becomes the master and enslaves the other because he learns that if he cares for the other, rather than destroying him, he can force the other to care for him. In this way the master realizes that his free existence is dependent upon others. The slave learns to subordinate his desires to the wants of others, and thereby becomes socialized. In this struggle both individuals ultimately realize that others are not things, but persons like themselves. At this stage, individuals have risen above "mere isolated individuality," but only as the individual realizes "that there is a true unity of will to which all equally owe obedience" does he become fully free. In this way, individuals learn that "the true objective self is neither itself nor some other particular self," and "is truly objective instead of being simply one object among, or by the side of, other objects."[94]

Hegel's Method

Dewey explained that Schelling and Hegel rejected Fichte's notion that, because absolute spirit requires opposition in order to achieve fulfillment, it "creates the world of sense and of nature" solely for the purpose of overcoming it. Dewey wrote, "it is obvious that such a view both involves a contradiction and makes the process of nature and of experience purely subjective." As Dewey realized, Schelling and Hegel objected that if Fichte's absolute succeeded in overcoming the opposition of nature, it would destroy the grounds for its own moral perfection, thereby "destroy[ing] itself."[95] Thus Fichte's moral ideal is unattainable. Of course Dewey rejected this sort of devaluation of nature, but this also clarifies why he referred to Green's ethical theory as "Neo-Fichtean." As we have already seen, in "Green's Theory of the Moral Motive," Dewey's main objection was that Green made the moral ideal unattainable because it was utterly transcendent.[96]

Hegel's relationship to Fichte and Schelling also takes Dewey to the issue of his alleged monism. When scholars think about the differences between Dewey's thought and Hegel's many correctly think of Dewey as a pluralist and, more questionably, Hegel as a monist. Dewey's explanation of Hegel's break with Schelling is revealing on this point. As I explained in chapter one, Hegel rejected Schelling's principle of identity, which proclaimed the absolute identity of nature and spirit. Hegel objected that the underlying unity was not "a common substratum, but . . . a unity of *activity* to be realized in and through diversity and opposition." Schelling's absolute identity, which he took to be the ultimate conclusion of philosophy, was only a starting point for Hegel. In Dewey's words, "Schelling . . . made the absolute simply an identity in which differences of subject and object, man and nature, were swallowed up."[97] In his second publication, "The Pantheism of Spinoza," Dewey had made the same objection to Spinoza's "identity philosophy," claiming that he had affirmed the unity of reality at the expense of the diversity of ordinary experience.[98] Dewey was inclined toward Hegel's idealism, rather than any of the other German idealists, precisely because he believed that Hegel had successfully accounted for the unity of reality without resorting to a monistic, identity philosophy. In contrast to Schelling, Hegel's absolute was a subject rather than a substance, meaning that it is "a spiritual principle which maintains itself as unity, not by abolishing distinctions, but by making them elements in its own self-conscious life. It is a principle of activity as against one of mere existende [sic]."[99] Apparently Dewey had reached a better understanding of this point just a few years before this lecture. In an 1894 letter to Alice, he wrote, "I can see that I have always been interpreting the dialectic wrong end up—the unity of the reconciliation of opposites, instead of the opposites as the unity in its growth." Dewey believed that Hegel's concepts of negation and *Aufhebung,* or sublation, provided for the continuing existence and affirmation of diverse elements—functions—within a unified reality.[100]

Dewey explained that Hegel's "idea of method was deepened and almost transformed by [his] conviction of the important place of opposition, of contradiction and negation in life." In his discussion of negation, Dewey described Hegel's three stages of historical development in more detail:

> First, the period of implicit unity when, apparently all was harmony; when man and Nature and God were one. Then, secondly, there was the period of negation and of discord, the period when the various elements of the original unity were isolated and set over against each other. In the third period, however, a true reconciliation takes place. It is seen that underlying the discord and opposition there is still a unity, nay, even more, it is seen that the very principle of difference, of negation, is itself an expression and a realization of this unity,—that the period of discord is an element in the process by which the real harmony maintains and extends itself.[101]

The fundamental truth of the dialectic, Dewey maintained, is that all thought, like reality itself, involves "a union of affirmative and negative, or of universal and particular factors." Approvingly, Dewey explained that Hegel always retained the notion that the negative was as real as, or more precisely, a component of, the positive. That which had not been negated could not really be called a positive because it had merely not been questioned. In Hegel's political philosophy this meant that social unity requires continual critique from the members of society. Moreover, the negation is not final, because in its fullest development it must give rise to a more inclusive positive and negate itself. This brings us to the third stage of the dialectic, the "negation of negations." This stage, however, is not "mere annihilation"; rather it is a determinate negation, "the statement of a positive in which all contradictions had been reconciled." Dewey also described the first stage of the dialectic as dogmatic thought, "thought which is not at all aware of its own conditions, limitations and relations." The second stage is skepticism, in which doubt at first appears to nullify all truth, but this is actually only doubt of unreflective, dogmatic truth. The skeptical period must give way to "the period of criticism" or of "self-conscious thought" in which truth "is aware of its own contradictions and relations."[102] As we have already seen with both Morris and Dewey, for this reason Hegelians do not take skepticism seriously as a philosophical position; it is merely a partial understanding, a stage on the path to truth.

Along the same line Dewey argued that Hegel's philosophical method surpassed Schelling's Romantic method, because he rejected Schelling's monism.

> This original defect of Schelling's also led, in Hegel's mind to another defect. Not perceiving that all difference is the first stop in the unfolding of the great spiritual reality which comprehends all things, Schelling really had no method by which he could trace the various phases either of thought or of the world. Schelling thus fell back on what he called intellectual intuition, a sort of direct perception of the original identity and of corresponding forms of mind and nature which grew out of it.[103]

Hegel's emphasis on difference within the unity of experience allowed him to build upon Fichte's and Schelling's dialectical method by claiming that reason, understood as logical relationships, is in the world, and thus the world is rationally comprehensible. According to Dewey, Hegel put thought in the world, denying Cartesian dualism, by asserting that relations are objectively real. Relations are not added to the data of experience by thought that exists apart from the data; rather, thought recognizes the logical relations latent in the world and articulates them in rational form. Thought and object, mind and world, are able to connect because they are equally real, but differentiated, functions within the process of experience.

The Historical Fallacy

Hegel's relationship to Fichte and Schelling is also relevant to Dewey's perception of whether or not Hegel committed the historical fallacy. According to Dewey, Schelling and Hegel objected that, for Fichte, "the realm of Nature and history [have] no true objective worth." For Dewey then, Fichte would be guilty of the historical fallacy because he made one part of experience, the subjective, more real than another, nature. Although Hegel agreed with Schelling that there is an underlying unity "between man and nature, between the objective and subjective worlds," Schelling made the same mistake as Fichte by positing "a common substratum" that grounds the world of experience.[104]

Dewey discussed Hegel's theory of causation in a way that bears directly on whether or not he faulted Hegel, as he did the British neo-Hegelians, with committing the historical fallacy. Dewey maintained that, on Hegel's theory of causation, there is no practical difference between materialism and idealism because a consistent materialism leads to idealism.[105] Materialism, for Hegel, disregards the fact that "the cause goes into its effect." When materialists claim that matter is the cause of the soul, they unwittingly concede that "it is the very nature of matter to become soul, that the soul is the real meaning, the real truth of matter, and this is precisely what is meant by idealism." Dewey's phrase, "the cause goes into its effect," is a virtual quotation of a passage I quoted in chapter one from Hegel's "Lesser Logic," as translated by William Wallace. Wallace renders the passage as "[the cause] is wholly passed into the effect."[106]

In 1902, Dewey objected to the

> purely metaphysical conception of causation . . . according to which the cause is somehow superior in rank and excellence to the effect. The effects are regarded as somehow all inside the womb of cause, only awaiting their proper time to be delivered. They are considered as derived and secondary, not simply in the order of time, but in the order of existence.

This theory of causation is an example of the historical fallacy because it holds that the cause is more real than the effect. According to Dewey, "Materialism arises just out of this fetich-like worship of the antecedent." The materialist believes that he can trace all effects back to material causes, and that this proves that reality is ultimately material because matter is the universal antecedent. Dewey went on to write that the idealist makes the same mistake in reverse because he "isolates and deifies . . . the later term," the consequent.

> To him [the idealist] the reality is somehow "latent" or "potential" in the earlier forms, and, gradually working from within, transforms them until it finds for itself a fairly adequate expression. It is an axiom with him that what is evolved in the latest form is involved in the earliest. The later reality is, therefore, to him the persistent reality in contrast with which the first forms are, if not illusions, at least poor excuses for being.[107]

While this might have been true of the neo-Hegelians, in §153 of the "Lesser Logic," Hegel argued not that the effect is more real than the cause, but that the two are implicitly identical to experience.[108] One could understand Hegel to have articulated the pragmatic principle that we only perceive a cause after we see its effect and, in the same way, we only perceive an effect after we discover its cause. According to Hegel, the distinction of cause and effect is introduced by the understanding (*Verstand*) into an essentially homogeneous continuum, but reason (*Vernunft*) reveals that they are not ontologically distinct. They are functions of our effort to understand our experience. Moreover, like Hegel, Dewey maintained throughout his philosophical development that cause and effect, means and ends, are not ontologically distinct but are integrally related. As early as 1893 Dewey stated that we separate "cause from effect . . . means from end," because we have "a partial and vague idea of the whole fact."[109]

Dewey also emphasized that Hegel saw nature as "a factor in the process of spirit itself" rather than an ontologically distinct realm. Accordingly, on Dewey's reading, Hegel was not guilty of the historical fallacy because he rejected the doctrine of metaphysical substance, depicting spirit as "a principle of activity," the process of development rather than an entity that develops.[110]

Ethics and Political Philosophy

Dewey continued with a discussion of Hegel's ethics and political philosophy that begins with an explanation of Hegel's criticism of formal reason. Dewey explained that Hegel criticized "merely formal" reason because he maintained that, rather than a process of abstraction, thinking should comprehend "the true meaning of the facts themselves," which is the universal. Because abstraction dissects the whole into parts (e.g., the table possesses the qualities of solidity and extension) it does not apprehend facts. Solidity and extension do not exist in and of themselves, but the table does; the table is a factual existence. The universal is not tacked onto the particular mechanically; it is organically integral to the fact. Dewey explained, "When this is discovered, thought ceases to be merely formal, a process of operation upon an outside material and becomes one with the content of the facts themselves." When there is a distinction between form and content, thought is merely understanding (*Verstand*); reason (*Vernunft*) comprehends facts in their interrelated unity.[111]

Hegel rejected Kant's and Fichte's transcendentalism precisely because it was a formalism that authoritatively imposes norms upon a foreign content. The notion of a beyond that presents itself to consciousness as "otherness" creates the feeling of being an alien in the world or, as Hegel often stated it, of not being "at home."[112] As we have already seen, Dewey also rejected the transcendent during the 1880s as he moved away from Christianity and the neo-Hegelian notion of a transcendent absolute spirit. This is precisely why Dewey rejected any moral theory that made the ideal otherworldly and unattainable.

When a person has understood his true good in a particular, specific way, it no longer seems like a law externally imposed upon his actions. In Dewey's words, if a person "translates his good into particular acts . . . it becomes his interest as well as his duty to perform the specific act." Duty and motive become one; a person fulfills his moral obligations because he understands that they coincide with his best interest. "In other words, the stage of doing a duty for the sake of a duty marked the point in the morality [sic] at which a man is sufficiently moralized to see that there is a good which should control his actions, but not sufficiently moralized to bring this good home to himself as his own good in every specific act."[113] The former stage is abstract, formal morality, what Hegel called *Moralität*; the latter stage is the ethical, *Sittlichkeit,* in the sense of actual, concrete morality. The particular and the universal, in both reason and morality, must be united. The individual will is not fully realized when it conforms to universal law—such as Kant's categorical imperative—but only when it is one with universal law.

Furthermore, for Hegel, ethical action is not purely individual. As Dewey explained, "The will finds complete expression only when it gets realized in actual institutions and when these institutions are so bound up with the very life purposes of the individual that they supply him his concrete motives." In such a society the law is not something external to, and beyond, the individual, nor is it something that simply ought to be. The law becomes concrete and is "the life and movement of existing social institutions." These institutions have an educative influence on individuals, teaching them that their "true interest is public rather than private" that their interests are "not hostile to, but one, with that of others." Dewey argued that Hegel understood this to be especially true in modern, civil society in which labor is specialized for the sake of efficiency, so that "the satisfaction of each is made dependent upon the labor of others." In such a society, "individuals are knit together through their mutual dependencies." For this reason, individuals should not seek to satisfy only themselves, but should labor "for the satisfaction of society as a whole." In Dewey's words, "It is the essence of civil society that the individual will . . . can [only] satisfy [its] private interests by contributing to the satisfaction of others by producing wealth," which Hegel viewed as social, "as distinct from mere property," which Hegel viewed as individual.[114] Hegel's ethics led Dewey quite naturally to his philosophy of religion and social philosophy.

Dewey examined Hegel's philosophy of religion because Hegel believed that religion could contribute to social unity. Dewey's description of Hegel's philosophy of religion is remarkably sympathetic:

> [T]he development of religion is that of the religious consciousness, of consciousness which appreciates, at least in the form of feeling that God is both the subject and object of life; that he is not unknowable nor faraway spirit, but is the spirit of all spirits. In other words, the development of religion is simply the progressive revelation of man to man, the revela-

> tion in which man discovers that the ground and aim of his existence is neither in man as a mere individual nor in a world of physical force external to him, but in a living process which unites within its activity him and all other persons, the process of nature itself. The development of religion, in other words, is man finding that the divine spirit is the source and end of all his activity and that therefore the absolute power of the universe is neither mere blind force nor simply an intelligent person outside of the world, that is, a living spirit who lives in and through the world.[115]

The key idea in this passage is that religions progress, or get closer to the truth with time. In this way, Dewey, like Hegel, adapted religion to a more forward looking, though not necessarily apocalyptic, metaphor in order to make it more credible in the face of the continual progress of scientific knowledge. Furthermore, it seems that God has completely disappeared from "religion." Religion is not about God; it is about man, and man's understanding of nature. Thus science serves a religious purpose. As Dewey wrote in 1889, in "The Value of Historical Christianity," "the Spirit of God . . . is not a mystery working only in miracles, in revivals, etc., but is the intelligence present in all man's science, is his inspiration for whatever is better than himself." Arguably, in the "Religion" chapter of the *Phenomenology of Spirit,* Hegel depicted religious practice as a collective reflection on what matters most to a people and, ideally, on what is most important to humanity.[116] According to Dewey, "Hegel conceived a natural religion which would unite the reason, avoiding all superstitions, with the positive course of history and the imagination and feelings." Such a religion would countenance "no division, no divorce of the worldly and the spiritual, or piety and virtue." Rather, "Man [would live] a single, concrete life in which science, art, religion and politics were as one."[117]

In much the same way, many years later in *A Common Faith* (1934), Dewey depicted God as humanity's highest ideals and aspirations.[118] Though scholars have argued for over one hundred years about whether Hegel was a theist, a pantheist, or more of a humanist who equated God with humanity, the following passage indicates that in this 1889 essay Dewey had already come very close to the humanistic view he held in *A Common Faith,* and thus had already moved to the Hegelian left of W. T. Harris regarding the philosophy of religion.

> God is neither a far-away Being, nor a mere philosophic conception by which to explain the world. He is the reality of our ordinary relations with one another in life. He is the bond of the family, the bond of society. He is love, the source of all growth, all sacrifice, and all unity. He has touched history, not from without but has made Himself subjected to all the limitations and sufferings of history; identified Himself absolutely with humanity, so that the life of humanity is henceforward not for some term of years, but forever, the Life of God.[119]

Dewey went on to describe two crucial characteristics of Hegel's notion of spirit: its "freedom and its self-revealing power." Spirit can be in a relationship of opposition to all of nature and "still retain and assert its one being." Natural things cannot endure a contradiction but "spirit can sustain itself even under infinite self-denial." This power is spirit's freedom. Yet the power to stand alone is merely abstract freedom. "Spirit attains to positive freedom, not when it withdraws from all positive relations and still maintains its identity, but only when it impresses its own identity upon all the material which seems to resist it." Dewey's exposition of the Hegelian theory of freedom sheds light on why the St. Louis Hegelians were critical of the individualism of Thoreau, and why Denton Snider referred to Brokmeyer's retreat into the wilderness as "his grand act of negation," and his transition from social recluse to institutionalist as a "spiritual transformation."[120] According to Hegel, a free act is neither antisocial nor arbitrary; rather, a free act is one that is determined solely by the self, on the basis of reasons, to be one that rises above particularity to the universal.[121] Hegel convinced Dewey and the St. Louis Hegelians that mere independence was only partial freedom. In order to attain positive freedom, spirit also reveals or manifests itself by "externaliz[ing] itself in nature," by returning "to itself through and by means of this externality," and by overcoming the dualism between the objective and the subjective, a dualism that merely articulates internal aspects of absolute spirit. When this occurs, "Nature is no longer a limit which has to be overcome by spirit, but simply a stage in the process by which self consciousness elevates itself to its own complete and objective being."[122] In the same way, individuals need both negative and positive freedom, the latter being the opportunity and ability to contribute to the construction of their world, including their society.

Though Dewey did not discuss Hegel's writings on the state in great detail, he rejected the notion that Hegel was an apologist for Prussian absolutism, but criticized him for advocating constitutional monarchy:

> Hegel's philosophy of the state has often been termed simply a philosophical extraction and justification of the then existing Prussian monarchy. While this, perhaps, is saying too much there can be no doubt that Hegel's discussion of the internal organization of the state is the most artificial and the least satisfactory portion of his political philosophy. He makes the ideal State most highly realized in the constitutional monarchy in whose structure simple monarchy, aristocracy and democracy are simply subordinate phases.

Dewey was correct to note that Hegel never embraced democracy, but he did not view Hegel's statism as inherently inimical to individualism. Rather, Dewey explained that Hegel believed it was the task of the modern state to work out the Christian principle of individuality "in its definite, outward realization." Moreover, in his discussion of Hegel's philosophy of history, he noted that Hegel claimed that, in the modern era, man began to examine human action rationally, seeking a foundation for law and morality within his own reason and will rather than in any external authority, and discovered that "society and the State were themselves [man's] own objective reason." Consequently, society and the state "did not need to be overthrown in order that the individual might be free, but it was in and through them that the individual was free."[123] When we combine this with the notion in the master/slave dialectic that individuals come together because they recognize that they need recognition from other free, self-conscious beings, we can see why Hegel scholars have argued that his political philosophy makes diversity as essential to community as opposition and negation are to the dialectic, rather than something we must learn to tolerate in order to achieve community.[124]

Finally, I will close this discussion of Dewey's lecture with a consideration of his claim, published in 1939, that he was influenced by "Hegel's idea of cultural institutions as an 'objective mind' upon which individuals were dependent," but that the notion of an "absolute mind" dropped out. Although this passage is often taken to describe Dewey's rejection of Hegel, I have already established reasons to believe that it is best viewed as a rejection of the neo-Hegelian's metaphysical reading of Hegel, in favor of a historicist reading in which the absolute is not a transcendent reality. This is consistent with the postulate that in the 1890s Dewey began to take Hegel's *Phenomenology of Spirit* more seriously than the British neo-Hegelians. Dewey also explained that whereas his confidence in Hegel's dialectic ultimately gave way, Hegel's "emphasis on continuity and the function of conflict persisted on empirical grounds."[125] In this passage, Dewey also referred to his continued rejection of philosophical dualisms of all kinds, according to the emphasis on continuity, and his notion of the necessity and inevitability of problematic situations that spur growth. He explained that he retained Hegel's emphasis on the "power exercised by cultural environment in shaping the ideas, beliefs, and intellectual attitudes of individuals," and thus came to believe that "the only possible psychology, as distinct from a biological account of behavior, was a social psychology." Perhaps the most relevant part of this passage is Dewey's explanation that

> There was a period extending into my earlier years at Chicago when, in connection with a seminar in Hegel's Logic I tried reinterpreting his categories in terms of "readjustment" and "reconstruction." Gradually I came to realize that what the principles actually stood for could be better understood and stated when completely emancipated from Hegelian garb.[126]

This passage indicates that Dewey retained the principles that Hegel's categories stood for; he simply sought to restate them more clearly. In the following section I show how Dewey began to emancipate these logical principles from Hegelian nomenclature.

Instrumental Logic

It is fruitful to view Dewey's philosophy, as it developed in Chicago and continued to develop until his death, as a philosophy of learning. This point is critical to a full understanding of his writings on logic. Completely out of step with the way logic was beginning to develop in the early twentieth century, Dewey's logic was not concerned with proof, but with learning or, as he generally stated it, "inquiry." Dewey's theory of learning was suggested in "The Reflex Arc Concept in Psychology," and was taking shape in his essays on the philosophy of education throughout the 1890s. In a series of publications on logic from 1900 to 1903 Dewey continued to develop his theory of learning.[127]

As we examine the early development of Dewey's logic, we must recall that in 1898 James had introduced pragmatism in "Philosophical Conceptions and Practical Results," a lecture he delivered at Howison's Philosophical Union at Berkeley. In that lecture, James turned American philosophers' attention to Peirce, whom he credited with the initial development of the pragmatic method for evaluating the meaning of ideas, although James extended it to a method of ascertaining the value of ideas. In 1903, Dewey acknowledged to James that he had been reading Peirce, and that he could see how far his thought had developed when he considered "how much I got out of Peirce this year and how easily I understand him; when a few years ago he was mostly a sealed book to me aside from occasional inspirations."[128] But the influence of Peirce was already apparent in Dewey's "Some Stages in Logical Thought," published in 1900.

In "Some Stages in Logical Thought," Dewey began to speak of the doubt-inquiry process Peirce had introduced in "The Fixation of Belief" (1877), and further elaborated in "How To Make Our Ideas Clear" (1878). Unconstrained by Hegel's triadic logic, Dewey described four stages in the doubt-inquiry process, but he defined these stages much more clearly in later writings.[129] Part of the ambiguity in "Some Stages in Logical Thought" is due to his thesis that the "different stages denote various degrees in the evolution of the doubt-inquiry function."[130] Like Hegel, Dewey correlated the thought process of the individual with the historical development of western thought. He claimed that these stages of development are "easily recognizable in the progress of both the race and the individual," but the difficulties Dewey had explaining the stages in this essay suggest that they are not so apparent.[131]

In the first stage, we are engaged in activities in which we employ settled beliefs that we take to be facts, without recognition that those beliefs were initially formulated to relieve specific doubts that had arisen in previous conflicting situations. These beliefs are based upon social customs, which "are no less real than physical events," and "habit[s] of understanding." According to Dewey, this stage of the doubt-inquiry process was analogous to "primitive communities" in which customs are to be followed uncritically, and "are made valid at once in a practical way against anyone who departs from them."[132] This stage corresponds to the first stage of Hegel's dialectic, the dogmatic stage, as Dewey described it in his 1897 lecture.

Even in a more advanced society, Dewey explained, the fixation of belief is essential to action, because "the necessities of action do not await our convenience"; in everyday life we do not always have the luxury to engage in exhaustive inquiry before we act. In this vein, Dewey made a comment about Hegel that is worth quoting in its entirety:

> The alternative to vacillation, confusion, and futility of action is importation to ideas of a positive and secured character, not in strict logic belonging to them. It is this sort of determination that Hegel seems to have in mind in what he terms *Verstand*—the understanding. "Apart from *Verstand*," he says, "there is no fixity or accuracy in the region either of the-

> ory or practice"; and, again, "*Verstand* sticks to fixity of characters and their distinctions from one another; it treats every meaning as having a subsistence of its own." In technical terminology, also, this is what is meant by "positing" ideas—hardening meanings.[133]

This characterization of Hegel's notion of *Verstand* is consistent with what I said about it in chapter one. The understanding was, for Hegel "analytic cognition" which is "a *positing* that no less immediately determines itself as a *presupposing*."[134]

The first stage is followed by the stage of "external connection," in which society has multiplied rules to the extent to which thought must inquire into which rule to apply in particular circumstances. In this stage, "doubt and inquiry are directed neither at the nature of the intrinsic fact itself, nor at the value of the idea as such, but simply at the manner in which one is attached to the other." In such a society, critical inquiry is used merely to refine the rules of the society, not to question them. Thus ideas, social customs, have a conservative function, the preservation of social institutions. "In Hebrew history," Dewey explained, we see the transition from this stage to the following one "in the growing importance of the prophet over the judge," which was a "transition from a justification of conduct through bringing particular cases into conformity with existent laws, into that effected by personal right-mindedness enabling the individual to see the law in each case for himself." In other words, the principle of subjectivity, in its most rudimentary form, began to emerge in ancient Hebrew culture, assuming we accept Dewey's equation of the emergence of the Hebrew prophets with the emergence of a greater awareness of individuality and the individual's ability to understand morality. But in this short essay it was impossible for Dewey to explicate the stages of inquiry *and* develop a full-blown philosophy of history. Although, Dewey continued, this was a profound change in the "conception of the relation between law and particular case[s]," the Hebrews did not apply it to the rules of logic; that development awaited the Greeks, who affected "a continuous and marked departure from positive declaration of custom."[135]

In the third, "subjective" stage, which emerged in ancient Greece, man realizes that "fixity" is not an essential property of ideas themselves, but rather something we attach to them. An idea is seen "as a manufactured article needing to be made ready for use." The "friction of circumstances" reveals the "fiction" of the idea. During this stage we enter into the "conversation of thoughts" or "dialogue—the mother of dialectic in more than the etymological sense." This conversation can take place between individuals, or it can occur as the process of reflection within the consciousness of one individual. Dewey emphasized that this is not a comfortable stage; it is one we seek to minimize as much as possible, because we are primarily acting, not thinking, beings. In Greece, we see "assemblies meeting to discuss and dispute, and finally, upon the basis of the considerations thus brought to view, to decide. The man of counsel is set side by side with the man of deed." The Greek emphasis upon discussion gave birth to logical theory, and a particularly profound development occurred when it was realized that the individual could conduct this discussion within himself by weighing pros and cons; this was the birth of reflection. The Sophists, however, took advantage of the negativity of this subjective stage by claiming that all ideas "are just expressions of an individual's way of thinking." Logical theory arose as an effort to counter the Sophists, who misunderstood the value of the subjective stage that is necessary because in situations that call for reflection "we cannot appeal directly to the 'fact,' for the adequate reason that the stimulus to thinking arises just because 'facts' have slipped away from us." The Sophists correspond to Hegel's second stage, the "period of negation and of discord."[136]

The "Socratic school" represents the third stage of logical thought because, instead of doubting all ideas wholesale, they doubted because they sought a "common denominator" that would bring "different ideas into relation with one another." Plato objectified the universals Socrates sought because he wanted a decisive standard to regulate reflection. For Aristotle, there was no longer a need to prove the existence of standards, but to establish rules of procedure in applying those standards, hence his codification of logical rules. With Aristotle there emerged "a distinctive type of thinking marked off from mere discussion and reflection. It may be called either reasoning or proof."[137] Yet Aristotelian logic required first principles that could serve as major premises in syllogisms, and this model of reflection was passed down to medieval logicians who rigidly limited inquiry by requiring that all ideas be subsumed under universal principles, and by denigrating matters of fact that paled by comparison to their first principles.

The final stage, "covering what is popularly known as inductive and empirical science," corresponds to Hegel's final stage in which the negation is negated, and it is realized that the negative is an essential component of every positive, and thus that the dialectic is a never-ending process.[138] As Dewey described it, in the final stage we seek inferences rather than proof. Proof, Dewey claimed, seeks to connect a proposition with another proposition we take to be secure. Inference, on the other hand, seeks propositions that take us beyond established facts and provide us with a more inclusive apprehension of the initiating situation. The doubt-inquiry process leads to the fixation, rather than the crystallization, of belief. In language similar to his letter to James in which he spoke of "the intellectual forces which have been gathering since the Renascence & Reformation," Dewey explained that "The growth . . . of freedom of thought during the Renaissance was a revelation of the intrinsic momentum of the thought-process itself." Renaissance intellectuals such as Galileo and Copernicus extended the process of inquiry "into the region of particulars, of matters of fact, with the view of reconstituting them through discovery of their own structure," rather than "by connecting them with some authoritative principles."[139]

In this final stage, ideas are always subject to revision. Specialization in the sciences, an important phenomenon in Dewey's day, was not a mere historical epoch, but a logical requirement, because knowledge must be based upon fact; consequently all apparent facts "must be resolved into their elements." "Every phase of experience must be investigated, and each characteristic aspect presents its own peculiar problems which demand, therefore, their own technique of investigation."[140] For Dewey this was far more than a purely logical advance, however; it was an expression of the democratic spirit, a leveling of facts:

> when interest is occupied in finding out what anything and everything is, any fact is just as good as its fellow. The observable world is a democracy. The difference which makes a fact what it is, is not an exclusive distinction, but a matter of position and quantity, an affair of locality and aggregation, traits which place all facts upon the same level, since all other observable facts also possess them, and are, indeed, conjointly responsible for them.[141]

Dewey ended the essay with the question he sought to answer in his contributions to the *Studies in Logical Theory*:

> Does not an account of thinking, basing itself on modern scientific procedure, demand a statement in which all the distinctions and terms of thought—judgment, concept, inference, subject, predicate and copula of judgment, etc., ad infinitum—shall be interpreted simply and entirely as distinctive functions or divisions of labor within the doubt-inquiry process?[142]

In 1903, Dewey, along with seven of his associates at the University of Chicago, published *Studies in Logical Theory*. The *Studies* is an anthology of eleven essays by Chicago philosophy professors and graduate students, to which Dewey contributed the introduction and four essays. All seven writers agreed on "the intimate connections of logical theory with functional psychology," and acknowledged "a pre-eminent obligation . . . to William James."[143] Dewey's focus in the *Studies* is a critique of the assumptions of traditional epistemology, exemplified in Rudolf Hermann Lotze's *Logic*.[144] Because Lotze was known as an idealist, scholars assume that Dewey attacked Hegelian logic in his critique of Lotze. But Lotze viewed his logic as an attack on Hegelian logic, and was criticized by Henry Jones, a British neo-Hegelian, in much the same way that Dewey criticized him.[145] Yet some of Dewey's contemporaries also viewed the *Studies* as an official break from idealism. F. C. S. Schiller, the noted English pragmatist, declared that Dewey had dealt a fatal blow to absolute idealism by "his admirable proof of the superfluity of an absolute truth-to-be-*copied*, existing alongside of the human truth which is *made* by our efforts."[146] Notice, however, that Schiller's description of the absolute idealist theory of truth is at odds with Dewey's understanding of Hegel's theory of truth; Schiller described a neo-Hegelian theory of truth.

In his introduction to the volume, Dewey noted that all of the authors agreed that "judgment is the central function of knowing, and hence affords the central problem of logic." Beyond that point, it is readily apparent that this was no ordinary treatise on logic because, Dewey affirmed, all the authors also agree that "the act of knowing is intimately and indissolubly connected with the like yet diverse functions of affection, appreciation, and practice."[147] Logic must be understood in its emotive and working context; otherwise it is distorted. This is the crux of Dewey's criticisms of the logic of Lotze, who held that logic studies the "universal forms and principles of thought which hold good everywhere both in judging of reality and in weighing possibility, *irrespective of any difference in the objects*."[148] Of course this criticism applies to a host of philosophers who have engaged in what Dewey called "traditional" or "epistemological" logic, because they have proceeded on the conviction that the principles of logic are universal. Dewey explained that philosophers have fallen into this error because they assumed that thought and being are ontologically distinct. Philosophers have believed that rational thought, because its principles seem universally applicable, had to be somehow above the stream of experience, in a different realm. Dewey's proposed "instrumental" logic would avoid this error.

This criticism is not new to Dewey's writings. We have already seen that, in his earliest essays, Dewey criticized British empiricism for positing an ontological distinction between thought and being. Moreover, as early as 1886, in "Psychology as Philosophic Method," Dewey began to criticize neo-Hegelians for claiming that philosophy and psychology are distinctly different. Ultimately, in his ethical writings, Dewey pointed out that neo-Hegelians made this distinction because they too believed in an ontological dualism. Philosophy, which the neo-Hegelians equated with logic, dealt with pure, eternal being; psychology dealt with the particulars of experience and required an empirical, rather than logical, methodology.

Dewey's objection to traditional logic stemmed from his commitment to functional psychology. Knowledge is a function of experience; it is always involved in the reconstruction or transformation of a specific, problematic situation. Dewey also reaffirmed his convictions that reality, which is "dynamic or self-evolving" can be properly defined only "in terms of experience," and that such a logic would be useful to both science and morality. Dewey expressed high hopes that instrumental logic would prove beneficial to our efforts to solve a myriad of complex practical problems:

> The value of research for social progress; the bearing of psychology upon educational procedure; the mutual relations of fine and industrial art; the question of the extent and nature of specialization in science in comparison with the claims of applied science; the adjustment of religious aspirations to scientific statements; the justification of a refined culture for a few in face of economic insufficiency for the mass, the relation of organization to individuality—such are a few of the many social questions whose answer depends upon the possession and use of a general logic of experience as a method of inquiry and interpretation.[149]

Epistemological logic, Dewey explained, is committed to a particular sort of metaphysics because it studies "the relation of thought as such to reality as such," and is, therefore, the study of "absolute entities and relations." In fact, Dewey claimed that viewing thought processes (or any processes for that matter) "apart from the limits of a historic or developing situation, is the essence of metaphysical procedure." Because epistemological logic is concerned with absolute entities and relations, it is concerned with proof and certainty. By way of contrast, instrumental logic "makes no pretense to be an account of a closed and finished universe. Its business is not to secure or guarantee any particular reality or value." Instrumental logic is a logic of experience; it studies inquiry, how we resolve problems and dilemmas that arise in specific situations. Because of this focus, instrumental logic is a logic of learning, rather than a logic of proof, and will facilitate "the methodic control of experience."[150]

Dewey equated instrumental logic with the "naïve point of view," a development of his earlier "psychological standpoint."[151] Like Hegel's absolute standpoint, which is contained within the natural consciousness, the naïve point of view makes no metaphysical assumptions.[152] For it, thought and being occur within experience, and we experience interrelated situations, wholes, rather than series of discrete, atomistic sensations. Further, situations are experienced in a temporal flow. From the naïve point of view there is no mystery about the relationship of thought to reality; we think about anything and everything and there is "a certain rhythm of direct practice and derived theory." We assume that we have unrestricted "passage from ordinary experience to abstract thinking, from thought to fact, from things to theories and back again. . . . The fundamental assumption is *continuity*."[153] The distinction between idea, or meaning, and fact is simply a useful division of labor in the effort to perform a specific task, rather than an ontological principle.

According to the naïve point of view, thinking always arises when a conflicting situation disrupts a specific practice or activity in which we are engaged. Thought is viewed as "derivative and secondary," prompted by tensions, conflicts, within a particular situation and for a particular purpose—resolution of the conflict. Normally, we are in an organic relationship with our environment, working to accomplish goals, thinking through problems when they arise, and moving ahead with our activities as problems are resolved. We rarely stop to reflect on why we were motivated to begin thinking, or why we decided to return to our temporarily interrupted activities, because the answers to those questions seem obvious, and because, ordinarily, there is no problem that requires us to reflect on thought "*überhaupt*." The measure of the success of thought, or theory, according to the naïve point of view, is simply the extent to which it disposes of the immediate problem "and allows us to proceed with more direct modes of experiencing, that are forthwith possessed of more assured and deepened value."[154] Truth is what resolves specific problems, and logic should help us understand how to validate particular thoughts, rather than thought overall.

Moreover, Dewey agreed with Hegel that "there is no difference of kind between the methods of science and those of the plain man." Scientists are simply more in control of the articulation of the problem, and the selection of "relevant material, both sensible and conceptual." Dewey described four stages of scientific inquiry, which are similar, but not entirely analogous, to the stages of the doubt-inquiry process. The disanalogies undercut his claim that scientific process is simply a refined version of the doubt-inquiry process as he articulated it here, but it is not difficult to see significant similarities between the two. Like the doubt-inquiry process, the first is the stage in which no inquiry occurs at all, because no problem has provoked it. In the second, "empiric stage," rather than engaging in the "conversation of thoughts," the scientist proceeds by gathering facts. Rather than analyze particulars in the third stage, the scientist moves into "the speculative stage" in which she formulates hypotheses, and makes distinctions and classifications. In the final stage, however, scientific inquiry concludes with "a period of fruitful interaction between the mere ideas and the mere facts: a period when observation is determined by experimental conditions depending upon the use of certain guiding conception." This is analogous to the final stage of the doubt-inquiry process, which ends with inference rather than proof, because, during this period, the scientist checks conclusions by experimental data and the need to solve a specific problem and thus further inquiry, and the "evolution of new meanings."[155] Despite the disanalogies, the methods are the same at crucial points. Both are stimulated by a problematic situation, are empirical as well as rational, include the dialectical interplay of idea and fact, and are open-ended.

Only "the epistemological spectator" sees the plain man and the scientist "rashly assuming the right to glide over a cleft in the very structure of reality." It is worthwhile to note here that Dewey depicted the epistemologist as a passive spectator, since we know Dewey believed that learning requires action. Because he studies thought as though it were in a vacuum, the epistemological logician is removed from the constraints of the plain man. "The epistemological logician deliberately shuts himself off from those cues and checks upon which the plain man instinctively relies, and which the scientific man deliberately searches for and adopts as constituting his technique."[156] The primary example of this error is the notion that thought and fact are representatives of distinct ontological realms. When we view thought and being in this way, we create a philosophical conundrum that can only be addressed on its own terms because it cannot be resolved by appeals to ordinary experience.

Why then, have philosophers been so consumed with traditional logic? According to Dewey, "a generic account of our thinking behavior, the generic account termed logical theory, arises at historic periods in which the situation has lost the organic character above described." Traditional logic arises when we encounter problems so vast and unsettling that we are forced to question thinking itself rather than thinking in a particular situation. At this point one is reminded of the beginning of the "First Part" of Descartes' *Discourse on Methods,* in which he explained, in the midst of the disintegration of the medieval world, that he had studied at "one of the most celebrated schools in all of Europe . . . learned there everything that others learned," but "found nothing there to satisfy me."[157] In times of immense cultural transformation, in which our frame of reference is radically undermined, we begin to ask, "What is thought?" or "What is the relationship of thought to the world?"; we begin to reflect upon logic in the generic sense. With this analysis, Dewey, like Nietzsche, put philosophy "on the couch" as it were, explaining its preoccupation with abstract, non-worldly issues as a function, or product, of existential anxiety. Though Dewey did not say so explicitly, the inference seems to be that because epistemological logicians seek to avoid existential anxiety, their logic ignores the limitations of real life and "assumes an activity of thought 'pure' or 'in itself,' that is, 'irrespective of any difference in its objects,'" and reaches "results which are not so much either true or false as they are radically meaningless."[158]

Reminiscent of Hegel's claim that every philosophy "is *its own time comprehended in thoughts*," Dewey also explained that "every system of philosophy . . .

has been evoked out of specific social antecedents, and has had its use as a response to them."[159] Epistemological logic's denial of its own historical context, and "of the significance of historic method" in logic, is indicative of how unrealistic and useless it is. When philosophers remove the varieties of thought from their functional context, they isolate them "from the conditions in which alone they have determinable meaning and assignable worth." Logic, Dewey asserted, should take its cue from biology and learn to study the elements of thought as instruments of adaptation to an environment. By ignoring "the chain of historic sequence," the epistemological logician has set "the vessel of thought . . . afloat to veer upon a sea without soundings or moorings."[160] Here we see Dewey's debt to James, who taught him to think of perceptions and conceptions as "biological sports," which we maintain if they are applicable to concrete situations.[161]

Extending his emphasis upon logic as the study of the history of thinking activities, Dewey asserted that psychology should be "the natural history of the various attitudes and structures through which experiencing passes." Psychology should examine the conditions under which various attitudes have emerged and the ways those attitudes have stimulated or inhibited the formation of other forms of reflection. When we treat logic "as an account of thinking as a response to its own generating conditions," such a psychology is "indispensable to logical evaluation." We shall then be able to evaluate the validity of various ways of thinking by reference to their "efficiency in meeting [the] problems" that provoked them. Thus, for Dewey, psychology became what it was for Hegel. In the introduction to the *Phenomenology of Spirit,* Hegel explained that the book was a study of "the way of the Soul which journeys through the series of its own configurations" on its path to self-knowledge. The *Phenomenology,* Hegel claimed, presented "the series of configurations which consciousness goes through along this road" and was, therefore, "the detailed history of the *education* of consciousness."[162]

In his next contribution to the *Studies,* Dewey focused more specifically on his criticisms of Lotze's logic. For our purposes, his methodology is revealing. Dewey proposed to examine the relationship of thought to its antecedent, its provocateur, as it were,

> indirectly rather than directly, by indicating the contradictory positions into which one of the most vigorous and acute of modern logicians, Lotze, has been forced through failing to define logical distinctions in terms of the history of readjustment and control of things in experience, and being thereby compelled to interpret certain notions as absolute instead of as historic and methodological.

Like Hegel, Dewey sought to critique traditional logic, and thereby promote his own theory, by revealing the contradictions into which it is inevitably led by its assumptions. Dewey was not pursuing Lotze per se; rather he claimed to have chosen "one of the most vigorous and acute of" traditional logicians, in order to examine traditional logic at its best. Revealing the contradictions in Lotze's theory, Dewey believed, would uncover the assumptions of traditional logic; in true dialectical fashion he examined the endpoint of Lotze's theory in order to articulate what was implicit from the very beginning. Once those problematic assumptions are identified, Dewey believed, we can productively move on to more inclusive assumptions that would avoid the contradictions of traditional logic. Dewey also explained that Lotze's unexamined assumptions are characteristic of the assumptions we all bring to the study of logic from our "concrete experience," and from "the logical theory which has got embodied in ordinary language."[163] This claim may appear problematic because Dewey maintained that the plain man employs the doubt-inquiry process, yet also claimed that we are easily led astray by the assumptions of traditional logic. Dewey's point was simply that we need to articulate what the plain man and the scientist do when inquiry is successful; that was the goal of his instrumental logic. Because Dewey's critique of Lotze was a critique of all of our implicit assumptions, it was, like Hegel's dialectic, an exercise in self-understanding and immanent cultural criticism.

Like the plain man, Lotze assumed that thought is reflective, "and thus presupposes a given material," something to reflect upon.[164] But because he assumed, unlike the plain man, that thought and being are ontologically distinct, he was forced to struggle with the issue of how thought, which is subjective, can gain its materials from something ontologically foreign to it, the objective, take those materials into the subjective realm, and shape them into results which are objective or true. When stated in this way, the problem seems obviously intractable, but Dewey argued that because philosophers have not examined their ontological dualism, they have not become so starkly aware of the contradictions created by that presupposition.

Lotze maintained that we receive impressions from external objects and, upon reception, they become ideas, or "mere psychical states or events." We receive series of ideas, some of which are associated coincidentally and some of which are associated coherently. That is to say, some series of ideas, the coherent, really belong together and provide us with knowledge; others merely occur together and are the source of error. Thought must actively distinguish between the merely coincident and the coherent associations of ideas; it must determine their worth. Dewey commended Lotze for avoiding "the extravagancies of transcendental logic," which asserts that impressions are predetermined, prior to our experience of them, by rational thought. Lotze also "avoids the pitfall of purely empirical logic" which does not distinguish between the association of ideas and their real worth, and thus cannot account for truth. For Lotze, "unreflective experience" passively receives impressions, while reflective thought "has to introduce and develop systematic connection—rationality."[165]

But according to Lotze, "the action of thought . . . is never anything but reaction"; it merely interprets relations it finds in our associations of ideas in order to determine which are coherent and which are merely coincidental. This brought Dewey to the contradiction he sought to uncover. Initially, impressions were simply the "crude material" of experience, but somehow, as they are associated, they become the content of thought. According to Dewey, Lotze maintained that reflective thought discovers relations in our associations of ideas "which have been prepared for it by the unconscious mechanism of the psychic states" themselves. In effect, Lotze described impressions as raw data, wholly undetermined, and ideas as determined, because the impressions have a mysterious ability to prepare themselves for reflective thought. Dewey argued not only that this is a contradiction within Lotze's logic, but also that this contradiction is necessary to his system. If our ideas were simply undetermined psychical states, they could not be adequate materials for thought. Consequently, Dewey argued,

> The idea forms a most convenient halfway house for Lotze. On one hand, as absolutely prior to thought, as material antecedent condition, it is merely psychical, bald subjective event. But as subject matter for thought, as antecedent which affords stuff for thought's exercise, it characteristically qualifies content.[166]

Once more, Dewey's historical fallacy makes its appearance. Lotze fell into this error because he assumed that thought works with atomistic, unrelated impressions. Dewey argued that in the doubt-inquiry process, we analyze experience into atomistic units (Hegel's *Verstand*), but that it is fallacious to then assume that experience is composed of those units. For Dewey, thought is reflective, as it is for Lotze. It works upon a material, but that material is a situation, replete with relations, rather than a series of atoms. But Dewey avoided the neo-Hegelian temptation to attribute transcendent rationality to these situations by, once more, invoking the psychological fallacy. He never spoke about situations-in-themselves, but only about situations as they are experienced. Dewey also argued that coincidence and coherence are functions that make sense only within a reflective context, rather than essential properties of ideas.

> The side-by-sideness of books on my bookshelf, the succession of noises that rise through my window, do not trouble me logically. They do not appear as errors or even as problems. One coexistence is just as good as any other until some new point of view, or new end, presents itself. If it is a question of the convenience of arrangement of books, then the value of their present collocation becomes a problem. Then I contrast their present state as bare conjunction over against another scheme as one which is coherent.[167]

As long as philosophers assume that thought and being are ontologically distinct, they have to resolve the dilemma of how the materials of thought, originating in a foreign reality, become suitable for thought. If relations are a posteriori, and the mind always shapes our impressions, thought is falsifying because we never experience impressions as they are in themselves; if relations are a priori, and the mind passively receives predetermined materials, thought is futile because there is nothing for it to add to our experience. If, however, thought and being are both within experience, as Dewey maintained, rather than distinct ontological realms, they have features in common that facilitate their interaction. Coincidence and coherence can both be found within situations, depending upon our specific purpose. When a situation "is in conflict within itself," thought is provoked and we begin a "search to find what really goes together and a correspondent effort to shut out what only seemingly goes together." To read those qualities back into a preexisting unmediated situation is fallacious, because they only emerged in inquiry. Like Hegel's notion of reason (*Vernunft*), which can reconstruct and apprehend the whole, Dewey claimed that the "redefining and re-relating" of conflicted situations "is the constructive process termed thinking."[168] In the same way, Hegel's "understanding" (*Verstand*) leads us into error if we stop with its analysis of the subject matter into constituent parts without proceeding to *Vernunft*. This is where, in Dewey's parlance, we fall into the psychological fallacy. We must move beyond the analysis of the components of an experience to an apprehension of the whole experience.

At this point we encounter passages that have led scholars to claim that Dewey publicly broke with idealism in the *Studies*. Dewey noted that the British neo-Hegelian philosopher, Henry Jones, had formulated a critique of Lotze's logic very similar to his own.[169] Jones had criticized Lotze for trying to find any existence antecedent to thought. Dewey noted that this position is often called neo-Hegelian, but added, parenthetically, "though, I think, with questionable accuracy." Dewey tried to carefully distinguish his critique from that of Jones, conceding that they agreed that reflection cannot arise from an "antecedent bare existence," or that there is such a thing as bare existence. They also agreed that "reflective thought grows organically out of an experience which is already organized, and that it functions within such an organism." They disagreed, however, on a fundamental point. Dewey rejected the notion that all of reality is organized by thought, and that there is some other type of thought—"Pure Thought, Creative or Constitutive Thought, Intuitive Reason, etc."—that organizes reality prior to the situations we encounter in experience.[170]

According to Dewey, "the more one insists that the antecedent situation is constituted by thought, the more one has to wonder why another type of thought is required; what need arouses it, and how it is possible for it to improve upon the work of previous constitutive thought." Like Lotze, neo-Hegelians run the risk of making human thought futile. In order to avoid this problem, neo-Hegelians abandon the logic of experience, the psychological standpoint, and formulate "a metaphysics of purely hypothetical experience." The neo-Hegelians posit a transcendent absolute spirit, but this does not help because one wonders why the absolute spirit "does such a poor and bungling job that it requires a finite discursive activity to patch up its products?" Neo-Hegelians resort to more metaphysics by explaining that the absolute spirit chooses to work in limited conditions, but

> Why and how should a perfect, absolute, complete, finished thought find it necessary to submit to alien, disturbing, and corrupting conditions in order, in the end, to recover through reflective thought in a partial, piecemeal, wholly inadequate way what it possessed at the outset in a much more satisfactory way?[171]

Dewey implied that neo-Hegelianism dies the death of a thousand qualifications, always finding a way to back-pedal and add another metaphysical doctrine post-hoc to explain its position. But neo-Hegelianism lands in the same position as Lotze because, if the absolute is limited, then the situations we encounter are not always entirely rational, and therefore we must encounter some bare existences that are not already suitable materials for thought.

Rather than argue that Hegel avoided this problem, however, in this essay Dewey began to refer to neo-Hegelians simply as absolute idealists, and one might conclude from this that he was also condemning Hegel. But Dewey's primary criticism of the neo-Hegelians was that they resorted to a transcendental logic in order to explain how the antecedents of thought could have the qualities (relations) needed to provoke thought. Both empiricist and transcendental logic commit the error of making "into absolute and fixed distinctions of existence and meaning . . . things which are historic or temporal in their origin and their significance." Both view thought as representational, instead of reconstructive. Consequently,

> The rock against which every such logic splits is that either existence already has the statement which thought is endeavoring to give it, or else it has not. In the former case, thought is futilely reiterative; in the latter, it is falsificatory.[172]

I have argued, however, that on Dewey's historicist reading, Hegel avoided the error of positing something beyond history, beyond possible experience, and did not encounter the problem inherent in all representational logics.

The *Studies in Logical Theory* received a variety of reactions. Dewey had sent proofs to James before the volume was published, and asked James's permission to dedicate the book to him. In a letter to Dewey, James expressed embarrassment that he had underestimated the extent to which Dewey and the other philosophers at Chicago were moving toward his philosophical position, but he was obviously delighted to have their company, and Dewey was also clearly flattered by James's praise. James explained to Dewey that he had not appreciated their increasing similarity because "you all have come from Hegel . . . I from empiricism, and though we reach much the same goal it superficially looks different from the opposite sides." In a letter to Schiller, James excitedly declared that the *Studies* "was splendid stuff, and Dewey is a hero. A real school and real thought. At Harvard we have plenty of thought, but no school. At Yale and Cornell, the other way about."[173]

Peirce reviewed the book for the *Nation,* but was much less enthusiastic than James. According to Peirce, "The Chicago school or group . . . are not making any studies which anybody in his senses can expect, directly or indirectly, in any considerable degree, to influence twentieth-century science."[174] This is especially clear in Peirce's letter to Dewey, written before the review appeared, in which he explained

> that your style of reasoning about reasoning has, to my mind, the usual fault that when men touch on this subject, they seem to think that no reasoning can be too loose, that indeed there is a merit in such slipshod arguments as they themselves would not dream of using in any other branch of science. You propose to substitute for the Normative Science which in my judgment is the greatest need of our age a "Natural History"

> of thought or of experience. Far be it from me to do anything to hinder a man's finding out whatever kind of truth he is on the way to finding out. But I do not think anything like a natural history can answer the terrible need that I see of checking the awful waste of thought, of time, of energy, going on, in consequence of men's not understanding the theory of inference.[175]

Peirce explained to Dewey that he hoped to publish a review in the *Nation,* and after this letter, Dewey may have preferred that Peirce's review never appear. Peirce recognized the *Studies* as a "Phänomenologie" of thought, which he equated with moral licentiousness:

> The effect of teaching that such a Natural History can take the place of a normative science of thought must be to render the rules of reasoning lax; and in fact I find you and your students greatly given over to what to me seems like a debauch of loose reasoning. Chicago hasn't the reputation of being a moral place; but I should think that the effect of living there upon a man like you would be to make you feel all the more the necessity for Dyadic distinctions,—Right and Wrong, Truth and Falsity.[176]

Unlike Dewey, Peirce sought a normative science of logic that would provide atemporal rules of reason. Consequently, Peirce was the first in a long line of critics who accused Dewey's instrumentalism of a debilitating relativism, an inability to establish transcendent values. Of course that was a risk Dewey took when he made the transition to a historicist reading of Hegel, and incorporated insights gained from that reading into his instrumentalism.

Notes

1. On Dewey's early rejection of idealism see Michael Buxton, "The Influence of William James on John Dewey's Early Work," *Journal of the History of Ideas* 45, no. 3 (July-Sept. 1984): 451-463; and Bruce Kuklick, *Churchmen and Philosophers: From Jonathan Edwards to John Dewey* (New Haven: Yale University Press, 1985), ch. 16.

2. Morton White, *The Origin of Dewey's Instrumentalism* (New York: Columbia University Press, 1943), 96-108, 134.

3. White, *The Origin of Dewey's Instrumentalism,* 110-113. See also George Dykhuizen, *The Life and Mind of John Dewey* (Carbondale: Southern Illinois University Press, 1973), 68-71, 82-83.

4. In this chapter and the next, I observe places where Dewey uses the term "idealism" without clearly defining it. It is noteworthy that he rarely used the term "absolute idealism" at all. In "Experience and Objective Idealism" (1906), as I will argue in chapter six, Robert Westbrook and others have claimed Dewey criticized "absolute idealism," but in fact the only form of idealism he explicitly attacked was neo-Kantianism, or what he often called "transcendental idealism." For Westbrook's dating of this transition in Dewey's thought see *John Dewey and American Democracy* (Ithaca: Cornell University

Press, 1991), 61. Westbrook characterizes "Experience and Objective Idealism" as a "critique of absolute idealism," 124 n. 9.

5. John Shook, *Dewey's Empirical Theory of Knowledge and Reality* (Nashville: Vanderbilt University Press, 2000), 215.

6. Dewey to William James, 6 May 1891.

7. Dewey to William Rainey Harper, 15 February 1894.

8. Harper's dismissal of Alice in 1904 instigated Dewey's resignation from the University of Chicago. Dewey claimed, however, that Alice's dismissal was "but one incident in the history of years." Dewey to William Rainey Harper, 10 May 1904. For a full history of the Dewey School see Katherine Camp Mayhew and Anna Camp Edwards, *The Dewey School* (New York: Atherton Press, 1966).

9. Dewey, "Interest in Relation to the Training of the Will" (1896), EW 5: 141.

10. See Dykhuizen, *The Life and Mind of John Dewey,* 87-91.

11. Dewey was increasingly involved in particular social and political problems, especially after he left Chicago in 1904, but the core of his philosophy was the promotion of intelligent action more generally. This is the central theme of Michael Eldridge, *Transforming Experience: John Dewey's Cultural Instrumentalism* (Nashville: Vanderbilt University Press, 1998).

12. Dewey to Alice Chipman Dewey and children, 20, 21 July 1894.

13. Harold E. Bergquist, Jr., "The Edward Bemis Controversy at the University of Chicago," *American Association of University Professors Bulletin* 58 (1972): 383-393. Cf. Dewey's concern about "academic materialism" in "Academic Freedom" (1902), MW 2: 62.

14. Dewey to Alice Chipman Dewey and children, 4, 5 July 1894.

15. Jay Martin does a good job of showing how overwhelmed Dewey was by the minutiae and politics of administration during his years in Chicago. Martin, *The Education of John Dewey* (New York: Columbia University Press, 2002), 183-186.

16. Dewey to Alice Chipman Dewey, 23 September 1894. Chicago was second only to New York in the rate of population growth from 1890 to 1900, increasing from a population of 1,099,850 to 1,698,575, a 54 percent rate of growth. See Bayrd Still, *Urban America: A History with Documents* (Boston: Little Brown, 1974), 210-211.

17. Dewey to Alice Chipman Dewey, 2 August 1894.

18. Dewey to Alice Chipman Dewey, 20 November 1894.

19. Dykhuizen, *The Life and Mind of John Dewey,* 105.

20. Tufts was Dewey's colleague at Michigan. When Tufts left to study in Germany in 1891, Mead was hired to take his place. James R. Angell was the son of James B. Angell, president of the University of Michigan; the younger Angell studied as an undergraduate with Morris, Dewey, and Tufts before going to Germany.

21. Dewey, "George Herbert Mead as I Knew Him" (1931), LW 6: 27. Cf. Jane Dewey, "Biography of John Dewey" in *The Philosophy of John Dewey,* ed. Paul Arthur Schilpp (Evanston, IL: Northwestern University Press, 1939), 25-26.

22. George Herbert Mead, "A New Criticism of Hegelianism: Is It Valid?" *The American Journal of Theology* 5 (1901): 87-88, 96.

23. Gary A. Cook, *George Herbert Mead: The Making of a Social Pragmatist* (Urbana: University of Illinois Press, 1993), 39. Cf. Hans Joas, *G. H. Mead: A Contemporary Re-examination of His Thought,* trans. Raymond Meyer (Cambridge, MA: MIT Press, 1997), 60.

24. Josiah Royce, *Lectures on Modern Idealism,* ed. Jacob Loewenberg (New Haven: Yale University Press, 1919), 85-86. One of Royce's last graduate students, Jacob Loewenberg, made a significant contribution to the post-World War II renaissance in Hegel studies by publishing an existentialist reading of Hegel's *Phenomenology of Spirit,* a reading Loewenberg claimed was inspired by Royce's *Lectures on Modern Idealism.*

Loewenberg, *Hegel's Phenomenology: Dialogues on the Life of the Mind* (LaSalle, IL: Open Court, 1965), x.

25. Joas, *G. H. Mead,* 53, 60.

26. Thomas L. Haskell, "Persons as Uncaused Causes: John Stuart Mill, the Spirit of Capitalism, and the 'Invention' of Formalism," in *Objectivity is Not Neutrality* (Baltimore: The Johns Hopkins University Press, 1998), 318-367. Haskell compares Mill's ultimate solution to this existential problem to that of James and Dewey. On James's depression brought on by the problem of free will and determinism see Ralph Barton Perry, *The Thought and Character of William James* (Boston: Little, Brown, 1935), 1: 321-326.

27. See the distinction Larry Hickman makes between narrow, "straight-line instrumentalism" and Dewey's instrumentalism. Hickman, *John Dewey's Pragmatic Technology* (Bloomington: Indiana University Press, 1990), 13, 153-154. The term "straight-line instrumentalism" comes from Langdon Winner, *Autonomous Technology* (Cambridge, MA: MIT Press, 1977). See also Hickman's "Habermas's Unresolved Dualism: *Zweckrationalität* as *Idée Fixe*," in *Perspectives on Habermas,* ed. Lewis Edwin Hahn (Chicago: Open Court, 2000), 501-513. In this article, Hickman argues that Dewey's richer conception of scientific technology allows his instrumentalism to avoid the pitfalls of the instrumental reason that has been criticized by Weber, the Frankfurt School, and Habermas, as narrowly goal and efficiency oriented without regard for moral issues. According to Hickman, Dewey's rich notion of inquiry, the "method of intelligence," allows him to integrate what Habermas calls the "empirical sciences" with the "human sciences." Although Hickman does not suggest this, my claim is that Dewey appropriated this richer notion of inquiry from Hegel's dialectic.

28. Ultimately, Dewey decided that even "experience" was overly weighted down by philosophical associations with Cartesian dualism, explaining in a new introduction to *Experience and Nature* (written in 1951): "Were I to write (or rewrite) *Experience and Nature* today I would entitle the book *Culture and Nature* and the treatment of specific subject-matters would be correspondingly modified. I would abandon the term 'experience' because of my growing realization that the historical obstacles which prevented understanding of my use of 'experience' are, for all practical purposes, insurmountable." Dewey, *Experience and Nature* (1925), LW 1: 361.

29. Jennifer Welchman, *Dewey's Ethical Thought* (Ithaca: Cornell University Press, 1995), 124.

30. Ibid.

31. Dewey to William James, 27 March 1903. Quoted by permission of the Houghton Library, Harvard University, call number bMS Am 1092.9 (128)-(144). I made minor spelling corrections to this quotation.

32. Dewey, "The Reflex Arc Concept in Psychology" (1896), EW 5: 97. William James, *The Principles of Psychology,* 2 vols. (New York: Dover Publications, 1950), 1: 24-26.

33. Dewey, "The Reflex Arc Concept in Psychology" (1896), EW 5: 104.

34. Ibid., 98, 104.

35. Ibid., 105-106. During these years there were two other essays in which Dewey discovered the psychological fallacy, in different forms, in the positions of his opponents. Dewey, "The Ego as Cause" (1894), EW 4: 94-95; and Dewey, "The Psychology of Effort" (1897), 5: 163.

36. Of course, Dewey's new psychology did not emerge newborn in this essay. Cf. Dewey, "The Theory of Emotion (1894-1895), EW 4: 163, 181. Darnell Rucker documents that Mead, Angell, and Moore were developing this interpretation of action simultaneously with Dewey. Rucker, *The Chicago Pragmatists* (Minneapolis: University of Minnesota Press, 1969), 58-60.

37. Andrew Backe has recently pointed out that the notion of an organic unity that "is realized through differentiation and opposition of elements" is not new to Dewey's thought, and that Dewey saw the argument in this article as a Hegelian critique of the reflex arc. According to Backe, "one credible inference to draw is that Hegel provided fundamental inspiration for Dewey's functionalism expressed in the paper." Backe, "Dewey and the Reflex Arc: The Limits of James's Influence," *Transactions of the Charles S. Peirce Society* 35, no. 2 (Spring 1999): 322.

38. Dewey, "The Reflex Arc Concept in Psychology" (1896), EW 5: 100.

39. Dewey, "The Evolutionary Method as Applied to Morality" (1902), MW 2: 14.

40. "Dreams are not something outside of the regular course of events; they are in and of it. They are not cognitive distortions of real things; they are more real things. There is nothing abnormal in their existence, any more than there is in the bursting of a bottle. But they may be abnormal, from the standpoint of their influence, of their operation as stimuli in calling out responses to modify the future. Dreams have often been taken as prognostics of what is to happen; they have modified conduct. A hallucination may lead a man to consult a doctor; such a consequence is right and proper. But the consultation indicates that the subject regarded it as an indication of consequences which he feared: as a symptom of a disturbed life. Or the hallucination may lead him to anticipate consequences which in fact flow only from the possession of great wealth. Then the hallucination is a disturbance of the normal course of events; the occurrence is wrongly used with reference to eventualities." Dewey, "The Need for a Recovery of Philosophy" (1917), MW 10: 27-28.

41. See especially Dewey, "The Good as Self-Realization" in *Ethics* (1908), MW 5: 351-357.

42. Westbrook, *John Dewey and American Democracy,* 69-70.

43. Welchman, *Dewey's Ethical Thought,* 129.

44. Dewey, *Psychology* (1887), EW 2: 216.

45. William Robert McKenzie, introduction in EW 5: xvi; Dewey, "The Discussion at Jacksonville," in "Interest in Relation to the Training of the Will" (1896), EW 5: 147.

46. Dewey, *Schools of To-Morrow* (1915), MW 8: 370; Dewey, "Introductory Word" (1918), MW 11: 352. For Dewey's criticisms of the way some theorists spoke of "self-expression" see Dewey, *How We Think* (1910), MW 6: 215, 225, 230; Dewey, *Democracy and Education* (1916), MW 9: 108; Dewey, *Experience and Nature* (1925), LW 1: 272; Dewey, "Philosophies of Freedom" (1928), LW 3: 98; Dewey, *How We Think,* rev. ed. (1933), LW 8: 180-181, 341. Dewey criticized aesthetic expression in the same way in *Democracy and Education* and *Art as Experience,* objecting to the association of the word art "not with specific transformation of things, making them more significant for mind, but with . . . emotional indulgences." Dewey, *Democracy and Education* (1916), MW 9: 143. Cf. Dewey, *Art as Experience* (1934), LW 10: 68, 112, 288. See also Dewey's response to critics of *Art as Experience,* in which he states that his "treatment of 'expression' is derived from a combination of criticisms I wrote many years ago about the idea of 'Self-expression' as put forward by some educational theorists." Dewey, "A Comment on the Foregoing Criticisms" (1948), LW 15: 100.

47. Dewey, *Democracy and Education* (1916), MW 9: 55; Dewey, *How We Think* (1910), MW 6: 230.

48. Dewey, "Mental Development" (1900), MW 1: 197.

49. Dewey, *Democracy and Education* (1916), MW 9: 182. I believe this bolsters Thomas Alexander's claim that "the best approach to what Dewey means by 'experience' is not to be gained by focusing primarily on the theme by which Dewey is generally known, his 'instrumentalism,' but instead by looking at experience in its most complete, most significant, and most fulfilling mode: experience as art. . . .When we explore experience which has been shaped into an aesthetically funded process, into 'an experience,'

we will discover Dewey's paradigmatic understanding of experience." Alexander, *John Dewey's Theory of Art, Experience and Nature: The Horizons of Feeling* (Albany: State University of New York Press, 1987), xiii.

50. Dewey, *How We Think* (1910), MW 6: 230.

51. Dewey, "Results of Child-Study Applied to Education" (1895), EW 5: 204.

52. See W. T. Harris, "Professor John Dewey's Doctrine of Interest as Related to the Will," *Educational Review* 11 (May 1896): 486-493.

53. "Annual Register," July 1896–July 1897 with announcements for 1897-1898 (Chicago: University of Chicago Press, 1897). According to the register, Dewey offered the course in the autumn, winter and spring quarters. The course is also listed in the 1897-1898 register. His use of Rosenkranz's biography of Hegel (see below), as well as other sources, indicates that Dewey read German rather well. Nevertheless, his students may have needed to read Hegel in translation. William Wallace's translation of Hegel's "Lesser Logic" was first published in 1873; its second edition was released in 1892. Wallace's translation of Hegel's *Philosophy of Mind* (translated from the *Encyclopädie*) was published in 1894. Hegel's *Aesthetics or Philosophy of Fine Art* was available only in partial translation at this time. William Bryant, one of the St. Louis Hegelians, published a translation of Part Two in 1879. Hegel, *The Philosophy of Art: Being the Second Part of Hegel's Æsthetik, in which Are Unfolded Historically the Three Great Fundamental Phases of the Art-Activity of the World,* trans., W. M Bryant (New York: D. Appleton and Co., 1879). Several other partial translations appeared during the 1880s. Another partial translation appeared in the Griggs' Philosophical Classics series, edited by G. S. Morris and Dewey. John Steinfort Kedney, *Hegel's Aesthetics: A Critical Exposition* (Chicago: S. C. Griggs and Company, 1885). The first third of Kedney's book was a translation of the beginning of Part One. Kedney's translation was followed by two more partial translations in 1886. Hegel, *The Philosophy of Art: An Introduction to the Scientific Study of Aesthetics,* ed. Karl Ludwig Michelet, trans. William H. Hastie (Edinburgh: Oliver and Boyd, 1886). Bernard Bosanquet, *The Introduction to Hegel's Philosophy of Fine Art* (London: Kegan Paul, Trench, 1886). The *Phenomenology of Spirit* was not translated in its entirety until 1910. Hegel, *The Phenomenology of Mind*, trans. J. B. Baillie (London: Swan Sonnenschein, 1910). A partial translation of Hegel's philosophy of law was published in 1873. James Hutchison Stirling, *Lectures on the Philosophy of Law: Together with Whewell and Hegel, and Hegel and Mr. W. R. Smith, a Vindication in the Physico-Mathematical Regard* (London: Longmans, Green and Co., 1873).

54. This lecture also makes it apparent that Dewey studied Hegel intensely and should dispel claims like Raymond Boisvert's that Dewey's allegiance was to "*Hegelianism,* the movement . . . not to a thorough assimilation of Hegel, the individual philosopher." Boisvert, *Dewey's Metaphysics* (New York: Fordham University Press, 1988), 27.

55. Dewey, "Hegel's Philosophy of Spirit: Lectures by John Dewey," University of Chicago, 1897. Unpublished manuscript, John Dewey Papers, Collection 102, Special Collections, Morris Library, Southern Illinois University, Carbondale, IL, 1.

56. Karl Rosenkranz, *Georg Wilhelm Friedrich Hegel's Leben* (Berlin: Duncker und Humblot, 1844); and Rudolf Haym, *Hegel und seine Zeit, Vorlesungen über Entstehung und Entwickelung, Wesen und Werth der Hegel'schen Philosophie* (Berlin, 1857). Dewey could have also relied on Edward Caird's *Hegel,* published in 1883, and Frederic Ludlow Luqueer's *Hegel as Educator,* published in 1896, for biographical information, both of which were explicitly based upon Rosenkranz's biography.

57. Dewey to W. T. Harris, 1 July 1882. See also Dewey to W. T. Harris, 22 October 1881.

58. Dewey, "Hegel's Philosophy of Spirit," 2.

59. Ibid., 3.

60. Ibid., 4.

61. Ibid., 6. Cf. Royce's claim that "Nothing is true, for them [the post-Kantian idealists], unless therein the sense, the purpose, the meaning of some active process is carried out, expressed, accomplished. Truth is not for these post-Kantian idealists something dead and settled apart from action. It is a construction, a process, an activity, a creation, an attainment." Later, Royce claimed that "It becomes manifest throughout the whole work [Hegel's *Phenomenology of Spirit*] that, for Hegel, thought is inseparable from will, that logic exists only as the logic of life, and the truth, although in a sense that we shall hereafter consider absolute, exists only in the form of a significant life process, in which the interests and purposes both of humanity and of the Absolute express themselves. The deduction of the categories of the thinking process, in so far as it is suggested in this work, is dialectical. It is based upon the method of antithesis, a method possessing for Hegel pragmatic significance and illustrating the way in which men live as well as the way in which men must think." Royce, *Lectures on Modern Idealism,* 86, 145.

62. Hegel, *Elements of the Philosophy of Right,* ed. Allen Wood, trans. H. B. Nisbet (Cambridge: Cambridge University Press, 1991), 20. Cf. Hegel's claim in the *Science of Logic* that "what is actual can act." Hegel, *Hegel's Science of Logic,* trans. A. V. Miller (Atlantic Highlands, NJ: Humanities Press, 1969), 546. Cf. Hegel's claim that "People are in the habit of saying '*it is only a conception*,' contrasting the concept, not merely with the idea, but with sensuous, palpable existence in time and space, as something more excellent than the concept. And then, because so much material of this kind is omitted from the abstract, the abstract is held to be a poorer thing than the concrete. The signification of abstraction on this view is that from the concrete, merely *for our subjective behoof, this or that mark* is detached, without any derogation from the *worth* and *value* of the several other *properties* and *qualities* that are left behind; and that these remain the *reality,* and are always perfectly valid, only over on the opposite side; so that it is merely an *incapacity* on the part of the understanding that it is unable to take up such treasures, but contents itself perforce with the starved abstraction." Hegel, *Hegel's Doctrine of Formal Logic: Being a Translation of the First Section of the Subjective Logic,* trans. H. S. Macran (Oxford: Clarendon Press, 1912), 129 (emphasis in the original).

63. In *The Origin of Dewey's Instrumentalism,* Morton White maintains that "when he [Hegel] attacked the mechanical approach [to human problems], he made way for the growth of social science and the emphasis on process; when he called the real 'rational,' he made way for the right Hegelians." From this, White concludes that Hegel's organicism and emphasis on process culminated in Dewey's social psychology, but "signs of right Hegelianism leave forever." This is a good example of errors that have arisen from speculating about Dewey's Hegelian deposit without exegesis of Hegel's writings. The notion that Hegel's assertion inevitably led to right Hegelianism is based on a misunderstanding of Hegel's meaning and is at odds with the way Dewey understood it. White, *The Origin of Dewey's Instrumentalism,* 98.

64. Dewey, *The Quest for Certainty* (1929), LW 4: 51. Although Dewey criticized Hegel in *The Quest for Certainty* for making "meanings and values" into absolutes, I think this is a dubious criticism that requires a defense, which Dewey did not provide. I also believe it is significant that Dewey criticized Hegel in a book that I read as a persuasive argument in favor of philosophy as *Bildung.* In the following chapter I will show that scholars should take Dewey's comments about Hegel after World War I with a grain of salt. Cf. Dewey's reading of Hegel in this lecture to Karl Löwith's claim that, with Hegel, "Philosophy becomes an eternally living activity, excluding any revival of past systems. The philosopher who is to do justice to this transitory nature must be the most persevering and productive spirit of his age, a man with the surest capacity for making distinctions in order to be able to differentiate what is valuable from what is worthless, and what is significant for the future from what is merely topical." Löwith, *From Hegel to Nietzsche: The Revolution in Nineteenth-Century Thought* (New York: Columbia Univer-

sity Press, 1964), 130. For a good discussion of Hegel's dictum and the ways it has been misunderstood see M. W. Jackson, "Hegel: The Real and the Rational," in *The Hegel Myths and Legends,* ed. John Stewart (Evanston, IL: Northwestern University Press, 1996), 19-25.

65. Dewey, "From Absolutism to Experimentalism" (1930), LW 5: 154.

66. Dewey, "Hegel's Philosophy of Spirit," 9.

67. Ibid., 15.

68. Ibid., 8.

69. Ibid., 9.

70. Ibid., 38. Cf. Hegel, *Phenomenology of Spirit,* trans. A. V. Miller (Oxford: Oxford University Press, 1977), §§73-74.

71. Dewey, "Hegel's Philosophy of Spirit," 19-20.

72. Ibid., 98, 15-16, 68, 77. Cf. Hegel, *The Philosophy of Right,* §§124, 260; and Hegel, *Phenomenology of Spirit,* "Absolute Freedom and Terror," §§582-595.

73. Dewey, "Hegel's Philosophy of Spirit," 37.

74. Ibid., 86. Similarly, Hegel wrote, "A history without such aim and such criticism would be only an imbecile mental divagation, not as good as a fairy tale, for even children expect a motif in their stories, a purpose at least dimly surmisable with which events and actions are put in relation." Hegel, *Philosophy of Mind, Translated from* The Encyclopaedia of the Philosophical Sciences, trans. William Wallace and A. V. Miller (Oxford: Clarendon Press, 1971), §549. Since Dewey is apparently talking about Hegel's later historical writings, Royce seems to have been more critical of Hegel than Dewey on this point. According to Royce, "It is easy to say that in Hegel's treatment of his ethicological parallelism, as one might call it, he becomes a formalist, and often appears to falsify history by interpreting its catastrophes and its warfare in terms of the categories of his system. But this offense, in so far as it can be charged against Hegel, in much less present in the *Phaenomenologie* than in his much later lectures on the philosophy of history." Royce, *Lectures on Modern Idealism,* 144.

75. Joseph Torrey, *A Theory of Fine Art* (New York: Scribner, Armstrong, and Co., 1874), 170ff.

76. Dewey, "The Significance of the Problem of Knowledge" (1897), EW 5: 3-24. Cf. Dewey, *Reconstruction in Philosophy* (1920), MW 12:79-201; and Dewey, *The Quest for Certainty* (1929), LW 4: 1-251.

77. Dewey, "Hegel's Philosophy of Spirit," 28.

78. In this lecture, Dewey seems to have followed Hegel's usage of "soul" as the emotional aspect of the self and "spirit" as the intellectual and more active aspect of the self.

79. Dewey, "Hegel's Philosophy of Spirit," 46. Cf. Dewey, "The Theory of Emotion" (1894), EW 4: 152-188. Dewey to William James, 6 May 1891.

80. Dewey, "Hegel's Philosophy of Spirit," 46, 66.

81. Dewey, "Imagination and Expression" (1896), EW 5: 195.

82. Dewey, "Hegel's Philosophy of Spirit," 25-26.

83. Ibid., 24-25, 23. Cf. Hegel, *Phenomenology of Spirit,* §§15-18, §§73-74.

84. Cf. Hegel, *Philosophy of Mind,* §379.

85. Dewey, "Hegel's Philosophy of Spirit," 29, 30.

86. Ibid., 30, 31. Cf. Hegel, *Phenomenology of Spirit,* §§84-86.

87. Dewey, "Hegel's Philosophy of Spirit," 36, 58. For Hegel's theory of habit see Hegel, *Philosophy of Mind,* §§409-410. John McCumber offers an account of Hegel's theory of habit that is quite similar to Dewey's. McCumber, "Hegel on Habit," *The Owl of Minerva* 21, no. 2 (Spring 1990): 155-165. See also Alfredo Ferrarin's comparison of Hegel's conception of habit to Aristotle's. Ferrarin, *Hegel and Aristotle* (Cambridge: Cambridge University Press, 2001), 278-283.

88. Dewey, "Hegel's Philosophy of Spirit," 43 (emphasis in the original).

89. Ibid., 49. Cf. Hegel, *Phenomenology of Spirit,* §401.

90. Dewey, "Hegel's Philosophy of Spirit," 52-53.

91. Cf. Hegel, *Hegel's Philosophy of Mind,* §§471-472; Hegel, *Phenomenology of Spirit,* §§167-175.

92. Dewey, "Hegel's Philosophy of Spirit," 55.

93. Cf. Hegel, *Hegel's Philosophy of Mind,* §§426-429; Hegel, *Phenomenology of Spirit,* §§167-177.

94. Dewey, "Hegel's Philosophy of Spirit," 56, 57. Cf. Hegel, *Hegel's Philosophy of Mind,* §§430-439; Hegel, *Phenomenology of Spirit,* §§178-196. Cf. Mead's claim that "the immediate analysis of consciousness reveals an essentially social nature of the self. From childhood up we see that the individual recognizes and formulates the personalities of others before he does his own; that the formation of his own personality is the result of the organization of that of others. . . . Immediate consciousness . . . must recognize others in order that it may state itself." Mead, "A New Criticism of Hegelianism: Is It Valid?" 95-96.

95. Dewey, "Hegel's Philosophy of Spirit," 21. Hegel, *The Logic of Hegel, Translated from* The Encyclopaedia of the Philosophical Sciences, 3rd edition, trans. William Wallace (Oxford: Clarendon Press, 1975), §234.

96. Dewey, "Self-Realization as the Moral Ideal" (1893), EW 4: 53; and Dewey, "Green's Theory of the Moral Motive" (1892), EW 3: 163.

97. Dewey, "Hegel's Philosophy of Spirit," 24. Cf. Hegel, *Phenomenology of Spirit,* §§15-16.

98. Dewey, "The Pantheism of Spinoza" (1882), EW 1: 10. It is significant that Schelling first proclaimed his identity philosophy in his *Vorlesungen über die Methode des academischen Studiums,* which he wrote in Spinoza's axiomatic mode.

99. Dewey, "Hegel's Philosophy of Spirit," 24. Cf. Hegel, *Phenomenology of Spirit,* §§17, 802.

100. Dewey to Alice Dewey, 9 October 1894. On sublation, see Hegel, *Science of Logic,* 106-108.

101. Dewey, "Hegel's Philosophy of Spirit," 16.

102. Ibid., 17, 18. Cf. Hegel's discussion of the role of skepticism in *Phenomenology of Spirit,* §§78-80. Dewey's periodization—dogmatic thought, skepticism, and criticism—may be based on Kant, *Critique of Pure Reason* (New York: Macmillan, 1929), 668-669.

103. Dewey, "Hegel's Philosophy of Spirit," 23. Cf. Hegel's critique of Romanticism in *Phenomenology of Spirit,* §§367ff.

104. Dewey, "Hegel's Philosophy of Spirit," 22, 23.

105. Recall Dewey's claim in Dewey to H. A. P. Torrey, 17 November 1883, that consistent use of the psychological standpoint would inevitably lead one to idealism.

106. Dewey, "Hegel's Philosophy of Spirit," 39. Hegel, *The Logic of Hegel,* §153.

107. Dewey, "The Evolutionary Method as Applied to Ethics" (1902), MW 2: 12.

108. Hegel, *The Logic of Hegel,* §153. Cf. Hegel, *Science of Logic,* 559.

109. Dewey, "The Superstition of Necessity" (1893), EW 4: 36.

110. Dewey, "Hegel's Philosophy of Spirit," 24, 25.

111. Ibid., 68.

112. Hegel, *Phenomenology of Spirit,* §462; and Hegel, *Introduction to the Lectures on the History of Philosophy,* trans. T. M. Knox and A. V. Miller (New York: Oxford University Press, 1987), 79.

113. Dewey, "Hegel's Philosophy of Spirit," 77-78.

114. Ibid., 80, 82.

115. Ibid., 102. Cf. Dewey's claim that, "God is no remote Being away from the world, that He is no Force which works in physical Nature alone, but . . . He is an ever present fact in life, in history, and in our social relations." Dewey, "The Value of Historical Christianity" (1889), LW 17: 531.

116. See Robert C. Solomon, *In the Spirit of Hegel: A Study of G. W. F. Hegel's* Phenomenology of Spirit (New York: Oxford University Press, 1983), 591-597.

117. Dewey, "Hegel's Philosophy of Spirit," 9, 7, 8. In this passage, Dewey was discussing Hegel's early theological writings, which, at that time, were published only in fragments in Rosenkranz's and Haym's biographies.

118. See Dewey's discussion of the term "God." Dewey, *A Common Faith* (1934), LW 9: 29ff.

119. Dewey, "The Value of Historical Christianity" (1889), LW 17: 531.

120. Dewey, "Hegel's Philosophy of Spirit," 32. Denton Snider, *The St. Louis Movement in Philosophy, Literature, Education, Psychology, with Chapters of Autobiography* (St. Louis: Sigma, 1920), 344, 13. Cf. Snider, *A Writer of Books in His Genesis; Written for and Dedicated to His Pupil-friends Reaching Back in a Line of Fifty Years* (St. Louis: Sigma, 1910), 391.

121. Hegel, *The Philosophy of Right,* §§11, 15, 23. Dewey's commitment to positive freedom is a constant in his political thought. Dewey, *Outlines of a Critical Theory of Ethics* (1891), EW 3: 343-345; Dewey, *Ethics* (1908), MW 5: 393; Dewey, *Human Nature and Conduct* (1922), MW 14: 115; Dewey, *The Public and Its Problems* (1927), LW 2: 340; and Dewey, *Ethics,* rev. ed. (1932), LW 7: 306. The best source on Dewey's and Hegel's theories of freedom is Joseph Charles Flay, "Hegel and Dewey and the Problem of Freedom" (Ph.D. diss., University of Southern California, 1965). See also Maxine Green, *The Dialectic of Freedom* (New York: Teachers College Press, 1988), 39-44.

122. Dewey, "Hegel's Philosophy of Spirit," 33-34.

123. Ibid., 84, 94, 98. This indicates that if Dewey studied Haym's biography of Hegel, *Hegel und siene Zeit,* he rejected its primary thesis that Hegel was an apologist for the conservative Prussian state. Either Dewey had not read Haym's book, or he was more influenced by Rosenkranz's biography, *Georg Wilhelm Friedrich Hegel's Leben.*

124. See for example, H. Tristram Engelhardt, Jr., "*Sittlichkeit* and Postmodernity: An Hegelian Reconsideration of the State," in Engelhardt and Terry Pinkard, eds., *Hegel Reconsidered: Beyond Metaphysics and the Authoritarian State* (Boston: Kluwer, 1994), 217-222.

125. Jane Dewey, "Biography of John Dewey," 18. I take Dewey's assertion that he became skeptical about the dialectic to be comparable to his claim in "From Absolutism to Experimentalism" that "The form, the schematism, of [Hegel's] system now seems to me artificial to the last degree." Dewey, "From Absolutism to Experimentalism" (1930), LW 5: 154. As I have argued in this and the previous two chapters, I believe Dewey rejected Hegel's formal system building, but the substance of Hegel's dialectical method is a significant element of the permanent deposit in his thought.

126. Jane Dewey, "Biography of John Dewey," 18.

127. On Dewey's logic as a theory of learning see Hickman, *John Dewey's Pragmatic Technology,* esp. ch. 2; and Tom Burke, *Dewey's New Logic: A Reply to Russell* (Chicago: University of Chicago Press, 1994), 3ff, 136-156. With regard to these early essays, this characterization of Dewey's logic is reinforced by Shook, *Dewey's Empirical Theory of Knowledge and Reality,* 184ff. The essays under consideration are Dewey, "Some Stages of Logical Thought" (1900); his four chapters in the *Studies in Logical Theory.* Cf. Dewey, "Lectures in the Theory of Logic, 1899-1900," which can be accessed in Steven Alan Nofsinger, ed., "John Dewey's 'Lectures in the Theory of Logic' delivered at the University of Chicago, fall and winter quarters (1899-1900)" (Ph.D. diss., Michigan State University, 1989).

128. Dewey to James, 27 March 1903. Dewey acknowledged his indebtedness to Peirce's *Monist* articles in a letter to Peirce. Dewey to C. S. Peirce, 23 December 1903.

129. I suspect this is one of the ways in which Dewey began to think Hegel's dialectic was artificial, and he was not alone in that opinion. On this point, some have suggested Hegel might have followed his own advice a little better: "Of course, the triadic form must not be regarded as scientific when it is reduced to a lifeless schema, a mere shadow, and when scientific organization is degraded into a table of terms." Hegel, *Phenomenology of Spirit,* §50. In that passage Hegel criticized Kant's formalism, which indicates that to be true to his own position, he could not consistently be dogmatic about the triadic form of his own logic if it proved to be an empty formalism. The substance behind the form of Hegel's logic was that any and every belief we hold will be challenged, negated, at some point, requiring us to modify it in the light of its negation or succumb to stagnation. For a recent discussion of problems of execution in Hegel's logic see Thomas J. Bole III, "The Cogency of the *Logic*'s Argumentation: Securing the Dialectic's Claim to Justify Categories," in *Hegel Reconsidered,* 79-102.

130. Dewey, "Some Stages in Logical Thought" (1900), MW 1: 165-166. Cf. Hegel's claim that "The same evolution of thought which is exhibited in the history of philosophy is presented in the System of Philosophy itself." Hegel, *The Logic of Hegel,* §14. Dewey discussed the stages of the process of inquiry much more clearly and precisely in *How We Think* (1910), MW 6: 179-356. Consistent with the view that Dewey's logic was a theory of learning rather than proving, *How We Think* was a book on the philosophy of education.

131. Dewey, "Some Stages in Logical Thought" (1900), MW 1: 151.

132. Ibid., 154.

133. Ibid., 156. Dewey quoted this passage from Hegel's "Lesser Logic." It is probably his translation from the German. In Wallace's translation we find: "Thought, as *Understanding,* sticks to fixity of characters and their distinctness from one another: every such limited abstract it treats as having a subsistence and being of its own." Later in the same section, we read: "It must be added, however, that the merit and rights of the mere Understanding should unhesitatingly be admitted. And that merit lies in the fact that apart from Understanding there is no fixity or accuracy in the region of theory or of practice." Hegel, *The Logic of Hegel,* §80.

134. Hegel, *Science of Logic,* 787, 788

135. Dewey, "Some Stages in Logical Thought" (1900), MW 1: 158.

136. Ibid., 160; and Dewey, "Hegel's Philosophy of Spirit," 16.

137. Dewey, "Some Stages in Logical Thought" (1900), MW 1: 163.

138. Ibid., 153-154, 157-158, 168.

139. Dewey to William James, 3 June 1891; and Dewey, "Some Stages in Logical Thought" (1900), MW 1: 167.

140. Dewey, "Some Stages in Logical Thought" (1900), MW 1: 169.

141. Ibid., 171.

142. Ibid., 174.

143. Dewey, et al., *Studies in Logical Theory* (1903), MW 2: 296-297.

144. Rudolf Hermann Lotze, *Logic,* trans. B. Bosanquet (Oxford: Clarendon Press, 1884).

145. Henry Jones, *A Critical Account of the Philosophy of Lotze: The Doctrine of Thought* (Glasgow: J. Maclehose and Sons, 1895).

146. Ferdinand C. S. Schiller, "In Defense of Humanism," *Mind* n.s. 13 (1904): 100.

147. Dewey, *Studies in Logical Theory,* MW 2: 296.

148. Ibid., 302.

149. Ibid., 313-314.

150. Ibid., 305, 315, 313, 306.

151. Ibid., 298.
152. Hegel, *Phenomenology of Spirit,* §26.
153. Dewey, *Studies in Logical Theory,* MW 2: 299, 306 (emphasis in the original).
154. Ibid., 299-300.
155. Ibid., 305-307.
156. Ibid., 311-312.
157. Rene Descartes, *Discourse on Method and Meditations,* trans. Laurence J. Lafleur (New York: Macmillan, 1960), 5, 9.
158. Dewey, *Studies in Logical Theory,* MW 2: 303-304.
159. Hegel, *The Philosophy of Right,* 21; and Dewey, *Studies in Logical Theory,* MW 2: 314.
160. Dewey, *Studies in Logical Theory,* MW 2: 309, 310, 312.
161. Dewey, "From Absolutism to Experimentalism" (1930), LW 5: 157.
162. Hegel, *Phenomenology of Spirit,* §§77-78.
163. Dewey, *Studies in Logical Theory,* MW 2: 317-18.
164. Ibid., 318.
165. Ibid., 321.
166. Ibid., 323.
167. Ibid., 326.
168. Ibid., 328, 330.
169. Henry Jones, *A Critical Account of the Philosophy of Lotze*.
170. Dewey, *Studies in Logical Theory,* MW 2: 333.
171. Ibid., 334.
172. Ibid., 336.
173. Dewey to James, March 1903. Dewey to James, 19 December 1903. Quoted by permission of the Houghton Library, Harvard University, call number bMS Am 1092.9 (128)-(144). James to Dewey, 23 March 1903. Quoted by permission of the Houghton Library, Harvard University, call number bMS Am 1092.9 (887). Cf. James to Schiller, 8 April 1903, in Perry, ed., *Thought and Character of William James* (Boston: Little, Brown: 1935), 2: 374, 521. James also contributed a positive review of the *Studies* to *The Psychological Bulletin* 1 (1904), titled "The Chicago School."
174. Charles S. Peirce, "John Dewey, *Studies in Logical Theory*" in *Collected Papers of Charles S. Peirce,* ed. Charles Hartshorne, Paul Weiss, and A.W. Burks (Cambridge, MA: Harvard University Press, 1958), 8: 189. According to Shook, Peirce claimed that Dewey did not clearly distinguish his logic from idealism in this book, but Peirce actually claimed that Dewey did not clearly distinguish his logic from "the German school of logicians, meaning such writers as Christoph Sigwart, Wundt, Schuppe, Benno Erdmann, Julius Bergmann, Glogau, Husserl, etc." Peirce, *Collected Papers,* 189-190. Cf. Shook, *Dewey's Empirical Theory of Knowledge and Reality,* 189.
175. Charles S. Peirce, "To John Dewey, on the Nature of Logic" in *Collected Papers,* 8: 180-184. I imagine Peirce understood quite well that Dewey was working within the German post-Kantian tradition, according to which logic was a descriptive science. Hegel's logic, which I characterized as descriptive in chapter one, followed Fichte's lead. As Daniel Breazeale explains, "Fichte insists that philosophers are mere historians of the mind and not its legislators, who would attempt to dictate, on the basis of pure thinking, how the mind 'ought' to act." Breazeale, "Fichte's Conception of Philosophy as a 'Pragmatic History of the Mind' and the Contributions of Kant, Platner, and Maimon," *Journal of the History of Ideas* 62, no. 4 (October 2001): 701.
176. Peirce, "To John Dewey, on the Nature of Logic."

Chapter Six

From Actualism to Brutalism, 1904–1916

Up to this point, I have argued that Dewey's Hegelianism should be understood in the context of a neglected American Hegelian tradition that tended toward center Hegelianism and viewed Hegel as a practical and politically liberal philosopher. I have also argued that from 1883 to 1891 Dewey can properly be called a neo-Hegelian philosopher because of his acceptance of a transcendent absolute. By 1891, however, Dewey rejected all transcendent realities as he moved away from organized religion and sought to articulate a philosophy of social involvement by firmly situating mind in the world rather than a separate metaphysical realm. Although other scholars have concluded that this rejection of the transcendent entailed the beginning of Dewey's rejection of Hegel, if not the decisive point of rejection, I have shown that it was a rejection of British neo-Hegelianism and an embrace of the sort of humanistic/historicist reading of Hegel that I outlined in chapter one. Through juxtaposition of Dewey's post-1891 interpretation of Hegel to recent readings of Hegel, I have shown that he anticipated a reading that is widely accepted in current Hegel scholarship. Finally, I have shown that, according to the humanistic/historicist reading of Hegel, his absolute, his theory of truth, the dialectic, his theory of learning, his philosophy of religion, and his ethics and political thought are far more similar to Dewey's instrumentalism than has been previously imagined.

Hegel's absolute standpoint is analogous to Dewey's psychological standpoint in that both are implicit in the natural, ordinary viewpoint and both reject metaphysical assumptions, particularly Cartesian dualism. Both philosophers engaged in phenomenological analysis of experience, and rejected talk of realities that exist beyond experience. They embraced functionalism and social psychology because they rejected the reification of the mind's functions as separate compartments within an inner reality. They also embraced the romantic depiction of human experience as far more than cognitive and analytical. Both philosophers espoused a theory of truth that included the logical coherence of our beliefs and an existential requirement: truth provides resolution of practical problems and hence a certain sense of satisfaction, unification, or comfort in the world. Dewey believed that his theory of inquiry, in which ideas function as means to action and are always subject to revision as they are tested in practice, was a restatement of Hegel's dialectic in more current terminology. Dewey was particularly impressed with Hegel's dialectic because it entailed that unity requires diversity. This aspect of Hegel's dialectic provided Dewey with a way to address the enduring metaphysical problem of the one and the many by ascribing both unity and diversity to reality, and it also provided a fruitful way to think about American society during a flood of immigration. Both philosophers supported a humanistic religion that would promote community and moral responsibility in this world by emphasizing moral behavior rather than doctrine. And although Dewey's political thought was more egalitarian than Hegel's, both viewed learning and growth as means to the human good, which they defined as growth through self-development and self-expression. Self-expression for both philosophers meant the continual enrichment of experience, but it also included the realization of positive freedom through commitment to our social responsibilities, and recognition from our peers.

In the light of the evidence I have assembled for Dewey's continuing Hegelianism, I find it particularly odd that scholars claim Dewey publicly broke from "absolute idealism" in the *Studies in Logical Theory* (1903), when in fact he never used that term in his contributions to that volume, nor did he mention Hegel. As John Shook has noted, Dewey's criticisms of Lotze are not properly viewed as criticisms of Hegel, and I would add that those criticisms are certainly not applicable to the historicist Hegel. In this chapter I point out that Dewey's last affirmation of Hegelian influence (until 1930) came in his 1905 American Philosophical Association address and that he first publicly criticized Hegel in his 1915 *German Philosophy and Politics,* thirty-three years after his initial conversion to Hegelian thought at Johns Hopkins in 1882. Though Dewey slowly lost interest in Hegel during the fifteen years after graduate school, the period during which he said he "drifted away" from Hegel, I argue that 1905 to 1915 is more accurately characterized as the drifting period.

I also analyze the way that Dewey criticized Hegel during World War I and consider reasons why his attitude toward Hegel may have changed at this time. To be specific, in 1915 Dewey implied that Hegel's philosophy assumed history was moving toward a predetermined end and doing so through necessary stages of development. The most obvious explanation for this transition, I believe, is that Dewey was reacting to hyperbole he encountered in the pro-German writings of German-American intellectuals like Hugo Münsterberg, a psychology professor at Harvard, and German intellectuals. These misgivings coincided with a series of tragedies in Dewey's life that seem to have made him suspicious of philosophies that posited a necessary historical teleology. Finally, I believe the three-way debate between pragmatists, realists, and idealists in which Dewey was engaged before World War I pressured him to become entrenched in the pragmatist camp and to participate in polemical caricaturing of idealism. Whereas in 1901, Dewey attributed "dialectical fireworks" to Hegel's followers, he began to speak as though Hegel committed those excesses himself.[1]

Personal Struggles

World War I impacted Dewey at a particularly difficult time in his life. During the twenty-five years leading up to the war, the Dewey family was battered by a series of emotional traumas that led him to reflect on the contingency of human existence and may well have made him more suspicious of any philosophy, like Hegel's, that might give the appearance of positing a necessary historical teleology, whether it really did or not.[2]

Shortly after the publication of *Studies in Logical Theory,* Dewey's already strained relationship with William Rainey Harper, president of the University of Chicago, collapsed. In 1902 the university acquired the Chicago Institute, run by Colonel Parker. Like the Dewey school, the Parker school included an elementary school and, quite naturally, many administrators at the university believed the two elementary schools should be merged to minimize duplication of effort. After a year of wrangling over the merger, in which Dewey sought to insure that he would continue to have control over the elementary school, the two finally merged in the fall of 1903 with Alice Dewey as principal of the resultant elementary school. Many of the faculty of the Parker school did not trust Alice Dewey, who had been openly critical of the school, and threatened to resign. Harper managed to quell their fears by ensuring that faculty of the Parker school without tenure could not be dismissed for at least three years and that Alice Dewey's appointment would be for only one year. But Harper failed to clearly communicate to John and Alice Dewey that her appointment was temporary, and when he informed them in the spring of 1904 that Alice's appointment would end prior to the fall 1905 semester, both were infuriated and immediately resigned from their positions at the university.[3] Alice Dewey, a talented and ambitious woman, seems to have taken this blow to her career very hard.[4]

Even before his resignation had been tendered to the trustees of the University of Chicago, Dewey contacted his old friend W. T. Harris, by then United States Commissioner of Education, and James McKeen Cattell, a friend from graduate school and professor of psychology at Columbia, for advice about future employment.[5] Cattell seized the opportunity and promptly contacted Nicholas Murray Butler, president of Columbia, who engineered an offer acceptable to Dewey without delay. The Deweys decided to take the family on a vacation to Europe during the summer and fall of 1904; hence Dewey stipulated that he would not begin teaching at Columbia until February 1905. While on vacation, their eight-year-old son Gordon died of typhoid fever, under circumstances similar to those surrounding the death of their son Morris, who died in 1894 of diphtheria in Milan during a family vacation. A child-centered family, the Deweys were shocked by the death of Morris, and the trauma was dramatically deepened by the death of Gordon, especially because he died suddenly after seeming to rally from the depths of the disease. Though shortly after Gordon's death the Deweys adopted an Italian boy, Sabino, their daughter Jane wrote that Alice "never fully recovered her former energy," and it seems their marriage suffered as well. The loss of her career and the death of two sons made Alice increasingly bitter, and according to Max Eastman, by the time of her death in 1927 she had become "impossible except for saints to live with."[6] Though his critics have accused Dewey of being naïve about historical progress, there is evidence in his poetry that this series of existential crises led him to reflect on the contingencies of human existence.[7]

Dewey also worked in a different professional environment after he left Chicago. Most notably, the Columbia philosophy department was not of his design and did not represent a particular school of thought. Dewey's new colleagues, including Felix Adler, co-founder of the Ethical Culture Society, Wendell Bush, William P. Montague, and F. J. E. Woodbridge, espoused a variety of philosophical viewpoints, and Dewey benefited from their affable criticisms of his thought. Of these colleagues, Woodbridge was undoubtedly the most influential on Dewey. Much like Morris, Woodbridge studied at Union Theological Seminary with an eye toward a ministerial career, but during a period of graduate study in Germany, decided to switch to philosophy. Deeply influenced by Aristotle, Woodbridge was also an empirical naturalist, and he seems to have convinced Dewey that a naturalistic metaphysics was possible and could ground his instrumentalism.[8] In time, Dewey's and Woodbridge's naturalistic philosophy became characteristic of the department, as can be seen by the graduate students it produced, many of whom went on to become prominent naturalistic philosophers—Irwin Edman, Horace L. Freiss, Sydney Hook, Ernest Nagel, John Herman Randall, Jr., and Herbert W. Schneider.[9]

Robert Westbrook correctly notes, "on the face of it, the years between Dewey's move to Columbia and American entry into World War I in 1917 were among the most professional of his career." The American Philosophical Association had been founded in 1901 and Dewey served as its president in 1905. It was in the context of the continuing professionalization of philosophy that Dewey focused his energy on the debate among pragmatists, realists, and idealists, a debate internal to the academic discipline of American philosophy. But as Westbrook also notes, "the impression . . . that Dewey retreated into an ivory tower in these years is misleading."[10] Dewey's rejection of the fact/value distinction, which was crucial to his theory of inquiry, undermined any philosophical founding of a professional devotion to truth without regard for moral and social issues. After World War I, Dewey published many works in which he advocated a fusion of technical philosophy and politics, and in an oft-quoted passage he summarized this view by writing that "Philosophy recovers itself when it ceases to be a device for dealing with the problems of philosophers and becomes a method, cultivated by philosophers, for dealing with the problems of men."[11]

Westbrook's characterization of these years is supported by Dewey's activities and social life beyond the Columbia philosophy department. Not only did he befriend Columbia historian Charles Beard, Dewey enjoyed meeting radical intellectuals in Greenwich Village, such as Bourne, Max Eastman, Charlotte Perkins Gilman, and Emma Goldman. In 1906 he defended Maxim Gorky's freedom to travel with a female companion to whom he was not married by inviting the couple to stay at the Dewey home. And in the space of just a few years prior to World War I, Dewey took part in the founding of the Teachers' League of New York (soon to become the New York Teachers' Union), the American Association of University Professors, and the National Association for the Advancement of Colored People.[12] In 1914 Dewey found a national platform for his social and political thought with the establishment of the *New Republic,* the principal medium for his political views for the next two decades. Dewey was also named as an editor of the *Dial* in 1918. Both magazines were established to give voice to liberal democrats.[13]

Despite Dewey's activities beyond the sphere of professional philosophy and his criticisms of its over-professionalization, he had to address the excesses of his discipline in terms that its practitioners would respect. Talk of an absolute mind, or a necessary historical teleology, would only discredit his efforts to reconstruct philosophy by associating him with theology or amateur philosophy. Heated polemics amongst pragmatists, realists, and idealists made it almost customary to exaggerate the views of ones' opponents. And because one might justifiably conclude that idealists ultimately lost the debate, as their philosophy went into decline until after World War II, it is no surprise that Dewey would prefer to distance himself from that camp.

That Dewey needed to distance himself from the idealist camp is seen in numerous articles, such as one published in 1906 by Warner Fite, professor of philosophy at the University of Texas. In that article, entitled "The Experience Philosophy," Fite equated pragmatism and idealism on the grounds that both were variants of subjective idealism. According to Fite, subjective idealism, pragmatism, personal idealism, and the radical empiricism of James all "deny that there is a world beyond experience; all, in substance, hold with Berkeley and Schopenhauer, that 'the world is my idea.'"[14] Dewey seems to have accepted this and other exaggerations that realists made about idealism in his efforts to join and unify the pragmatist ranks. He made no effort to articulate his realist reading of Hegel in opposition to these exaggerations, though he strenuously objected to the claim that pragmatism was a form of subjective idealism. Dewey did so by appealing to his version of Hegel's notion of alienation and return. In "The Realism of Pragmatism," Dewey argued that "States of consciousness, sensations and ideas as cognitive, exist as tools, bridges, cues, functions—whatever one pleases—to affect a realistic presentation of things, in which there are no intervening states of consciousness as veils, or representatives."[15] The problematic alienates us from the world in a veil of consciousness; completed inquiry, in which we come to integrate the problematic into the whole, allows us to return to ourselves, to our ordinary "naïve realism."[16] Incidentally, "The Realism of Pragmatism," published in 1905, was the first time Dewey used the term "pragmatism" in print, thus publicly associating himself with the new philosophical movement.

Hegel as Brutalist

Although in his 1897 lecture, Dewey portrayed Hegel as "the great actualist," in 1915 he substituted a new term, describing Hegel instead as a "brutalist." This new description of Hegel manifested itself rather abruptly because, as late as his 1905 presidential address to the American Philosophical Association, Dewey continued to acknowledge his indebtedness to Hegel on an issue central to his philosophical development. In that address, Dewey criticized philosophers for reducing experience to a dispassionate search for knowledge.

> Sensationalist and idealist, positivist and transcendentalist, materialist and spiritualist, defining this object [the object of knowledge] in as many differing ways as they have different conceptions of the ideal and method of knowledge, are at one in their devotion to an identification of Reality with something that connects monopolistically with passionless knowledge, belief purged of all personal reference, origin, and outlook.[17]

Dewey's presidential address was part of an ongoing debate in which he, as a self-described pragmatist, continued to defend his thought from realist and idealist factions within American academic philosophy. But it can be readily seen that this passage goes beyond that debate to an assessment of philosophy itself. It is apparent that Dewey believed realists, and some idealists, were guilty of equating experience with knowing experience, and we have already seen that as early as the "The Reflex Arc" article Dewey's thinking about the psychological standpoint had developed into an opposition to philosophers' proclivity to reduce experience to knowing experiences. This theme persisted throughout Dewey's mature works, in which he continued to argue that in order to fully understand human experience, philosophers must learn to appreciate its entire range, emotional as well as cognitive. Emotional experiences are not less real, or less important, than knowing experiences. Noting this development of the psychological standpoint in "The Reflex Arc," Westbrook claims that Dewey's opposition to the knowledge/experience equation was also a break from idealism.

Attached to the sentence quoted above, however, is a footnote that scholars, including Westbrook, seem to have overlooked. But for our purposes that footnote is vastly important:

> Hegel may be excepted from this statement. The habit of interpreting Hegel as a Neo-Kantian, a Kantian enlarged and purified, is a purely Anglo-American habit. This is no place to enter into the intricacies of Hegelian exegesis, but the subordination of both logical meaning and of mechanical existence to *Geist,* to life in its own developing movement, would seem to stand out in any unbiased view of Hegel. At all events, I wish to recognize my own personal debt to Hegel for the view set forth in this paper, without, of course, implying that it represents Hegel's own intention.[18]

Dewey's conviction that experience includes more than knowledge may well have been at odds with British neo-Hegelianism, or even post-1900 American idealism, but it was not a break from Hegel. Hegel, Dewey implied, held the same expansive meaning of experience as he did.

This footnote also demonstrates that Dewey continued to distinguish Hegel from neo-Kantians and continued to see Hegel as subordinating logical and "mechanical existence" to "life in its developing movement." Hegel's logic, for Dewey, was a logic of life. Furthermore, although Dewey continued to acknowledge his debt to Hegel at this late date, he was unconcerned about allegiance to Hegel's intention. Dewey was no disciple of Hegel, even though he believed crucial elements of his presidential address were based on insights gleaned from his study of Hegel's writings. Finally, in addition to being a component of his debates with realists and idealists, Dewey's presidential address is part of a sustained attack on the "epistemological industry," an attack worth considering in some detail.[19]

Dewey's primary complaint about epistemology-centered philosophy was that it was based on too narrow an understanding of the task of philosophy, and in his presidential address, he argued that this conception of philosophy was reinforced by the professionalizing currents of the day. Unlike "the common man," Dewey explained, "the professional man, the philosopher" is engaged in a search for truth through "passionless imperturbability" and "absolute detachment." Epistemologists attempted to study beliefs in a laboratory setting, as it were, removed from the context in which they function. In that setting, beliefs seem neat and tidy, hence the philosopher/epistemologist searches for a "ready-made and finished reality" that corresponds to neat and tidy beliefs. But Dewey wrote that "beliefs are personal affairs, and personal affairs are adventures, and adventures are, if you please, shady." The common man lives in a world "of affection," with "the gallantry of adventure, the genuineness of the incomplete, the tentative." There is no finished reality to discover, because "the world has meaning as somebody's, somebody's at a juncture."[20] Dewey acknowledged his debt to Hegel in this article because Hegel taught him not to equate philosophy with epistemology and not to subordinate life to logic. This reveals an element of the Hegelian deposit in Dewey's thought that has been completely ignored. Hegel provided him with a conception of philosophy that Dewey believed was at odds with professional American philosophy. Like the St. Louis Hegelians, Dewey found in Hegel a philosophy of lived experience.

Dewey published two essays in 1906 that shed further light on this point. In "The Experimental Theory of Knowledge," Dewey wrote that

> experiences of failure, disappointment, non-fulfilment of the function of meaning and contention may lead the individual to the path of science—to more careful and extensive investigation of the things themselves, with a view to detecting specific sources of error, and guarding against them, and regulating, so far as possible, the conditions under which objects are bearers of meanings beyond themselves. But impatient of such slow and tentative methods (which insure not infallibility but increased probability of valid conclusions), by reason of disappointment a person may turn epistemologist.[21]

The scientific method, as Dewey understood it, is much more than a matter of following certain procedures in a certain order; it is an attitude of "careful investigation of the things themselves." Like the supernaturalist, the epistemologist shies away from things that cause discomfort and postulates entities, be they God or an inaccessible thing-in-itself, that he hopes will bring certainty and assurance. For Dewey, the scientist unflinchingly examines the source of the discomfort until the problem is solved. The advance of modern science is a psychological advance, a sign of maturity, an overcoming of psychological weakness. This brings to mind Dewey's conviction that Kant's postulation of an inaccessible thing-in-itself "does violence to science" and Hegel's elimination of the thing-in-itself makes him "the quintessence of the scientific spirit."[22] Kant's thing-in-itself is unscientific for Dewey, because it blocks the road to further inquiry. The historicist Hegel, on the other hand, rejects transcendent realities, leveling reality to the sphere in which we actually live and directly access "things themselves."

The second 1906 essay is "Experience and Objective Idealism," published in *The Philosophical Review.* In this essay, as in others, Dewey was frustratingly vague about what he meant by idealism and who he intended to criticize. Consequently, many scholars have construed the essay as an attack on absolute idealism.[23] In the first paragraph Dewey distinguished idealism "in its subjective form, or sensationalism," apparently meaning Berkeley, from idealism "in its objective or rational form." According to Dewey, the latter form of idealism claims to correct the former by arguing that "thought . . . supplies the factors of objectivity and universality lacking in sensationalism." In other words, according to objective idealism, thought supplies logical categories that are not found in sensations. Claiming that objective idealism is "half opposed to empiricism and half committed to it," Dewey began to refer to it as "Neo-Kantianism," finally providing an important clue to what he meant by "objective idealism" in the essay.[24] We know that in his presidential address, Dewey continued to exclude Hegel from the class of neo-Kantian philosophers, and that during the 1890s he labeled certain British neo-Hegelians, particularly T. H. Green and F. H. Bradley, neo-Kantians because they postulated a transcendent absolute that went beyond possible experience. According to Dewey, philosophers such as Kant, Green, Bradley—"epistemologists" broadly speaking—err when they attempt to explain experience by appealing to something that goes beyond possible experience; they violate the psychological standpoint or, as he began to call it in 1905, "the postulate of immediate empiricism."[25]

There is also evidence that philosophers who were engaged in these debates with Dewey understood him to mean Kantianism by "objective idealism." In a critique of "Experience and Objective Idealism," published in the same journal six months after Dewey's article, John E. Russell concluded that Dewey's term "objective idealism" meant Kantian transcendentalism. And four years later, as this debate continued in the pages of *The Philosophical Review,* R. H. Bode published an article in which he attempted to clarify the terms of the debate. Bode concluded that "objective idealism," as it was being used in this extended debate, meant Kantian transcendentalism.[26]

Dewey's attitude toward Hegel changed, however, in his most notorious book, *German Philosophy and Politics,* published in 1915. Although warmly received at the time, many Dewey scholars are now embarrassed by the book because it seems to fit neatly into the genre of ill-conceived works published by Anglo-American authors who attempted to demonstrate a substantial connection between German militarism and German philosophy.[27] Sydney Hook, for one, found the book doubly embarrassing because Dewey insisted on republishing it in 1942 with a new introduction that alleged to connect Nazism with previous German militarism.[28] Because of the book's pariah status within the Deweyan corpus, it has been studied little and is little understood.

And *German Philosophy and Politics* is indeed an odd book. Rather than point to the usual suspects in German philosophy (e.g., Hegel, Schopenhauer or Nietzsche) Dewey laid the primary blame for German militarism at the feet of Kantian dualism.[29] To Dewey's credit, he acknowledged the precariousness of "singl[ing] out some one thing in German philosophy as of typical importance in understanding German national life." Yet Dewey asserted that he was committed to just that project and explained that Kant's doctrine of "the two realms, one outer, physical and necessary, the other inner, ideal and free" is the element of German philosophy that has defined German national character. This dualism facilitated a "combination of self-conscious idealism with unsurpassed technical efficiency and organization in the varied fields of action."[30] More explicitly, Dewey claimed that Kantian philosophy allowed an absolute devotion to transcendent ends, ends that could not be checked by practical and humane considerations, and an overdeveloped technical efficiency in the achievement of those ends. For Dewey, the German people were militaristic because, in the phenomenal realm at least, they were devoted to what the Frankfurt School later called instrumental reason, reason that could efficiently solve technical problems but could not critique ends.[31] The German people were not, Dewey added, consciously devoted to Kantian philosophy; rather, "Kant detected and formulated the direction in which the German genius was moving, so that his philosophy is of immense prophetic significance."[32] In this regard, *German Philosophy and Politics* was Hegelian intellectual history. Dewey's claim was that Kant had understood, and been a vehicle for, the German *Volksgeist.*

Dewey's debt to Hegel is also evident in the substantive criticism he directed against Kantian dualism. As I explained in chapter one, Hegel was most concerned with countering Kantian philosophy because he believed Kant's moral formalism, according to which we have absolute rights and duties regardless of our social context, was typical of the thinking that led to the French Reign of Terror. As Dewey wrote in *German Philosophy and Politics,* "Empirically grounded truths . . . do not inspire such violent loyalty to themselves as ideas supposed to proceed directly from reason itself." Empirical truths are open to question and debate, "while truths of pure reason have a paradoxical way . . . of escaping from the arbitrament of reason." Rather than a "logic of experience," rational truths provide the foundation for a "logic of fanaticism."[33]

Yet Hegel does not emerge from the book unscathed. Dewey also repeated the principal claim of his 1897 lecture on Hegel's philosophy of spirit, but with a significant new twist. Dewey explained that one of the most important elements Hegel contributed to the development of German idealism was "his bottomless scorn for an Idea, an Absolute, which merely ought to be and which is only going to be realized after a period of time. 'The Actual is the Rational and the Rational is the Actual'—and the actual means the actuating force and movement of things." Dewey also noted that, although "It is customary to call [Hegel] an Idealist. . . . In one sense of much abused terms, he is the greatest realist known to philosophy. He might be called a Brutalist."[34] It is this last comment, Hegel as "Brutalist," that signals a decisive change in Dewey's attitude toward Hegel. He continued to cast doubt on the accuracy of characterizing Hegel as an idealist, but he proceeded to elaborate on what he meant by calling Hegel a Brutalist in a discussion of Hegel's theory of the state.

In the account that followed, Dewey associated Hegel with the "purely artificial cult of race" in Germany, which he described as a crucial component of Germany's geopolitical ambitions. Dewey also claimed Hegel had absorbed Fichte's ideas of the state and history.[35] In his discussion of Hegel's philosophy of the state, Dewey suddenly rejected, without explaining why, Rosenkranz's characterization of Hegel as a politically liberal philosopher in favor of Rudolf Haym's characterization of Hegel as an apologist for the conservative Prussian state, actually quoting Haym. Dewey also quoted, without citation, passages from §258 of Hegel's *Philosophy of Right* to support this reading of Hegel.[36] Hegel's brutalism, according to Dewey, arises from his identification of the actual with the rational coupled with his conviction that reason, which Dewey equated with both God and the state, drives history with no regard for the rights and interests of the individual. For Hegel, he implied, it is the duty of the individual to completely subordinate his interests to the state.[37] Comparison with S. W. Dyde's 1897 translation of *The Philosophy of Right,* the only one then available, indicates that Dewey used his own translation of passages from *The Philosophy of Right.* Readers may find H. B. Nisbet's 1991 translation less objectionable; in fact Dewey's is rather loose. Allen Wood, an expert on Hegel's moral and political thought who advocates a humanist/historicist reading, writes that it is "a gross distortion to associate Hegel's view with the image of individuals having to sacrifice themselves to the ends of the state. Such sacrifices may be required in some circumstances, but it is precisely the *abnormality* of such circumstances which makes the state an end in itself."[38] Regardless of which commentator is right about Hegel's conception of the individual's relation to the state, it is clear that Dewey's reading of Hegel's political thought is not consistent with the reading that gained ascendancy during the post-World War II renaissance in Hegel studies; and more important for our purposes, it is not consistent with the reading he himself had espoused in his 1897 lecture.

An important element of this shift in Dewey's characterization of Hegel is revealed in his discussion of Hegel's philosophy of history. Despite what Dewey said about Hegel ten short years before in his presidential address, he now implied that Hegel subordinated life to logic by postulating a necessary historical teleology. Whereas the common man, he explained in 1905, lives in an incomplete and tentative world, Hegel envisioned a completed world beyond ordinary existence. Dewey reiterated this reading of Hegel's philosophy of history in *Democracy and Education,* published in 1916.

> But since Hegel was haunted by the conception of an absolute goal, he was obliged to arrange institutions as they concretely exist, on a stepladder of ascending approximations. Each in its time and place is absolutely necessary, because a stage in the self-realizing process of the absolute mind. Taken as such a step or stage, its existence is proof of its complete rationality, for it is an integral element in the total, which is Reason.[39]

In this passage Dewey even suggested a theological reading of Hegel by implying that his absolute was a supernatural being. In *German Philosophy and Politics,* Dewey's notion of Hegel as brutalist is completed in his claim that Hegel's necessary teleology is fulfilled through war. Having construed his philosophy of history in nationalistic terms, Dewey contended it was inevitable that Hegel would articulate a "philosophical justification of war."[40] Hegel had become, for Dewey, the bellicose philosopher of Prussian conservatism.

In addition, in his 1942 introduction to the second edition of *German Philosophy and Politics,* Dewey distinguished Hegel's concepts of *Vernunft* (reason) and *Verstand* (understanding) in a way that would be difficult to defend with reference to Hegel's writings, and in fact he provided no defense of his reading. According to Dewey, *Vernunft* is the agent that moves creative history, and *Verstand* is "reflection, inquiry, observation and experiment to test ideas and theory."[41] Hegel scholars too numerous to list have viewed Hegel's notion of *Verstand* as a moment, or stage, of *Vernunft,* the stage of analysis that must be completed by synthesis.[42] This latter reading, I have already argued, is analogous to Dewey's requirement that inquiry move beyond the analysis of a problem into its components toward a vision of the whole in order to avoid the historical fallacy.

Dewey never acknowledged the weakness of the arguments he made in *German Philosophy and Politics.* As Hook notes, "The characteristics of the German mind as described by Dewey are, to be sure, logically compatible with Kantian dualism but they are just as compatible with Cartesian dualism."[43] Although Dewey found Cartesian dualism lurking behind virtually all Anglo-American philosophy, he never suggested that it explained British or American imperialism which, one might argue, was more aggressive than Germany's. One might also expect Dewey to shun the sort of intellectual history he employed in *German Philosophy and Politics* on philosophical grounds. By ignoring economic, political, diplomatic, and social pressures that pushed Germany into war, Dewey was, in essence, ignoring the environmental context of ideas, a mistake he had often pointed to in the philosophy of others.[44] Dewey did, however, express concern that Americans might succumb to the same sort of a priori absolutism that had swept Germany. In a reply to William Ernest Hocking in the *New Republic,* Dewey wrote that *German Philosophy and Politics* was "addressed to American, not German readers" because of his discomfort at Woodrow Wilson's and William Jennings Bryan's (Wilson's Secretary of State) rhetorical appeals to "immutable principles." Where Hocking argued that Americans had been too pragmatic in their dealings with Germany and should now invoke absolute moral truths, Dewey asserted that Americans, like Germans, needed to beware of politicians who practiced realpolitik under the guise of absolute moral principles.

The Germans did not support such a bloody war out of "practical expediency," Dewey proclaimed; they supported it because they had been misled by the idealistic rhetoric of politicians. For Dewey it was a fact that "men act pragmatically" and a mistake to allow the reality of those actions to be masked by high-sounding rhetoric. According to Dewey, the German people had fallen into a duplicity that tempts us all.

> What is at issue is the difference between an activity which is aware of its own character, which knows what it is about, which faces the consequences of its activities and accepts responsibility for them, and an activity which disguises its nature to the collective consciousness by appeal to eternal principles and the eulogistic predicates of pure idealism.[45]

Two years after the publication of *German Philosophy and Politics,* Randolph Bourne claimed Dewey's ultimate decision to support the American war effort demonstrated that his philosophy was committed to technological efficiency with no ability to critique ends.[46] In so doing, Bourne assumed the dualism between means and ends that Dewey had always opposed on Hegelian grounds. In Dewey's moral thought, means and ends were dialectically related within a larger whole, the act. Further, if Dewey was wrong to support Wilson's decision to enter the war, it was as difficult for Bourne to blame it on Dewey's philosophy as it was for Dewey to blame German militarism on Kantian dualism. Bourne seems to have misunderstood that, like Hegel, Dewey always warned that the separation of fact and value, means and ends, which followed from Kant's dualism, was inherently dangerous. Kantianism had led, argued Dewey, to a mentality that was committed to absolute ends that could not be subjected to empirical, or even rational, evaluation. Furthermore, claimed Dewey, Kantian dualism had encouraged a commitment to technological efficiency in the phenomenal realm.

Dewey's decision to republish *German Philosophy and Politics* in 1942 indicates that his remarks about Hegel in that book represent an enduring change in his thought. At the time of the original publication of the book, war had been raging in Europe for a year, and it is easy, perhaps too easy, to conclude that Dewey had been caught up in anti-German hysteria. Yet in 1915 widespread anti-German hysteria had not begun in the United States and, in fact, most Americans still favored President Wilson's policy of neutrality.[47] Moreover, it was *after* the publication of *German Philosophy and Politics* that Dewey engaged in heated polemics about American involvement in World War I. At this time he was only mildly involved in the "preparedness versus pacifism" debate, opposing universal military training for schoolboys.[48]

It is not difficult to understand why Dewey would reject a necessary historical teleology; it requires something that exists beyond history, an ahistorical, unchanging purpose to history. Yet we have no textual clues as to why Dewey came to believe that Hegel posited such a teleology. Undoubtedly, the most satisfying explanation of the change in Dewey's attitude toward German thought and culture is that the rhetoric he encountered from German and German-American intellectuals made him, like many other American intellectuals, reexamine his perception of Germany. Bruce Kuklick goes to the heart of this issue when he writes that

> From a later perspective, the ethical issues that separated the Allies from the Central Powers were unclear, it they existed at all. But in 1914 the British were astute and the Germans inept in their use of propaganda, and in the United States opinion leaders supported the Allies. The New England elite was outstanding in its unanimous hostility to Germany.[49]

A prime example of extravagant, and rather alarming, pro-German rhetoric can be found in the wartime writings of Hugo Münsterberg. Born in Germany, Münsterberg completed the Ph.D. in psychology at Leipzig in 1885 under the direction of Wilhelm Wundt. He then earned an M.D. at Heidelberg in 1887. William James brought Münsterberg to Harvard in 1892 to take over his psychological laboratory.

As early as 1913, in *American Patriotism and Other Social Studies,* Münsterberg articulated the sort of rhetoric about duty that seems to have animated Dewey in *German Philosophy and Politics.* According to Münsterberg, "systematic education" in Germany "with sharp training and hard discipline early inculcates into every mind a habit of hard work. This energy for doing one's duty in spite of all selfish temptations, moreover, is greatly strengthened by the years of military service, the great national high school of labor and disciplined effort."[50] Münsterberg quickly followed this book with *The War and America* in 1914. In this second book he admitted that the British had been more effective than the Germans in their propaganda, argued that Germany did not start the war but was forced into it by the actions of Russia and France, and depicted the war as unavoidable. Though the "war might have been delayed a month, perhaps a year," Münsterberg claimed, political tensions in Europe made it inevitable. War was brought on by the natural growth of European empires, including both the Central and the Allied Powers, thus "no one is to be blamed." Each nation entered the war convinced that it was "fighting for a just and solemn cause and that it was performing its national duty."[51] It was in his defense of war as a positive good that Münsterberg wrote a passage that may have been the most provocative to Dewey:

> It is as if at the eastern frontier at the town of Königsberg a little old-fashioned man had left the grave, Immanuel Kant, and whispered into the heart of everyone: "There is only one thing worth while in life, and that is the moral will." And all are ready to give their lives to protect those boundaries against the Russian onslaught. Never was the moral will of the nation more alive and more pure.[52]

Münsterberg continued this Kantian theme in a third volume, *The Peace and America*, but it is difficult to know whether Dewey had time to read *The Peace and America* before he published *German Philosophy and Politics.*[53]

Münsterberg's defense of Germany was only a small part of the flood of pro-German publications during the war, most of which emanated from Germany. In a letter "To the Civilized World" published in the *New York Times* in 1914, a galaxy of notable German scholars, including Rudolf Eucken, Ernst Haeckel, Karl Lamprecht, Max Planck, Wilhelm Windelband, and Wilhelm Wundt, protested the "lies and calumnies with which our enemies are endeavouring to stain the honour of Germany in her hard struggle for existence—a struggle which has been forced upon her." The letter went on to condemn those "who have allied themselves with Russians and Serbians" and incited "Mongolians and Negroes against the white race."[54] Two years after its publication, Dewey identified the moment as one of sudden and profound disillusionment with the German intellectual tradition that had figured so prominently in his own intellectual formation.

> But I doubt if a single outsider who had previously refrained from committing himself as to the justice of the cause did not conclude that if that was all that Germany had to say for herself, bad indeed must be her cause. . . . I doubt if anyone can reread, say, the Address to the Civilized World, without being again overcome by those old sensations of incredulity and amazement. Was it possible that men to whom we had been trained to look up could lend their names, even in a moment of patriotic fervor, to such a farrago?[55]

Dewey's heightened concern about the notion of inevitable historical progress was not unique among American intellectuals. As Franklin H. Giddings wrote in 1916, whereas "the nineteenth century had closed in a blaze of scientific glory" and hopes for the future, World War I raised disturbing doubts about the notion of progress.[56] Nicholas Murray Butler eloquently encapsulated the trauma many intellectuals felt:

> The peoples who are engaged in this titanic struggle are not untamed barbarians or wild Indians of the virgin forest. They are the best-trained and most highly educated peoples in the world. They have had every advantage that schools and universities can offer, and they have been associated for generations with literature and science and art and everything that is fine and splendid in what we call civilization.

For Butler, and others, civilization had proven to be a "thin veneer" over the "passions of jealousy, envy, hatred, and malice."[57]

Although Dewey publicly criticized Hegel during the war, I believe the Hegelian deposit I have identified can be found throughout his published writings after the war. Even in *Democracy and Education,* Dewey demonstrated a continuing commitment to *Bildung,* particularly in the fourth chapter of the book, "Education as Growth."[58] Moreover, scholars should be careful about assuming that his wartime writings demonstrate a reasoned rejection of Hegel. Westbrook has argued persuasively that during World War I, Dewey's "judgment faltered." Of course Westbrook meant primarily that Dewey's political judgment was at fault, but he also notes that during the war Dewey "proved susceptible to an idealization of the moral qualities of his country, the very sort of ideological blindness against which he had warned in the period of [American] neutrality."[59] To his credit, Dewey quickly abandoned his unrestrained Americanism as repression of dissent and free speech swept the nation, but he never defended his wartime characterization of Hegel with scholarly evidence.

Dewey's Continuing Commitment to *Bildung*

A full discussion of Hegelianism in Dewey's mature thought would require analysis of his most important later works, but such an analysis goes well beyond the scope of the current book. I would add, however, that I believe Dewey's clearest expression of Hegel's conception of philosophy as *Bildung,* and his abiding commitment to it, is in the last chapter of *Experience and Nature,* ostensibly a metaphysical treatise. Not only did Dewey explicitly describe philosophy as criticism in that chapter, but as the queen of all criticism: "philosophy is inherently criticism, having its distinctive position among various modes of criticism in its generality; a criticism of criticisms, as it were." Like Hegel, Dewey argued that philosophy is not the creator of value; philosophy's

> business is to accept and to utilize for a purpose the best available knowledge of its own time and place. And this purpose is criticism of beliefs, institutions, customs, policies with respect to their bearing upon good. This does not mean their bearing upon the good, as something itself attained and formulated in philosophy. For as philosophy has no private store of knowledge or of methods for attaining truth, so it has no private access to good. As it accepts knowledge of facts and principles from those competent in inquiry and discovery, so it accepts the goods that are diffused in human experience. It has no Mosaic nor Pauline authority of revelation entrusted to it. But it has the authority of intelligence, of criticism of these common and natural goods.[60]

Philosophy is immanent cultural criticism, the effort to promote the actualization of ideals latent within the culture.

Anticipating objections to this conception of philosophy, Dewey asserted that it does not denigrate that revered discipline in any way. Cultural criticism is not the private purview of "those who are insensitive to the positive achievements of culture and over-sensitive to its evils." As Dewey explained,

> "Social reform" is conceived in a Philistine spirit, if it is taken to mean anything less than precisely the liberation and expansion of the meanings of which experience is capable. No doubt many schemes of social reform are guilty of precisely this narrowing. But for that very reason they are futile; they do not succeed in even the special reforms at which they aim, except at the expense of intensifying other defects and creating new ones. Nothing but the best, the richest and fullest experience possible, is good enough for man. The attainment of such an experience is not to be conceived as the specific problem of "reformers" but as the common purpose of men. The contribution which philosophy can make to this common aim is criticism.[61]

Nevertheless, in a previous chapter of *Experience and Nature,* "Experience as Precarious and Stable," Dewey also mentioned what I suspect many will agree is an important difference between his mature philosophy and the philosophy of Hegel. Unlike Dewey, who had fully embraced the philosophical implications of Darwinian biology, Hegel, and other philosophers of change (e.g., Bergson and Heraclitus) could not conceive of sheer randomness. I disagree with Dewey that, for Hegel, change "is not, as it is in experience, a call to effort, a challenge to investigation." But even if Hegel rejected the notion of a glorious conclusion of history, as I maintain he did, Dewey is correct to state that he did not see change as "a potential doom of disaster and death."[62] Hegel never considered the possibility of the utter annihilation of the human race, a prospect that seemed possible after World War I, and even more possible by the time of Dewey's death in 1952.

In addition to statements of the *Bildung* conception of philosophy, Dewey demonstrated his commitment to it through acts of self-expression throughout his professional life. The Laboratory School in Chicago, his work with Jane Addams at Hull House, and his continuing efforts to advocate educational reform are all prime examples of Dewey acting as a philosopher of *Bildung*. Dewey worked tirelessly for social and political reform after he left Chicago, involved in various capacities in organizations such as the AAUP, the American Federation of Teachers, the American Civil Liberties Union, and the NAACP. He engaged in countless political debates as a public speaker and through the publication of numerous editorials, and lectured on philosophy and educational and social reforms in Japan, China, Turkey, and South Africa. Throughout all of these activities, the central thrust of Dewey's reform efforts was the expansion of meaningful human freedom and opportunities for human growth. Dewey lived the life of a philosopher of *Bildung,* in the study as well as out.

Like Hegel, Dewey always eschewed reductive and dualistic explanations in favor of a holistic approach in which the parts are seen as functions within a dynamic whole. He called for continual human growth through self-development, and employed a Hegelian method of immanent cultural criticism. Like Hegel, in his mature work Dewey continued to reject the Enlightenment tendency to reduce experience to cognition, and in fact he developed that theme most fully in *Experience and Nature* and *Art as Experience,* by arguing for the aesthetic nature of experience. He continued to examine experience in its organic wholeness, rather than as raw material in need of intellectual synthesis. Experience, for Dewey, does not need to be constructed out of a mass of disconnected sense data; rather, it needs to be analyzed, reconstructed, and thus directed, when possible, toward desirable ends. Again like Hegel, Dewey believed that when properly reconstructed, experience yields truth in the sense of coherent beliefs, but more importantly, in the sense of satisfaction or unification of the self in its never-ending efforts to cope with and, ideally, find harmony within, its social and natural environment. Dewey continued to understand logic as a theory of learning rather than proof, and thus as a critical tool of human growth or self-development. Self-development for both philosophers is a striving toward one's potential, but it also includes positive freedom, understood as liberation through commitment to one's social responsibilities, and recognition of our worth by our peers.

If I have succeeded, Hegel should no longer be viewed as an embarrassment to Dewey. I hope that by drawing upon recent Hegel scholarship to clarify Dewey's debt to Hegel, this study will promote a rapprochement of Dewey and Hegel scholarship and a historical and philosophical interest in the American *Bildung* tradition of philosophy.

Notes

1. Dewey, "The Present Position of Logical Theory" (1901), EW 3: 134.

2. For a recent discussion of Dewey's "crisis" during these years see Bruce Wilshire, *The Primal Roots of American Philosophy: Pragmatism, Phenomenology, and Native American Thought* (University Park: Pennsylvania University Press, 2000), 121ff. Jay Martin also provides insight into the tribulations Dewey and his family experienced during this time. Martin, *The Education of John Dewey: A Biography* (New York: Columbia University Press, 2002), 263-299.

3. There are ample records to indicate that Dewey's resignation from the University of Chicago was sparked by more than the loss of Alice's job. Evidence in Dewey's correspondence indicates that he and Harper had almost constant disagreements over the budget for the Dewey school for a number of years. See William Rainey Harper to Dewey, 9 February 1904, 10 February 1904, 29 February 1904; and Dewey to William Rainey Harper, 12 February 1904, 19 April 1904; and Dewey to James McKeen Cattell, 13-15 April 1904. See also Brian Hendley, *Dewey, Russell, Whitehead: Philosophers as Educators* (Carbondale: Southern Illinois University Press, 1986), 18-19.

4. Martin, *The Education of John Dewey,* 306-310.

5. Dewey to William Torrey Harris, 25 April 1904; and Dewey to James McKeen Cattell, 12 April 1904.

6. Jane Dewey, "Biography of John Dewey," in *The Philosophy of John Dewey,* ed. Paul Arthur Schilpp (Evanston, IL: Northwestern University Press, 1939), 35; George Dykhuizen, *The Life and Mind of John Dewey* (Carbondale: Southern Illinois University Press, 1973), 115. See Robert Westbrook's discussion of this issue, as well as the numerous sources he cites. Robert Westbrook, *John Dewey and American Democracy* (Ithaca: Cornell University Press, 1991), 151. Further evidence of family difficulties after Gordon's death can be found in Max Eastman, "John Dewey," *Atlantic* (December 1941): 680-681.

7. See Dewey's 1905 poem about the deaths of Gordon and Morris. John Dewey, *The Poems of John Dewey,* ed. Jo Ann Boydston (Carbondale: Southern Illinois University Press, 1977), xviii, 30. Philip W. Jackson's article on Dewey's poetry supports the claim that Dewey himself, and the family as a whole, was devastated by these events. Jackson, "John Dewey's Poetry," *American Journal of Education* 9 (1982): 65-78. During World War I, Dewey also published an eloquent critique of the "dream of automatic uninterrupted progress." Dewey, "Progress" (1916), MW 10: 234.

8. In 1957 John Herman Randall, Jr. wrote that Woodbridge "encouraged Dewey to cut loose from the remaining idealistic formulations in his philosophy of experience, to think and talk more naturalistically, and to develop an empirical metaphysics as the ontological implication of his conception of human life and culture." Like most scholars who talk about the Hegelianism in Dewey's mature thought, however, Randall was not specific about the "idealistic formulations" that disappeared from Dewey's writings. John Herman Randall, Jr., "The Department of Philosophy," in *A History of the Faculty of*

Philosophy of Columbia University, ed. Jacques Barzun (New York: Columbia University Press, 1957), 127-128. For others who agree that Woodbridge's influence was important see Westbrook, *John Dewey and American Democracy,* 119; Steven C. Rockefeller, *John Dewey: Religious Faith and Democratic Humanism* (New York: Columbia University Press, 1991), 362; and Alan Ryan, *John Dewey and the High Tide of American Liberalism* (New York: W. W. Norton, 1995), 164-166.

9. Randall, "The Department of Philosophy," 102-145.

10. Westbrook, *John Dewey and American Democracy,* 119-120. Recently, Louis Menand has reinforced this periodization of Dewey's thought and activities in *The Metaphysical Club* (New York: Farrar, Straus and Giroux, 2001), 360.

11. Dewey, "The Need for a Recovery of Philosophy" (1917), MW 10: 46.

12. The NAACP was founded in 1910, the Teachers' League of New York in 1913 and the AAUP in 1915.

13. Dykhuizen, *The Life and Mind of John Dewey,* 180.

14. Warner Fite, "The Experience Philosophy," *The Philosophical Review* 15, no. 1 (January 1906): 1.

15. See Dewey's reply to Stephen Sheldon Colvin's "Is Subjective Idealism a Necessary Point of View for Psychology?" *Journal of Philosophy, Psychology and Scientific Methods* 2 (1905): 225-231. Dewey, "The Realism of Pragmatism" (1905), MW 3: 154.

16. Dewey, "The Need for a Recovery of Philosophy" (1917), MW 10: 39.

17. Dewey, "Beliefs and Realities," (1905), MW 3: 86.

18. Ibid. As was customary with A.P.A. presidential addresses, this paper was published the following year in the *Philosophical Review,* but Dewey changed the title to "Beliefs and Existences" with the following explanatory footnote: "The substitution of the word 'Existences' for the word 'Realities' (in the original title) is due to a subsequent recognition on my part that the eulogistic historic associations with the word 'Reality' (against which the paper was a protest) infected the interpretation of the paper itself, so that the use of some more colorless word was desirable" (MW 3: 83).

19. Dewey first used the term "epistemological industry" in "Psychology and Philosophic Method," which was initially published in the *University* [of California] *Chronicle* 2 (1899): 159-179. The essay was reprinted separately as "'Consciousness' and Experience" in *The Influence of Darwin on Philosophy* (New York: Henry Holt, 1910), 242-270. See "'Consciousness' and Experience" (1899), MW 1: 122.

20. Dewey, "Beliefs and Existences" (1905), MW 3: 84-85.

21. Dewey, "The Experimental Theory of Knowledge" (1906), MW 3: 122.

22. Dewey, "The Present Position of Logical Theory" (1891), EW 3:134, 138.

23. See Westbrook, *John Dewey and American Democracy,* 124 n. 9.

24. Dewey, "Experience and Objective Idealism" (1906), 3:128, 130.

25. Dewey, "The Postulate of Immediate Empiricism" (1905) MW 3: 158-167; and "Immediate Empiricism" (1905) MW 3: 168-170.

26. John E. Russell, "Objective Idealism and Revised Empiricism (for Discussion)," *The Philosophical Review* 15, no. 6 (Nov. 1906): 627-633. R. H. Bode, "Objective Idealism and Its Critics," *The Philosophical Review* 19, no. 6 (Nov. 1910): 597-609. Unfortunately, Dewey's use of terms did not improve in later writings. In *Democracy and Education,* for example, he notes that although Hegel's philosophy "is usually termed absolute or objective idealism, it might better be termed, for educational purposes at least, institutional idealism." Dewey, *Democracy and Education* (1916), MW 9: 309.

27. In the textual apparatus to volume 8, the editors of the *Collected Works of John Dewey* provide a lengthy list of book reviews, mostly positive, of *German Philosophy and Politics*: *A.L.A. Booklist* 12 (1915): 6; *American Review of Reviews* 52 (1915): 248; *Independent* 83 (1915): 24-25; *New York Times Book Review* (18 July 1915): 257; *Springfield Daily Republican,* 10 June 1915; Francis Hackett, review of *German Phi-*

losophy and Politics, by John Dewey, *New Republic* (17 July 1915): 282-284, with a footnote by Walter Lippmann, 284-285; William Ernest Hocking, "Political Philosophy in Germany," *New Republic* (2 October 1915): 234-236; Frank Thilly, review of *German Philosophy and Politics,* by John Dewey, *Philosophical Review* 24, no. 5 (Sept. 1915): 540-545; James H. Tufts, review of *German Philosophy and Politics,* by John Dewey, *International Journal of Ethics* 26, no. 1 (Oct. 1915): 131-133; George Santayana, review of *German Philosophy and Politics,* by John Dewey, *Journal of Philosophy, Psychology and Scientific Methods* 12, no. 24 (25 Nov. 1915): 645-649; F. C. S. Schiller, review of *German Philosophy and Politics,* by John Dewey, *Mind* 25, no. 98 (April 1916): 250-55; *Nation* (29 July 1915): 152-53.

28. Sidney Hook, "Introduction" MW 8: xxx-xxxi. The thesis that there is a continuity between Imperial and Nazi Germany significant enough to equate Germany's war aims in World War I with those of the Third Reich has been hotly debated since the publication of Fritz Fischer's *Griff nach der Weltmacht: die Kriegszielpolitik des kaiserlichen Deutschland 1914-18* (published in English translation as *Germany's Aims in the First World War*) in 1961, and is a subtext of the recent *Historikerstreit* in which Jürgen Habermas participated. See Charles S. Maier, *The Unmasterable Past: History, Holocaust, and German National Identity* (Cambridge, MA: Harvard University Press, 1988), 4; and David Blackbourn and Geoff Eley, *The Peculiarities of German History: Bourgeois Society and Politics in Nineteenth-Century Germany* (New York: Oxford University Press, 1984), 28ff. The complexities of this debate underscore the extraordinary simplicity of Dewey's arguments in *German Philosophy and Politics.*

29. Dewey claimed Nietzsche's philosophy had little influence in Germany, characterizing it as "a superficial and transitory wave of opinion." Dewey, *German Philosophy and Politics* (1915), MW 8: 151. The following year he criticized efforts to connect German militarism to Nietzsche in "On Understanding the Mind of Germany" (1916), MW 10: 216-233.

30. Dewey, *German Philosophy and Politics* (1915), MW 8: 151.

31. See especially Max Horkheimer and Theodor Adorno, *The Dialectic of Enlightenment,* trans. John Cumming (New York: Continuum, 1996), 81-127. Axel Honneth has recently noted this similarity between Dewey and Horkheimer and Adorno in "The Logic of Fanaticism: Dewey's Archaeology of the German Mentality," trans. Jason Murphy, in *Pluralism and the Pragmatic Turn: The Transformation of Critical Theory,* eds. William Rehg and James Bohman (Cambridge, MA: MIT Press, 2001), 321-322. Honneth also notes the similarity of Dewey's and Hegel's criticism of the formalism of Kant's ethics. But he goes on to assert without evidence or argumentation "the fact that . . . Hegel . . . conceived of war as a rational, purifying means for the realization of . . . the moral task of the state." Honneth also never questions Dewey's characterization of Hegel as, like the later Fichte, opposed to Kantian cosmopolitanism (327). Thus Honneth misses the degree to which *German Philosophy and Politics* displays evidence of Dewey's continuing Hegelianism.

32. Dewey, *German Philosophy and Politics* (1915), MW 8: 152.

33. Ibid., 159.

34. Ibid., 191.

35. Dewey's equation of Fichte's and Hegel's views of the state is questionable indeed. Hegel was quite worried about Fichte's nationalism and authoritarian elements in his vision of the state. See George Armstrong Kelly, *Idealism, Politics, and History: Sources of Hegelian Thought* (Cambridge: Cambridge University Press, 1969), 248-306.

36. Dewey, *German Philosophy and Politics* (1915), MW 8: 192-193. This is the only passage in Dewey's published works in which he mentioned Rudolf Haym.

37. Dewey ignored passages in the *Philosophy of Right* that contradict his reading of §258. Two paragraphs after the passage Dewey quoted, Hegel wrote, "The state is the

actuality of concrete freedom. But *concrete freedom* requires that personal individuality [*Einzelheit*] and its particular interests should reach their full *development* and gain *recognition of their right* for itself. . . . The principle of modern states has enormous strength and depth because it allows the principle of subjectivity to attain fulfillment in the *self-sufficient extreme* of personal particularity, while at the same time *bringing it back to substantial unity* and so preserving this unity in the principle of subjectivity itself." Hegel, *Elements of the Philosophy of Right,* ed. Allen W. Wood, trans. H. B. Nisbet (Cambridge: Cambridge University Press, 1991), §260 (emphasis in the original). Moreover, in his *Lectures on the Philosophy of World History,* Hegel wrote that "the universal spirit or world spirit is not the same thing as God. It is the rationality of spirit in its worldly existence." Hegel, *Lectures on the Philosophy of World History: Introduction: Reason in World History* (New York: Cambridge University Press, 1975), 213.

38. Wood, "Editor's Introduction" in Hegel, *Philosophy of Right,* xxvi.

39. Dewey, *Democracy and Education* (1916), MW 9: 64.

40. Dewey, *German Philosophy and Politics* (1915), MW 8: 118.

41. Ibid., 441.

42. A good example can be found in Lewis Hinchman, *Hegel's Critique of the Enlightenment* (Gainesville and Tampa: University Presses of Florida, 1984), 73-75. Hinchman claims to "dispel the widely held belief that Hegel scorned 'mere' understanding for the sake of higher reason which could dispense with the labor of finite thought." He does show by employing textual evidence to argue that Hegel viewed the understanding as a necessary component of reason. Cf. Steven B. Smith's penetrating discussion of Hegel's concept of rational necessity. In that discussion Smith casts significant doubt not only on the characterization of Hegel's concepts of reason and understanding that we encounter here in Dewey, but also on the notion that Hegel believed in the sort of necessary historical teleology that Dewey claimed he did. Smith, *Hegel's Critique of Liberalism: Rights in Context* (Chicago: University of Chicago Press, 1989), 204-217.

43. Sydney Hook, "Introduction," MW 8: xxviii.

44. Although, in *German Philosophy and Politics,* Dewey rejected "the doctrine of the economic interpretation of history in its extreme form," it is difficult to imagine any philosophical reason for him not to employ an economic interpretation of the history of Imperial Germany in a more moderate form in this book, or to supplement intellectual history with other considerations. Dewey, *German Philosophy and Politics* (1915), MW 8: 140. In fact, in "The Bearings of Pragmatism on Education," Dewey compared pragmatism to the "the theory of 'economic interpretation of history' in its broad sense." Dewey (1908), MW 4: 178. A Deweyan intellectual history, it seems, would require a willingness to consider a host of causal factors, some of which were obviously related to any analysis of World War I (e.g., diplomatic history). In his reply to Hocking, Dewey suggested that the "class stratifications, and . . . efficiently organized hierarchy of subordinations" of German society "give appeal to a priori concepts a certain solid backing" that might be lacking in American society. But Dewey left this social analysis undeveloped. Dewey, "Reply to William Hocking's 'Political Philosophy in Germany'" (1915), MW 8: 419.

45. Dewey, "Reply to William Ernest Hocking's 'Political Philosophy in Germany'" (1915), MW 8: 420.

46. See Randolph Bourne, "Twilight of Idols," "A War Diary," and "The Collapse of American Strategy" in *The Radical Will: Selected Writings, 1911-1918,* ed. Olaf Hansen (Berkeley: University of California Press, 1977). It is odd that Bourne did not recognize that his critique of Dewey was substantially the same as Dewey's claims about the use of Kantianism by Germans because, before Dewey decided to publicly support Wilson, Bourne described *German Philosophy and Politics* as one of the few examples of "origi-

nal and illuminating interpretation" written by an American during the period of American neutrality (310).

47. Alan Dawley, *Struggles for Justice: Social Responsibility and the Liberal State* (Cambridge, MA: Belknap Press of the Harvard University Press, 1991), 184ff. The fact that Wilson won reelection in 1916 running on a platform of neutrality indicates that as late as November of that year many Americans still favored American neutrality. Thomas J. Knock, *To End All Wars: Woodrow Wilson and the Quest for a New World Order* (New York: Oxford University Press, 1992).

48. Dewey, "Universal Service as Education" (1916), MW 10: 183-190; and "Universal Military Training" (1917), MW 10: 377-393.

49. Bruce Kuklick, *The Rise of American Philosophy: Cambridge, Massachusetts, 1860-1930* (New Haven: Yale University Press, 1977), 437.

50. Hugo Münsterberg, *American Patriotism and Other Social Studies,* reprint of 1913 ed. (Freeport, New York: Books for Libraries Press, 1968), 105. In the following discussion of intellectuals during the war I am indebted to conversations with James Campbell, and to an unpublished draft of the fifth chapter of his history of the A.P.A., "Philosophers in Wartime: The A.P.A. and World War One."

51. Hugo Münsterberg, *The War and America* (New York: Appleton, 1914), 43.

52. Ibid., 206-207.

53. Hugo Münsterberg, *The Peace and America* (New York: Appleton, 1915). Before his death in 1916, Münsterberg managed to publish a fourth volume in support of the German war effort entitled *Tomorrow, Letters to a Friend in Germany* (New York: Appleton, 1916). A Columbia University colleague of Dewey's, George Stuart Fullerton, also published a defense of German culture in 1915, but it drew less obviously on Kantian themes. Fullerton, *Germany of To-day* (Indianapolis: Bobbs-Merrill, 1915).

54. Quoted in Ralph Haswell Lutz, ed., *Fall of the German Empire, 1914-1918,* 2 volumes, trans. David G. Rempel and Gertrude Rendtorff (Stanford, CA: Stanford University Press, 1932), 1: 74-75.

55. Dewey, "Our Educational Ideal in Wartime" (1916), MW 10: 180.

56. Franklin H. Giddings, "Introduction" to *Towards an Enduring Peace: A Symposium of Peace Proposals and Programs, 1914-1916,* ed. Randolph Bourne (New York: American Association for International Conciliation, 1916), vii.

57. Nicholas Murray Butler, *A World in Ferment: Interpretations of the War for a New World* (New York: Scribner, 1918), 89-90.

58. Dewey, *Democracy and Education* (1916), MW 9: 46-58. Without acknowledging it, Dewey nicely defined *Bildung* in the opening paragraph of chapter two, "Education as a Social Function": "1. The Nature and Meaning of Environment.—We have seen that a community or social group sustains itself through continuous self-renewal, and that this renewal takes place by means of the educational growth of the immature members of the group. By various agencies, unintentional and designed, a society transforms uninitiated and seemingly alien beings into robust trustees of its own resources and ideals. Education is thus a fostering, a nurturing, a cultivating, process. All of these words mean that it implies attention to the conditions of growth. We also speak of rearing, raising, bringing up—words which express the difference of level which education aims to cover. Etymologically, the word education means just a process of leading or bringing up. When we have the outcome of the process in mind, we speak of education as shaping, forming, molding activity—that is, a shaping into the standard form of social activity. In this chapter we are concerned with the general features of the way in which a social group brings up its immature members into its own social form." Ibid., 14.

59. Westbrook, *John Dewey and American Democracy,* 205. As evidence of Dewey's uncritical Americanism during the war, Westbrook discusses Dewey's 1918 essay, "America in the World," in which he proclaimed that the United States had abolished a

plethora of social ills including political discrimination on the basis of race and ethnicity. According to Dewey, "To us language, literature, creed, group ways, national culture, are social rather than political, human rather than national, interests. Let this idea fly abroad; it bears healing in its wings." Dewey, "America in the World" (1918), MW 11: 71.

60. Dewey, *Experience and Nature* (1925), LW 1: 305.

61. Ibid., 307-308.

62. Ibid., 149-150.

Selected Bibliography

Unpublished

Angell, James B., Papers. Bentley Historical Library. University of Michigan.

Angell, James Rowland, Personal Papers. Manuscripts and Archives, Yale University Library.

Burnett, Joe R. to Herbert Schneider, 10 June 1971. Center for Dewey Studies file, "'Glenmore School for the Cultural Sciences,' 1892." Southern Illinois University Carbondale.

Byrne, Margaret Myers. "Great Scot: The Life and Philosophical Communities of Thomas Davidson." Unpublished manuscript.

Calhoun, Robert. "An Introduction to the Philosophy of Thomas Davidson, with Illustrative Documents." Ph.D. diss., Yale University, 1923.

Davidson, Thomas, Papers. Manuscripts and Archives, Yale University Library.

"Dewey, John, Correspondence." Center for Dewey Studies. Southern Illinois University Carbondale.

Dewey, John. "Hegel's Philosophy of Spirit: Lectures by John Dewey," University of Chicago, 1897. Unpublished manuscript, John Dewey Papers, Collection 102, Special Collections Research Center, Morris Library, Southern Illinois University Carbondale.

Dewey, John, Papers. Special Collections. University of Vermont Library.

Dowler, Lawrence. "The New Idealism and the Quest for Culture in the Gilded Age." Ph.D. diss., University of Maryland, 1974.

FBI New York File No. 100-25838. New York, 29 Apr. 1943 (copy at Center for Dewey Studies, Carbondale, IL).

Flay, Joseph Charles. "Hegel and Dewey and the Problem of Freedom." Ph.D. diss., University of Southern California, 1965.

Gilman, Daniel Coit, Papers. Special Collections. The Johns Hopkins University.

Haag, Alvin S. "Some German Influences in American Philosophical Thought from 1800 to 1850." Ph.D. diss., Boston University, 1939.

Harris, William Torrey, Papers. Missouri Historical Society.

Huenemann, Calvin Victor. "Denton J. Snider: A Critical Study." Ph.D. diss., University of Wisconsin, 1953.

Kwon, Teck-Young. "A. Bronson Alcott's Literary Apprenticeship to Emerson: The Role of Harris's *Journal of Speculative Philosophy*." Ph.D. diss., University of Nebraska, Lincoln, 1980.

Rogers, Dorothy G. "'Making Hegel Talk English': America's First Women Idealists." Ph.D. diss., Boston University, 1998.

Savage, Willinda. "The Evolution of John Dewey's Philosophy of Experimentalism as Developed at the University of Michigan." Ph.D. diss., University of Michigan, 1950.

Schneider, Herbert. "Reminiscences about John Dewey at Columbia, 1913-1950." Unpublished manuscript, Special Collections Research Center, Morris Library, Southern Illinois University Carbondale.

———. "John Dewey: A Talk Delivered by Professor Herbert W. Schneider in the Ira Allen Chapel, the University of Vermont, on October 26, 1949, at the Celebration of John Dewey's Ninetieth Birthday Anniversary." Unpublished manuscript. John Dewey Papers. Special Collections. University of Vermont Library.

———. Oral History Interview of John Dewey, 29 June 1967. Unpublished manuscript, Special Collections Research Center, Morris Library, Southern Illinois University Carbondale.

Watson, John. "Idealism and Social Theory: A Comparative Study of British and American Adaptations of Hegel, 1860-1914." Ph.D. diss., University of Pennsylvania, 1975.

Published

Abrams, M. H. *Natural Supernaturalism: Tradition and Revolution in Romantic Literature.* New York: W. W. Norton, 1971.

Adams, Herbert Baxter. "The Germanic Origin of New England Towns." *Johns Hopkins University Studies in Historical and Political Science,* vol. 1. *Local Institutions.* Baltimore: Johns Hopkins University Press, 1882.

Addams, Jane. *Twenty Years at Hull-House with Autobiographical Notes.* New York: Macmillan, 1920.

Adler, Felix. "The Freedom of Ethical Fellowship." *International Journal of Ethics* 1, no. 1 (Oct. 1890): 16-30.

Alcott, Bronson A. *The Journals of Bronson Alcott.* Edited by Odell Shepard. Boston: Little, Brown, 1938.

Alexander, Thomas. *John Dewey's Theory of Art, Experience and Nature: The Horizons of Feeling.* Albany: State University of New York Press, 1987.

Althaus, Horst. *Hegel: An Intellectual Biography.* Translated by Michael Tarsh. Cambridge: Polity, 2000.

Anderson, Paul Russell. *Platonism in the Midwest.* Philadelphia: Temple University Publications, 1963.

Annual Register. July 1896–July 1897 with announcements for 1897-1898. Chicago: University of Chicago Press, 1897.

Aronowitz, Stanley. "Introduction." In Max Horkheimer, *Critical Theory: Selected Essays.* New York: Continuum, 1995.

Backe, Andrew. "Dewey and the Reflex Arc: The Limits of James's Influence." *Transactions of the Charles S. Peirce Society* 35, no. 2 (Spring 1999): 312-326.

Baillie, J. B. "Introduction." In *The Phenomenology of Mind,* by G. W. F. Hegel. Translated by J. B. Baillie. New York: Humanities Press, 1949.

Bakewell, Charles. "Thomas Davidson." In *Dictionary of American Biography, under the Auspices of the American Council of Learned Societies,* 5: 96. New York: C. Scribner's Sons, 1928.

Barns, William E., ed. *The Labor Problem.* New York: Arno Press, 1971.

Beineke, John A. "The Investigation of John Dewey by the FBI." *Educational Theory* (Winter 1987): 43-52.

Beiser, Frederick C. *The Fate of Reason: German Philosophy from Kant to Fichte.* Cambridge, MA: Harvard University Press, 1987.

Bender, Thomas. *New York Intellect: A History of Intellectual Life in New York City, from 1750 to the Beginnings of Our Own Time.* New York: Knopf, 1987.

———. *Intellect and Public Life: Essays on the Social History of Academic Intellectuals in the United States.* Baltimore and London: Johns Hopkins University Press, 1993.

Benne, Kenneth, ed. *Essays for John Dewey's Ninetieth Birthday.* Urbana: Bureau of Research and Service, College of Education, University of Illinois, 1950.

Bergquist, Harold E., Jr. "The Edward Bemis Controversy at the University of Chicago." *American Association of University Professors Bulletin* 58 (1972): 383-393.

Blackbourn, David and Geoff Eley. *The Peculiarities of German History: Bourgeois Society and Politics in Nineteenth-Century Germany.* New York: Oxford University Press, 1984.

Blau, Joseph. "Rosmini, Domodossola, and Thomas Davidson." *Journal of the History of Ideas* 18, no. 4 (Oct. 1957): 522-528.

———. "John Dewey's Theory of History." *Journal of Philosophy* 57, no. 3 (4 February 1960): 89-100.

Blewett, John, ed. *John Dewey: His Thought and Influence.* New York: Fordham University Press, 1960.

Bode, R. H. "Objective Idealism and Its Critics." *Philosophical Review* 19, no. 6 (Nov. 1910): 597-609.

Boisvert, Raymond. *Dewey's Metaphysics.* New York: Fordham University Press, 1988.

———. *John Dewey: Rethinking Our Time.* Albany: State University of New York Press, 1998.

Bosanquet, Bernard. "The Communication of Moral Ideas as a Function of an Ethical Society." *International Journal of Ethics* 1, no. 1 (Oct. 1890): 79-97.

Bostwick, Arthur E. "List of Books Written by Denton J. Snider, Litt. D., with Annotations." *St. Louis Public Library Monthly Bulletin* (Aug. 1924), 1-8.

Bourne, Randolph. *The Radical Will: Randolph Bourne Selected Writings, 1911-1918.* Edited by Olaf Hansen. Berkeley: University of California Press, 1977.

________. *War and the Intellectuals: Collected Essays, 1915-1919.* Indianapolis: Hackett Publishing Co. Inc., 1999.

Bradley, F. H. *Appearance and Reality.* London: Oxford University Press, 1969.

Brent, Joseph. *Charles Sanders Peirce: A Life.* Revised and enlarged edition. Bloomington: Indiana University Press, 1998.

Buckham, John Wright. "A Group of American Idealists." *Personalist* 1 (Apr. 1920): 18-31.

———. "A Vermont Boyhood." *Vermont History* 30, no. 3 (July 1962): 203-210.

Buckham, John Wright and George Stratton. "A Biographical Sketch." In *George Holmes Howison: A Selection of His Writings with a Biographical Sketch,* 1-122. Berkeley: University of California Press, 1934.

Buckham, Matthew. "Burlington as a Place to Live In." *The Vermont Historical Gazeteer* 1, no. 8 (1867): 724.

———. *The Very Elect.* Boston: Pilgrim Press, 1912.

Buford, Thomas. "What We are About." *Personalist Forum* 1, no. 1 (1985): 1-4.

Burgess, John W. *Reminiscences of an American Scholar: The Beginnings of Columbia University.* New York: AMS Press, 1966.

———. *Political Science and Comparative Constitutional Law.* Boston: Ginn, 1896.

Burke, Tom. *Dewey's New Logic: A Reply to Russell.* Chicago: University of Chicago Press, 1994.

Butler, Nicholas Murray. *A World in Ferment: Interpretations of the War for a New World.* New York: Scribner, 1918.

Buxton, Michael. "The Influence of William James on John Dewey's Early Work." *Journal of the History of Ideas* 45, no. 3 (July-Sept. 1984): 451-463.

Caird, Edward. *Hegel.* 1883. Reprint. Hamden, CT: Archon Books, 1968.

Canfield, James. *American Review of Reviews* 34 (Aug. 1906): 164-166.

Carafiol, Peter. *Transcendent Reason: James Marsh and the Forms of Romantic Thought.* Tallahassee: University Presses of Florida, 1982.

Catalogue of the University of Vermont, 1878-79. Burlington: University of Vermont.

Chandler, Kenneth. "Dewey's Phenomenology of Knowledge." *Philosophy Today* 21 (1977): 43-55.

Cohen, Morris Raphael. "The New Realism." *Journal of Philosophy* 10, no. 8 (10 Apr. 1913): 197-211.

———. *A Dreamer's Journey.* Boston: Beacon Press, 1949.

Colapietro, Vincent M. "Transforming Philosophy into a Science: A Debilitating Chimera or a Realizable Desideratum?" *American Catholic Philosophical Quarterly* 72, no. 2 (Spring 1998): 245-278.

Conkin, Paul. *Puritans and Pragmatists.* New York: Dodd, Mead, 1968.

Cook, Gary A. *George Herbert Mead: The Making of a Social Pragmatist.* Urbana: University of Illinois Press, 1993.

The Correspondence of John Dewey. Edited by Larry A. Hickman. Charlottesville, VA: InteLex Corporation, 2001.

Coughlan, Neil. *Young John Dewey: An Essay in American Intellectual History.* Chicago: University of Chicago Press, 1973.

Curti, Merle. *Social Ideas of American Educators.* New York: Charles Scribner's Sons, 1935.

Dalton, Thomas C. *Becoming John Dewey: Dilemmas of a Philosopher and Naturalist.* Bloomington: Indiana University Press, 2002.

Davidson, Thomas. "Antonio Rosmini." *The Fortnightly Review* 36 (Nov. 1881): 553-584.

———. "Noism." *The Index* (29 Apr. 1886): 525.

———. *The Education of the Greek People.* New York: Appleton, 1894.

———. "American Democracy as a Religion." *International Journal of Ethics* 10 (Oct. 1899): 21-41.

———. *The Education of the Wage-Earners: A Contribution Toward the Solution of the Educational Problem of Democracy.* Boston: Ginn, 1904.

———. "Autobiographical Sketch." *Journal of the History of Ideas* 18, no. 4 (Oct. 1957): 531-536.

———. *The Philosophy of Goethe's Faust.* Edited by Charles M. Bakewell. New York: Haskell House Publishers, Ltd., 1969.

Davidson, Thomas and Daniel G. Brinton. *Giordano Bruno: Philosopher and Martyr. Two Addresses.* Philadelphia: David McKay Publisher, 1890.

DeArmey, Michael. "Thomas Davidson's Apeirotheism and Its Influence on William James and John Dewey." *Journal of the History of Ideas* 48, no. 4 (Oct.-Dec. 1987): 691-707.

Descartes, Rene. *Discourse on Method and Meditations.* Translated by Laurence J. Lafleur. New York: Macmillan Publishing Co., 1960.

Dewey, John. *Leibniz's New Essays Concerning the Human Understanding: A Critical Exposition.* Chicago: S. C. Griggs, 1888.

———. *The Collected Works of John Dewey, 1882-1953: The Electronic Edition.* Edited by Larry A. Hickman. Charlottesville, VA: InteLex Corporation, 1996.

———. *The Poems of John Dewey.* Edited by Jo Ann Boydston. Carbondale: Southern Illinois University Press, 1977.

Dickey, Laurence. *Hegel: Religion, Economics, and the Politics of Spirit, 1770-1807.* Cambridge: Cambridge University Press, 1987.

Diehl, Carl. *Americans and German Scholarship, 1770-1870.* New Haven and London: Yale University Press, 1978.

Diggins, John Patrick. *The Promise of Pragmatism: Modernism and the Crisis of Knowledge and Authority.* Chicago: University of Chicago Press, 1994.

Dilthey, Wilhelm. *Die Jugendgeschichte Hegels und andere Abhandlungen zur Geschichte des deutschen Idealismus.* Leipzig: B. G. Teubner, 1905.

Dye, James Wayne. "Denton J. Snider's Interpretation of Hegel." *The Modern Schoolman* 46 (Jan. 1970): 153-167.

Dykhuizen, George. *The Life and Mind of John Dewey.* Introduction by Harold Taylor. Edited by Jo Ann Boydston. Carbondale: Southern Illinois University Press, 1973.

———. "John Dewey at Johns Hopkins (1882-1884)." *Journal of the History of Ideas* 22, no. 1, (Jan.-March 1961): 103-116.

———. "John Dewey in Chicago: Some Biographical Notes." *Journal of the History of Philosophy* 3, no. 2 (Oct. 1965): 217-233.

Eastman, George Herbert. Review of *John Dewey: Philosophy, Psychology and Social Practice,* by Joseph Ratner. *Studies in Philosophy and Education* 4 (1965): 95-104.

Eastman, Max. "John Dewey." *Atlantic Monthly* 168 (1941): 672-691.

Easton, Lloyd D. *Hegel's First American Followers: The Ohio Hegelians: John B. Stallo, Peter Kaufmann, Moncure Conway, and Aug. Willich, with Key Writings.* Athens: Ohio University Press, 1966.

Eisele, Christopher J. "John Dewey and the Immigrants." *History of Education Quarterly* 15, no. 1 (Spring 1975): 67-85.

Eldridge, Michael. *Transforming Experience: John Dewey's Cultural Instrumentalism.* Nashville: Vanderbilt University Press, 1998.

Elkins, Stanley. *Slavery: A Problem in American Institutional and Intellectual Life,* 3rd edition, revised. Chicago: University of Chicago Press, 1976.

Elton, William. "Peirce's Marginalia in W. T. Harris's *Hegel's Logic.*" *Journal of the History of Philosophy* 2, no. 1 (Apr. 1964): 82-84.

Emerson, Ralph Waldo. *The Letters of Ralph Waldo Emerson.* 6 volumes. Edited by Ralph L. Rusk. New York: Columbia University Press, 1939.

———. *Selections from Ralph Waldo Emerson.* Edited by Stephen E. Wheeler. Boston: Houghton Mifflin, 1957.

Engelhardt, H. Tristram and Terry Pinkard, eds. *Hegel Reconsidered: Beyond Metaphysics and the Authoritarian State.* Boston: Kluwer, 1994.

Evans, Henry Ridgley, ed. "A List of the Writings of William Torrey Harris." *Report of the Commissioner of Education for 1907.* (Washington, D.C.: Government Printing Office, 1908): 37-72.

Everett, Charles. *Fichte's Science of Knowledge: A Critical Exposition.* Chicago: S. C. Griggs, 1884.

Feffer, Andrew. *The Chicago Pragmatists and American Progressivism.* Ithaca: Cornell University Press, 1993.

Fellman, Michael. *Inside War: The Guerrilla Conflict in Missouri during the American Civil War.* New York: Oxford University Press, 1989.

Ferrarin, Alfredo. *Hegel and Aristotle.* Cambridge: Cambridge University Press, 2001.

Feuer, Lewis Samuel. "Letters from the Past: Letters of H. A. P. Torrey to William T. Harris." *Vermont History* 25, no. 3 (July 1957): 215-219.

———. "H. A. P. Torrey and John Dewey." *American Quarterly* 10 (1958): 34-54.

———. "James Marsh and the Conservative Transcendentalist Philosophy: A Political Interpretation." *New England Quarterly* 31, no. 1 (March 1958): 3-31.

———. "John Dewey's Reading at College." *Journal of the History of Ideas* 19, no. 3 (June 1958), 415-421.

———. "John Dewey and the Back to the People Movement in American Thought." *Journal of the History of Ideas* 20, no. 4 (Oct.-Dec. 1959): 545-568.

———. "Prefatory Note." *Vermont History* 30, no. 3 (July 1962): 201-203.

———. Introduction to *The Later Works of John Dewey, 1925-1953,* volume 15, edited by Jo Ann Boydston. Carbondale: Southern Illinois University Press, 1989.

Fichte, J. G. *The Vocation of Man.* Translated by William Smith. Chicago: Open Court, 1906.

Findlay, J. N. *Hegel: A Re-examination.* London: Allen and Unwin, 1958.

Firda, Richard Arthur. "German Philosophy of History and Literature in the *North American Review:* 1815-1860." *Journal of the History of Ideas* 32, no. 1 (Jan.-March 1971): 133-142.

Fisch, Max H. "Philosophical Clubs in Cambridge and Boston." *Coranto* 2, no. 1 and no. 2; 3, no. 1 (Fall and Spring 1964, Fall 1965): 16-18, 12-23, 16-29.

Fischer, Fritz. *Germany's Aims in the First World War.* New York: W. W. Norton, 1967.

Flay, Joseph Charles. *Hegel's Quest for Certainty.* Albany: SUNY Press, 1984.

Flower, Elizabeth and Murray G. Murphey. *A History of Philosophy in America.* 2 volumes. New York: Capricorn Books, 1977.

Forster, Michael N. *Hegel's Idea of a* Phenomenology of Spirit. Chicago: University of Chicago Press, 1998.

Fott, David. *John Dewey: America's Philosopher of Democracy.* New York: Rowman and Littlefield, 1998.

Franco, Paul. *Hegel's Philosophy of Freedom.* New Haven: Yale University Press, 1999.

Fredrickson, George M. *The Inner Civil War: Northern Intellectuals and the Crisis of the Union.* New York: Harper and Row, 1968.

Friedrich, Carl J. *The Philosophy of Hegel.* New York: Modern Library, 1953.

Fukuyama, Francis. "The End of History." *The National Interest* 16 (Summer 1989): 3-18.

Fullerton, George Stuart. *Germany of To-day.* Indianapolis: Bobbs-Merrill, 1915.

Garrison, Jim. "Dewey's Philosophy and the Experience of Working: Labor, Tools and Language." *Synthese* 105 (1995): 87-114.

———. *The End of History and the Last Man.* New York: Free Press, 1992.

Garza, Abel, Jr. "Hegel's Critique of Liberalism and Natural Law: Reconstructing Ethical Life." *Law and Philosophy* (1991): 371-398.

Geiger, George Raymond. *John Dewey in Perspective.* New York: Oxford University Press, 1958.

Geitz, Henry, Jürgen Heideking, and Jurgen Herbst, eds. *German Influences on Education in the United States to 1917.* Washington, D.C.: German Historical Institute, and Cambridge: Cambridge University Press, 1995.

Giddings, Franklin H. "Introduction." In *Towards an Enduring Peace: A Symposium of Peace Proposals and Programs, 1914-1916,* edited by Randolph Bourne, vii-xi. New York: American Association for International Conciliation, 1916.

Gierke, Otto. *Natural Law and the Theory of Society, 1500 to 1800.* Translated by Ernest Barker. Cambridge: Cambridge University Press, 1950.

Gilman, Charlotte Perkins. *The Living of Charlotte Perkins Gilman.* New York: Arno Press, 1972.

Goetzmann, William, ed., *The American Hegelians: An Intellectual Episode in the History of Western America.* New York: Alfred A. Knopf, 1973.

Good, James A. "Dewey's 'Permanent Hegelian Deposit' and the Exigencies of War." *Journal of the History of Philosophy* (forthcoming).

———. "The Value of Thomas Davidson." *Transactions of the Charles S. Peirce Society* 40, no. 2 (Spring 2004): 289-318.

———. "The 'Eclipse' of Pragmatism: A Reply to John Capps." *Transactions of the Charles S. Peirce Society* 39, no. 1 (Winter 2003): 77-86.

———. "Introduction." In *Autobiography and Miscellaneous Writings by Moncure Daniel Conway,* 3 vols. 1905; 1909. Reprint. Bristol, England: Thoemmes Press, 2003.

———. "Introduction." In *The Journal of Speculative Philosophy, 1867-1893.* Reprint. Bristol, England: Thoemmes Press, 2002.

———. "Introduction." In *Psychology; or a View of the Human Soul; including Anthropology,* by Frederich Augustus Rauch. 1840. Reprint. *The Early American Reception of German Idealism,* vol. 1. Bristol, England: Thoemmes Press, 2002.

———. "Introduction." In *The Remains of the Rev. James Marsh, D.D.: Late President and Professor of Moral and Intellectual Philosophy, in the University of Vermont; with a Memoir of His Life,* by James Marsh. 1843. Reprint. *The Early American Reception of German Idealism,* vol. 2. Bristol, England: Thoemmes Press, 2002.

———. "Introduction." In *Prose Writers of Germany,* edited by Frederic Henry Hedge. 1847. Reprint. *The Early American Reception of German Idealism,* vol. 3. Bristol, England: Thoemmes Press, 2002.

———. Review of *The Soul's Economy: Market Society and Selfhood in American Thought, 1820-1920,* by Jeffrey Sklansky. In *Register of the Kentucky Historical Society* 100, no. 4 (Autumn 2002): 536-538.

———. "A 'World-Historical Idea': The St. Louis Hegelians and the Civil War," *Journal of American Studies* 34, no. 1 (Dec. 2000): 447-464.

———. Review of *Reading Dewey: Interpretations for a Postmodern Generation,* edited by Larry A. Hickman. *Transactions of the Charles S. Peirce Society* 35 (Winter 1999), 240-247.

Good, James A. and Michael DeArmey. *The St. Louis Hegelians.* 3 volumes. Bristol, U.K.: Thoemmes Press, 2001.

Green, Maxine. *The Dialectic of Freedom.* New York: Teachers College Press, 1988.

Greer, Colin. *The Great School Legend: A Revisionist Interpretation of American Public Education.* New York: Basic Books, 1972.

Grier, Philip T. "The End of History, and the Return of History." *The Owl of Minerva* 21, no. 2 (Spring 1990): 131-144.

Guizot, Francois Pierre Guillaume. *General History of Civilization in Europe, from the Fall of the Roman Empire to the French Revolution.* New York: Appleton, 1867, 1877.

Hackett, Francis. Review of *German Philosophy and Politics,* by John Dewey. *New Republic* (17 July 1915): 282-284.

Hall, G. Stanley. "Anti-Materialism." JSP 6, no. 3 (July 1872): 216-222.

———. "Notes on Hegel and his Critics." JSP 12, no. 1 (Jan. 1878): 93-103.

———. "Philosophy in the United States." *Mind* 4, no. 13 (Jan. 1879): 89-105.

———. Review of *Psychology,* by John Dewey. *American Journal of Psychology* 1 (1888): 154-159.

Hance, Allen. "Pragmatism as Naturalized Hegelianism: Overcoming Transcendental Philosophy?" In *Rorty and Pragmatism: The Philosopher Responds to His Critics,* ed. Herman J. Saatkamp, Jr., 100-125. Nashville: Vanderbilt University Press, 1995.

Hansen, Jonathan M. *The Lost Promise of Patriotism: Debating American Identity, 1890-1920.* Chicago: University of Chicago Press, 2003.

Harmon, Frances. *The Social Philosophy of the St. Louis Hegelians.* New York: Columbia University, 1943.

Harris, David H., ed. *A Brief Report of the Meeting Commemorative of the Early Saint Louis Movement in Philosophy, Psychology, Literature, Art and Education.* St. Louis: n.p., 1922.

Harris, Errol E. *An Interpretation of the Logic of Hegel.* Lanham, MD: University Press of America, 1983.

———. "In Memoriam: John Neimeyer Findlay (1903-1987)." *The Owl of Minerva* 19, 2 (Spring 1988): 252-253.

Harris, H. S. *Hegel's Development: Toward the Sunlight, 1770-1801.* Oxford: Clarendon Press, 1972.

———. *Hegel's Development: Night Thoughts (Jena 1801-1806).* Oxford: Clarendon Press, 1983.

———. "The Hegel Renaissance in the Anglo-Saxon World Since 1945," *The Owl of Minerva* 15 (Fall 1983): 77-106.

Harris, William Torrey. "Philosophy of History." *Missouri Republican,* 8 Oct. 1861.

———. "Preface," JSP 1, no. 1 (1867), iii.

———. "To the Reader." JSP 1, no. 1 (1867): 2.

———. "What Shall We Study?" *Journal of Education* 2 (Sept. 1869): 1-3.

———. "Immortality of the Soul." JSP 4, no. 2 (1870): 97-111.

———. "Theism and Pantheism," JSP 5, no. 1 (Jan. 1871): 86-94.

———, ed. "Correspondence," JSP 6, no. 2 (Apr. 1872): 175-181.

———. *A Statement of the Theory of Education in the United States by Many Leading Educators.* Washington, D.C.: Government Printing Office, 1874.

———. "Trendelenburg and Hegel." JSP 9, no. 1 (Jan. 1875): 70-80.

———. "Defense of Hegel against the Charge of Pantheism as Made in Hickok's Logic of Reason." JSP 9, no. 3 (July 1876): 328-334.

———. "Do the Public Schools Educate Children Beyond the Position Which They Must Occupy in Life?" New Haven, CT: Board of Education. *Report* (1882): 33-50.

———. "Analysis and Commentary [of Karl Rosenkranz's Pädagogik als System]." JSP 15, no. 1 (Jan. 1881): 52-62.

———. "Books That Have Helped Me." *Forum* 3 (March 1887): 145.

———. "The Definition of Social Science and the Classification of the Topics Belonging to its Several Provinces." *Journal of Social Science* 22 (June 1887): 1-7.

———. "The Psychology of Manual Training." *Educational* 9 (May 1889): 571-582.

———. "The Philosophic Aspects of History." *Proceedings of the American Historical Association,* (1890): 247-254.

———. *Hegel's Logic: A Book on the Genesis of the Categories of the Mind: A Critical Exposition.* Chicago: S. C. Griggs, 1890.

———. "Professor John Dewey's Doctrine of Interest as Related to the Will." *Educational Review* 11 (May 1896): 486-493.

———. *Psychologic Foundations: An Attempt to Show the Genesis of the Higher Faculties of the Mind.* New York: Appleton, 1898.

———. "An Educational Policy for Our New Possessions." National Education Association *Proceedings* (1898): 69-79.

———. "A Brief for Latin." *Educational Review* 17 (Apr. 1899): 313-316.

———. "The Relation of Women to the Trades and Professions." *Educational Review* 20 (Oct. 1900), 217-229.

———. "Co-education of the Sexes." *Report of the Commissioner of Education* 2 (1900-1901): 141-147.

———. "Why Women Should Study the Law." *Ohio Educational Monthly* 50 (July 1901): 289-292.

———. "The Kindergarten as a Preparation for the Highest Civilization." *Atlantic Educational Journal* 6 (July-Aug. 1903): 35-36.

———. "Religious Instruction in the Public Schools." *Independent* 55 (6 Aug. 1903): 1841-1843.

———. "The School City." *School Bulletin* 32 (March 1906): 113-114.

Hartmann, Klaus. "On Taking the Transcendental Turn." *The Review of Metaphysics* 20 (Dec. 1966): 238.

———. "Hegel: A Non-Metaphysical View." In *Hegel: A Collection of Critical Essays*. Edited by A. MacIntyre. Garden City, New York: Doubleday, 1972.

Harvey, Mary Jane. "Henry James Describes Vermont." *Vermont History* 23 (1955): 348.

Haskell, Thomas L. *The Emergence of Professional Social Science: The American Social Science Association and the Nineteenth-Century Crisis of Authority*. 2d ed. Baltimore: Johns Hopkins University Press, 2000.

———. *Objectivity is Not Neutrality: Explanatory Schemes in History*. Baltimore: Johns Hopkins University Press, 1998.

Hawkins, Hugh. *Pioneer: A History of the Johns Hopkins University, 1874-1889*. Ithaca: Cornell University Press, 1960.

Haym, Rudolf. *Hegel und seine Zeit, Vorlesungen über Entstehung und Entwickelung, Wesen und Werth der Hegel'schen Philosophie*. Berlin, 1857.

Hegel, G. W. F. *Aesthetics: Lectures on Fine Art*. 2 vols. Translated by T. M. Knox. Oxford: Clarendon Press, 1975.

———. *Elements of the Philosophy of Right*. Edited by Allen Wood. Translated by H. B. Nisbet. Cambridge: Cambridge University Press, 1991.

———. *Encyclopedia of the Philosophical Sciences in Outline and Critical Writings*. Edited by Ernst Behler. Translated by Steven A. Taubeneck. New York: Continuum, 1990.

———. *Encyklopädie der philosophischen Wissenschaften im Grundrisse*. Mit Einleitung und Erläuterungen hrsg. von Karl Rosenkranz. Berlin: L. Heimann, 1870.

———. *Faith and Knowledge*. Translated by Walter Cerf and H. S. Harris. Albany: State University of New York, 1977.

———. *Hegel's Doctrine of Formal Logic: Being a Translation of the First Section of the Subjective Logic*. Translated by H. S. Macran. Oxford: Clarendon Press, 1912.

———. *Hegel's Early Theological Writings*. Translated by T. M. Knox. Chicago: University of Chicago Press, 1948.

———. *Hegel's Introduction to Aesthetics: Being the Introduction to the Berlin Aesthetics Lectures of the 1820s*. Translated by T. M. Knox. Oxford: Clarendon Press, 1979.

———. *Hegel's Philosophy of Mind, Translated from* The Encyclopaedia of the Philosophical Sciences. Translated by William Wallace and A. V. Miller. Oxford: Clarendon Press, 1894, 1971.

———. *Hegel's Philosophy of Right*. Translated by S. W. Dyde. London: G. Bell and Sons, 1896.

———. *Hegel's Political Writings*. Translated by T. M. Knox with an introductory essay by Z. A. Pelczynsky. Oxford: Clarendon Press, 1964.

———. *Hegel's Science of Logic*. Translated by A. V. Miller. Atlantic Highlands, NJ: Humanities Press, 1969.

———. *Hegels Theologische Jugendschriften*. Edited by Hermann Nohl. Tübingen: Mohr, 1907.

———. *The Introduction to Hegel's Philosophy of Fine Art.* Translated with notes and prefatory essay by Bernard Bosanquet. London: Kegan Paul, Trench, 1886.

———. *Introduction to the Lectures on the History of Philosophy.* Translated by T. M. Knox and A. V. Miller. New York: Oxford University Press, 1987.

———. *Lectures on the History of Philosophy.* 3 volumes. Translated by E. S. Haldane and Frances H. Simson. Lincoln: University of Nebraska Press, 1995.

———. *Lectures on the Philosophy of World History.* Translated by H. B. Nisbet with an introduction by Duncan Forbes. Cambridge: Cambridge University Press, 1975.

———. *The Logic of Hegel, Translated from* The Encyclopaedia of the Philosophical Sciences, 3rd edition. Translated by William Wallace. Oxford: Clarendon Press, 1975.

———. *The Phenomenology of Mind.* Translated by J. B. Baillie. London: Swan Sonnenschein, 1910.

———. *The Phenomenology of Spirit.* Translated by A. V. Miller. Oxford: Clarendon Press, 1977.

———. *The Philosophical Propadeutic.* Translated by A. V. Miller. Edited by Michael George and Andrew Vincent. Oxford: Basil Blackwell, 1986.

———. *The Philosophy of Art: An Introduction to the Scientific Study of Aesthetics.* Edited by Karl Ludwig Michelet. Translated by William H. Hastie. Edinburgh: Oliver and Boyd, 1886.

———. *The Philosophy of Art: Being the Second Part of Hegel's Æsthetik, in which Are Unfolded Historically the Three Great Fundamental Phases of the Art-Activity of the World.* Translated by William M. Bryant. New York: Appleton, 1879.

———. *The Philosophy of History.* Translated by J. Sibree with an introduction by C. J. Friedrich. New York: Dover, 1956.

———. *Three Essays, 1793-95: The Tübingen Essay, Berne Fragments, The Life of Jesus.* Edited and translated with introduction and notes by Peter Fuss and John Dobbins. Notre Dame, IN: University of Notre Dame Press, 1984.

Herbst, Jurgen. *The German Historical School in American Scholarship: A Study in the Transfer of Culture.* Ithaca, NY: Cornell University Press, 1965.

Hickman, Larry A. *John Dewey's Pragmatic Technology.* Bloomington: Indiana University Press, 1990.

———. "Habermas's Unresolved Dualism: *Zweckrationalität* as *Idée Fixe.*" In *Perspectives on Habermas,* ed. Lewis Edwin Hahn, 501-513. Chicago: Open Court, 2000.

———, ed. *Reading Dewey: Interpretations for a Postmodern Generation.* Bloomington: Indiana University Press, 1998.

Hicks, Steven V. *International Law and the Possibility of a Just World Order: An Essay on Hegel's Universalism.* Amsterdam: Rodopi, 1999.

Higham, John. *From Boundless to Consolidation: The Transformation of American Culture, 1848-1860.* Ann Arbor, MI: William L. Clements Library, 1969.

Hinchman, Lewis. *Hegel's Critique of the Enlightenment.* Gainesville and Tampa: The University Presses of Florida, 1984.

Hocking, William Ernest. "Political Philosophy in Germany." *New Republic* (2 October 1915): 234-236.

Hocutt, Max O. "The Logical Foundations of Peirce's Aesthetics." *Journal of Aesthetics and Art Criticism* 21, no. 2 (Winter 1962): 157-166.

Hodgson, Shadworth H. *The Philosophy of Reflection.* 2 volumes. London: Longmans, Green, 1878.

———. "Illusory Psychology." *Mind* 11, No. 44. (Oct. 1886): 478-494.

———. "'Illusory Psychology.'—A Rejoinder." *Mind* 12, no. 46. (Apr. 1887): 314-320.

Hoffman, Franz. "Letter on the Philosophy of Baader." JSP 1, no. 3 (1867): 190-192.

———. "Die Hegelsche Philosophie in St. Louis in den vereinigten Staaten Nordamerika's." *Philosophische Monatshefte.* (1871): 58-63.

Honneth, Axel. "The Logic of Fanaticism: Dewey's Archaeology of the German Mentality." Translated by Jason Murphy. In *Pluralism and the Pragmatic Turn: The Transformation of Critical Theory,* edited by William Rehg and James Bohman, 319-337. Cambridge, MA: MIT Press, 2001.

Hollinger, David A. *In the American Province: Studies in the History and Historiography of Ideas.* Bloomington: Indiana University Press, 1985.

Hook, Sidney. *The Metaphysics of Pragmatism.* Chicago: Open Court, 1927.

———. *The Hero in History: A Study in Limitation and Possibility.* Boston: Beacon Press, 1943.

———. *From Hegel to Marx.* New York: Humanities Press, 1950.

———. "Some Memories of John Dewey." *Commentary* 14 (September, 1952): 245-253.

———. *Education and the Taming of Power.* LaSalle, IL: Open Court, 1973.

———. *John Dewey: An Intellectual Portrait.* New York: Prometheus Books, 1995.

Hook, Sidney, William O'Neill, and Roger O'Toole, eds. *Philosophy, History and Social Action: Essays in Honor of Lewis Feuer.* Boston: Kluwer, 1988.

Hoopes, James. "Objectivity and Relativism Affirmed." *American Historical Review* 98, no. 5. (Dec., 1993): 1545-1555.

———. *Community Denied: The Wrong Turn of Pragmatic Liberalism.* Ithaca: Cornell University Press, 1998.

Horkheimer, Max and Theodor Adorno. *The Dialectic of Enlightenment.* Translated by John Cumming. New York: Continuum, 1996.

Houlgate, Stephen, ed. *Hegel and the Philosophy of Nature.* Albany: State University of New York Press, 1998.

Howison, George Holmes. *The Limits of Evolution, and Other Essays Illustrating the Metaphysical Theory of Personal Idealism.* New York: Macmillan, 1901.

Hughes, H. Stuart. *The Sea-Change: The Migration of Social Thought, 1930-1945.* New York: Harper and Row, 1975.

Huson, Timothy. "Hegel's Concept of the Self-Standing Individual as an Essential Moment of the Community." *International Studies in Philosophy* 32 (2000): 47-66.

Hylton, Peter. *Russell, Idealism, and the Emergence of Analytic Philosophy.* Oxford: Clarendon Press, 1990.

In Memoriam Henry A. P. Torrey, LL.D.: Marsh Professor of Intellectual and Moral Philosophy in the University of Vermont. Address at the Annual Meeting of the Associate Alumni, 23 June 1903. Burlington, VT: Published by the University, 1903.

Inwood, M. J. *A Hegel Dictionary.* Oxford: Blackwell Publishers, 1992.

Jackson, Philip W. *John Dewey and the Philosopher's Task.* New York: Teachers College Press, 2002.

James, William. *The Correspondence of William James.* 11 volumes. Edited by Ignas K. Skrupskelis and Elizabeth M. Berkeley. Charlottesville: University Press of Virginia, 1998.

———. *Memories and Studies.* New York: Longmans, Green, and Co., 1917.

———. "Philosophical Conceptions and Practical Results." *University Chronicle* 1 (1898): 287-310.

———. *Pluralistic Universe: Hibbert Lectures on the Present Situation to Philosophy.* New York: Longmans, Green, and Co., 1909.

———. *Pragmatism: A New Name for Some Old Ways of Thinking.* Indianapolis: Hackett, 1981.

———. *The Principles of Psychology.* 2 volumes. New York: Dover, 1950.

———. *Varieties of Religious Experience.* Edited by Martin E. Marty. New York: Penguin Books, 1982.

Jay, Martin. *The Dialectical Imagination: A History of the Frankfurt School and the Institute of Social Research, 1923-1950.* Berkeley: University of California Press, 1973.

Joas, Hans. *G. H. Mead: A Contemporary Re-examination of His Thought.* Translated by Raymond Meyer. Cambridge, MA: MIT Press, 1997.

Jones, Henry. *A Critical Account of the Philosophy of Lotze: The Doctrine of Thought.* Glasgow: J. Maclehose and Sons, 1895.

Jones, Howard Mumford. *Revolution and Romanticism.* Cambridge, MA: Harvard University Press, 1974.

Jones, Marc Edmund. *George Sylvester Morris: His Philosophical Career and Theistic Idealism.* New York: Greenwood Press, 1968 [c1948].

Kallen, Horace M. "Individuality, Individualism, and John Dewey." *Antioch Review* 19, no. 3 (Fall 1959): 299-314.

Kant, Immanuel. *Critique of Pure Reason.* New York: Macmillan, 1929.

———. *Critique of Judgement.* Translated with an introduction by J. H. Bernard. New York: Hafner Press, 1951.

———. *Metaphysical Foundations of Natural Science.* Translated by J. Ellington. Indianapolis: Bobbs-Merrill, 1970.

Katz, Michael. *Class, Bureaucracy and Schools: The Illusion of Educational Change in America.* New York: Praeger, 1971.

Kaufmann, Walter. "The Hegel Myth and Its Method." *Philosophical Review* 60, no. 4. (Oct. 1951): 459-486.

———. "Hegel's Early Anti-Theological Phase." *Philosophical Review* 63, no. 1 (Jan. 1954): 3-18.

———. *From Shakespeare to Existentialism: Studies in Poetry, Religion, and Philosophy.* Boston: Beacon Press, 1959.

———. *Hegel: A Reinterpretation.* Notre Dame, IN: University of Notre Dame Press, 1965.

———. *Tragedy and Philosophy.* Garden City, NY: Doubleday Anchor, 1969.

———, ed. *Hegel's Political Philosophy.* New York: Atherton, 1970.

Kedney, John. *Hegel's Æsthetics: A Critical Exposition.* Chicago: S. C. Griggs, 1885.

Kelly, George Armstrong. *Idealism, Politics and History: Sources of Hegelian Thought.* Cambridge: Cambridge University Press, 1969.

———. *Hegel's Retreat from Eleusis: Studies in Political Thought.* Princeton, NJ: Princeton University Press, 1978.

Kestenbaum, Victor. *The Phenomenological Sense of John Dewey.* Atlantic Heights, NJ: Humanities Press, 1977.

Kloppenberg, James T. *Uncertain Victory: Social Democracy and Progressivism in European and American Thought, 1870-1920.* Oxford: Oxford University Press, 1986.

Knight, William, ed. *Memorials of Thomas Davidson: The Wandering Scholar.* Boston: Ginn, 1907.

Knox, T. M. "Hegel and Prussianism." *Philosophy* 15 (1940): 51-63, 313-314.

Kroeger, A. E. "The Difference between the Dialectic Method of Hegel and the Synthetic Method of Kant and Fichte." JSP 6, no. 2 (Apr. 1872): 184-187.

Kuklick, Bruce. *Churchmen and Philosophers: From Jonathan Edwards to John Dewey.* New Haven: Yale University Press, 1985.

Kurita, Osamu. "John Dewey's Philosophical Frame of Reference in His First Three Articles." *Educational Theory* 21 (Summer 1971): 338-346.

Lamont, Corliss, ed. *Dialogue on John Dewey.* New York: Horizon Press, 1959.

Lamprecht, Sterling. "An Idealistic Source of Instrumentalist Logic." *Mind* 33 (Oct. 1924): 415-427.

Lasch, Christopher. *The New Radicalism in America, 1889-1963: The Intellectual As a Social Type.* New York: Knopf, 1965.

———. *The True and Only Heaven: Progress and Its Critics.* New York: Norton, 1991.

Lataner, Albert. "Introduction to Davidson's 'Autobiographical Sketch.'" *Journal of the History of Ideas* 18, no. 4 (Oct. 1957): 529-531.

Le Duc, Thomas. *Piety and Intellect at Amherst College, 1865-1912.* New York: Arno Press, 1946.

Leidecker, Kurt F. *Yankee Teacher: The Life of William Torrey Harris.* New York: Philosophical Library, 1946.

Levine, Barbara, ed. *Works About John Dewey, 1886-1995.* Carbondale: Southern Illinois University Press, 1995.

Lieber, Francis, ed. *Encyclopedia Americana.* Philadelphia: Lea and Blanchard, 1829–1833.

Lindsey, Julian I. "Coleridge and the University of Vermont." *Vermont Alumni Weekly,* 15 (1936), nos. 13-15.

Lloyd, Brian. *Left Out: Pragmatism, Exceptionalism, and the Poverty of American Marxism, 1890-1922.* Baltimore: Johns Hopkins University Press, 1997.

Locke, John. *An Essay Concerning Human Understanding.* Edited by Peter Nidditch. Oxford: Clarendon Press, 1988.

Loewenberg, Jacob. *Hegel's Phenomenology: Dialogues on the Life of the Mind.* LaSalle, IL: Open Court, 1965.

Lotze, Rudolf Hermann. *Logic.* Translated by B. Bosanquet. Oxford: Clarendon Press, 1884.

Löwith, Karl. *From Hegel to Nietzsche: The Revolution in Nineteenth-Century Thought.* Translated by David E. Green. New York: Columbia University Press, 1964.

Luqueer, Frederic Ludlow. *Hegel as Educator.* New York: Macmillan, 1896.

Lutz, Ralph Haswell, ed. *Fall of the German Empire, 1914-1918.* 2 volumes. Translated by David G. Rempel and Gertrude Rendtorff. Stanford, CA: Stanford University Press, 1932.

MacDiarmid, Hugh. *Scottish Eccentrics.* London: Routledge, 1936.

Maier, Charles S. *The Unmasterable Past: History, Holocaust, and German National Identity.* Cambridge, MA: Harvard University Press, 1988.

Maker, William. "The Science of Freedom: Hegel's Critical Theory." *Bulletin of the Hegel Society of Great Britain* 41-42 (2000): 1-17.

Marcuse, Herbert. *Reason and Revolution: Hegel and the Rise of Social Theory.* London: Oxford University Press, 1941.

Marsh, James. Introduction to *Aids to Reflection,* by Samuel Taylor Coleridge. Burlington, VT: Chauncey Goodrich, 1829.

———. *The Remains of the Rev. James Marsh, D.D.: Late President and Professor of Moral and Intellectual Philosophy, in the University of Vermont; with a Memoir of His Life.* Edited by Joseph Torrey. Boston: Crocker and Brewster, 1843.

———. *Coleridge's American Disciples: The Selected Correspondence of James Marsh.* Edited by John J. Duffy. Amherst: University of Massachusetts Press, 1973.

Martin, Jay. *The Education of John Dewey: A Biography.* New York: Columbia University Press, 2002.

Mayhew, Katherine Camp and Anna Camp Edwards. *The Dewey School.* New York: Atherton Press, 1966.

McClay, Wilfred. *The Masterless: Self and Society in Modern America.* Chapel Hill: University of North Carolina Press, 1994.
McCumber, John. "Hegel on Habit." *The Owl of Minerva* 21, no. 2 (Spring 1990): 155-165.
McDermott, John, ed. *The Philosophy of John Dewey.* Chicago: University of Chicago Press, 1981.
———. "Introduction." In *The Later Works of John Dewey, 1925-1953,* volume 11, edited by Jo Ann Boydston. Carbondale and Edwardsville: Southern Illinois University Press, 1987.
———. "The Confrontation between Royce and Howison." *Transactions of the Charles S. Peirce Society* 30, no. 4 (Fall, 1994): 779-790.
McIntyre, Stephen. "'Our Schools are Not Charitable Institutions': Class, Gender, Ethnicity, and the Teaching Profession in Nineteenth-Century St. Louis." *Missouri Historical Review* 92 (Oct. 1997): 27-44.
McLachlan, James. "The Idealist Critique of Idealism: Bowne's Theistic Personalism and Howison's City of God." *The Personalist Forum* 13, no. 1 (Spring 1997): 89-106.
Mead, George Herbert. "A New Criticism of Hegelianism: Is It Valid?" *The American Journal of Theology* 5 (1901): 87-96.
Metz, Rudolf. *A Hundred Years of British Philosophy.* New York: Macmillan, 1950.
Morris, George Sylvester. "Friedrich Adolf Trendelenburg." *The New Englander* 33 (1874): 287-336.
———. "Vera on Trendelenburg." JSP 8, no. 1 (Jan. 1874): 92-94.
———. *British Thought and Thinkers: Introductory Studies, Critical, Biographical and Philosophical.* Chicago: S. C. Griggs, 1880.
———. *Kant's Critique of Pure Reason.* Chicago: S. C. Griggs, 1882.
———. *Philosophy and Christianity.* New York: Robert Carter, 1883.
———. *Hegel's Philosophy of the State and of History: An Exposition.* Chicago: S. C. Griggs, 1887.
Morrissey, Charles T. *Vermont: A History.* New York: W. W. Norton, 1981.
Mueller, Gustav Emil. *Hegel: The Man, His Vision and Work.* New York: Pageant Press, 1968.
Mumford, Lewis. *The Golden Day: A Study in American Experience and Culture.* New York: Boni and Liveright, 1926.
Münsterberg, Hugo. *American Patriotism and Other Social Studies,* reprint of 1913 ed. Freeport, New York: Books for Libraries Press, 1968.
———. *The War and America.* New York: Appleton, 1914.
———. *The Peace and America.* New York: Appleton, 1915.
———. *Tomorrow, Letters to a Friend in Germany.* New York: Appleton, 1916.
Murray, J. Clark. "A Summer School of Philosophy." *The Scottish Review* 19 (Jan.–Apr. 1892), 98-113.
Niebuhr, Reinhold. *Moral Man and Immoral Society: A Study in Ethics and Politics.* New York and London: Scribner's, 1932.

Norton, Robert E. *The Beautiful Soul: Aesthetic Morality in the Eighteenth Century.* Ithaca: Cornell University Press, 1995.

Novick, Peter. *That Noble Dream: The "Objectivity Question" and the American Historical Profession.* New York: Cambridge University Press, 1988.

O'Malley, J. J., et al., eds. *The Legacy of Hegel: Proceedings of the Marquette Hegel Symposium, 1970.* The Hague: Martinus Nijhoff, 1973.

Parker, Theodore. "The Transient and Permanent in Christianity." *Christian Examiner* 28 (1839): 272-313.

Passmore, John. *A Hundred Years of Philosophy,* 2nd ed. London: Duckworth, 1966.

Peirce, Charles S. "Nominalism versus Realism." JSP 2, no. 1 (1868): 57-61.

———. "Questions Concerning Certain Faculties Claimed for Man." JSP 2, no. 2 (1868): 103-114.

———. "Some Consequences of Four Incapacities." JSP 2, no. 3 (1868): 140-157.

———. "What Is Meant by 'Determined.'" JSP 2, no. 3 (1868): 190-191.

———. "Grounds of the Validity of the Laws of Logic." JSP 2, no. 4 (1869): 193-208.

———. *Collected Papers of Charles S. Peirce.* 8 volumes. Edited by Charles Hartshorne, Paul Weiss, and A.W. Burks. Cambridge, MA: Harvard University Press, 1931-1960.

Perry, Charles Milton, ed. *The St. Louis Movement in Philosophy: Some Source Material.* Norman: University of Oklahoma Press, 1930.

Perry, Ralph Barton. *The Thought and Character of William James.* Boston: Little, Brown, 1935.

Pinkard, Terry. *Hegel's Dialectic: The Explanation of Possibility.* Philadelphia: Temple University Press, 1988.

———. *Hegel: A Biography.* Cambridge: Cambridge University Press, 2000.

Pippin, Robert. *Hegel's Idealism: The Satisfactions of Self-Consciousness.* Cambridge: Cambridge University Press, 1989.

———. *Idealism as Modernism: Hegelian Variations.* London: Cambridge University Press, 1997.

Pochmann, Henry A. *New England Transcendentalism and St. Louis Hegelianism: Phases in the History of American Idealism.* Philadelphia: Carl Shurz Memorial Foundation, 1948.

———. *German Culture in America: Philosophical and Literary Influences, 1600–1900.* Madison: University Press of Wisconsin, 1957.

Popper, Karl. *The Open Society and Its Enemies,* rev. ed. Princeton, NJ: Princeton University Press, 1950.

Porter, Frank C. "Lewis Orsmond Brastow, D.D." *Yale Divinity Quarterly* 9 (Jan. 1913): 75.

Porter, Noah. *Kant's Ethics: A Critical Exposition.* Chicago: S. C. Griggs, 1886.

Quandt, Jean B. *From the Small Town to the Great Community: The Social Thought of Progressive Intellectuals.* New Brunswick, NJ: Rutgers University Press, 1970.

Randall, John Herman. *From the German Enlightenment to the Age of Darwin.* Volume 2. *The Career of Philosophy.* New York: Columbia University Press, 1962.

———. "The Department of Philosophy." In *A History of the Faculty of Philosophy of Columbia University,* edited by Jacques Barzun. New York: Columbia University Press, 1957.

Ratner, Joseph. "Reply to George Eastman." *Studies in Philosophy and Education* 4 (1965): 105-107.

Ratner, Sydney and Jules Altman, eds. *John Dewey and Arthur F. Bentley: A Philosophical Correspondence, 1932-1951.* New Brunswick: Rutgers University Press, 1964.

Reck, Andrew J. *Recent American Philosophy: Studies of Ten Representative Thinkers.* New York: Pantheon Books, 1962.

———. "Idealism in American Philosophy Since 1900," in *Contemporary Studies in Philosophical Idealism,* ed. John Howie and Thomas O. Buford (Cape Cod, MA: Claude Stark, 1975), 17-52.

———. "Idealist Metaphysics in William James's *Principles of Psychology* (1887)." *Idealistic Studies* 9 (1979): 214-221.

———. "The Influence of William James on John Dewey in Psychology (1887)." *Transactions of the Charles S. Peirce Society* 20, no. 2 (Spring 1984): 87-118.

Redding, Paul. *Hegel's Hermeneutics.* Ithaca: Cornell University Press, 1996.

Ripalda, José María. *The Divided Nation, The Roots of a Bourgeois Thinker: G. W. F. Hegel.* Translated by Fay Franklin and Maruja Tillman. Amsterdam: Van Gorcum, Assen, 1977.

Ritter, Joachim. *Hegel and the French Revolution: Essays on the Philosophy of Right.* Translated with an introduction by Richard Dien Winfield. Cambridge, MA: MIT Press, 1982.

Roberts, John. *William T. Harris: A Critical Study of His Educational and Related Philosophical Reviews.* Washington, D.C.: National Education Association, 1924.

Robertson, George Croom. Review of *Psychology,* by John Dewey. *Mind* 12, no. 47 (July 1887): 439-443.

Rockefeller, Steven C. *John Dewey: Religious Faith and Democratic Humanism.* New York: Columbia University Press, 1991.

Rockmore, Tom. *On Hegel's Epistemology and Contemporary Philosophy.* Atlantic Highlands, NJ: Humanities Press International, 1996.

———. *Cognition: An Introduction to Hegel's* Phenomenology of Spirit. Berkeley: University of California Press, 1997.

Rogers, Dorothy G. "Introduction." In *Women in the St. Louis Idealist Movement, 1860–1925,* 4 vols. (Bristol, England: Thoemmes Press, 2003).

———. *America's First Women Philosophers: Transplanting Hegel, 1860-1925* (London and New York: Continuum, 2005).

Rorty, Richard. *The Consequences of Pragmatism.* Minneapolis: University of Minnesota Press, 1982.

Rose, Anne C. *Transcendentalism as a Social Movement, 1830-1850.* New Haven and London: Yale University Press, 1981.

Rosenfield, Leonora Cohen. *Portrait of a Philosopher: Morris R. Cohen in Life and Letters.* New York: Harcourt, Brace, 1948.

Rosenkranz, Karl. *Georg Wilhelm Friedrich Hegel's Leben* (Berlin: Duncker und Humblot, 1844.

———. "The Difference of Baader from Hegel." Translated by William Torrey Harris. JSP 2, no. 1 (1868): 55-56.

———. *Hegel als Deutscher Nationalphilosph.* Leipzig: Duncker und Humblot, 1870.

———. "Hegel as Publicist." Translated by G. Stanley Hall. JSP 6, no. 3 (July 1872): 258-279.

———. "Hegel's Philosophy of History." Translated by G. Stanley Hall. JSP 6, no. 4 (Oct. 1872): 340-350.

———. "Introduction to Hegel's *Encyclopedia of the Philosophical Sciences.*" Translated by Thomas Davidson. JSP 5, no. 3 (July 1871): 234-250.

Rosenstock, Gershon. *F. A. Trendelenburg: Forerunner to John Dewey.* Carbondale: Southern Illinois University Press, 1964.

Rosmini-Serbati, Antonio. *The Philosophical System of Antonio Rosmini-Serbati.* Translated, with a sketch of the author's life, bibliography, introduction and notes by Thomas Davidson. London: Kegan Paul, Trench and Co., 1882.

Ross, Dorothy. *G. Stanley Hall: The Psychologist as Prophet.* Chicago and London: University of Chicago Press, 1972.

———. *The Origins of American Social Science.* Cambridge: Cambridge University Press, 1991.

Roth, Robert J. *British Empiricism and American Pragmatism: New Directions and Neglected Arguments.* New York: Fordham University Press, 1993.

Royce, Josiah. "Schiller's Ethical Studies." JSP 12, no. 4 (Oct. 1878): 373-392.

———. *Lectures on Modern Idealism.* Edited by Jacob Loewenberg. New Haven: Yale University Press, 1964.

Royce, Josiah, Joseph LeConte, George Howison, and Sydney Edward Mezes. *The Conception of God: A Philosophical Discussion Concerning the Nature of the Divine Idea as a Demonstrable Reality.* New York: Macmillan, 1898.

Rucker, Darnell. *The Chicago Pragmatists.* Minneapolis: University of Minnesota Press, 1969.

Russell, Bertrand. "Logic as the Essence of Philosophy." In *Readings on Logic,* ed. Irving M. Copi and J. A. Gould, 75-88. New York: Macmillan, 1972.

Russell, John E. "Objective Idealism and Revised Empiricism (for Discussion)." *Philosophical Review* 15, no. 6 (Nov. 1906): 627-633.

Ryan, Alan. *Bertrand Russell: A Political Life.* New York: Hill and Wang, 1988.

———. *John Dewey and the High Tide of American Liberalism.* New York: W. W. Norton, 1995.

Ryan, Frank. "The Kantian Ground of Dewey's Functional Self." *Transactions of the Charles S. Peirce Society* 28, no. 1 (Winter 1992): 127-144.

Salter, William M. "A Service of Ethics to Philosophy." *International Journal of Ethics* 1, no. 1 (Oct. 1890): 114-119.

Sanborn, F. B. and William Torrey Harris. *A. Bronson Alcott: His Life and Letters.* 2 volumes. Boston: Roberts Brothers, 1893.

Santayana, George. Review of *German Philosophy and Politics,* by John Dewey. *Journal of Philosophy, Psychology and Scientific Methods* 12, no. 24 (25 Nov. 1915): 645-649.

Savage, Daniel. *John Dewey's Liberalism: Individual, Community, and Self-Development.* Carbondale: Southern Illinois University Press, 2002.

Schelling, F. W. J. *Vorlesungen über die Methode des academischen Studiums.* Tübingen: J. G. Cotta, 1803.

Schiller, Ferdinand C. S. "In Defense of Humanism." *Mind* 13, no. 52 (Oct. 1904): 525-542.

———. Review of *German Philosophy and Politics,* by John Dewey. *Mind,* 25, no. 98 (Apr. 1916): 250-255

———. "Instrumentalism and Idealism." *Mind* 34, no. 133 (Jan. 1925): 75-79.

Schilpp, Paul Arthur, ed. *The Philosophy of John Dewey.* Evanston, IL: Northwestern University Press, 1939.

Schmidt, James. "A *Paideia* for the '*Burger als Bourgeois*': The Concept of 'Civil Society' in Hegel's Political Thought." *History of Political Thought* 11, no. 3 (Nov. 1981): 469-477.

Schmitt, Carl. *Political Romanticism.* Translated by Guy Oakes. Cambridge, MA: MIT Press, 1986.

Schneider, Herbert. *History of American Philosophy,* 2d ed. New York: Columbia University Press, 1963.

———. Review of *F. A. Trendelenburg: Forerunner to John Dewey*, by Gershon Rosenstock. *Journal of the History of Philosophy* 4, no. 3 (July 1966): 266.

Schuyler, William. "German Philosophy in St. Louis." *Bulletin of the Washington University Association,* no. 2 (23 Apr. 1904): 72-73.

Services in Remembrance of Rev. Joseph Torrey and of Geo. Wyllys Benedict, Professors in the University of Vermont. Burlington: Free Press Steam Book and Job Office, 1874.

Seth, Andrew. *Hegelianism and Personality.* Edinburgh: William Blackwood and Sons, 1887.

Sheehan, James. *German History: 1770-1866.* Oxford: Oxford University Press, 1989.

Shirk, Evelyn. "Alfred Henry Lloyd: Beyond Labels." *Transactions of the C. S. Peirce Society* 15, no. 4 (Fall 1979): 269-282.

Shook, John. *Dewey's Empirical Theory of Knowledge and Reality.* Nashville: Vanderbilt University Press, 2000.

Sidgwick, Henry. "The Morality of Strife." *International Journal of Ethics* 1, no. 1 (Oct. 1890): 1-15.

Skrupskelis, Ignas K. "The Royce-Howison Debate on the Conception of God." *Transactions of the Charles S. Peirce Society* 30, no. 4 (Fall 1994): 791-802.

Small, Albion and George E. Vincent. *An Introduction to the Study of Society.* Dubuque, IA: Brown Reprints, 1971.

Smith, Elizabeth Lee, ed. *Henry Boynton Smith, His Life and Work.* New York: A. C. Armstrong and Son, 1881.

Smith, John. "Foreword." In Josiah Royce, *Lectures on Modern Idealism.* Edited by Jacob Loewenberg. New Haven: Yale University Press, 1964.

Snider, Denton. *The American State.* St. Louis: n.p., 1874.

———. *Social Institutions in their Origin, Growth, and Interconnection, Psychologically Treated.* St. Louis: Sigma, 1901.

———. *The State, Specially the American State, Psychologically Treated.* St. Louis: Sigma, 1902.

———. *Modern European Philosophy: The History of Modern Philosophy, Psychologically Treated.* St. Louis: Sigma, 1904.

———. *The American Ten Years' War, 1855-1865.* St. Louis: Sigma, 1906.

———. *Abraham Lincoln, an Interpretation in Biography.* St. Louis: Sigma, 1908.

———. *Lincoln in the Black Hawk War, an Epos of the Northwest.* St. Louis: Sigma, 1910.

———. *A Writer of Books in His Genesis; Written for and Dedicated to His Pupil-friends Reaching Back in a Line of Fifty Years.* St. Louis: Sigma, 1910.

———. *Lincoln and Ann Rutledge; an Idyllic Epos of the Early North-west. Souvenir of Abraham Lincoln's Birth-day, 1912.* St. Louis: Sigma, 1912.

———. *Lincoln in the White House; a Dramatic Epos of the Civil War.* St. Louis: Sigma, 1913.

———. *Lincoln at Richmond; a Dramatic Epos of the Civil War.* St. Louis: Sigma, 1914.

———. *The St. Louis Movement in Philosophy, Literature, Education, Psychology, with Chapters of Autobiography.* St. Louis: Sigma, 1920.

———. *Biography of Ralph Waldo Emerson.* St. Louis: W. H. Miner, 1921.

Solomon, Robert. *In the Spirit of Hegel: A Study of G. W. F. Hegel's* Phenomenology of Spirit. New York: Oxford University Press, 1983.

Spencer, Herbert. *Social Statistics: Or, the Conditions Essential to Human Happiness Specified, and the First of them Developed.* London: John Chapman, 1851.

Stace, W. T. *The Philosophy of Hegel: A Systematic Exposition.* London: Macmillan, 1924.

Stewart, Jon, ed. *The Hegel Myths and Legends.* Evanston, IL: Northwestern University Press, 1996.

Still, Bayrd. *Urban America: A History with Documents.* Boston: Little Brown, 1974.

Stirling, James Hutchinson. *The Secret of Hegel: Being the Hegelian System in Origin, Principle, Form, and Matter.* 2 volumes. London: Longman, Green, Longman, Roberts, and Green, 1865.

———. *Lectures on the Philosophy of Law: Together with Whewell and Hegel, and Hegel and Mr. W. R. Smith, a Vindication in a Physico-Mathematical Regard.* London: Longman, Green, 1873.

Stormer, John A. *None Dare Call it Treason.* Florissant, MO: Liberty Bell Press, 1964.

Suratt, Judy. "Alice Chipman Dewey." *Notable American Women: A Biographical Dictionary.* 4 volumes. Edited by Edward T. James. Cambridge, MA: Harvard University Press, 1971-1980.

Taylor, Bob Pepperman. "John Dewey in Vermont: A Reconsideration." *Soundings* 75, no. 1 (Spring 1992): 175-198.

Taylor, Charles. *Hegel.* Cambridge: Cambridge University Press, 1975.

Tesconi, Jr., Charles A. and Van Cleve Morris. *The Anti-Man Culture: Bureautechnocracy and the Schools.* Urbana: University of Illinois Press, 1972.

Thilly, Frank. Review of *German Philosophy and Politics,* by John Dewey. *Philosophical Review* 24, no. 5 (Sept. 1915): 540-545.

Thomas, Geoffrey. *The Moral Philosophy of T. H. Green.* Oxford: Clarendon Press, 1987.

Tibbetts, Paul. "John Dewey and Contemporary Phenomenology on Experience and the Subject-Object Relation." *Philosophy Today* 15 (1971): 250-275.

Tiles, J. E. *Dewey.* London and New York: Routledge, 1988.

Toews, John. *Hegelianism: The Path Toward Dialectical Humanism, 1805-1841.* New York: Cambridge University Press, 1980.

Torrey, H. A. P. "The 'Theodicy of Leibniz.'" *Andover Review* 4 (Oct.-Dec. 1885): 511.

———. Review of *Facts and Comments* by Herbert Spencer. *Philosophical Review* 12, no. 2 (March 1903): 193-199.

Torrey, Joseph. *A Theory of Fine Art.* New York: Scribner, Armstrong, 1874.

Townsend, Harvey G. "The Pragmatism of Peirce and Hegel." *Philosophical Review* 37, no. 4 (July 1928): 297-303.

Troen, Selwyn K. "Operation Headstart: The Beginnings of the Public School Kindergarten Movement." *Missouri Historical Review* 66, no. 2 (Jan. 1972): 211-229.

Tufts, James H. Review of *German Philosophy and Politics,* by John Dewey. *International Journal of Ethics* 26, no. 1 (Oct. 1915): 131-133.

Van Bunge, Wiep. "Spinoza in English, 1700-1900." *Intellectual News* nos. 6-7 (Winter 2000): 65-70.

Vera, Augusto. "Trendelenburg as Opponent of Hegel." Translated by Anna Brackett. JSP 7, no. 1 (Jan. 1873): 26-32.

Wallace, Robert M. "Hegel on 'Ethical Life' and Social Criticism." *Journal of Philosophical Research* 26 (Jan. 2000): 571-591.

Warren, Austin. "The Concord School of Philosophy." *New England Quarterly* 2 (Apr. 1929): 199-233.

Watson, John. *The Philosophy of Kant, in Extracts.* Kingston, Ontario: Bailie, 1882.

———. *Philosophical Essays Presented to John Watson.* Kingston, Ontario: Queen's University, 1922.

Welchman, Jennifer. "From Absolute Idealism to Instrumentalism: The Problem of Dewey's Early Philosophy." *Transactions of the Charles S. Peirce Society* 25, no. 4 (Fall 1989): 407-419.

———. *Dewey's Ethical Thought.* Ithaca: Cornell University Press, 1995.

Wells, Harry K. *Pragmatism: Philosophy of Imperialism.* New York: International Publishers, 1954.

Wenley, R. M. *The Life and Work of George Sylvester Morris: A Chapter in the History of American Thought in the Nineteenth Century.* New York: Macmillan, 1917.

Westbrook, Robert B. *John Dewey and American Democracy.* Ithaca: Cornell University Press, 1991.

Westhoff, Laura. "The Popularization of Knowledge: John Dewey on Experts and American Democracy." *History of Education Quarterly* 35, no. 1 (Spring 1995): 27-47.

Westphal, Kenneth R. *Hegel's Epistemological Realism: A Study of the Aim and Method of Hegel's* Phenomenology of Spirit. Dorchrecht: Kluwer, 1989.

———. "Is Hegel's 'Phenomenology' Relevant to Contemporary Epistemology?" *Bulletin of the Hegel Society of Great Britain* (2000): 41-85.

White, Morton. *The Origin of Dewey's Instrumentalism.* New York: Columbia University Press, 1943.

Whitman, Walt. *The Complete Writings of Walt Whitman.* 10 volumes. New York and London: G. P. Putnam's Sons, 1902.

———. *Social Thought in America: The Revolt Against Formalism,* new ed. Boston: Beacon Press, 1957.

Whittaker, Frederick William. *Samuel Harris: American Theologian.* New York: Vantage Press, 1982.

Whittemore, Robert C. *Makers of the American Mind.* New York: William Morrow, 1964.

Wiebe, Robert. *The Search for Order, 1877-1920.* New York: Hill and Wang, 1967.

Wiener, Philip H. and Frederic H. Young. *Studies in the Philosophy of Charles Sanders Peirce.* Cambridge, MA: Harvard University Press, 1952.

Wiggerhaus, Rolf. *The Frankfurt School: Its History, Theories and Political Significance.* Translated by Michael Robertson. Cambridge, MA: MIT Press, 1994.

Willey, Thomas E. *Back to Kant: The Revival of Kantianism in German Social and Historical Thought, 1860-1914.* Detroit: Wayne State University Press, 1978.

Williams, Daniel Day. *The Rise of the Andover Liberals.* New York: Octagon Books, 1941; reprint, Dallas, TX: Taylor, 1970.

Wilson, Daniel. "Science and the Crisis of Confidence in American Philosophy." *Transactions of the Charles S. Peirce Society* 23, no. 2 (Spring 1987): 235-262.

———. *Science, Community, and the Transformation of American Philosophy, 1860-1930.* Chicago: University of Chicago Press, 1990.

Wilson, Jackson. *In Quest of Community: Social Philosophy in the United States, 1860-1920.* New York: John Wiley and Sons, 1968.

Winner, Langdon. *Autonomous Technology.* Cambridge, MA: MIT Press, 1977.

Wright, Elvirton. *Freshman and Senior.* Boston and Chicago: Congregational Sunday-School and Publishing Society, 1899.

Zammito, John H. *The Genesis of Kant's* Critique of Judgment. Chicago: University of Chicago Press, 1992.

———. *Kant, Herder, and the Birth of Anthropology.* Chicago: University of Chicago Press, 2002.

Ziegler, Howard. *Frederick Augustus Rauch: American Hegelian.* Lancaster, PA: Franklin and Marshall College, 1953.

Index

About the Author

James A. Good is Professor of History at North Harris College in Houston, Texas, where he lives with his wife and youngest daughter. His primary research interests are the history of American philosophy and the American reception of German idealism. His next major project is a history of the American Philosophical Association since 1927.